The Spirit of Biography

Literature Advisory Boards

Studies in Modern Literature

A. Walton Litz, Series Editor
Princeton University

Consulting Editors
Joseph Blotner
University of Michigan
George Bornstein
University of Michigan
Jackson R. Bryer
*University of Maryland
at College Park*
Keith Cushman
*University of North Carolina
at Greensboro*
Richard J. Finneran
University of Tennessee at Knoxville
Daniel Mark Fogel
Louisiana State University
Carolyn G. Heilbrun
Columbia University
Paul Mariani
*University of Massachusetts
at Amherst*
Thomas C. Moser
Stanford University
Linda Wagner-Martin
University of North Carolina
Patricia C. Willis
Yale University

Nineteenth-Century Studies

Juliet McMaster, Series Editor
University of Alberta

Consulting Editors
Carol Christ
*University of California
at Berkeley*
James R. Kincaid
University of Southern California
Julian Markels
Ohio State University
G. B. Tennyson
*University of California
at Los Angeles*

Studies in Speculative Fiction

Eric S. Rabkin, Series Editor as of 1989
University of Michigan
Robert Scholes, Series Editor 1984–1988
Brown University

Studies in Modern Literature, No. 102

Contemporary American Literary Critics

No. 64
Poets, Poems, Movements
Thomas Parkinson

No. 105
*D. H. Lawrence in Changing Times:
A Normative Progress*
Mark Spilka

The Spirit of Biography

by
Jeffrey Meyers

Ann Arbor / London

Copyright © 1989
Jeffrey Meyers
All rights reserved

Produced and distributed by
UMI Research Press
an imprint of
University Microfilms Inc.
Ann Arbor, Michigan 48106

Library of Congress Cataloging in Publication Data

Meyers, Jeffrey.
　The spirit of biography / by Jeffrey Meyers.
　　p. cm.—(Studies in modern literature ; no. 102)
　Essays previously published in various publications between 1970 and 1989.
　Bibliography: p.
　Includes index.
　ISBN 0-8357-2001-2 (alk. paper)
　1. Biography (as a literary form) 2. Authors—20th century—
Biography—History and criticism. I. Title.
CT21.M47　1989
809—dc20　　　　　　　　　　　　　　　　　　　　　　　　89-33823
　　　　　　　　　　　　　　　　　　　　　　　　　　　　　　　CIP

British Library CIP data is available.

The paper used in this publication meets the minimum requirements of
American National Standard for Information Sciences—Permanence of Paper for Printed
Library Materials, ANSI Z39.48-1984. ∞ ™

For Donald Greene

*Through Jonathan Swift's dark grove he passed, and there
Plucked bitter wisdom that enriched his blood.*
                              Yeats, "Parnell's Funeral"

Contents

Introduction *1*

1 Freud, Hitler and Vienna *3*

2 Filial Memoirs of Tolstoy *15*

3 George Painter's *Marcel Proust* *29*

4 André Malraux and the Art of Action *47*

5 "To Die for Ireland": The Character and Career of Sir Roger Casement *69*

6 E. M. Forster and T. E. Lawrence: A Friendship *91*

7 D. H. Lawrence, Katherine Mansfield and *Women in Love* *101*

8 Murry's Cult of Mansfield *119*

9 The Quest for Katherine Mansfield *137*

10 Memoirs of D. H. Lawrence: A Genre of the Thirties *149*

11 Wyndham Lewis and T. S. Eliot: A Friendship *175*

12 Wyndham Lewis: Portraits of an Artist *187*

13 The Quest for Wyndham Lewis *201*

14 Hemingway: Wanted by the FBI *215*

x   Contents

15   Memoirs of Hemingway: The Growth of a Legend   *223*

16   The Quest for Hemingway   *241*

17   Poets and Tennis   *255*

18   The Death of Randall Jarrell   *263*

Notes   *277*

Bibliography   *297*

Index   *299*

Introduction

The eighteen essays included in this volume, published between 1970 and 1989, concern biographical aspects of European, English and American writers of the twentieth century. At a time when virtually all significant works in the modern period have been exhaustively analyzed and interpretive criticism has almost come to a dead end—apart from the rare brilliant article, most textual explications are either far-fetched or familiar—the historical and biographical approaches, which bring new facts and new learning (often based on unpublished material in archives) to illuminate literary works, seem to be the most useful and innovative way to discuss modern novels and poetry. I have been particularly interested in the life in the work, in the relations between biography, culture, politics and literature.

Literary biography combines the drudgery of research with the excitement of the chase and attempts to probe the mystery of artistic creation. My biographical works have considered the literary idealist in politics, the marriages of modern writers, the lives of Katherine Mansfield, Wyndham Lewis, Ernest Hemingway, and Robert Lowell and his circle. This book is unified by these interests, and attempts to suggest the mood of the modern age by considering the bitter wisdom that evolves from the life and works of some of the best writers of the period.

"Freud, Hitler and Vienna" considers the conjunction of a genius and a madman during a period of cultural achievement and political chaos; and Freud's ideas influence many of the subsequent chapters. "Filial Memoirs of Tolstoy" concerns the troubled relations of fathers and children. The essay on Painter's *Proust,* which begins with a brief biography of the biographer, is a tribute to the greatest literary biography of the century. The chapters on Malraux and on the Irish revolutionary Roger Casement are concise life-histories that discuss the relation of art and action and the destructive effects of homosexuality—a major theme in the life of Proust and a vital bond between Forster and T. E. Lawrence. The dynamics of literary friendships are also the subject of the essays on D. H. Lawrence and Mansfield, Mansfield and Murry, Lewis and

Eliot. Four of the chapters—on Tolstoy, D. H. Lawrence, Hemingway and Lewis—analyze how the biographer evaluates and interprets personal memoirs and imaginative portraits of his subject. Three essays provide practical accounts of how I did the research and wrote the lives of Mansfield, Lewis and Hemingway. The narrative of Hemingway and the FBI—based on material acquired through the Freedom of Information Act—describes Hemingway's spy network in wartime Cuba and reveals that he was actually persecuted by the FBI. "Poets and Tennis," inspired by my lifelong interest in the sport, describes its literary manifestations. "The Death of Randall Jarrell"—based on his autopsy report, coroner's report and death certificate—interprets the medical evidence, analyzes his motivation and conclusively proves that he committed suicide.

The factual basis and biographical orientation of these essays stand in direct opposition to the currently fashionable abstractions of critical theory, which too often confuse or ignore rather than clarify and explain the literary text. My critical position is similar to the one expressed in a letter of 1842 by the young cultural historian, Jakob Burckhardt: "My own substitute [for abstract thought] is my effort to achieve with every day a more intense immediacy in the perception of essentials. By nature I cling to the tangible, to visible reality and to history. But I have a bent for incessantly looking for parallels in co-ordinating facts and have thus succeeded on my own in arriving at a few generalized principles."

1

Freud, Hitler and Vienna

"Conscience is a Jewish invention."

Adolf Hitler

I

In Vienna, during the decade before the Great War, an astounding concentration of creative genius coincided with the final stages of political collapse. The work of Hofmannsthal, Musil, Broch, Schnitzler, Kraus, Werfel and Zweig in literature; Mahler, Wolf and Schönberg in music; Krafft-Ebing, Adler and Rank in psychology; Wittgenstein and Buber in philosophy; Kokoschka and Reinhardt, Herzl and Schumpeter, suggested that Austria had achieved self-awareness only at the moment of dissolution. As Musil wrote, "Yes, maybe Kakania [Austria] was, despite much which speaks to the contrary, a country for geniuses; and probably that is another reason why it succumbed."

Freud and Hitler also lived in Vienna during these formative years of psychoanalysis, logical positivism, atonal music, abstract painting and functional architecture, and they represented two radical ways of diagnosing and curing the psychological and political illnesses of the capital. "Politics is magic," said Hofmannsthal. "He who knows how to summon the forces from the deep, him they will follow." Both Freud and Hitler, who were profoundly influenced by Viennese culture and politics, rejected rationalism and recognized the importance of subconscious forces. But while Freud attempted to understand and control the forces from the deep, Hitler unleashed and exploited them—with tragic consequences for Freud (when Hitler triumphantly returned to Vienna in 1938) as well as for all the Jews of Europe.

The Austro-Hungarian Empire had been created in the seventeenth century to protect Europe from the infidel invasions of the Turks, who had reached the gates of Vienna in 1682. At the turn of the twentieth century, Vienna was still the capital of an empire of nearly fifty million people that stretched from the

Rhine to the Dneister, from the Po Valley to the Carpathians and from Saxony to Montenegro. Like its Ottoman rival, the Hapsburg Empire was a political fossil that preserved, well into modern times, many of the ideas and institutions that had been destroyed, elsewhere in Europe, by the revolutions of 1848. In the final years of Hapsburg power conditions were characteristically described as "always desperate, but never serious."

Vienna represented a state of mind in a state of siege. The lack of political reality was expressed in a social artificiality and pretense that emphasized external appearances and adornments, elaborate titles and gradations. The traditional Austrian Biedermeier attitudes: sentimentality, nostalgia for the past, lighthearted aestheticism, love of spectacle, fondness for the countryside, indifference to reform and passivity toward bureaucracy mingled uneasily with more modern currents: the protests against censorship and rigid sexual conventions, the alienation of intellectuals and high suicide rate, the nationalist and anti-Semitic movements. Those who lived blindly and happily in the past could agree with the music critic, Max Graf, that "We who were born in Vienna, and grew up there, had no idea, during the city's brilliant period before the First World War, that this epoch was to be the end and still less did we suspect that the Hapsburg Monarchy was destined to decline." But more apocalyptic artists, like Oskar Kokoschka and the satirist, Karl Kraus, recognized the impending doom during "the last days of mankind." The painter wrote that "My early black portraits arose in Vienna before the World War; the people lived in security, yet they were all afraid. I felt this through their cultivated form of living, which was still derived from the Baroque; I painted them in their anxiety and pain." On the death of Franz Josef in 1916, Kraus remarked that he could believe the Emperor had died, but could not convince himself he had ever lived. And he ironically called Austria, with its quixotic mixture of repression and freedom, "an isolation cell in which one was allowed to scream."

II

In this contradictory and stimulating atmosphere of Vienna, Jewish genius flowered as richly as it had under the Moslem caliphs of Granada. The Austrian Jews were not completely freed from legal constraints until 1867, but as William Johnston writes in *The Austrian Mind*, "No other ethnic group produced so many thinkers of transcendent originality."

In 1910 the 175,000 Jews of Vienna comprised nearly nine percent of the population, and the city had, after Warsaw and Budapest, the largest Jewish community in Europe. Jews controlled the great financial houses as well as the Marxist Social Democratic party, which in 1907 had won the largest number of seats in the Reichsrat. Jews dominated artistic and cultural life, and formed the majority in the professions of medicine, law and journalism.

Jewish success, as well as Jewish failure, stimulated the deep-rooted political anti-Semitism, and Jews became the obvious scapegoats during the twenty years of economic depression that followed the great Bourse crash of 1873. This political anti-Semitism, which first developed in modern Austria, was fed by the racial theories of men like Houston Stewart Chamberlain (who lived in Vienna from 1889 until 1909), and by fear of Jewish fecundity, economic envy, *völkisch* rejection of materialism and, as Freud adds in *Moses and Monotheism*, by the Jews' traditional resistance to persecution and oppression, and their role as "parricides" who reject the Christian God. Anti-Semitism was also exacerbated by the intense self-hatred that afflicted many assimilated and converted Jews, and by the heavy migration of orthodox rural Jews into Vienna. After 1900, the Jews and the Turks were the only minorities whose people wore their traditional clothing on the streets of the city. These, and other irrational factors, inspired an abundance of journals like the Social Catholic *Deutsches Volksblatt*, edited by Ernst Vergani, which combined crude sex and anti-Semitic prejudice with a popular version of current racial theories.

The two most powerful advocates of political anti-Semitism were the Pan-German Georg von Schönerer and the Christian Socialist mayor of Vienna, Karl Lueger. Both men had an immense influence on the young Adolf Hitler, who absorbed their ideas and learned how to exploit their prejudices, how to appeal to a mob and how to deal violently with political opponents. Schönerer was elected to the Reichsrat in 1873, the year of the financial crash, represented the very district where Hitler was born in 1889 (at the height of Schönerer's anti-Semitic fulminations), and was defeated in 1907, when Hitler first came to Vienna. Besides Pan-Germanism, Schönerer's virulent and largely negative program included hostility toward Czechs and other minorities, hatred of the Jews and the Catholic Church, fear of socialism and contempt for liberalism.

As early as 1887 Lueger made the macabre but novel proposal of putting "all the Jews upon a large ship, to be sunk on the high seas with loss of all aboard, as a great service to the world." Despite the opposition of the Emperor, Lueger became mayor of Vienna in 1897 and died in office in 1910, while Hitler was living in the capital. When criticized for his social relations with his political scapegoats, Lueger made the characteristic remark, "I decide who is a Jew," which epitomized the split between his ruthless public character and his genial informality in private. In his posthumously published autobiography, *The World of Yesterday,* Stefan Zweig provided an extremely naive expression of the Jews' ambivalent attitude toward Lueger:

> An able and popular leader was Dr. Karl Lueger, who mastered this unrest and worry and, with the slogan "the little man must be helped," carried with him the entire small bourgeoisie and the disgruntled middle class. . . . It was exactly the same worried group which Adolf Hitler later collected around him as his first substantial following. Karl Lueger was also his prototype

in another sense, in that he taught him the usefulness of the anti-semitic catchword, which put an opponent before the eyes of the broad classes of the bourgeoisie. . . . [But] his official anti-semitism never stopped him from being helpful and friendly to his former Jewish friends. . . . The Jews, who had trembled at this triumph of the anti-semitic party, continued to live with the same rights and esteem as heretofore.

Thirty years later, when Lueger's "helpful and friendly" anti-Semitism had led directly to Hitler and the Anschluss, Zweig went into exile and killed himself in Brazil, "exhausted by long years of homeless wandering." Hitler eventually became more nationalistic and anti-Semitic than Schönerer, more popular and powerful than Lueger. The Nazi reign of terror, as well as Theodor Herzl's idea of Zionism, which provided a persuasive political response for many of Hitler's victims, both had their origins in Vienna.

III

Freud was born in Moravia in 1856, came to Vienna at the age of four and lived there until the penultimate year of his long life. Though Freud was irritated by Pierre Janet's remark that "the idea of a sexual aetiology for the neuroses could only arise in the atmosphere of a town like Vienna," this *aperçu* contained an element of truth. For the rigid convention of silence about sex in a society of libertine men and frequently repressed, neurotic and frigid women led to an overt inhibition and a covert emphasis on sexual matters. The psychoanalytic investigation of the subconscious emerged in a city where the superficial calm concealed a hidden volcano.

Johnston has some illuminating ideas about the relation of Freud's thought to the concepts of memory, repression, father-figures, duplicity and helplessness in his Viennese environment:

> Freud's psychotherapy mirrors that fact that Vienna was a stronghold of memory. In Vienna everyone exemplified what in 1895 Freud ascribed to hysterics: they suffer largely from reminiscences. In this citadel of memory, Freud exploited Breuer's discovery that reliving a trauma could dispel its symptoms. . . .
> A public life veiled in dissimulation paralleled the repression that Freud discerned in individuals. In this schema of neurosis we see Hapsburg society writ small. . . .
> When Freud spoke of father-figures, he could have had in mind this macrocosmic father [the Emperor], whose deportment both the ambitious and the lethargic emulated. Secretiveness blanketed public life, prompting a search for latent meanings behind every event. . . . Duplicity aggravated the mechanisms of neurosis which Freud was seeking. When he spoke of superego censoring id, he knew what press censorship meant: a story would be missing from the front page, unleashing a fresh spate of rumours. Helpless—Freud would say castrated—before the bureaucracy, the populace indulged fantasies that belittled the omnipotent personages who manipulated them. Most Austrians harboured feelings of paranoia towards the state.

Freud's seminal works were written early in the century and he was at the height of his powers during the years before the Great War, which marked the beginning of his international recognition. The First International Psychoanalytical Congress took place in Salzburg in 1908, he delivered the influential lectures at Clark University in Worcester, Mass. in 1909, founded four psychoanalytical journals, including *Imago,* between 1909 and 1913, and published *Leonardo da Vinci* in 1910, "The Psychology of Love" in 1910–1912, *Totem and Taboo* and the *History of the Psychoanalytical Movement* in 1913.

The prevalence of official anti-Semitism in professional, academic and governmental circles, and a violent hostility to his ideas, were primarily responsible for Freud's profound dislike of Vienna. In the months before his marriage in 1886 he doubted if he could earn a living in the capital and seriously thought of moving either to a provincial city or to another country. Ernest Jones quotes Freud as saying, "I hate Vienna almost personally. . . . It is a misery to live here: this is no atmosphere in which one can maintain the hope of achieving anything difficult." And he even stated, quite unreasonably, "I have lived here for fifty years and have never come across a new idea here." But there was an element of ambivalence in Freud's hatred, for he was reluctant to leave the city, even when his life was threatened by the Nazis, and he once admitted, "I feel an unrestrained affection for Vienna and Austria, although I know her abysses."

Freud's insistence on the sexual etiology of neurosis and his claim that psychoanalytic sessions could often cure hysteria conflicted with the traditional concepts of therapeutic nihilism in Viennese psychiatry, and the fact that almost all of his followers were Jewish made his ideas and his movement a special target of anti-Semitism. Despite his international recognition, Freud was not made a full Professor—in a field where the hierarchy of titles was particularly important—until 1919, and even then he called it an "empty title" because it did not include membership on the Board of the Faculty.

Freud never voted in elections until the end of Lueger's tenure, and in 1926 he told Max Eastman, "Politically I am just nothing." Though Freud was an atheist who felt that religion was merely an infantile indulgence, his sense of Jewish identity inevitably sharpened with the intensification of anti-Semitism after the Austrian defeat in the Great War. In the late 1920s he wrote: "My language is German. My culture, my attainments are German. I considered myself a German intellectual, until I noticed the growth of anti-semite prejudice in German Austria. Since that time, I considered myself no longer a German. I prefer to call myself a Jew." And in a famous letter to his fellow members of the Vienna B'nai B'rith Lodge, he defined his Jewish characteristics in terms of intellectual freedom and ideological independence, and ended with a reference to Ibsen's *Enemy of the People:* "It was only to my Jewish nature that I owed the two qualities that have become indispensable to me throughout my difficult life. Because I was a Jew I found myself free of many prejudices which restrict others in the use of the intellect: as a Jew I was prepared to be in opposition and to renounce agreement with the 'Compact majority.'"

IV

Freud belonged to the comfortable and cultured middle-class of Vienna, while Hitler dwelled among the homeless and uprooted outcasts at the very bottom of society. Hitler lived in Vienna for five and a half years between 1907 and 1913, during the most impressionable and formative period of his life; and like Freud, his character and opinions were profoundly marked and molded by the city.

Hitler emphasizes the importance of the years in Vienna in a long section in *Mein Kampf*, which he wrote in a German prison after the failure of the first *putsch* in 1924, and categorically states: "In this period there took shape within me a world picture and a philosophy which became the granite foundation of all my acts. In addition to what I then created, I have had to learn little; and have had to alter nothing." He then adds, with an element of self-pity, that his experiences in "this city of lotus-eaters" was almost entirely negative and was (for a man who lacked a formal education) "the hardest, the most thorough, school of my life": "To me Vienna represents, I am sorry to say, merely the living memory of the saddest period of my life. Even today this city can arouse in me nothing but the most dismal thoughts. . . . Five years of hardship and misery. Five years in which I was forced to earn a living, first as a day labourer, then as a smaller painter; a truly meagre living which never sufficed to appease even my daily hunger."

Hitler first visited Vienna in May 1906 and sent home enthusiastic postcards about his youthful passions, Wagnerian music and Baroque architecture. He came to live in the capital in October 1907, full of illusory expectations, but soon began his descent into poverty and degradation. He was refused admission as a student of painting to the Vienna Academy of Fine Arts in 1907 and again in 1908. And he still had not recovered from that shock when, sixteen years later, he described the traumatic incident with a characteristic combination of astonishment, rage and violence: "I was so convinced that I would be successful that when I received my rejection, it struck me as a bolt from the blue. . . . They rejected me, they threw me out, they turned me down. . . . The whole Academy ought to be blown up." Hitler was so ashamed of his failure that he never revealed it to his family and tried to keep it hidden from his roommate, August Kubizek. Shattered by his rejection, Hitler wandered aimlessly around the city, from the impressive new buildings on the Ring to the brothel district, until he ran out of money in December 1909.

The furnished room that Hitler first shared with Kubizek was rather grim, and his friend relates that "It was not necessary for us to go out to study the mass misery of the city—it was brought into our own home. Our own damp and crumbling walls, bug-infested furniture and the unpleasant odor of kerosene were typical." Hitler states that in the "socially backward" Vienna, "dazzling riches and loathsome poverty alternated sharply." He was clearly in the "loathsome" camp and came to hate the rich as his hunger and filth intensified. His description of the poor man in Vienna is clearly a portrayal of his own shameful decline: "He walks the streets, hungry; often he pawns and sells his last possessions; his clothing becomes more and more wretched; and thus he sinks into eternal surroundings which, on top of his physical misfortune, also poison his soul. . . . The more I witnessed it, the greater grew my revulsion for the big city which avidly sucked men in and then so cruelly crushed them."

By the end of 1909 Hitler was forced to give up his room, disappeared without even notifying Kubizek and was desperate enough to join the ranks of the city's tramps. He slept in doss-houses, park benches or (wrapped in newspapers) on the streets; and eked out a meagre subsistence by running errands, beating carpets, carrying luggage at the Bahnhof and shovelling snow. In June 1910 he entered the prison-like Home for Men on the Meldemannstrasse, with its "sordid scenes and repulsive filth." He spent his last three Viennese years in the Home, where he eventually took up the trade of water-color copyist. Hitler describes this period of his life as years of great loneliness. He avoided contact with the Viennese, whom he condemned as too easygoing and frivolous, made no friends and lived in solitude among the homeless tramps and drunkards.

It was almost inevitable that Hitler, who experienced poverty and misery in an intensely anti-Semitic atmosphere, and who longed for and envied both wealth and culture, should enthusiastically adopt the prevailing hostility to Jews. But there was also a personal reason. Hitler, who once said "The Jew is always within us," was haunted by the fear that he might be partly Jewish. His crude friend, Reinhold Hanisch, reports, "Hitler at that time looked very Jewish, and I often joked with him that he must be of Jewish blood."

Hitler writes in *Mein Kampf* that he was converted to anti-Semitism (which he relates to Jewish politics), while living in Vienna: "In this period my eyes were opened to two menaces of which I had previously scarcely known the names . . . Marxism and Jewry." And in a notorious passage he describes his first meeting with a Jew, whose strange appearance made him stand out in the urban crowd:

> One day I suddenly encountered an apparition in a black caftan and black hair locks. Is this a Jew?, was my first thought. For, to be sure, they had not looked like that in Linz. I observed the man furtively and cautiously, but the longer I stared at this foreign face, scrutinizing feature for feature, the more my first question assumed a new form: Is this a German? As always in such cases, I now began to try to relieve my doubts by books. For a few hellers I bought the first anti-Semitic pamphlets of my life.

Hitler added nothing new to the abundant anti-Semitic literature that expressed the racial theories of men like Count Gobineau and Houston Chamberlain, and were adopted by Schönerer and Lueger, but like his political mentors he made it a cornerstone of his party program. During these repressed and ascetic years he was particularly fascinated by the sexual activities of the Jews. He states that "The relation of the Jews to prostitution, and even more to white-slave traffic, could be studied in Vienna as perhaps in no other city of western Europe," and he was outraged by the fantastic "nightmare vision of the seduction of hundreds of thousands of girls by crooked-legged Jew bastards." As Alan Bullock observes, "Hitler's Jew is no longer a human being, he has become a mythical figure, a grimacing, leering devil invested with infernal powers, the incarnation of evil, into which Hitler projects all that he hates and fears—and desires."

It is possible to see Hitler's attitude toward Austria and Germany, as well as toward Jews, in terms of Freudian psychology. Hitler called Vienna, with its extraordinary mixture of races, "the symbol of incest." And he identified his aged, exhausted yet tyrannical father, whom he intensely disliked, with the Emperor and the city from which "the last flush of life flowed out into the sickly, old body of the crumbling empire." Hitler had succeeded in usurping his young mother's affection for his father by becoming the spoiled darling of the only person he ever loved, and he wished to extinguish the authority and power of the threatening Austrian fatherland by the triumph of the more potent German motherland:

> The protection of the German race presumed the destruction of Austria . . . above all else, the Royal House of Hapsburg was destined to bring misfortune upon the German nation. . . . Since my heart had never beaten for an Austrian monarchy but only for a German Reich, the hour of this state's downfall could only seem to me the beginning of the redemption of the German nation.

And in another crucial passage, despite his confused and inconsistent use of the words fatherland and mother country, Hitler—who was strengthened by his mother and oppressed by his father—describes the political opposition of Austria and Germany in terms of parental conflict:

> My most ardent and heartfelt wish: the union of my beloved homeland with the common fatherland: the German Reich. . . . I address myself to all those who, detached from their mother country . . . are persecuted and tortured for their loyalty to the fatherland, and who now, with poignant emotion, long for the hour which will permit them to return to the heart of their faithful mother.

Hitler's forcible annexation of Austria to Germany was a political expression of his subconscious desire for a "return to the heart of his faithful mother"—who had died of breast cancer in December 1907 while he was separated from her and living in Vienna. Hitler's Anschluss, which was specifically prohibited by the Treaty of Versailles, symbolically absorbed and replaced the Austrian father-image through a forbidden and "incestuous" union with the German mother-image.

The extraordinary transformation of Hitler from the young tramp of Vienna to the conqueror of Europe suggests the demonic possibilities of mediocrity. When Hitler moved to Munich in May 1913 in order to avoid military service in Austria his political beliefs—which had evolved from his personal guilt, fear, anger and destructiveness—were fully developed. His intense German nationalism, his contempt for Viennese cosmopolitanism, his hatred of parliamentary democracy, Marxist Socialism, Jews and Jewish thought, were to dominate his actions for the rest of his life.

V

According to Nazi ideology, psychoanalysis had soul-destroying consequences; it was alien to the German nature and had been refuted by German science. The Nazis lost no time in attacking Freud, and his books were burned in Berlin as early as May 1933. The following year, Freud wrote with foreboding to his son, Ernst: "The future is uncertain; either Austrian fascism or the swastika. In the latter event we shall have to leave; native fascism we are willing to take in our stride up to a certain point; it can hardly treat us as badly as its German cousin." Freud was more aware than most Viennese Jews of Hitler's overwhelming need for revenge, self-justification and self-redemption, of his urge to dominate and subdue the city that had once "sucked him in and cruelly crushed him."

The annexation of Austria was inevitable after the remilitarization of the Rhineland and the establishment of the Rome-Berlin axis. Despite, or perhaps because of the humiliation of the Austrian government, there was a spontaneous and enthusiastic welcome when the Nazi troops crossed the border on March 11, 1938, and when Hitler drove through the cheering crowds of Linz. (He immediately transformed the cemetery where his family was buried into an artillery range to destroy any possible evidence of his Jewish blood.) And during his reception at the Hapsburg palace twenty-five years after his undignified departure from the city, Hitler proudly told the Burgermeister of Vienna: "Be assured that this city is in my eyes a pearl. I will bring it into that setting which is worthy of it and I will entrust it to the care of the whole German nation."

This "care," needless to say, did not extend to the Jews. Two nights after the Anschluss, as Hitler complacently observed that "A good political action saves blood," the swastika was hoisted above St. Stephen's Cathedral and the first of the 76,000 arrests began. The street named for Heine was appropriately renamed for Schönerer; the atrocities of the Austrian Nazis—a prolonged Kristallnacht—exceeded anything that had happened in the Reich; and after three months in Austria the Nazis accomplished what had taken five years to do in Germany. Rabbis were forced to scrub the pro-Schuschnigg slogans off the pavements, synagogues were desecrated, Jewish homes and shops were wrecked and looted, and Jews were driven out of governmental and industrial positions, the public schools and even the public parks.

Though shocked and threatened by these outrages, Freud was not surprised by them, for he had little reason to change his "judgment of human nature, above all the Christian-Aryan variety." His denial, in *Civilization and Its Discontents,* of the supremacy of culture over instinct, and his belief in the elemental destructive urge in the human soul, had been tragically confirmed when, as he said in *Moses and Monotheism,* "The German people retrogressed into all but prehistoric barbarism."

Even the Nazis hesitated to condemn a man of Freud's fame and stature, and the personal intervention of both Roosevelt and Mussolini (through Freud's Italian translator) helped to secure his eventual release. Before he left, the Nazis confiscated Freud's substantial bank account and forced him to pay an exit tax of 12,000 Dutch gulden. Freud's Psychoanalytic Society was dissolved; his publishing company destroyed; his books banned, confiscated and reduced to pulp; another stock of books recalled from Switzerland for destruction; his children expelled from their professions. In a moving letter of May 12 Freud wrote to his son, Ernst, in London and likened himself to a biblical patriarch: "Two prospects keep me going in these grim times: to rejoin you all and—to die in freedom. I sometimes compare myself with the old Jacob who, when a very old man, was taken by his children to Egypt, as Thomas Mann is to describe in his next novel." On June 4, 1938, after continuous persecution, the old and frail Freud signed the absurd statement that he had been well treated by the Nazis, added the superb postscript: "I can heartily recommend the Gestapo to anyone," and, escorted by Ernest Jones, was allowed to leave the city where he had lived and worked for 78 years. Freud was forced to leave his four aged sisters in Vienna, and they were all killed in concentration camps in 1943.

A few days after he arrived in his London refuge (where he died in 1939 from the cancer of the jaw that had tormented him during the last two decades of his life), Freud wrote with defensive irony to his lifelong friend and disciple, Max Eitingon: "The feeling of triumph on being liberated is too strongly mixed with sorrow, for in spite of everything I still greatly loved the prison from which I have been released. The enchantment of the new surroundings (which make one want to shout 'Heil Hitler!') is blended with discontent caused by little peculiarities of the strange environment."

Thomas Mann, the first and most brilliant exponent of Freudian thought in literature, has made an illuminating speculation about the final, tragic conjunction of Freud and Hitler in Vienna: "I have a private suspicion that the élan of the march on Vienna had a secret spring: it was directed at the venerable Freud, the real and actual enemy, the philosopher and revealer of neuroses, the great disillusioner, the seer and sayer of the laws of genius." Hitler saw Freud, who was nourished by the same ambivalent and cosmopolitan atmosphere and who recognized, but could not cure, the disease of modern civilization that Hitler represented, as the personification of Jewish culture and conscience, intellect and insight, that he hated, feared—and destroyed—in Vienna.

2

Filial Memoirs of Tolstoy

I

The writer of a memoir is always writing about himself. The autobiographical emphasis becomes a problem when the author is describing a father who is also a great literary figure. He is torn between veneration and rivalry, between a desire to emphasize the father's greatness and to reveal his human failings, between a need to bask in his reflected glory and to tell the story of his own development. Two masterpieces of English autobiography, Edmund Gosse's *Father and Son* and J. R. Ackerley's *My Father and Myself,* succeed brilliantly because their subject is frankly dual and the author is free to discuss the true focus: his relations with his father. Though both books deal with powerful personalities, neither one has to confront a writer of genius, a glamorous and mythical public figure.

Tolstoy fathered thirteen children between 1863 and 1888, of whom three died in infancy and two in childhood. Five of the eight surviving children wrote memoirs, which were published between 1914 and 1975. These seven firsthand accounts provide a portrait of his patriarchal life and contribute to our understanding of the social history of nineteenth-century Russia. Despite their wealth of detail and their unique perspective on Tolstoy's life, these memoirs, though revealing, are disappointingly diffuse.

Tolstoy was a famous writer before most of his children were born. He was also an extremely wealthy aristocrat, a feudal lord in a society that was, in many respects, still medieval. Tolstoy's children inherited a privileged life, supported by the labor of innumerable peasants, whom their father ruled like a deity. The parents' marriage was extremely happy and productive—of books and children—for seventeen years. But Tolstoy's spiritual crisis shattered their security and led to thirty years of bitter conflict with his sons and his wife Sofia. Tolstoy wanted to give away all his possessions and disinherit his wife and children; Sofia fought to keep the money that would allow the family to maintain their luxurious way of life.

In about 1879, after completing *Anna Karenina,* Tolstoy began to experience the spiritual crisis that led to a religious conversion and a dramatic change in his life. The family's move to Moscow in 1881 intensified his hatred of materialistic society. In 1883 he renounced his property—in land, copyrights and money—and gave Sofia the income from all his works published before 1881. He abandoned literary works for religious tracts and became a prophet, moralist and reformer. The saintly sybarite tried to imitate the simple life of the peasants. He wore bast sandals and coarse peasant blouses, did manual labor with his former serfs, made shoes, and gave up hunting, meat, wine and tobacco. He was tempted by suicide and feared he might hang himself from the beam of his study. After a period of repentant worship in the Orthodox Church, he adopted primitive Christianity, attempted to purify religion of dogmas and mysteries, and tried to simplify the message of the Gospels. In 1891 he publicly renounced the copyright of all works written after 1881; in 1892 he divided his estates among his wife and children. He broke with the Church for distorting Christ's teachings and was excommunicated in February 1901. Tolstoy's unusual beliefs attracted hordes of parasitic, foolish and fanatic followers, whom Sofia called "the Dark Ones." Dressed in greasy sheepskin coats and muddy felt boots, they invaded the household and intensified the domestic conflicts. Yet Tolstoy was not able to put his principles into practice. He still fathered children, though he preached purity and hated his wife; still lived in comfort while advocating asceticism. After Tolstoy's conversion, his children lived in an atmosphere of religious mania. Sofia's emotional instability, irrational behavior and desperate demands for money finally drove Tolstoy to flight, illness and death.

In the final months of his life, the octogenarian Tolstoy—influenced by his most educated, principled and power-hungry disciple, Vladimir Chertkov—became completely alienated from his wife and sons. Chertkov transcribed his diaries and controlled his manuscripts, which had, until then, been the responsibility of Sofia. In June 1910 she had a nervous breakdown. In July Tolstoy made a secret will that rejected Sofia, named Chertkov literary executor and renounced the rights to *all* his works. He fled from home on October 28 and—surrounded by three of his children: Sergei, Tatiana and Alexandra—died on November 7 in the remote railway station at Astapovo. A famous photograph shows the pathetic Sofia, shut out of Tolstoy's bare room and staring through the window at his deathbed. It was highly ironic that all the wealth and property at the root of this bitter struggle was expropriated, a few years later, by the Bolsheviks.

There is no writer today comparable in status to those giants of the nineteenth century—Dickens, Hugo, Tolstoy—who had an immense cultural impact and were internationally revered. Tolstoy (like Leonardo, Darwin and Whitman) had a long white beard, resembled Jehovah and was treated like a god at home.

His noble lineage and extensive estates, his impressive appearance and austere way of life, his sharp intellect and superior wisdom, his force of character and fame as a writer, the adoration of his young wife as well as of the peasants, servants, retainers, visitors and disciples inspired an awed reverence in his children. Yet Tolstoy, a genius and religious fanatic, could not give them the love, care and attention that most fathers provide. His spiritual principles, which brought public veneration, destroyed the lives of those around him. The memoirs tend to contrast the early idyllic years with the traumatic domestic quarrels that divided Tolstoy from his wife and children during the last three decades of his life.

Children of that class and period were not close to their parents. This was especially true in the large Tolstoy household in which the numerous children, competing for their parents' attention, were brought up by nurses, maids, governesses and tutors. Tolstoy, sixteen years older than Sofia, begot his last child at the age of sixty. The four oldest children—Sergei, Tatiana, Ilya and Leo—born between 1863 and 1869, during the period of their parents' happiness, tend to idealize their childhood. Confused and distressed by their father's withdrawal from the family and condemnation of their way of life, their books express resentment even as they try to hide it. Alexandra, born a generation later in 1884, never experienced the good years of her parents' marriage. She suffered most from her parents' frustration and rage, and wrote the best book about them. Alexandra's suffering gave her insight into herself and her parents, and provoked her into overstepping, if only in a limited way, the polite, hagiographic conventions of filial memoirs. Contemporary memoirs, by contrast, justify the sensational denigration of parents in the interest of "truth."

The sons do not want to reveal too much about the unpleasant aspects of the Tolstoys' tempestuous relationship, but their loyalty to Sofia gives them an excuse to attack their father. The children generally give a brief sketch of Tolstoy's distinguished family history and omit the events of his life before his marriage in 1862. There is no reference, for example, to Tolstoy's selling part of his estate to pay off youthful gambling debts; or to Sofia's shock, sense of pollution and permanent jealousy of his early loves when Tolstoy showed her, to relieve his guilt just before their marriage, the revelations of sexual debauchery in his diary; or to Tolstoy's illegitimate child by the peasant, Aksinya, who continued to serve on his country estate, Yasnaya Polyana.

These memoirs seem to confirm Freud's oedipal theory, for the sons (Ilya, Leo and Sergei) sympathize with Sofia and the daughters (Alexandra and Tatiana)—who also vie with each other in flirtatious attempts to attract their father—sympathize with Tolstoy. The sons, though loyal to their mother, have difficulty making a convincing case for the melodramatic and masochistic, irritable and despotic, destructive and devouring Sofia.

The children deal with this difficult situation with varying degrees of honesty and self-justification. They all begin with a child's point of view and all portray themselves as victims. They criticize their father, but are proud of being his offspring. They identify themselves as Tolstoy's children, but reveal that they were crippled by their father. The strain of suicide runs through these memoirs: Tolstoy feared suicide, young Leo threatened to kill himself, Sofia's sister, Aunt Tanya, attempted to poison herself, Sofia tried to drown herself. Four main themes emerge from these memoirs: the relations with their father (the sons were oppressed by him, the daughters had their social and sexual lives destroyed by his jealousy), the reaction to their parents' quarrel, the attitude toward Chertkov and the account of Tolstoy's flight and death.

II

Tolstoy, My Father by Ilya, the second son and third of thirteen children, was published in 1914 and revised shortly before his death in 1933. In boyhood Ilya—who was anti-intellectual and disliked poetry, music, languages, tutors and studies—adored his mother and feared his father. According to Ilya, Tolstoy never showed affection, was harsh in argument, had an aristocratic pride and taught his children to be arrogant. In old age—when he became a consultant to the Hollywood film, *Anna Karenina*—Ilya's bald head, thick nose and unkempt beard bore a striking resemblance to his father's.

Ilya states that when Turgenev had resolved his old quarrel with Tolstoy and visited Yasnaya Polyana in 1878, he expressed disapproval of the "queer ideas" that distracted Tolstoy from his literary work. But after relating the story of the lost woodcock—which Turgenev claimed he had shot and Tolstoy's dog could not find, and which had fallen into the fork of a tree—Ilya lamely concludes: "This is all I can recall about that delightful, ingenuously warmhearted man with the childlike eyes and childlike laugh."

The memoir becomes more interesting when Ilya shifts from the lyric to the tragic mode, from his sunny childhood to his gloomy adolescence, from a united family to a father estranged from his wife and children. Soon after his fiftieth year Tolstoy's personality changed: "he became taciturn, morose, and irritable, and our former jovial buoyant companion and leader was transformed before our eyes into a stern and censorious preacher." Sofia's interests, which he had formerly shared, no longer concerned him. And she refused (after a life of luxury) to dispose of their property and imitate the primitive existence of the peasants. Only Marya, the fifth child, who died in 1906, allied herself with her father. (Sergei Tolstoy reveals that Sofia, who suffered an almost fatal attack of puerperal fever when Marya was born in 1871, liked the pale and ugly girl far less than her other children.)

Yet Tolstoy could not live up to his own principles and seemed (at least to his enemies) to be a hypocrite. Ilya agrees that "he talked about the criminality of wealth and the evil of money, yet he himself possessed half a million; he talked about the simple workman's life, yet he himself lived in a fine manor house, slept on an expensive mattress, and ate tasty, satisfying food; he condemned private property and talked of six feet of land, yet he himself possessed over twenty thousand acres; his family spent more in a week than any peasant family could spend in a year." When Tolstoy fled from his wife and home, Sofia—a "pathologically suspicious . . . pitiful, half-mad" old woman, not accountable for her actions—became hysterical and reacted violently.

When Sofia tracked down Tolstoy in the provincial railway station, the doctors, following his orders, prevented her from seeing him. Ilya finds it "deplorable" that she was not allowed a final opportunity for reconciliation. His book aims to protect Sofia from the venom that "has been gratuitously splattered over her memory by my father's so-called friends and supporters," and argues that it was impossible for her to agree to his irrational desires. Ilya maintains that "she was a wonderful woman, an ideal mother, and would have been an ideal wife for any ordinary man," but concedes that she was not the ideal wife for Leo Tolstoy.

The proprietary and polemical title, *The Truth about My Father* (1924), by Tolstoy's third son Leo, implies that the truth has not been told in previous books. The memoir was written, after the Bolshevik Revolution, during exile in Paris. Leo discusses Tolstoy's works and ideas as well as his life, but Ilya gives a more vivid version of the stories that appear in both books: the disciple Feinerman who (like St. Martin) gave away his coat to a poor peasant (Ilya admires this, Leo disapproves); Tolstoy calling for cutlets on a fast day to signal his break with the Orthodox Church; the half-blind Aunt Marya praying to a swarm of flies she had mistaken for an icon.

Leo's object is to "set forth a general and accurate picture of the life and work of my Father, illustrated by my personal recollections." Leo is much more sympathetic to his mother and hostile to Chertkov than Ilya. He claims that Tolstoy's good fortune was exemplified in Sofia, the source of his greatest happiness. He naively attributes the estrangement between his parents (which began about 1880) to the secret will that Tolstoy made during the last months of his life. And he calls "the Dark Ones" stupid, boring and greedy.

Like Sergei and Tatiana, Leo portrays the household (before Tolstoy's crisis) as vigorous, joyous, tranquil. All inspiration and happiness came from his father, who had four main occupations: writing, shooting, the family and the estate. Leo agrees with Ilya that Tolstoy's greatest fault was pride. Though Tolstoy liked to instruct his children in mathematics, he was an impatient and terrifying teacher: "He set us problems to solve, and woe betide those of us who did not manage them. On such occasions he grew angry, and wept and fell into fits of despair. His anger had the effect of making our minds a complete blank." Though Tolstoy took lessons from the village cobbler and made his son a pair of elastic-sided boots, Leo never wore them. (Tatiana mentions that the boots he made for Marya were too small.)

Leo's stories are sometimes pointless, his analyses superficial and his conclusions misleading. He mentions the visit of William Jennings Bryan, but can "remember very little, however, of this very serious man." He merely announces that Tolstoy's excommunication from the Orthodox Church, which had profound and traumatic consequences, "produced a very painful effect on the sensitive soul of my father." According to Leo, Tolstoy's brother Sergei did not marry Sofia's sister Tanya because "a strong sentiment of duty in the noble heart of Count Sergei compelled him to marry the mother of his first two children." In fact, as Leo's brother Sergei later revealed, Uncle Sergei had an affair with Aunt Tanya before jilting her—and did not marry his gypsy wife until eighteen years later.

Leo's arguments are often confusing and contradictory. He states that even Tolstoy did not consider himself a Tolstoyan and argues that "all who had tried to apply my father's ideas to practical life have had to confess themselves sometimes disenchanted." Yet he believes that Tolstoy's nihilistic ideas led directly to the Russian Revolution: "Negation of the State and its authority, negation of the law and the Church, of war, and property and the family, negation of everything in the face of a single Christian ideal: what could be expected to happen when such poison permeated the half-civilised brains of the Russian *moujiks* [peasants]?"

Leo criticizes Tolstoy's beliefs and joins the army. Though he claims to have been a convinced Tolstoyan, he also states that his five-year nervous malady was cured when he definitely renounced Tolstoyism. In *The Tolstoy Home* (1950), Tatiana describes her trip to Paris in 1894, in response to Leo's urgent telegram begging her to bring him back to Russia. He had had a complete nervous breakdown, had been "in a very desperate state of mind, weeping and complaining and losing hope," and had threatened to commit suicide. Leo eventually became a writer and published a novel, *Chopin's Prelude,* which attacked the ideas in Tolstoy's "The Kreutzer Sonata."

Leo attempts to shift the blame for Tolstoy's flight and death from Sofia to Chertkov, a handsome former Guards officer who came from one of the noblest and richest Russian families. Chertkov—the Rasputin of the Tolstoy court—"unhappily acquired too great an influence over him, and thus, taking advantage of his weakness, compelled him to make a [secret] will," which broke the bonds between himself and his family. Leo believes Sofia was right to resist Tolstoy's desire to impoverish his family and was the first to reveal that she attempted suicide after Tolstoy had left her.

The seven articles in *Family Views of Tolstoy* (1926), edited by his English friend and biographer Aylmer Maude, were obtained by the Austrian scholar René Fülöp-Miller during a trip to Russia. Three of the authors (Vera Nagorny,

N. Apostolov and Sofya Stakhovich) are not members of the Tolstoy family; but Tatiana writes on the land question, Sergei on humor and on music, and Alexandra carves out her territory on Tolstoy's homeleaving and death.

Tatiana, the eldest daughter, expresses a familiar theme by stating that during the first seventeen years of Tolstoy's marriage "life flowed smoothly and happily. My father was head of the family, and to him everyone submitted absolutely." It was therefore quite unreasonable of him to demand a radical change in the way of life he himself had provided. Tatiana compromised by accepting her share of the estate when it was divided in 1892 but asking that her heirs "hand over the land to the absolute ownership of the peasants."

In his chapter on humor, Sergei, the eldest son, explains the amusing stories that led to characteristic family expressions: "Ankov Cake" meant an elegant way of life, "The Architect's Fault" meant a tendency to blame others, "For Prokhor" meant showing off. The pedantic and rather condescending essay on music by the composer and musicologist, Sergei, concludes that Tolstoy (who was a talented pianist) liked simple folk songs and composers who expressed themselves in intelligible musical language, and preferred Haydn and Mozart to the Romantics of the nineteenth century.

Alexandra, the youngest daughter, who survived to bear the torch of Tolstoy's memory until 1979, trumped all her siblings by becoming his sole confidante on his final flight. He awakened Alexandra before dawn on the morning of October 28, told her he was leaving and promised to let her know his destination. When Tolstoy fell ill at Astapovo and became delirious, he expressed fear that he would be unable to continue his travels. While he was expiring inside the simple shack, "a separate life was going on outside the walls. Newspaper correspondents swarmed, catching every word; the telegraphists were unable to keep pace with the telegrams handed in to them." Tolstoy's last significant words, which preached universal rather than individual love, were: "I only ask you to remember that there are many people besides Leo Tolstoy in the world, but you only regard that one Leo." Alexandra's vivid and moving account of Tolstoy's final illness shows that he was more afraid of confronting Sofia than of facing death.

The Tragedy of Tolstoy (1933), by Alexandra, is the liveliest, best written and most thorough memoir. She analyzes her bitter relationship with her mother—to whom the title of her book refers. She gives the fullest account of Sofia's mental illness, deranged behavior and profound guilt. She portrays Tolstoy as a celebrity who attracted and sustained a small army of followers at Yasnaya Polyana and drew vast crowds wherever he travelled.

Alexandra declares it is her duty to tell the truth, for only she remained with her parents until the end. She states that she was obliged to write frankly after Sofia's unreliable diaries were published in the late 1920s. She describes how Sofia composed "a post-dated diary, using father's diary and interpreting the events and moods noted there to suit herself." Yet Sofia's efforts to redeem her reputation merely ruined it forever.

Alexandra frankly mentions unpleasant details that the others omit. She portrays the violinist S. I. Taneyev, with whom Sofia (reenacting "The Kreutzer Sonata") became infatuated in 1896, as a man with "small eyes and a kind, red face that was always glistening as if oiled, framed in a small beard; his fat body seemed packed into his clothes." She describes the pleurisy, pneumonia and typhus that nearly killed Tolstoy in the Crimea in 1901 (when he was visited by Chekhov and Gorky), Uncle Sergei's fatal cancer of the tongue in 1904 and Sofia's operation for a uterine tumor in 1906.

Alexandra tries to make her father love her, calls him a lonely man within the vast family and (like Sergei and Tatiana) states that Sofia managed the estates badly. She calls Tatiana the cleverest of all the children, says Sofia always dreamed of a brilliant match for her favorite and contrasts their attitudes towards their mother: "[Tatiana] could not be persuaded that mother was guided by any motives of self-interest, she saw in her only a nervously disturbed woman, an exhausted mother, and she loved her."

Alexandra describes the children in the family and her brothers' hostility to Tolstoy's ideas. Both Alexandra and Tatiana retrospectively envied Marya, who had the greatest spiritual power, was closest to Tolstoy, took no part in the family pastimes and toiled instead among the peasants of the village. She renounced her share of the estates, objected to her Orthodox wedding service and, partly because of her poor health and sacrificial work, was unable to bear children. Like the sixth son, Andrei, Leo sided with Sofia and incited her against Tolstoy. As an adult, Leo expressed one of the dominant themes of all the children's memoirs: "Nothing can be worse than being the son of a great man. Whatever you do, people compare you with your father."

Sofia not only loved Tatiana more than Marya but also loved Ivan (her youngest child) more than Alexandra. Sofia had attempted to abort Alexandra; and Tolstoy tried to leave home the very night she was born. When the seven-year-old Ivan died of scarlet fever in 1895, Sofia, overcome by grief, cruelly wailed: "'Why is God so unjust to me? Why? Why did he take Vanichka from me? Why not Sasha (Alexandra)? . . . You are my cross,' she concluded, 'Yes—Vanichka died and you remained, to my sorrow.'" Alexandra was a complete contrast to Tatiana. She was unattractive, survived Ivan, replaced Sofia as Tolstoy's copyist, did not marry and sided with her father. She aroused her mother's hostility and bitterly resented her lack of love.

Alexandra explains, better than any of the others, how Sofia provoked Tolstoy's Lear-like escape from her domestic tyranny. She describes Sofia's hysterical screams and Tolstoy's pleading voice, her paranoid jealousy of Chertkov and threats of suicide: "You have no pity, you have a heart of stone, you love nobody but Chertkov. I shall kill myself, you will see, I shall take poison!" Sofia deliberately tormented her husband, poisoned his existence and drove him to his death. Sofia shot at the photographs in Tolstoy's study with an air pistol and tore Chertkov's picture into shreds. Alexandra told Sergei that she "had seen mother torture father and drive everybody away, convinced that everyone was guilty with the single exception of herself, press father for his author's rights, for his diaries, force him to be photographed with her, and said that [Sofia's] motives were those of financial interest." (Sofia published and sold all of Tolstoy's works written before 1881 and in 1910 was offered, but was unable to accept, a million rubles for these rights.)

Though Alexandra adores Tolstoy, their relations are sometimes difficult. He calls her homely and fat, and criticizes her innocent buying and training of horses. Alexandra quotes his explicit condemnations of her suitors' "vile manifestations of passion." Alexandra cries over her broken romance, listens to the phonograph record of Glinka's "Calm Down, Ye Storms of Passion" and (like Anna Freud) swears she will never marry and leave her father.

Alexandra was the only child who got on well with Chertkov. She explains that Chertkov was important to her father because he devoted his whole life to Tolstoy, was occupied with his works and was his closest friend. Sofia's hatred of Chertkov was based on her abnormal jealousy, her wish to justify herself in the eyes of future generations by representing Tolstoy and Chertkov in the worst light, and her desire to retain the royalties of her husband's publications.

Alexandra's chapters on Tolstoy's sudden departure, final illness and death are taken from her essay in *Family Views of Tolstoy*. After his death, as sole heir of his will, she defied the bitter opposition of the family and carried out her father's instructions. Alexandra emigrated to Japan in 1929 and to America in 1931, started the Tolstoy Foundation to aid refugees in 1939 and published a pedestrian biography of Tolstoy in 1953.

Tolstoy Remembered, by Sergei, was written late in life and published posthumously in 1949. The chronological entries, based on his diary, recycle many of the anecdotes in the memoirs of Ilya and Leo: the shepherd gored by a bull, the summer visit to Samara in 1873, the move to Moscow in 1881. Sergei narrates his progress through school and university; his negotiation of the French and English rights to Tolstoy's works; and his trip to Canada with the persecuted religious sect, the Dukhobors, who were defended and supported by Tolstoy. He offers good character sketches of Tolstoy's brother and sister as well as of his military, political, musical and artistic friends; provides the most extensive account of the uneasy friendship between Tolstoy and Turgenev, and quotes Turgenev's perceptive criticism of Dostoyevsky: his "heroes—on every second page—are either delirious, in hysterics or in a fever. This does not happen in real life."

Sergei is more critical of his mother than Ilya and Leo. He reveals that she was jealous by nature and jealous of Tolstoy's past, that she had a sharp tongue and dominating character, that she spent more money than ever in response to his tirades against luxury, that she became increasingly nervous and unbalanced after the death of Ivan and her own serious illness in 1906, that she provoked her husband's flight by searching through his private diaries (Tolstoy wrote: "All my movements, every word, day and night, must be known to her, under her constant vigilance. . . . I feel uncontrollable indignation, repulsion"). Sergei relates that her attempted suicide was intended to provoke his pity, that she knew she was responsible for driving him away and causing his final illness, and that the family decided not to bury her next to Tolstoy.

Sergei, like Alexandra, explains the reasons for Tolstoy's attraction to Chertkov. When they first met in 1883, Tolstoy was drawn to Chertkov's "contempt of public opinion, his daring independence towards those in authority, his readiness to suffer for his convictions and, particularly, his perseverance in achieving his plans." Chertkov was banished from Russia for his dangerous Tolstoyan ideas and spent 1897 to 1907 in England.

The most interesting aspect of the memoir is Sergei's barely suppressed hostility to his father. "His judgments were law, his advice compelling," Sergei writes, "I could never stand the glance of his small, penetrating, steel-blue eyes [Tatiana says Tolstoy's eyes were grey] . . . and he liked to ask questions which one did not like to answer." Like Leo, Sergei "felt that he obliterated our personalities, so that sometimes we wanted to escape."

As a student, Sergei was confused and moved between extremes: "from the life of society to the life of the radical intelligentsia, from Father's teachings of Christianity to the teachings of science and of atheism, from a simple way of life to one of drunkenness and revelry." As an adult, he had no sympathy with Tolstoy's views. Tolstoy, consequently, treated him with coldness and irony. When Sergei asked his advice about which career to follow, Tolstoy irritably answered: "Work is easy to find: there are many useful jobs to be done. Sweeping the streets is a useful employment." Like Leo, Sergei suffered periods of neurasthenia for several years.

Sergei shrewdly saw some of his own inner conflicts reflected in his father. After his religious crisis, Tolstoy denied everything he had previously loved and believed in: "Brought up as a churchgoer, now he was critical about the church rites; a farmer who had loved farming, now he denied the right to own land; a man of great culture himself, he now turned against European culture and knowledge; a great artist himself, he denied all art that did not correspond to his own conception of pure art. His opinion of the idle rich, including members of his family, was that they were a gang of madmen." He cleaned his room, pumped water, chopped wood. But the luxury at Yasnaya Polyana denied everything he believed in and he could not completely change his life as long as he remained there.

The estates yielded little; most of their substantial wealth came from his writings. Tolstoy's secret will appealed, paradoxically, to a legal authority he had already repudiated. When he fled in 1910 he did not know his destination, and was more interested in covering his tracks than in reaching the Caucasus or Bulgaria. At Astapovo, he was conscious of dying of pneumonia—like his beloved Marya in 1906. When Sergei washed him for the last time, "his body seemed strong and young for its age. He had been ill for such a short time that he had not [had] time to grow thin. His expression was calm and concentrated."

Sergei attempts to be honest, but lacks analytical power and perception. Sergei, who says that soon after his marriage his pregnant wife visited her father and wrote that she would not return, characteristically concludes: "It is hard to say what caused the break between us."

The Tolstoy Home, by Tatiana, consists of her diaries for the years 1878 to 1911. They begin when she was only fourteen, continue until the year after Tolstoy died and were published in the year of her death, 1950. All the Tolstoy children were taught to keep diaries "in order to know, in many years' time, what I was like [as a young woman], and also because everything is clearer to your mind when you have written it down." But the diary tends to be gloomy and unreliable, Tatiana explains, because "one keeps it always in the worst possible, saddest moments, when one feels lonely and has nobody to complain to." The minute particulars of Tatiana's diaries, apparently unchanged by a retrospective point of view, provide a complete picture of daily life in the Tolstoy household. The book is more about herself, her moods and her long search for someone to fall in love with and marry, than about her father. A conventional girl, Tatiana is torn between her mother and father, arrogance and humility, property and charity, luxury and sacrifice.

Tatiana is more critical than her brothers of Sofia, who constantly complains of how unhappy she is. She tells her mother that even the most savage landowners did not employ the methods that Sofia used at Yasnaya Polyana. Tolstoy forgave the peasants who stole wood or could not pay the rent, but Sofia—who violated his principles by bringing in armed guards to suppress the peasants—was a harsh and exacting mistress. Tatiana feels that Sofia does not understand Tolstoy and has an unrealistic conception of his views. She dislikes Sofia's exasperating opposition to "what Papa considers to be right and what is right too." But in 1890 she pities rather than condemns Sofia because "she does not believe anything at all, either her own or Papa's ideas; [and] she is the more lonely, because since she says and does so many things which are unreasonable, of course all the children are on Papa's side [an exaggeration], and she feels her isolation terribly, and then she loves Papa more than he loves her, and is as delighted as a child if he addresses the least kind word to her." Though Tatiana dislikes Chertkov's meddling in Tolstoy's work and forcing the family to follow his advice and instructions, she thinks Sofia is absurd in urging her son Andrei to avenge her honor and kill Chertkov.

Tatiana vainly tries to defend Tolstoy against accusations that he denies the concept of property but continues to live in luxury, and maintains "there is absolutely no clash between his life and his convictions." He could see only two ways to achieve peace of mind: "one was to abandon the house, of which he had been thinking for some time, and the other, to give all the land to the peasants and make the rights of his books common property." He begged Sofia to acquiesce, either out of conviction or out of love for him. Tolstoy hated making a will, giving away possessions he no longer considered his own and asking his family to renounce what he himself had never given up.

The most interesting aspect of this book (as of Alexandra's and Sergei's) is Tatiana's account of her relations with Tolstoy. He had the ability to make everyone who disagreed with him feel acutely uncomfortable. When she was eighteen, Tolstoy said she was liked for her country wildness, girlish clumsiness and naiveté, but urged her to try reaping to get rid of her fat. He condemned his children's lack of spiritual and intellectual interests, called their innocent life "a ceaseless orgy" and described his visits to slaughterhouses to convince them to become vegetarians. Tatiana admits that she is fond of money and a comfortable life, that she finds working with peasants both unnatural and harmful. She is horrified to discover that Marya, carrying her equalitarian principles to an extreme, has started a flirtation with a peasant. But on her train journey to Leo in Paris, she dutifully preaches vegetarianism to Poles who are trying to tell her about *their* great writer, Henryk Sienkiewicz.

Tatiana regrets that she has no direct dealings with Tolstoy and very little opportunity to speak to him after he has withdrawn from the family. She complains that Tolstoy is bad-tempered, hostile and nasty—mocking her illness (which makes her howl and leave the table) and telling her that she is the worst of all his children. She finds it difficult to become intimate with the austere and lonely old man, though she feels he would have welcomed her attentions, for "a funny, silly, false shame keeps me from going to him." Like Alexandra, she tries to compel him to love her, and feels guilty about abandoning him when the family is in Moscow. "If ever I am long away from home," she relates, "he always greets me coldly when I get back and I have to spend some time with him to establish intimacy again. My way of life is revolting to him, firstly because I do nothing at all; secondly, I do things he hates, such as riding horseback, chattering frivolously, dressing very trimly, eating terribly." Just after Tolstoy's death, she sadly notes that indolence and scruples "made me afraid of boring Him, of taking Him away from people who, it seemed to me, were more interesting and necessary to Him than I was. I did not believe sufficiently in His affection for me."

Tatiana fears that Tolstoy will disapprove of her husband and become angry about her long-desired marriage. She fails to make a brilliant match and in 1895 finally weds Mikhail Sukhotin, a harmless widower with six children, fifteen years older than she. Unlike Alexandra, Tatiana does not mention Tolstoy's fierce jealousy and hostility toward any man who engaged her affections and threatened to take her away from him.

Tatiana's *Tolstoy Remembered* (the same title as Sergei's book) was written shortly before the Great War and first published in French in 1975. The chapters on childhood and adolescence (1864–1878) cover the period before the diaries of *The Tolstoy Home*. Tolstoy appears as a remote and forbidding figure. He feels no fondness for young children and seems unaware of their presence. He is either working or tired, appears absorbed in his lonely search for truth, and judges himself and others with implacable severity. Tatiana agrees with Leo that Tolstoy was a stern and impatient mathematics teacher, who would get angry, raise his voice and reduce her to "a state of total idiocy." The two main concerns of these chapters are Tatiana's deep attachment to her English governess, Hannah Tracey, and the family's visit to the steppes of Samara, when they lived among the Moslem Bashkirs and took a cure by drinking *kumiss* (fermented ass's milk). Tatiana (like Sergei) describes Tolstoy's contest of strength with an enormous Russian and his organization of a wild horse race.

In the random third section, "Flashes of Memory," Tolstoy is miraculously transformed from the gruff patriarch into "the dearest and most luminous being in my life." Tatiana repeats the story, from *Family Views of Tolstoy,* about writing an essay on Henry George, sending it to Tolstoy under a pseudonym, receiving a letter of praise from him and then revealing that she was the author. And she records her father telling Chekhov, whose stories Tolstoy admired, that his plays were even worse then Shakespeare's.

The final section, "My Father's Death," which is more extensive than the title suggests, concerns Tolstoy's religious crisis and thirty-year quarrel with Sofia. More analytical than her diaries and her chapters on childhood, it gives the clearest account of the events that led to his escape from home. Like Ilya, Tatiana insists that she is now breaking silence to protest against certain (unspecified) books by friends of her father "that give a false picture of the relations between my parents, and a portrait of my mother distorted by prejudice." And, like Alexandra, Tatiana claims that *she* "was associated more closely than any other person with [Tolstoy's] inner life."

Tolstoy's desire to free himself from the sin of ownership and his belief that life in Moscow was a cesspit inevitably led to an increasing gulf between the parents and a state of painful tension that could not be resolved. Tatiana thinks that Tolstoy's very soul was more important than the happiness and well-being of the children and that Sofia ought to have submitted to his wishes. In *The Tolstoy Home* the young Tatiana had condemned working with the peasants as unnatural and even harmful; but she now contradicts her earlier judgment and recalls that sharing the work of the peasants each summer "was the most wonderful time for us!"

Tatiana delineates the crucial changes in Sofia's life that intensified her possessiveness and jealousy, and led to the final tragedy: the death of her youngest and favorite child, Ivan; her period of religious exaltation; her compensatory infatuation with Taneyev; her increasing hysteria and mental illness. She also notes that a reporter from the *Voice of Russia* notified the family that Tolstoy was dying in Astapovo.

Tatiana left Russia in 1925 and lived with her daughter in Rome during the last twenty years of her life. After her father's death, she maintained a cult to his memory and created a Tolstoy Room in her house which contained all his works, hundreds of photographs and a wooden box with relics she had brought from Russia: "a lock from Tolstoy's beard, his paperknife whittled from a piece of oak from Yasnaya Polyana, the satchel in which he kept his manuscripts" and the ring he had given Sofia for copying *Anna Karenina*.

III

Despite the sympathetic portrayal of their mother in the memoirs of Ilya, Leo and Sergei and the recent feminist attempts by Anne Edwards and Cathy Porter to rehabilitate Sofia, Alexandra's and Tatiana's interpretation of Tolstoy's character and of their parents' quarrel has prevailed. Sofia was right to reject Tolstoy's unreasonable demands, but she had an odious personality and a hysterical response to his wishes. The ideal mother portrayed by Ilya and Leo was cruel to Marya and Alexandra; and her mad scenes and horrific displays had a traumatic effect on the lives of all the children. Her desperate efforts enabled the family to maintain their luxurious existence until Tolstoy's death. And if she had prevented his secret will, the foreign royalties would have kept the children wealthy, after the Revolution and in exile. Despite the intense scrutiny of these memoirs, Tolstoy the man, artist and prophet remains enigmatic and elusive, for no single memoir manages to capture his complexity. In *Tolstoy Remembered*, Tatiana expresses the bitter paradox at the core of these seven memoirs: "Those who understand Tolstoy don't imitate him. And those who imitate him don't understand him."

These inevitably biased narratives must be read with cautious scepticism. All memoirs are self-exploratory; they reshape experience by describing the personalities and arranging the events of one's life. A memoir that takes another person as its primary focus must still try to understand and explain the relationship between author and subject. During Tolstoy's lifetime—and after his death—his children benefited from and were stifled by his overwhelming personality. Their memoirs demonstrate the continuing struggle between their natural desire to establish their own self-image and to venerate their world-famous father. Alexandra and Tatiana both claim to have been closest to their father and to remain the true keepers of the Tolstoyan flame. But the shifting viewpoints, gradual revelations and conflicting attitudes of the sons and daughters in these memoirs illustrate the difficulty of discovering the truth.

3

George Painter's *Marcel Proust*

I

George Painter's biography of Proust grew out of a lifelong fascination with *Remembrance of Things Past*. And his own Proustian parody idealizes his origins and describes an early epiphany: "I was born [in 1914] in Birmingham, an unreal city in the English Midlands, ugly and black to outsiders, but to natives and exiles beautiful and haunting, navel of the labyrinth of place and time. Wandering alone in a public park there at the age of six towards a dead tree which I never reached, I had a moment of vision, a sense of personal identity and the reality beyond appearances, that marked me for life."[1]

His father was a musician, singer and schoolmaster; his mother an artist; and his parents gave him reading, solitude and holidays in the West Country. Painter said: "I've been interested in Proust since my school days, first read him when I was 14 and in search of literature in the local public library in Birmingham. I was browsing through the shelves and saw *Swann's Way,* and something attracted me about the title. I took the book and was immediately bowled over and have gone on reading and thinking about Proust, and in the end writing about him, ever since."[2]

Painter's preparation for his eventual career as a biographer was scholarly and archival. He was educated at King Edward's School, Birmingham, and at Trinity College, Cambridge. A brilliant student, Painter won three scholarships and three prizes, and graduated with first class honors in both parts of the Classical Tripos. He taught Latin for a year at Liverpool University before joining the Department of Printed Books at the British Museum in 1938. He married his cousin in 1942, had two daughters and served in the army from October 1941 until July 1946. In 1954 he became Assistant Keeper in charge of ten thousand fifteenth-century printed books, the largest and finest collection of incunabula in the world: "They needed a classical scholar because so much of it would be medieval Latin, and they chose me, rightly or wrongly, and I did that for twenty years."[3] His training in Classics—with its close attention to the text, interest in factual details and careful sifting of evidence—influenced his approach to biographical research. His Classics masters taught Painter "to read and write both Latin and Greek, for the sheer pleasure of discovering and experiencing, and reconstructing and reliving the ancient writer from the writing, the individual from his world." He learned to view biography as a process "of finding evidence and trying to express what seemed to be its meaning in a context of human life."[4]

Though Painter's professional life was scholarly, he felt his talents were also artistic. In 1951, at the age of thirty-seven, he published *The Road to Sinodun* [near Dorchester]: *A Winter and Summer Monodrama*, a volume of poems written during 1940–1941 "in plain English that rhymed and scanned," which were influenced by the bitterly ironic mode of Housman and Eliot. They did not attract much attention, sold about forty copies and brought in royalties of less than two pounds. He then realized that "the creations, minds, and lives of my favourite writers were . . . far more interesting to me than my own; and most interesting of all was the mysterious relationship between these creations and these minds and lives."[5] Painter's true vocation turned out to be biography: a literary form that combines the drudgery of research with the excitement of the chase and attempts to probe the mystery of artistic creation.

Painter, an extraordinarily learned man, is an authority in four fields: Classics, incunabula, medieval history and cartography, and French literature. He has translated André Gide's two satirical novels, *Marshlands* and *Prometheus Misbound* (1953), Marcel Proust's *Letters to His Mother* (1956) and André Maurois' *The Chelsea Way; or, Marcel in England: A Proustian Parody* (1967); produced a scholarly study (with R. A. Skelton and T. E. Marston), *The Vinland Map and The Tartar Relation* (1965) and *Studies in Fifteenth-Century Printing* (1984); and published four biographies: *André Gide* (1951), *Marcel Proust* (1959, 1965), *William Caxton* (1976) and the first of three projected volumes on *Chateaubriand* (1977).

Painter has remarked that his book about a lifelong invalid was conceived, appropriately enough, when he was ill: "During a bout of influenza in 1947 I first read a volume of Proust's letters, and found in them the very people and situations in his actual life that reappear transformed to the level of high art in *A la recherche du temps perdu*. . . . I resolved to write his biography in order to explain him to myself, little knowing that the task would demand eighteen years: six of preliminary research and thinking, and twelve of writing."[6]

Painter has explained why the gestation period was unusually long: "Work at the British Museum was arduous and exacting, a 42-hour, 5½-day week with 36 days annual leave, and it would have been neither possible nor legitimate to write there, or even read. . . . I worked or wrote in the evenings, at weekends, on holiday, at mealbreaks, while commuting in the train, all the time I could, from five minutes to all day, very slowly, very painfully, averaging nothing, or a sentence, or a paragraph."[7] He has also confessed: "I write with torture, and it's probably a self-punishment," and has described the biographer—not the subject—as a sacrificial victim: "Biography is often thought of as the vampire art—the vampire feeding upon his subject. For me it's the exact opposite. My subject has fed upon me. He's taken my life-blood while I've tried to give him life. I've sacrificed my own life, I've sacrificed my personality, and I've done it willingly."[8]

Painter won the Duff Cooper Prize for the second volume of *Proust* and the James Tait Black Prize for his life of Chateaubriand—a "great invisible presence" in Proust's novel. He was elected Fellow of the Royal Society of Literature in 1965 and awarded an honorary doctorate by Edinburgh University in 1979. He has lived in Hove, on the Channel coast near Brighton, since 1970; and calls himself reclusive and unsociable ("my friends are all dead").[9]

II

Painter first expressed in *André Gide* his fundamental principle of biography: his belief that the life-writer must treat the works as a part of, not a supplement to, his subject's life. And he elaborated his biographical principles in two important interviews: with Simon Blow in the *Guardian* (1977) and with Phyllis Grosskurth (the biographer of J. A. Symonds and Havelock Ellis) in *Salmagundi* (1983).

In his Foreword to *Gide* Painter declared: "no one so far has attempted to describe the actual nature and content of his work, and to show its organic growth from the history of his mind and heart. Before the work of a great writer can be appreciated as a whole, it must be seen as an evolutionary sequence from his first book to his last, and its relationship (hidden, but essential and organic) with the man himself must be restored."[10] Gide's works, like Proust's, are essentially autobiographical and developed directly from his personal experience. So a consideration of his works has to be integrated with a discussion of his life in order to reveal their significant interrelationship. The works of art justify the investigation of the life, which in turn illuminates the works and makes us value them more highly. Painter's particular contribution to modern biography is his scholarly skill in re-creating the sources of the novel in order to reveal or come close to the creative act itself. Whereas most biographers seek to discover living informants to ascertain the facts, Painter emphasizes an imaginative grasp of Proust's novel through searching and sifting the elemental components of the text.

Painter illustrates the "organic relationship" of Proust's life and art by showing how the young amateur, dilettante, flatterer and snob, who frequented luxury hotels, great restaurants and society drawing-rooms, was transformed into the magnanimous, reclusive and brilliant novelist. His biographical research directly informs our understanding of the novel because all the facts, episodes and characters in the life have their parallel in the novel. Painter shows how Proust's genius evolved from his early works—*Pleasures and Days, Jean Santeuil,* the Ruskin translations and *Contre Sainte-Beuve*—at the same time that he discovered the technique of unconscious memory.

Proust cultivated this technique—paradoxically triggered by the banal act of dipping a piece of sponge cake into a cup of tea—in order to focus his creative imagination on the reality he had experienced. Through the great theme of Time Regained, the novel's art redeemed the chaotic nature of experience and distilled it into an intelligible and beautiful form. The ritual of the *madeleine* became, for Proust, the missing key: "it was reality itself, freed from the mask of time and habit, 'a fragment of pure life preserved in its purity, which we can only know when it is so preserved, because, in the moment when we live it, it is not present to our memory but surrounded by sensations which suppress it.'"[11]

Painter believes that biography is now "the most living literary art form," for like the novel it reaches a wide audience and exerts a powerful cultural influence by portraying the struggles and achievements of literary heroes. He states that he writes biography "because I read it and most of all feel the necessity for it when I'm reading my favourite writers." The urge to read and to write biography comes from an intuitive grasp of the life between the lines, from a desire to know *more* about the cultural milieu in which the work of art was created. He adopted as his literary models three long, sometimes multi-volumed, exhaustively researched and elegantly written biographies: Ernest Jones' *Freud* (1953–1957), Leslie Marchand's *Byron* (1957) and Richard Ellmann's *Joyce* (1959). "I don't think any biography had any direct influence on mine in style or method," he explains, "except that reading in 1939 Steegmuller's *Flaubert and Madame Bovary* and in 1940 Newman White's *Shelley,* long before I ever thought of becoming a practitioner, left the lessons that biography could be live and entertaining (Steegmuller) and large in scale (White), and helped me to want mine to be both."[12] He justly feels that his own book has had a certain influence "in the approach to [large-scale] biography and the increase of interest in biography in the last twenty years." "In great works of art," Painter concludes, "human life is being expressed at a deeper, more intense, more clear-sighted level than anything we can achieve ourselves. That's why we write biographies."[13]

Unlike most biographers, Painter never read anyone else on his subject and denied himself one of the great pleasures of research by scrupulously avoiding anyone who had ever known Proust. One of his fundamental principles is the need "to work entirely from primary sources.... Letters, documents, reminiscences, memoirs certainly, but they've got to be used critically because people don't remember properly.... [But] you must never believe anything you read in print when you're writing a biography."[14] He used only written evidence but felt that evidence was not enough, and brought his subject back to life with fact fired by his imagination: "You've got to see the connections, to see it as it's happening in real life, and not just as a literary abstraction."[15]

Painter even declared, rather perversely, that he would not have liked to know the people who lived in Proust's world, that "if somebody had said, 'Proust's calling this evening, do look in and meet him,' I wouldn't have wanted to. I wouldn't have turned my head to see him across the street.... [He couldn't] tell me anything ... which I wouldn't find much more intensely, acceptably and deeply in [his] works." Though he met, for example, Marthe Bibesco and Violet Schiff, he maintained: "I've never, practically never, obtained information by word of mouth, and usually when I've done so, I've regretted it. It turned out to be quite incorrect.... All the people who could have told me anything had already put it into print, some of them many times over."[16]

Painter identified with his subject in terms of his method and his artistic approach. Like Proust, he seeks to imagine rather than simply find the facts in a journalistic fashion. By avoiding the people who had actually known Proust, by refusing to hear how a friend felt about an incident Proust has described, he remains completely loyal to the Proustian vision. Painter's biography, an elaborate critical reading of Proust's long novel, is illuminating in the same way as the novel is. It belongs with Ellmann's *Joyce* and Douglas Day's *Malcolm Lowry*—lives of authors of one great work which the biography helps to elucidate.

Painter's belief that recollection is more significant than actual experience is closely connected to the central theme of Proust's novel, the recovery of the past through memory, and to the central technique. For "just as the Japanese amuse themselves by filling a porcelain bowl with water and steeping in it little crumbs of paper which until then are without character or form," so, through Painter's act of creation as well as evocation, intangible people "take on colour and distinctive shape, become ... permanent and recognisable ... [and assuming] their proper shapes and growing solid, spring into being" (I.36).

But Painter's position is somewhat paradoxical. Though he believes "it's the biographer's duty to get inside that mind and live the life of that subject," he retains a profound scepticism about his ability to get inside the minds of Proust's surviving friends. Like Proust, Painter feels his vision will be sharper and imagination stronger if he remains aloof. As an invalid whose asthmatic attacks led to moments of intense pain and exhaustion; as a Jew and Dreyfusard pardoning rebuffs and flattered by condescension; as a homosexual doomed to constant duplicity and obliged to make a secret of life; and as a writer whose great work, by its very existence, profaned his mother while it triumphantly vindicated his dedication to art, Proust, with all his worldliness and charm, also stood clearly outside the society he portrayed and anatomized with such subtlety and perception.

Though scrupulous in its factual research and textual analysis, Painter's view of biography is novelistic. He believes the life-writer follows the same process as the fiction-writer, and knows by instinct how to convey the passage of time and when to end the book: "The artist has creative imagination, the artistic biographer has recreative imagination. You look at your evidence and your facts and their relationships, and they begin to come alive. . . . We live our lives hour by hour, day by day, and you've got to produce the feeling of day to day living, of this slow and sometimes very rapid movement in the texture of your book. . . . You have your solution to which you're applying all these ingredients, and there comes a point when the solution is saturated, when the law of diminishing returns comes, when you feel this is enough to get this thing right. Then you stop."[17]

III

The biographical principles expressed in the Foreword to *Gide* and in the retrospective interviews with Simon Blow and Phyllis Grosskurth were arrogantly and categorically stated (rather than carefully argued) in the Preface to the first volume of *Marcel Proust: A Biography* (1959). The Preface laid the intellectual and aesthetic foundations of this work, but the dogmatic tone provoked the hostility of a number of critics. Painter later acknowledged that the Preface was a contentious challenge and a strategic error (and did not write a Preface to the second volume of *Proust* or to *Chateaubriand*). As he told Grosskurth: "I was a very naughty young man [i.e., age 45] to use such words and I probably wouldn't do it now. I must say that sometimes when I read the preface, I don't altogether like the tone of it."[18]

But he also defended the Preface and declared: "It was an indispensable manifesto, historically necessitated by the then state of thought or *idées reçues* on literary biography or Proust, and I think it did its work, angered only those whom the cap fitted or those who cannot bear to be told things they don't think already, and has been generally assimilated whether directly or indirectly to the point of seeming obvious and axiomatic (it was both to me when I wrote it), instead of paradoxical and heretical."[19]

Though Painter claims his biography is "not intended as a controversial work," he recklessly abandons the scholar's false humility and debt to his predecessors, and announces that "the subject has never yet been treated with anything approaching scholarly method"—that is, with exhaustive research based on a carefully conceived theory of biography. He also defiantly declares: "I have endeavoured to write a definitive biography of Proust: a complete, exact and detailed narrative of his life, that is, based on every known or discoverable primary source, and on primary sources only. . . . I think I may claim that something like nine-tenths of the narrative here given is new to Proustian biography, or conversely that previous biographers have used only about one-tenth of the discoverable sources." Though Painter stresses his objective scholarly method, the most striking characteristic of the biography is the imaginative range and psychological depth. Painter's unhappily phrased claim that ninety percent of his material is new cannot be verified and is doubtless exaggerated. He must have meant, by this assertion, that the meaning he has invested in the material and the interpretation he gives to the facts—if not the actual facts themselves—are entirely new.

Painter next attacks "one of the dogmas of Proustian criticism, that his novel can and must be treated as a closed system" and read entirely without reference to Proust's biography and background. In opposition to this dogma, he reiterates his belief that "no aspect of Proust or his work . . . can be studied without an accurate and detailed knowledge of his life." Anticipating attacks on this point, he adds: "I hope those who judge . . . my work will consider whether the facts are true, rather than whether the critical approach demanded by the facts happens to be fashionable at the present moment."[20]

Painter's Preface then considers the vital question of the relation between Proust's art and life ("one of the chief meanings of Time Regained"), mentions his attempt to identify all the originals or components that were fused into Proust's people and places ("though he invented nothing, he altered everything"), and reveals his obsessive desire to connect every aspect of the novel to factual reality. "By discovering which aspects of his originals he chose or rejected," Painter observes, "how he combined many models into each new figure, and most of all how he altered material reality to make it conform more closely to symbolic reality, we can observe the workings of his imagination at the very moment of creation. . . . *A la recherche* turns out to be not only based entirely on his own experiences: it is intended to be the symbolic story of his life . . . it is not, properly speaking, a fiction, but a creative autobiography" (I.xii–xiii). Painter's method is to find the factual source for every aspect of the novel. And his biography emphasizes the factual basis by providing two separate indexes: the first of real persons and places, the second of fictitious characters and places in Proust's novel; and by cross-referencing each index to the other.

It is ironic that even the most sober aspects of Painter's Preface—his discussion of the bibliography, references and citations to Proust's work—provide points of contention. For he states that they would not appear in the first volume and would be postponed until the second, in order to prevent rival scholars from appropriating his sources and rushing into print before he could complete his work. "To avoid needless repetition," Painter writes, "—and also, I confess, to avoid laying all my cards on the table before the game is finished [though he certainly has done this in the Preface]—I have postponed giving a full bibliography of the sources used, together with detailed references for each statement, till the second and final volume, which will appear in two years' time." Painter concludes that "it seemed imperative to give references to the standard *Pléiade* edition of the original text in three volumes" (I.xv) rather than to the superb English translation by C. K. Scott-Moncrieff—though the difficult French text would scarcely serve the needs of the "general reader" to whom Painter addressed his book.

IV

When the first volume of *Marcel Proust* was published, many of the critics concentrated on the Preface rather than on the book and disputed Painter's controversial assertions: that previous scholarship was worthless (it is difficult to see how Painter could dismiss his predecessors if he had never read anyone else on his subject), that his biography was definitive, that nine-tenths of the narrative was new, that Proust's "creative autobiography" could not be understood without a knowledge of his life, that Proust "invented nothing," that every aspect of the book was based on reality, that all the fictional characters could be connected to their multiple original models, that no scholarly sources would be given in the first volume and that the French rather than the English edition of the novel would be cited in the notes. Publishing the biography in two volumes instead of one was a serious mistake, for it aroused expectations that could not be gratified for several years and diminished the impact of the entire book.

Critics recognized and praised Painter's solid scholarship, lucid interpretations, powerful prose style and penetrating portrayal of Proust as a flawed but heroic figure. But his "heretical" belief that "biography is an essential and preliminary part of criticism"[21] came into conflict with the prevailing theories of New Criticism—associated with the writings of I. A. Richards, T. S. Eliot and John Crowe Ransom—which held that works of art should be treated independently of the biography and intentions of the author, and of the social conditions at the time of its production. The fallacy of this view, of course, was that critics attempting to treat the work of art as a closed system were perfectly aware of the social and biographical background and used this knowledge, intentionally or not, when formulating their critique of the novel. Painter played a significant role in leading readers away from the once stimulating but ultimately sterile strictures of the New Criticism.

The English novelists who reviewed the first volume were much more sympathetic than the American critics and scholars. Painter's attempt "to bring [Proust's] friends and acquaintances to life as they were when he knew them" was praised by L. P. Hartley. Writing in the *Spectator* (October 16, 1959), he admired the complete evocation of Proust's society and felt that it *was* the definitive biography of the author and companion to the novel. In an early review in the *New Statesman* (September 19, 1959), Pamela Hansford Johnson, who had contributed an essay to Painter's edition of Proust's *Letters to His Mother* in 1956, called it "the finest biography of our time" and emphasized its blend of "intensive scholarship, imaginative sympathy, love and cool thinking." In the *Observer* (September 20, 1959), Angus Wilson, who had been Painter's colleague at the British Museum, pronounced it "brilliant and scholarly." He particularly valued the "depiction of place and people, his revelation of the raw material for the novel." The review in the *Daily Telegraph* by Anthony Powell, whose multi-volumed *Dance to the Music of Time* was profoundly influenced by Proust, concluded: "Mr. Painter has done his work so well that it is hard to speak in moderate terms of his skill and unobtrusive wit."

The reviewers in American journals (outside the English old-boy network) recognized Painter's merits but were far more critical of his biographical approach and arrogant claims. The drama critic Richard Gilman, writing in the Catholic weekly, *Commonweal* (October 16, 1959), questioned the biographical premises but commended Painter's scholarship, acknowledged that he had identified all the originals and agreed that he had, as he claimed, achieved the definitive biography. Gilman wondered, however, if Painter could deliver what he had promised in the second volume. In the *Yale Review* (December 1959), the excellent French scholar, W. H. Frohock, said "Painter's industry and learning are admirable." But he criticized Painter's "arrogantly assumed omniscience"; and stated that much of the material was quite familiar, and nine-tenths of it was certainly *not* new.

Two of the American reviews were particularly negative. In the *New York Herald Tribune Book Review* (August 16, 1959), Marvin Lowenthal, editor of Montaigne's *Autobiography,* agreed with Frohock that the new material was indeed familiar, perversely claimed that André Maurois and Richard Barker give "a far more vivid picture" of Proust, and called Painter's richly detailed volume "a singularly padded and jerky biography" which "constantly relapses into . . . a Handbook to Proust." The most antagonistic review came in the *Nation* (October 3, 1959) from Mina Curtiss, translator and editor of the *Letters of Marcel Proust* (1949), who seemed to resent the invasion of her scholarly territory and to express a personal grudge. She mentioned that only one-tenth of the material was new. She disputed Painter's facts, felt he had demeaned the power of Proust's imagination by linking it to actual events, called his work a series of "defective detective stories," and claimed that he lacked the humility and love that she presumably possessed.[22]

In the Preface of 1959 Painter had promised that detailed references would be given in the second volume, "which will appear in two years' time." In the fourth impression of the first volume (1965), he changed this to "six years' time" in order to match the publication of the second volume. During their interview, Grosskurth remarked: "when you published the first volume of *Proust* in 1959, you said that Volume Two would appear six years later." Painter, overcome by vanity (or perhaps by faulty memory), replied: "Did I now? That was a very good guess." And Grosskurth naively agreed: "You did, and it appeared exactly six years later."[23]

The reviews of the second volume were even more enthusiastic and vituperative than those of the first. Critics who admired the book praised the new interpretation of the material; those who disliked it either resented the mass of detail or the darker, more complex picture of Proust which interfered with their preconceived view of the writer. The literary critic John Gross, in *Encounter* (October 1965), felt the second half of Proust's life was less interesting, but that Painter "has sifted the evidence scrupulously, and rearranged an unwieldy mass of materials with admirable clarity. . . . In a word, he is indispensable." The philosopher Stuart Hampshire, writing in the *New Statesman* (July 9, 1965), perceived that Proust's "art was rooted in his own pathological condition." Hampshire felt that the second volume, which subordinated biography to the composition of the novel, "will be found slightly disappointing, as if there had been some loss of confidence in the interval; the detached, assured tone is gone." This change may have occurred because Painter had been attacked by certain critics, had come to regret the tone of the Preface to the first volume and had taken much longer than anticipated to complete the second.

The critics in America were generally harsher in their judgments than the English. On the front page of the *New York Times Book Review* (November 7, 1965), the distinguished English biographer, Peter Quennell, commented that Painter "attaches too much importance to Proust's relations with his mother" (though this was one of the most convincing aspects of the book); but agreed with his fellow-countrymen that the life illuminated the work: "I have seldom read a biography that provides so convincing an account of how a masterpiece evolves." The most intelligent review was written on the front page of the *Washington Post Book Week* (November 7, 1965) by a leading American Proust scholar, Roger Shattuck. He said the book was "organized in clusters around the crucial moments in Proust's life . . . [and] backed by Painter's psychological perceptiveness and sturdy prose style." Shattuck called it "a great biography" that achieves "a new level of accuracy and understanding, and stands in its own right as a work of art." In the *New York Review of Books* (November 11, 1965), Anne de Colleyre, a French poet and critic of Proust, noted Painter's cast of mind and psychological penetration: "Painter is a snob, as were Stendhal and Baudelaire, and his snobbishness provides him not only with a biased view of French history but also a remarkable literary insight." And she convincingly concluded: "It is a major biography in English, distinguished by thorough scholarship, honesty in acknowledging the frailty of genius, and a cogent style."

In the *Virginia Quarterly Review* (Winter 1966), Milton Hindus, author of *The Proustian Vision* (1954) and *A Reader's Guide to Marcel Proust* (1962), felt the need to defend Proust against Painter's methodology and unwelcome revelations about Proust's character. Hindus upheld the New Critics' viewpoint, denied that everything in the novel was based on Proust's own experience and objected to Painter's thesis that the work could not be fully understood without a knowledge of Proust's life. But Hindus' critical point was not a vital issue. Since Proust's novel, his fictional manifestation of reality, was utterly convincing, it did not greatly matter whether Proust had transformed or invented experience. Hindus also disliked the "pretentious style" (which everyone else had admired), and (like Marvin Lowenthal) rather perversely insisted that Richard Barker's superficial biography of 1958 was superior. Unable to bear the truth about his idol or accept the frailty of genius, Hindus attacked Painter's "voyeuristic fascination with the most intimate details of his private life."

In July 1960, just after the publication of the first volume, Marie Riefstahl-Nordlinger, an English friend who had introduced Proust to Ruskin and helped him translate the Master's work, attacked Painter in a cruelly wounding article. It had been originally broadcast on November 1, 1959 over the French Service of the BBC and then reprinted, disguised as a review, in *X*, a short-lived London quarterly. Though Riefstahl-Nordlinger tried to undermine Painter's authority by listing a series of minor factual errors, she was actually attempting to discredit his fundamental principles of biography, to dispute his right to gain access to intimate information and to question the entire point of his enterprise. She was even more possessive and proprietary about Proust than Curtiss and Hindus; and, like them, self-righteously felt that she alone was the sole repository of truth about her idol. Painter's quarrel with Riefstahl-Nordlinger is important because it reveals the resistance of the old guard to the new purpose and method of biography: to illuminate the artist's imagination by utilizing every available piece of evidence. Painter easily won the argument, partly because the points at issue were trivial, mainly because Riefstahl-Nordlinger, ostensibly disputing factual details, never directly addressed the much more serious issues that had originally inspired her outburst.

In a dignified and persuasive response in *X* in October 1960, Painter reiterated his admiration (fully expressed in his book) for his unexpected adversary; answered in considerable detail some fourteen trivial points "on which Mme. Riefstahl-Nordlinger accuses me of inaccuracy, negligence, misrepresentation, ignorance, malice, invention, mistranslation and prying"; and stated: "I can find no justification, in the factual objections which she makes to this small fraction of my work, for her imputations against my integrity, my scholarship and my taste." Invoking the recent example of Ellmann's *Joyce,* Painter strongly objected to Riefstahl-Nordlinger's assertion that "biography is a rather dubious business," and concluded with a fundamental principle of his work: "I am staggered by her remarks that an attempt 'to observe the workings of Proust's imagination' (surely one of the primary duties of the biographer, and one for which she herself has given invaluable evidence) can appeal 'only to the clinically minded.' "[24]

The dispute with Riefstahl-Nordlinger was revived and publicized, after the review of the second volume appeared in the *Times Literary Supplement,* when John Lehmann defended his distant cousin's little known attack on Painter. In the *Times Literary Supplement* of August 19, 1965, Painter responded to Lehmann's "ignorant and baseless smear" with a magnificently persuasive defense: "I answered the fourteen factual points with which she backed her imputations on my integrity as a scholar, showing that in most she was mistaken and I was right; in some I had relied on her own previous words, which she then clarified or retracted; others were matters of opinion, based in my case on evidence; but none involved the validity of any important conclusion, still less of my good faith."[25] The astonishing aspects of all these contradictory reviews is not that Painter's work received its just praise, but that it also provoked, from supposedly qualified critics, such violent and self-interested abuse.

V

Painter explains that the first volume of *Marcel Proust*—which concludes with the death of Proust's father in 1903—analyzes the autobiographical material used in the novel and that "a discussion of his methods of synthesis will appear in the second volume" (I.xii). Painter places the vast quantity of material in its organic order, and maintains the narrative thrust of the story through four long but necessary digressions: on the topography of the symbolic landscape, Illiers (chapter 2), on Proust's hosts, hostesses and acquaintances in society (chapter 10), on the Dreyfus affair (chapter 13) and on Proust's study of Ruskin (chapter 14). Painter links the thematic clusters of the narrative by means of clear transitions: "It is time for a further glimpse of Montesquiou," "It is time to tell the strange story of the Vinteuil Septet" (II.5, 242). His style is lucid, leisurely and elegant; with a rich particularity of detail (though he could have been more precise about what Proust's circle ate and drank at their memorable banquets) and a fine dramatic flair.

The span of Proust's life (1871–1922) extends from the Franco-Prussian War till after the Great War. Painter, with an impressive mastery of the background, places his subject in the social, political and cultural context. He vividly re-creates, for example, the disasters that occurred when the Seine overflowed its banks in the summer of 1910, which led to renovations in Proust's building, prolonged attacks of asthma and interruptions in his work: "The bears in the Jardin des Plantes were rescued in imminent danger of drowning; it was feared that the crocodiles might escape from their flooded pools; and the poor giraffe had to be left, knee-deep, to die of exposure. Sewers burst in the streets, or rose hideously in cellars, and rats fled through the boulevards" (II.158).

Painter's "palace of pleasure" exhibits a Proustian fascination with society (as well as a tendency to overload the narrative with lists of titles and proper nouns): "In their drawing-rooms flourished a gay elegance, a fantastic individuality, a chivalrous freedom, a living interplay of minds, morals and emotions" (II.315). Like Proust himself, Painter loves the definitive epigram and is fond of recording witty *mots*. Léon Daudet said: "I wouldn't have trusted [the surgeon] to cut my hair"; a cocotte "first posed in tights and spangles at the Théâtre du Châtelet, then put on more clothes to become an actress, and lastly took everything off to be an artist's model" (I.101, 217). He reveals how Proust transformed the dross of the frequently empty, heartless and corrupt society into the gold of literature, and made those people appear more interesting in fiction than they ever were in reality.

Painter portrays all the major characters in Proust's life with subtlety and vividness, and painstakingly unravels the strands of his personal relationships. Charles Haas, the model for Charles Swann, was, he said, "the only Jew ever to be accepted by Parisian society without being immensely rich" (I.92). Painter provides complex reasons to explain the social eminence of Count Robert de Montesquiou, the model for the monstrous Baron de Charlus: it "was based partly on his snob-value as a titled intellectual, partly on his hypnotic power of imposing himself on the fashionable world, and partly on the gift his hated relatives possessed for intermarriage with the great" (I.125). Painter describes Montesquiou's manners, his Wildean wit ("It's bad enough not to have any money, it would be too much if one had to deprive oneself of anything," I.127), his behavior (he never realized his artistic potential but merely "dressed, collected, scribbled, quarrelled, fascinated and terrorised," I.133), and his sexual tastes (his carnal relations with the divine Sarah Bernhardt were followed by a week of uncontrollable vomiting). More importantly, Painter shows how their relations changed as Proust transformed Montesquiou in his fiction; how Proust's suffering in love unexpectedly revealed another side of his friend's peculiar personality and inspired a rare letter "of genuine, winning sympathy with which this saturnine man revealed, sometimes, the goodness that still lingered in his corroded heart" (II.206).

The appearance, conversation and character of Proust himself are also vividly delineated. Lucien Daudet remembered "his moonlike paleness and jet-black hair, his over-large head drooping on his narrow shoulders, and his enormous eyes, which seemed to take in everything at once without actually looking at anything" (I.186). Proust—who slept in the day, worked by night and found the sun "a very strange object"—would often converse with his friends till dawn, "growing ever more brilliant to stave off the moment of parting. . . . His conversation was full of the most piercing psychological observations, and anecdotes of gentle but penetrating irony" (I.257, 294). Claude Debussy, however, felt Proust was "longwinded and precious and a bit of an old woman" (I.291).

Painter provides particularly interesting accounts of Proust's military service, when, among the discipline and love of comrades, he experienced the delightful illusion of being normal and accepted; of his duel, when he exchanged shots at twenty-five yards and showed considerable coolness and courage (he was also fearless of danger during wartime air-raids); and of his almost imperceptible sinecure as a librarian.

One of Painter's great strengths as a biographer is his ability to represent the complex motives of human behavior, to trace the recurrent patterns of Proust's life, and to delineate the major themes of the novel. He gives many reasons for Proust's courtship and flattery of Montesquiou—amiable, utilitarian, aesthetic, psychiatric—and concludes that Proust felt his own destiny as a man and a writer was linked to Count Robert. In a similar fashion, Painter explains that Proust did not object when his mother tried to find him a wife, "whether from desire to please her, or to conceal his perversion, or from confidence that he could always refuse any actual candidate for his hand, or because he had not yet entirely renounced the possibility of marriage" (I.247).

When tracing the dominant patterns of Proust's life, Painter notes that his "passion for Ruskin took precisely the same course as his love-affairs or ardent friendships. There was a prelude of tepid acquaintance; a crystallisation and a taking fire; and a falling out of love, from which he emerged free, but changed and permanently enriched" (I.256). He also observes that during Proust's ascent to the heights of the Faubourg Saint-Germain, he continued simultaneously his descent toward Sodom. And Painter concisely lists the major themes of *Remembrance of Things Past* as "the unreality of the phenomenal world, the poetic nature of the past in which the only true reality is hidden, the impossibility of knowing another person, the continual process of change in the self, feelings and memory" (I.69).

Painter told Grosskurth: "I went off Freud when I went off left-wing politics and the Popular Front before the war. . . . He was again and again presenting his theories as if he were scientifically proving them, and his texts contained no proof at all." Yet Painter qualified his "rejection" by adding, "Obviously there is a great deal of what Freud does say that is true" and by acknowledging, "Things like the Oedipus complex, love of one's mother and hostility against one's father, the encouragement of homosexuality by failure with [the] heterosexual love object, particularly when the family is involved in it, hostility between brothers, between children of the same parents—all of these I mention."[26]

Proust's doctor-father, who invented the principle of the *cordon sanitaire* and helped banish cholera from Europe, allowed his bewildering son to lead the life he wished. Proust's most profound and influential relationship was with his formidable and sacrificial mother. Painter observes early on that Proust "grew to believe, resentfully, that she loved him best when he was ill and he tried to win her love by being ill. . . . [Asthma] was the mark of his difference from others, his appeal for love, his refuge from duties which were foreign to his still unconscious purpose; and in later life it helped him to withdraw from the world and to produce a work 'de si longue haleine.' . . . Her blood made him a tribesman of Abraham, her over-anxious love a native of the Cities of the Plain" (I.4, 12).[27]

Painter establishes that the loss and recovery of his mother's good-night kiss, described in the "Overture" to *Swann's Way,* was not an act of love but a surrender to his blackmail. Withheld at first by the command of his father and then indulgently bestowed, it symbolizes the nourishing but destructive adoration that prevented him from loving another woman and the mutual hatred "which persisted at the root of their love" (II.301). Proust consistently made heterosexual choices that were certain to fail, so that he would be free at last to choose his true desire. The mother's death, which marked the great watershed of Proust's life and is described at the beginning of the second volume, is poignantly rendered. After Proust had kissed his mother for the last time, he told a friend: "Today I have her still, dead, but accepting my caresses—tomorrow I shall lose her forever" (II.49).

One of Painter's principal points is that Proust's sexual experience, far from being exclusively homosexual, was partly based on his physical relations with women: "readers who have felt all along that Proust's picture of heterosexual love is valid and founded on personal experience will be glad to find their instinct justified" (I.xii). The female characters desired by the Narrator were not merely transposed from men, but began as women to whom Proust was attracted in real life: "In his novel Proust rejected his own inversion, and created the Narrator from the lost but real heterosexual part of his own divided nature; he used homosexuality, like snobbism and cruelty, as a symbol of universal original sin" (II.313).

Freud has taught modern biographers that it is essential to examine the sexual life of their subject, which was formerly considered either unknowable or unsuitable to know. By dealing with unpleasant truths and discussing Proust's perverse sexuality, Painter inevitably demythologizes (as the nineteenth-century biographers had idealized) the great writer; but he also brings us close to the inner man by providing the most sophisticated and complex view of Proust. A frank and full knowledge of Proust's homosexuality increases our understanding of the man and his novel, and enables us to participate in the transformation of life into art.

Painter's sensational disclosures about Proust's homosexual aberrations show that even the basest vices—the donation of his parents' furniture to a male brothel, the desecration of his mother's photograph, the indulgence in flagellation, the torture of rats with hatpins—were redeemed by his art. In a brilliant and discriminating summary that binds together the themes of Proust's life, Painter traces his vicious descent into the violence and cruelty of Sodom:

> [It] had begun with love for his equals (Reynaldo and Lucien), progressed through platonic affection for social superiors (Fénelon, Antoine Bibesco, and the rest) to physical affection for social inferiors (Ulrich and Agostinelli), and now ended, disillusioned with all, in a sterile intercourse with professional catamites. He was experimenting with evil—an evil which perhaps does not exist anywhere in the realm of natural or unnatural sex, except as a moral nullity, a mirage for the desperate—and testing his power to associate with it unscathed.

Painter emphasizes that one of the greatest novels ever written was created, paradoxically, from the basest material. Though he makes a moral judgment on these disheartening events, he also encourages compassion and forgiveness: though this vice "revealed itself in acts which are at once abominable and absurd, [it] should be absolved with awe and sympathy by all of his sinful fellow-humans" (II.266–267).

Proust began his novel in July 1909, installed the famous cork walls in his bedroom, and started the long process of expansion and enrichment of his prearranged plan which would continue until the day of death. *Swann's Way*, rejected for publication by André Gide and praised by Henry James as the greatest French novel since *The Charterhouse of Parma*, was published in November 1913. *Within a Budding Grove* won the postwar Goncourt Prize for the intellectual non-combatant in 1919 and led to the Legion of Honor the following year. From then on Proust raced to complete his novel against the threat of death: "'Death pursues me, Céleste,' he said, 'I shan't have time to finish my corrections'" (II.356). But when he reached the moribund condition of one of his characters, he hastened to add some notes on the death of Bergotte.

It may have been possible to cure Proust's asthma, but he unconsciously preferred his illness and did not want to be cured. It freed him for isolation and for work, "widening," as he said, "by cutting down the undergrowth of pointless friendships, the avenues that lead to my solitude" (II.330). He spent the two years between 1905 and 1907 almost entirely confined to bed, indulging his regimen of insomnia, fumigation and drugs. When he contracted pneumonia and died in November 1922, his masterpiece, though still imperfect, was complete.

In the midst of an acute analysis of the relation of Proust's *Contre Sainte-Beuve* to *Remembrance of Things Past*, one third of the way through the second volume, Painter suddenly, and more clearly than ever, expounds his exalted biographical credo:

> The biographer's task is to . . . discover, beneath the mask of the artist's every-day, objective life, the secret from which he extracted his work; show how, in the apparently sterile persons

and places of that external life, he found the hidden, universal meanings which are the themes of his book; and reveal the drama of the contrast and interaction between his daily existence and his incommensurably deeper life as a creator. (II.126)

Painter's *Marcel Proust* triumphantly fulfills what he believes to be the author's highest purpose: to communicate "the state of vision in which the book was written, so that the writer's revelation becomes the reader's" (II.35).

4

André Malraux and the Art of Action

I

André Malraux always admired intellectual men of action: Trotsky, Mao, De Gaulle, and he believed "A man is what he does." The pattern and meaning of Malraux's complex life becomes clearer when he is compared to Gabriele D'Annunzio, T. E. Lawrence and Marie-David de Mayrena, who belonged to a vanished breed of mythomanic adventurers, who believed their own lies and turned them into legends, and who were able to live out their private fantasies. D'Annunzio and Lawrence, who reached the peak of their careers just as Malraux began his own brilliant trajectory through art, war and politics, were the most immediate and influential models of the literary adventurer. In the 1920s Malraux wanted to be, like D'Annunzio, a stylish revolutionary *condottiere* who could inspire and lead a people to nationalistic glory. His first wife, Clara, reports in her perceptive but bitchy memoirs that after Malraux's arrest in Indochina he boasted, "Don't lose heart: I'll certainly end up by being Gabriele D'Annunzio." "Where did I find the strength to shout that I did not care a damn in hell for Gabriele D'Annunzio, that grotesque, indecent clown? The funny thing is," writes Clara forty years after the incident, "that he has really become Gabriele D'Annunzio."

Throughout his life Malraux was obsessed by T. E. Lawrence, whom he saw as the archetypal scholar, soldier and writer, as well as the Nietzschean precursor of Malraux's own fight against destiny and attempt at self-transcendence. Both Lawrence and Malraux deliberately disguised their family background and the major events of their lives, and created their own exotic legends as an attractive alternative to reality. As Malraux writes of the Lawrencean hero of *The Walnut Trees of Altenburg* (1943): "He could perhaps have found some means of destroying the mythical person he was growing into, had he been compelled. But he had no wish to do so. His reputation was flattering. What was more important, he enjoyed it."

Both Lawrence and Malraux possessed a formidable erudition in their youth, despised academic pedantry, were fascinated by remote civilizations and cultures, began their careers with archeological expeditions to the East and carried out explorations in the desert. Both flamboyantly led the underdog in a foreign war and became fascinated with flying. Both were war heroes who shifted from a military to a political career at a crucial moment in history, and became the intellectual and ideological supporters of nationalistic leaders: Feisal and De Gaulle. While Lawrence deliberately regressed from a Lieutenant-Colonel to a private in the Tank Corps, Malraux, who adopted Lawrence's guerrilla tactics when he fought with the Resistance, began as a private in the Tank Corps and became a Lieutenant-Colonel. Malraux's capture of Strasbourg, the last French city in German hands, at the head of the Alsace-Lorraine Brigade, was the symbolic equivalent of Lawrence's capture of Damascus, the last Arab city in Turkish hands, at the head of the Bedouin legions. In *The Walnut Trees of Altenburg* Malraux observes, "Intellectuals are like women . . . soldiers make them dream," and in his own life he attempted to turn his dream of Lawrence into reality.

Malraux planned to write the life of Lawrence as early as 1929 and a chapter from this book, "Lawrence and the Demon of the Absolute" (1946), was written in 1942 at the same time as *The Walnut Trees of Altenburg*, in which Vincent Berger's tribal warfare among the Senussi of the Libyan desert and his relation to Enver Pasha and the Pan-Turk movement are clearly based on Lawrence's achievements in the Arab Revolt. In his essay on Lawrence, Malraux remarks, "Whoever writes his memoirs (except to deceive) judges himself. There were in this book [*Seven Pillars of Wisdom*], as in all memoirs, two *personae:* the one who said I and the author." This statement is revealing because Malraux's *Antimemoirs* (1967) were influenced by Lawrence's confessional mode and by his two *personae,* and also because Malraux's analysis and judgment of Lawrence represent a synthesis of his own dominant characteristics:

> His pride; his appetite for glory and deceit, his scorn of this desire; his implacable will; his distrust of ideas; his need for relief from his intelligence; his anguished self-consciousness which led him to try to see himself through the eyes of others; his lack of all faith and the search for the limits of his strength.

Finally, just as Malraux, when a student in 1914, is said to have met D'Annunzio in Paris, so in an interview with *L'Express* in 1971 Malraux claimed to have met Lawrence; and he discussed the English hero with a deferential reverence that he usually reserved for deities like De Gaulle.

> Lawrence, I've met him once. Once only, in a bar of a grand hotel, in Paris, I no longer know which one. We were not equals, you know. He had in his pocket the *Seven Pillars,* his collaboration with Churchill during the peace conference, his rupture with the world and that halo of mystery that the Intelligence Service gave him. Of course the true mystery was not

there. I doubted it without being sure of it at the time. I was a little French writer with only the Prix Goncourt in my pocket. It was light. He was extraordinarily elegant. Of an elegance of today, not of his time. A pullover with a rolled neck, a kind of nonchalance and distance.

I don't remember the subjects we discussed. I remember simply that he was then passionate for motors, those of motorcycles and boats. It was a relatively short time before his death. Did he want to die? I have often asked myself that question without being able to answer it.

Unfortunately this statement, so appropriate to Malraux's mythomania, deserves to be true but is patently false. It is significant that on this momentous occasion Malraux, who had a phenomenal memory, did not remember the name of the hotel nor the subjects discussed. Apart from the fact that Lawrence never mentions meeting Malraux, Lawrence did not drink nor frequent the bars of grand hotels; he did not collaborate with Churchill at the Paris Peace Conference of 1919, but at the Cairo Conference of 1921; he had never been in the Intelligence Service, though he did intelligence work for the Arab Bureau in Cairo during 1915–1916; he was not at all elegant, but self-consciously shabby (the pullover with a rolled neck comes from the well-known photograph taken at the end of Lawrence's life and reproduced in the *Letters*); and though Malraux claimed to have met Lawrence in Paris after he won the Prix Goncourt in 1933, Lawrence did not leave England between 1933 and his death in 1935. For Malraux the next best thing to actually meeting Lawrence was saying that he had met him.

"As late as 1946 it was rumored that Malraux was working on studies of [Mayrena] and of T. E. Lawrence whom," writes Frohock, "he thought of as another adventurer of this sort." In the *Antimemoirs* Malraux regrets "There are no real soldiers of fortune left. . . . The myth of Rimbaud is fading"; and he writes at great length about Mayrena, whose legend was still vivid in Indochina during the 1920s and whom Malraux acknowledged as a model for Perken in *The Royal Way* (1930).

Marie-David de Mayrena, an obscure French traveller and soldier, who has been dropped from the more recent editions of *La Grande Encyclopédie,* was compounded in Malraux's imagination of Rajah Brooke, who carved himself the kingdom of Sarawak in Borneo; of Rimbaud, a hopeless adventurer who came to grief in the wilderness of Abyssinia; and of Kurtz in Conrad's *Heart of Darkness* (1899). For like Kurtz, Mayrena was "hot-headed, impulsive, tough and without scruples, and capable of going forward to explore dangerous but useful paths."

The real Mayrena, the son of a captain in the French navy, was born in Toulon in 1842. He accompanied an expedition to Cochin-China in 1860s, fought in the Franco-Prussian War, took part in missions to Malaysia in the early 1880s, and in 1888 was sent by Constans, the Governor-General of Indochina, to explore the Moi region of the Mekong basin. Mayrena penetrated that unknown territory, formed a confederation with the tribes against their traditional Siamese enemies, forced the wild Mois to recognize his authority and proclaimed himself Marie I, King of the Sedangs. He then ceded political control to France and kept the right of economic exploitation for himself. But when Constans was replaced, the colonial administration quickly lost interest in the Mois and refused to recognize Mayrena's kingdom; and he embarked on an unsuccessful tour of Hong Kong, London and Brussels in search of financial and political support. Frustrated in his ambitions, he abandoned the Mois and retired to the island of Tioman, near Singapore, where he died of a snakebite in 1890.

Conrad's friend, Sir Hugh Clifford, knew Mayrena on Tioman, and described him as an "absurd anachronism," a pretentious and even ludicrous figure who tried to bribe embarrassed colonial officials with colorful but worthless decorations from the Kingdom of the Sedangs. But Malraux, who interpreted Mayrena subjectively and used him for his own purposes, believes "the more Mayrena found himself doomed to obscurity, the more the legend grew. He became very Parisian . . . a disreputable hero, destined less for kingship than for assassination, [but] redeemed by the *feeling he inspired*"—not by the reality of his actions. Malraux quotes Mayrena as complaining, "my enemies take me for an impostor," and comments (in a twice qualified phrase that applies to himself as well as his hero), "Mayrena tells lies. But not all the time, or at least not always undiluted lies."

II

Like D'Annunzio and Lawrence, Malraux was a talented virtuoso who in the course of his life was a "book dealer, editor, poet, publisher, explorer, archeologist, detainee, novelist, reviewer, aviator, revolutionary, politician, orator, soldier, guerrilla leader, minister and philosopher." Malraux's family came from the Dunquerque-Calais region in Flanders. His grandfather was a master-cooper and wine merchant who also owned a fishing fleet that he failed to insure and lost at sea in a storm near Newfoundland. Always incautious, he died by splitting open his own skull with a blow from a double-edged axe. Malraux's father, Fernand, was born in 1879 and married Berthe Lamy, the daughter of a farmer from the Jura, in 1900. Malraux was born in Paris in 1901, and after his parents' separation four years later he grew up and went to school in Bondy, the farthest and greyest of the Paris suburbs, where his mother kept a small grocery store. Malraux's parents were divorced in 1915 and his father, who remarried and moved to Orleans, had two other sons, Roland and Claude. He killed himself in 1930. Though Malraux claimed to have been a student at the Lycée Condorcet and the Ecole des Langues Orientales, there is no record of his enrollment there, and he left school without a diploma. It is not surprising therefore that he stated: "Almost all writers I know love their childhood; I hate mine."

Malraux entered the book trade by finding rare volumes on the bookstalls along the Seine and selling them to antiquarian dealers. In 1920 he worked on art books for the publisher Simon Kra, wrote articles for *avant-garde* magazines and met artists like Cocteau, Tzara, Artaud, Cendrars, Aragon, Satie and Derain. The following year he published in an expensive limited edition his first book, the Surrealistic fantasy *Lunes en papier,* and married the wealthy and attractive Jewish intellectual, Clara Goldschmidt. Clara relates that "When I used to weep and lament over trifles Malraux would say, 'You are bringing out your little portable wailing wall.'"

The aesthete and idler of the early twenties was very different from the heroic and committed Malraux of subsequent years. He avoided military service with a false medical report and spent the first years of his marriage studying anthropology and oriental art, travelling in Europe and North Africa, and gambling on the stock exchange until he lost all of Clara's money. She records that when "confronted with our economic disaster . . . he simply replied, 'You don't really suppose that I'm going to *work,* do you?'" Instead of work, Malraux planned an expedition to the East that marked the first turning point of his life, for during the twenties his career was dominated by Indochina, just as it was by Spain in the thirties, the Resistance in the forties, art in the fifties and Gaullist politics in the sixties.

III

During his studies of Khmer art Malraux had read about the once glorious Royal Way in the jungles of Cambodia, and to solve his financial problems the future custodian of French culture, decided as he told Clara, that "We'll go to some little Cambodian temple, we'll take away a few statues, and we'll sell them in America; and that will give us enough to live quietly for two or three years." And Clara adds, "In short, we knew nothing whatever about the country to which we were going, and from it expected everything." This expedition, which turned out disastrously, was thus motivated by a mixture of careful planning and romantic enthusiasm.

Malraux procured some rather vague credentials from the School of Oriental Studies in Paris, and in 1923 sailed for the East with Clara and his friend Louis Chevasson. He made his way to Pnom Penh, and on the strength of his Parisian papers commandeered ox-carts and guides who took him to the Buddhist temple of Banteay-Srey, about forty miles north of Angor Wat. Malraux sawed the sculpture off the temple and loaded it first on the ox-carts and then on the riverboat going to Pnom Penh. The entire adventure in the jungle lasted less than a week, but its sequel was far more protracted. For when they arrived in the capital the police boarded the boat, discovered the stolen statues and arrested Malraux and Chevasson. Malraux remained cool, adopted a cavalier attitude and attributed only slight importance "to an event whose only effect would be the delaying of our plans for a few days."

When Malraux was brought to trial he sent Clara back to France to gather support for him among the intellectuals of Paris, and assumed a perversely contemptuous attitude in court. He "vehemently claimed responsibility for the adventure; sarcasms were directed at the authorities and insults (or words interpreted as such) at the judges." Walter Langlois, in his authoritative account of Malraux's years in Indochina, states that Malraux's lawyer "maintained that no crime had been committed because the ruined Banteay Srei had never been officially classified as an 'historical monument' by the colonial government. Even if it had been, the classification would be invalid because the temple was not under the jurisdiction of the authority." This was the best argument his lawyer could make for a client who had been flagrantly caught with stolen goods, but it was not very convincing and Malraux was condemned to three years in prison. After an appeal in Saigon, this was reduced to one year with a suspended sentence and was later annulled in Paris. Clara's petition for clemency, which was signed by an impressive number of French writers and artists who admired Malraux's bold but unsuccessful venture, had been particularly effective. Malraux was fortunate to escape without punishment, and things ended as they began with the adventurer on the loose and the sculpture back in the temple. When the School of Oriental Studies restored Banteay Srey in 1925, the stolen statues were removed from storage in the museum in Pnom Penh and replaced in the temple wall, and unless they were looted or destroyed during the war in Cambodia, they are still there today.

Malraux sailed home in November 1924 swearing vengeance on the dull-witted colonial officials who had subjected him to a humiliating defeat in court. He returned to Saigon the following year, and in June 1925 founded *L'Indochine* with Paul Monin, a liberal lawyer and politician. Their daily, and later weekly, newspaper aggressively supported the nationalistic Young Annam League and crusaded against colonial injustice in a rather bombastic and ineffectual way until it was suppressed by the authorities in February 1926. As Langlois writes:

> In spite of his courageous public stand, pessimism eroded Malraux's indomitable spirit during his last two months in Indochina. Weakened by illness, exhausted from the unequal struggle against the ponderous colonial bureaucracy, and somewhat disillusioned by the lack of widespread upper-class Annamite support for his liberal program, he began to feel that effective reforms in the colony could be initiated only in France.

Malraux had left France as the non-political creator of Surrealistic fantasies; and when he came home (with some hashish for Clara) after his Indochina trial and newspaper career early in 1926, he had been transformed into an extreme opponent of colonialism. Nervous, intense, energetic, he was a brilliant talker, with a brooding expression and a cigarette dangling from the side of his mouth in a manner that would soon be adopted by generations of film stars. Jean Prévost's description of Malraux in 1926 reveals that the handsome and elegant adventurer, who seemed to have risked death in the jungle, made a powerful impression on his friends:

> He couldn't look you in the eye. His gaze followed an invisible bee in every direction. He would shift his shoulders as if a knife were sticking in his back. A punished child, a tense rebel, who had experienced everything but death, that was Malraux on his return from Asia. He tried to shield himself from others and from things behind polite forms, doctrines, crazy fantasies. Pen in hand he flayed at life. His genius could deal with it. Action more than years made a man. Danger had given his heart muscle.

And in that same year Maurice Sachs was overwhelmed by the qualities that Malraux shared with Lawrence: adventurousness, will-power and intelligence:

> I've met Malraux. He makes a very vivid impression. In his look he has the air of adventure, of melancholy and of irresistible will-power, a fine profile of a Renaissance Italian, and yet a very French appearance. He speaks very fast, very well, with the air of knowing everything, dazzles you with his self-confidence and leaves you with the impression that you've met the most intelligent man of the century.

In 1926 Malraux published *The Temptation of the West,* a cultural dialogue between an occidental in Asia and an oriental in Europe which, influenced by Spengler's *Decline of the West* (1918, 1922), attacked colonialism indirectly by celebrating the superiority of Eastern civilization. In 1928 he brought out his first novel, *The Conquerors,* which describes the failure of the 1925 insurrection in Canton, the headquarters of the Kuomintang. In a letter of 1929 Malraux explained how this novel formulates one of the major concerns in his work: "The fundamental question of Garine is much less how to participate in revolution than how to escape what he calls the absurd. The whole of *The Conquerors* is a perpetual quest, and I have moreover insisted on the phrase: to escape the idea of the absurd by seeking refuge in what is human."

Malraux had made a brief trip from Saigon to Hong Kong to purchase type for *L'Indochine* at the time of the nationalist rising in Canton; and in a famous letter to Edmund Wilson in 1933, Malraux said that he organized the Young Annam movement in Saigon and then became *commissaire* in charge of propaganda and information for the Kuomintang, first in Indochina (1924) and then in Canton (1925). Though Malraux was in Hong Kong for a few days in the latter part of 1925, he did *not* go to Canton during the insurrection; and there is absolutely no evidence to substantiate his claim to political power. It is therefore ironic that during Malraux's dispute with Trotsky about the ideology of *The*

Conquerors, the self-styled *commissaire,* who supposedly served the Comintern and the Kuomintang in 1925, was accused by the revolutionary hero of "carrying responsibility for the strangulation of the Chinese revolution."

In 1928, the year of *The Conquerors,* Malraux purged himself of his last Surrealistic fantasy, *Royaume farfelu,* and joined the publisher Gallimard as an editor of art books and organizer of exhibitions. Gallimard also published the distinguished journal, *Nouvelle Revue Française,* whose leading contributor, André Gide, soon became Malraux's close friend. Maurice Sachs, who recognized the fraudulent D'Annunzian element in Malraux's genius, writes:

> The figure who made the greatest effect at the *NRF* was André Malraux, and he had dazzling qualities: a uniquely lively and agile intelligence, a fine voice, a warm and persuasive manner of speaking, an admirable face, though it was beginning to be spoiled by the many tics he could not control or get rid of, elegant in everything, in his bearing, in his manner, in the gestures of his very beautiful hands, and besides his understanding, his attention, his curiosity, much generosity. And yet a bit of a charlatan! He seemed false because he believed that to be less than everything is to be nothing. And yet one could not know him without growing fond of a being so courageous, coldly heroic, passionate with almost as much impartiality as one could find in passion, compassionate, helpful, the friend of suffering mankind, yet not very human, too rational, sometimes crazy, never ordinary and all the same fairly *farfelu.* He never took me seriously and I do not know if that made me see that there was an element of farce in his seriousness, of superficiality in his knowledge, but something fine and lovable in his whole being.

During 1929–1931 Malraux, always an enthusiastic traveller, visited Persia, Afghanistan, India, Malaya and China (the setting of *Man's Fate*) and studied the masterpieces of Eastern art, one of the dominant interests of his life. In 1930 he published *The Royal Way,* a fascinating and underrated novel about a search for sculpture in the jungle, which was based on his experiences in Cambodia, inspired by the heroic adventurer Mayrena and strongly influenced by the dark fate of Kurtz in *Heart of Darkness.*

In 1933 Malraux won the Prix Goncourt, France's most important literary award, for *Man's Fate.* Malraux's greatest novel, which describes Chiang Kai-shek's destruction of his former Communist allies in Shanghai in 1927, concerns the conflict of mind and will and the possibilities of transcending Pascal's concept of the human condition: Gisors with opium and Katov with self-sacrifice, Chen through assassination and Kyo through suicide, Clappique in gambling and Ferral in eroticism. Malraux's portrayal of Ferral and Valerie is a brilliant and sophisticated analysis of the relationship between love, freedom and power that is also reflected in the marriage of Kyo and May, whose betrayal of her husband is based on Clara's confession of infidelity on her voyage from Indochina to France. As in Conrad's *Victory* and Camus' *The Plague,* which are ideologically close to Malraux, the tragic victory of the defeated men (Chen,

Katov and Kyo, who was modelled on Chou En-lai) is far more significant than the fate of those who survive the abortive insurrection (Clappique, Ferral and Gisors). Though Malraux's ideas evolve from his portrayal of revolutionary politics, his dominant theme, the affirmation of man's dignity and grandeur in tragic defeat, has two serious limitations. The opiate withdrawal and reflective wisdom of old Gisors diminishes the mode of action in the novel, and the ultimate transcendence and dignity are achieved only at the moment of death and with no hope of social amelioration. Zarathustra's answer is also Malraux's: "Die at the right time. He that consummates his life dies his death victoriously, surrounded by those who hope and promise."

IV

The royalties from the vast sales of *Man's Fate,* which inevitably followed the award of the Prix Goncourt, financed Malraux's next *farfelu* adventure: his flight over the Arabian desert in 1934 (it was too dangerous to land in that wild territory) in order to discover the Queen of Sheba's city. This flight, as bizarre as the great jungle robbery and as fantastic as his plan to rescue Trotsky from exile in remote Alma Ata, furnished an abundance of mythomanic material.

Malraux's imagination was stimulated by a number of sources and models. The first Book of Kings relates how the fabulously wealthy Queen of Sheba "came to Jerusalem with a very great train, with camels that bare spices, and very much gold, and precious stones: and when she was come to Solomon, she communed with him of all that was in her heart." And Malraux wrote in 1934 that Sheba's ruined city, which had decayed before the rise of Islam in the seventh century, was an "immense petrifaction still filled—beneath the five kilometres of its livid marble—with the dreams of millions of men, and the deaths of a few." In the *Natural History* Pliny describes the sixty glorious temples of the Queen; and Sheba appears as an apparition to tempt Flaubert's St. Anthony. Though a stranger in a Djibouti hotel once confided to Malraux "that somewhere beyond the Yemen desert, half hidden by the sand, the real capital of the Queen of Sheba still stands," the most powerful and direct inspiration came from Rimbaud's and Lawrence's penetration of the forbidden deserts of Abyssinia and Arabia.

Only the demands of a recent marriage prevented Saint-Exupéry from piloting Malraux, who boldly announced his search in the *Nouvelles littéraires.* In the beginning of March 1934 Malraux set out in a single engine plane with his friend Corniglion-Molinier on a ten-hour non-stop flight of 1250 miles from Djibouti in French Somaliland to the Arabian desert, and back again. And on March 10 Malraux cabled *L'Intransigeant,* a Paris newspaper with a strong interest in aviation that had commissioned Malraux to write about his expedition: "Have discovered legendary city of Queen of Sheba. 20 towers or temples still standing. Is *north* of Rub' al Khali [the Empty Quarter]. Have taken photos for Intransigeant. Greetings. Corniglion-Malraux."

This astonishing news was elaborated in a series of ten articles (seven by Malraux and three by Corniglion), "Au-dessus du désert d'Arabie," which appeared in the newspaper between May 3 and May 13, 1934. Like D'Annunzio's flight over Vienna, Malraux's flight over Arabia was clearly a publicity stunt; and Malraux had to produce a good newspaper story to justify the expenses and the risks of the journey. He knew that he was free to say whatever he liked as there was no way to verify his account and almost impossible to prove it was false.

Malraux begins with a good deal of potted history, based mainly on rumor and myth, and ends with his post-flight reception at the royal court of Ethiopia, whose king was the putative descendent of the great Queen. The crux of the story is presented by Malraux on May 9 when he related that they flew over the city of Saba (Sheba), for which he gives no latitudinal or longitudinal bearings; that the Bedouins fired muskets at the low-flying plane; and that the mysterious city was "like an enormous monument, like the towers of Notre Dame . . . blind towers . . . trapezoid towers . . . vast terraces . . . propylaea . . . walls 40 meters high . . . broken statues." To corroborate this marvellous description the newspaper published Malraux's large but indistinct photograph, blurred by the dust of the desert, that does not correspond to his verbal description and looks more like an ordinary Bedouin village than a ruined city.

Janet Flanner, who has followed the scholarly controversy provoked by Malraux's assertions, reports that the French Orientalist, Jules Barthoux, said that "Malraux had consulted with him about Sheba's city in 1930 but what he had just flown over was unfortunately a ruin called Wabar, the Arabic name for some large rodents that lived in its rocks." But Wabar is in the middle of the Empty Quarter about 600 miles northeast of Sana, and in *Arabia Felix* (1932) the explorer Bertram Thomas states that "today it is an untrodden desert owing to the drying up of its water. There are to be found in it great buildings which the wind has smothered in sand"—and which would *not* be visible from the air. Flanner then quotes the opinion of another expert:

> The University of Pennsylvania's Professor of Assyriology said, also in the *Herald Tribune*, that Malraux had undoubtedly found somebody's ruined city, but not Sheba's, which was authoritatively believed to be in the south of Arabia Felix, at Marib—a well-known theory, which, for some reason, Malraux refused to subscribe to; though in his flight, he passed over Marib to take a peek at it, out of curiosity, and later reported that he thought it small.

Malraux, like Lawrence, frequently provides more than one version of the crucial events of his life, and his account of the flight over Sheba in *Antimemoirs* contradicts the sensational articles in *L'Intransigeant*. In 1934, as we have seen, Malraux claimed to have flown over Saba and seen 20 towers and walls 40 meters high; in 1967 he claimed to have flown over Mareb and seen massive ramparts, horse-shoe walls and cuboid buildings. Both Saba and Mareb are *south*, not north of the Empty Quarter, as Malraux claimed in his original cable to the newspaper. In any case, the distance from Sana in the south (which Malraux recognized from the air by its fort) to Harad, the first village north of the Empty Quarter, is about 700 miles, or 2 1/2 times farther than the minimum direct distance from Djibouti to Sana (275 miles). So it was clearly impossible for Malraux, who states that he flew for five hours at a maximum speed of 130 miles per hour (*Antimemoirs,* p. 70), to reach either Wabar or a site north of the Empty Quarter, which would be about 900–1000 miles from Djibouti.

Langlois, a scholar devoted to Malraux in more than one sense, has attempted to explain away one contradiction in Malraux's two accounts: "To simplify the narrative in *Antimemoirs* Malraux speaks of Mareb as the goal of the expedition, but the site actually sought—and found—was an unnamed ruin some 100 miles to the north." This statement presents two serious difficulties. First, Malraux never attempted to simplify the extremely complex narrative of *Antimemoirs,* which constantly shifts backwards and forwards in time and has an almost Jamesian impenetrability. Second, if the vague "unnamed ruin" which Langlois believes Malraux actually found were 100 miles north of Mareb, it would be (like Wabar) *inside* the completely uninhabited Empty Quarter. Yet in both accounts Malraux states that he was prevented from landing near the village because the Bedouin fired rifles at his low-flying airplane. (In *Seven Pillars of Wisdom* Lawrence relates how *his* Bedouin soldiers fled in terror the first time they saw a Turkish airplane.) Therefore, Malraux must have changed the name of the ruins he claimed to discover in order to confuse matters and make it more difficult to prove precisely what he did or did not find. It is also possible that after rejecting in 1934 the authoritative theory that Mareb was in fact ancient Sheba, he then did more reading, became convinced that Mareb *was* Sheba and decided that if there were any ruins to be found they would *have* to be found in Mareb.

In the *Antimemoirs* version Malraux states that "The ruins of Mareb, the ancient Saba or Sheba, lie in the Hadhramaut [a district of southern Arabia, on the Arabian Sea], *south* of the desert, north-east of Aden"; and he mentions the well-known legend of the rat who loosened a stone of the Mareb dam, which then burst open and destroyed the Kingdom of Sheba. Malraux also refers to the explorers who died in their attempt to reach Mareb by land, and he quotes Arnaud, another of the admired breed of vanished adventurers, who declared: "Leaving Mareb, I visited the ruins of ancient Sheba, which in general have nothing to show but mounds of earth." (In the *Journal Asiatique* for 1845 Thomas Joseph Arnaud had reported: "Not a trace of a building is to be seen, not a single large stone to be found.") But Malraux is undaunted by Arnaud's denial and makes no attempt to reconcile the contradiction between Arnaud's statement and his own rich description. In the crucial passage of *Antimemoirs*, which as we have seen is entirely different from his description of 1934, Malraux declared that when he flew over Mareb 90 years after Arnaud had been there, he saw

> the ruins encroach on the desert. Those massive oval ramparts, whose debris was clearly visible against the soil, could they be temples? How to make a landing? To one side lay the dunes, in which the plane would overturn; to the other, a volcanic soil with rocks projecting from the sand. Closer to the ruins, the ground was caved in everywhere. We flew still lower, and went on photographing. The horse-shoe walls opened on empty space: the town, built of sun-dried bricks like Nineveh, must have similarly reverted to the desert. We turned back to the main mass: an oval tower, more ramparts, cuboid buildings. Tiny flames flickered against the dark patches of Bedouin tents scattered outside the ruins. They must be firing at us. On the other side of the walls we begin to make out the mysterious traces of things whose purpose we could not fathom. The flat H on the tower overlooking the ruins, what did it represent? Part of an observatory?

Malraux concludes, rather vaguely, by remarking that "Sheba, or Mareb, whatever one likes to call it, is still in the hands of the [Bedouin] dissidents. . . . One day, perhaps, a scientific expedition from independent Aden will clear up 'the mystery of Sheba.'"

Malraux would have been surprised to find that this mystery had been cleared up as early as 1936, only two years after his flight, when St. John Philby, father of the notorious spy, political rival of Lawrence, convert to Islam, friend of King Saud of Saudi Arabia, and one of the greatest modern explorers of the desert, went by car to examine and to photograph "the only piece of the Arabian peninsula that was entirely unexplored." (Philby either ignores or is unaware of Arnaud.)

Philby visited both Shabwa (Saba) and Mareb (the transliteration from the Arabic accounts for the difference in spelling), which are 115 miles apart and which Malraux claimed to have discovered in his first and in his second versions. Philby provides a plan of the original *foundations* of the ruins of Shabwa (190 miles east of Sana), but his photographs merely show some piles of rocks. Pliny's *Natural History* had also aroused Philby's archeological expectations and he reports with some irritation in the *Geographical Journal* of 1938 that

> Pliny's account of Shabwa . . . is grossly inaccurate. As for the number of its temples, there could never have been 60 nor even six within the exiguous space enclosed by the city walls. One outstanding temple of supreme magnificence it certainly had, and two other ruin heaps within the walls may also some day prove to be temples. But 3 is a very different matter from 60. The whole ruin-field lay before us, disappointingly small and insignificant. . . . Not a

single ancient building stood intact, not a pillar of the 60 temples erect. The ancient capital of the Himyarites was just a jumble of fallen debris.

It was considerably more difficult and dangerous to inspect Mareb (85 miles east of Sana), for the Imam of Yemen forbade all visitors and the inhabitants were openly hostile. But Philby, who ventured close enough to study the village with binoculars, did *not* find massive ramparts, oval towers, cuboid buildings and observatories in Mareb any more than he did in Shabwa.

> I did pay a flying visit to the threshold of the Sheban capital, Marib. It was a rather risky experiment as it had to be done hurriedly and secretly with a single car and only two guides. . . . The town or village of modern Marib stands on a low hillock and appeared in the distance, as I saw it through my glasses, as a group of buildings occupying the slopes and summit of the hill and forming a fine silhouette against the dull background of the sandy plain beyond. Doubtless the ancient capital occupied a much larger area around the hillock, but it was not possible to make out any of the detail. I should like to have had a nearer view, but in the circumstances that was impossible.

Janet Flanner believes that Malraux flew "over a majestic archeological ruin in Arabia Felix [Yemen] which was, after all, apparently *not* Sheba's city." Langlois is even more credulous, accepts Malraux at his own valuation, and concludes with a lyrical but totally unrealistic series of abstractions that are meant to explain the significance of Malraux's search for Sheba's city: the Sabaean adventure "permitted Malraux simultaneously to act and to prove his existence as a man, to dream under the stimulus of that action, and to record his poetic *cortège de rêves*. [Malraux could have done all this in bed in Paris.] In retrospect it also furnished him with a certain deepened metaphysical awareness."

Langlois also links the Sabaean with the Cambodian adventure and confidently concedes: "Malraux knew that only hard facts would silence those who were attacking him (as they had done once before after his return from the jungles of Cambodia) as an irresponsible adventurer or a fraud." We have seen that Malraux could not possibly have flown to a village *north* of the Empty Quarter. Bertram Thomas stated there were no visible ruins at Wabar and Philby provides the "hard facts" that "clear up the mystery of Sheba." His descriptions prove that there were not 20 nor even 2 "towers or temples still standing" at Saba, as Malraux claimed in 1934 when he reduced Pliny's number by two-thirds. And Philby also confirms Arnaud's statement, quoted by Malraux himself, that there was "nothing to show but mounds of earth."

It would be more profitable, however, to attempt to understand Malraux's motives than to admire or condemn him, for as he says in the *Antimemoirs*, "To know a man nowadays is above all to know the element of the irrational in him, the part he is unable to control." Having announced with considerable publicity and fanfare that he was about to undertake a flamboyant and heroic adventure, Malraux felt obliged to discover something spectacular. Given his predisposition to mythomania (that is, lies), his unwillingness to disappoint either his own expectations or those of his newspaper audience, and the impossibility of refuting or verifying the facts of his story, Malraux had virtually no choice but to invent an exciting and imaginative alternative to the dull reality of the empty desert—he owed this much to the Bible, to Pliny and to Flaubert. By the time of the *Antimemoirs* (not conventional, but selective and highly embellished memoirs) the search for Sheba, which had hardened into a legend that was impossible to deny, provided the ideal quest for the romantic adventurer. So Malraux brought the archeological theory up to date, switched to Mareb, and heightened and shaped the exotic story until it fitted into the pattern of his fictionalized autobiography. Malraux flew over Arabia not to discover Sheba's city, but to realize his fantasies and create a legendary *persona* worthy of Lawrence and Rimbaud.

V

After 1933, when *Man's Fate* was published and Hitler took power, Malraux became a deeply committed anti-fascist and a powerful spokesman for the Left. His flight over Arabia took place between January 1934 when he made an unsuccessful trip to Berlin with Gide to demand the release of the Bulgarian Dimitrov, who had been falsely imprisoned for starting the Reichstag fire, and the summer of 1934 when he attended the Congress of Writers in Moscow. Malraux, who awed Gide with "his dazzling and staggering flow of words" and who impressed Spender as "the most brilliant and dynamic conversationalist I had met," dominated the 1935 Congress of Writers in Paris, which was attended by Forster, Huxley, Gide, Martin du Gard, Aragon and Ehrenburg. In that year Malraux published his fourth novel, *Days of Wrath,* which dealt with conditions inside the Nazi concentration camps and created that atmosphere of psychological stress that was later portrayed in the political novels of Silone, Koestler and Orwell.

There is a considerable difference between Malraux's political crusading in Indochina and his profound commitment in Spain. In July 1936, two days after the outbreak of the Civil War, which began like the October Revolution with cinemas open and visitors strolling in the streets, Malraux, internationally famous as a Left-wing writer, arrived in Madrid. He immediately began to buy aircraft—often outdated and delapidated—for the Republican Government, and to recruit mercenaries—who were paid fifty thousand francs a month—for his flying squadron of volunteers.

Malraux's headquarters in Madrid was the Hotel Florida on the Gran Vía where Hemingway and Dos Passos, Pablo Neruda and Rafael Alberti, and the

Russian journalists Mikhail Koltzov and Ilya Ehrenburg often met. The latter describes Malraux in Spain as:

> a man who is always in the grip of a single absorbing passion. I knew him during the period of his infatuation with the East, then with Dostoyevsky and Faulkner, then with the brotherhood of workers and the revolution. In Valencia he thought and spoke only about the bombing of fascist positions and when I started to say something about literature, he twitched and fell silent.

Malraux, who was not a Communist, saw the Party "not as a means of persuasion but as a means of action"; and even before the Communists decided to form the International Brigade, he organized the Escadre España (the international air force) and commanded it with boldness and courage. He flew on 65 missions as a bombardier and gunner, and was wounded during a raid, which led Hemingway to remark that Malraux must have acquired his tic at well over 10,000 feet.

The first battle of Malraux's squadron, which provided moral as well as military support, took place in August 1936 at Medellín, the birthplace of Cortez in Estremadura, when six planes flying low enough to fire pistols destroyed a motorized column of Franco's forces. In December 1936 during a bombing raid on Teruel, northwest of Valencia, Malraux's antiquated planes fought bravely against the modern Nazi Henkels. An episode in this battle provided the moving and vivid image of human fraternity that Malraux used both in *Man's Hope* and in his film, *L'Espoir*. During his political tour of America in 1937 Malraux described how:

> On December 27 one of the planes of my squadron was brought down in the Teruel region—behind our lines. It had fallen very high, at about 2,000 meters above sea level, and snow covered the mountains. In this region there are very few villages, and it was only after several hours that the peasants arrived and began constructing stretchers for the wounded and a coffin for the dead. When all was ready the descent began. . . . [Later] I raised my eyes: the file of peasants extended now from the heights of the mountain to its base—and it was the grandest image of fraternity I have ever encountered.

The Escadre España fought at Toledo, Madrid, Jarama and at Guadalajara, the headquarters of the Russian air squadron northeast of the capital, where in March 1937 they bombed the Italian troops who were eventually defeated in battle. After Guadalajara Malraux's patched-up and punished planes literally fell apart after seven months of combat, and the squadron was replaced by a more professional and modern air force.

Malraux had separated from Clara (who refused to divorce him) in 1936, three years after the birth of their daughter Florence; and when he visited New York and Los Angeles, Harvard, Princeton and Berkeley in March 1937 to raise funds for the Loyalist cause, he was accompanied by Josette Clotis. Armand

Petitjean, who heard Malraux speak at a Loyalist rally in France, describes the inspiring effect of Malraux's speech, which seemed to embody the highest values of humanity:

> I must admit that it was magnificent. Never in my life have I seen such self-mastery, such power of a man, of *homo loquens*, of the man himself over other men. Malraux, I did not like you overmuch, but when you spoke, not for us in the hall but for those in the trenches, you gave us some idea of human greatness. And the proof is that it was not you we were applauding, but Spain.

During the next two years of the Civil War Malraux moved from action to art, published *Man's Hope* (1937) and wrote and directed *L'Espoir* (1938), which was based on certain episodes in the novel. During an interview in 1970 Malraux said, "I believe myself that the Spanish Revolution was the last great expression of hope" before the Second World War brought what he called "the return of Satan." Though Malraux considered *Man's Hope* his greatest achievement, this novel, which attempts to combine reportage, propaganda and ideology with a fictional account of Malraux's experience of contemporary history, is more ambitious but certainly less successful than *Man's Fate*. For the lengthy philosophical discussions about art, politics and heroism, faith, death and the apocalyptic vision, are not well integrated into the violent and episodic events of the book. As Gide observed of Malraux's novels: "The excessive use of abstract terms is often prejudicial to the narration of the action. One must not try simultaneously to make the reader visualize and to make him understand." Malraux's characters do not always embody his thematic abstractions, and Hernandez's philosophical refusal to save himself when another prisoner cuts the rope that binds them remains unconvincing in the context of the action.

The triumphant affirmation of the novel was extremely effective as Loyalist propaganda. Malraux writes about the siege of the Alcázar in Toledo in 1936 as if the fascists were about to surrender when, in fact, a supporting force broke through the Republican defences around the city, rescued the fortress and achieved a legendary victory. Malraux was also excellent in conveying the heroic spirit of men in war; and the famous descent from the mountain, inspired by the plane crash at Teruel, became the poignant finale of the film and of the novel:

> It had begun to drizzle. The last stretchers, the peasants from the mountains, and the last mules were advancing between the vast background of the rocky landscape over which the dark rain-clouds were massing, and the hundreds of peasants standing motionless with raised fists. The women were weeping quietly, and the procession seemed to be fleeing from the eerie silence of the mountains, its noise of clattering hoofs and clogs linking the everlasting clamour of the vultures with the muffled sound of sobbing.

Malraux filmed *L'Espoir* in Barcelona during the war while the city was constantly under attack by enemy bombers based on Majorca. *L'Espoir* was influenced by the cinematic realism of Eisenstein and foreshadows postwar films by Rossellini and De Sica. Its many outdoor sequences convey a vivid feeling of what Spain was like during the Civil War and how the Republicans fought with insufficient and obsolete equipment. The film is both subtle and persuasive as propaganda, moving and effective as art; it is a tribute to the foreign fighters in Spain and portrays the values and ideals of the Republicans. Its greatest scenes are the destruction of a strategic piece of artillery by a suicidal car driver, the peasant's initial failure to recognize his village and identify an enemy airfield from a plane, and the procession of the wounded aviators from the mountain. *L'Espoir* is a truly extraordinary achievement since Malraux had no previous film experience, shot the film in the midst of the Civil War and grasped the significance of the historical events that he portrayed just after they had occurred. James Agee rightly calls *L'Espoir* "one of the few wonderful film records of men in courage and sorrow.... Homer might know it, I think, for the one work of our time which was wholly sympathetic to him." Ironically, when Malraux left Spain in January 1939 to complete in the French Pyrenees the film that celebrates the glories of the Loyalist struggle, Franco's army was approaching Barcelona and the war was all but lost.

VI

Malraux's military and artistic achievements during the Second World War equalled his record in Spain. Early in the war he enlisted as a private in the Tank Corps and was captured with his unit during the fall of France. But in November 1940 he put on carpenter's overalls, carried a plank on his shoulder and walked out of the prisoner of war camp at Sens. He made his way to the Unoccupied Zone, joined Josette and her family in the south of France, and temporarily opted out of the war. Sartre "found him living in lordly style in a villa at Saint-Jean Cap-Ferrat," where he was writing *The Walnut Trees of Altenburg*, published in Switzerland in 1943. This superb novel contains the greatest scene in Malraux's fiction: a description of how in the Great War the victorious Germans, horrified at the success of their gas attack when they personally confront their Russian victims, wearily carry the suffering enemy back to the healing safety of their own lines. As Malraux writes of his hero, Vincent Berger: "What he liked about war was the masculine comradeship, the irrevocable commitments that courage imposes."

Under the name of "Colonel Berger" Malraux became active in the Resistance in the spring of 1944 and commanded 1500 *maquis* in the Dordogne region of southwest France. In the *Antimemoirs* and again in his commemorative speech on the Resistance leader Jean Moulin, in *Oraisons funèbres*, Malraux recalls a silent and symbolic incident from this period that reveals the same striking visual image of man in nature, and the same tribute to heroism and human solidarity, as in the descent from the mountain in Teruel:

> I thought, too, of the dawn rising over a cemetery in Corrèze surrounded by woods white with hoar-frost. The Germans had shot some maquisards, and the inhabitants were to bury them in the morning. A company had occupied the cemetery, submachine-guns at the ready. In that region, the women do not follow the hearse, they wait for it beside the family grave. At day-break, on each of the tombs on the hillside like the scattered stones of ancient amphitheatres, a woman in black could be seen standing, and not praying.

On D-Day in June the elite SS Division *Das Reich* was sent north to reinforce the defences at Normandy, and Malraux was ordered to delay them. E. H. Cookridge reports that on June 7 Malraux's *maquis*

> went into action. In a series of ambushes and skirmishes, the long German tank columns were halted and forced to abandon the main road. . . . The Division arrived in Normandy ten days behind schedule, completely disorganized, leaving many disabled tanks behind with its men hardly able to fight.

In July 1944, four months after he joined the *maquis*, Malraux's driver was killed as their car overturned during an ambush by an SS platoon. Malraux escaped from the car, was shot in the right leg, captured and sent to St. Michel prison in Toulouse. During his interrogation he justified the Resistance movement by telling the German officer: "Every struggle presupposes a soul. . . . In 1940 France suffered one of the most appalling defeats in her history. Those who are fighting you are guarantors of her survival." Like Dostoyevsky, Malraux was also placed before a firing squad in a mock execution, and his description of this traumatic event in *Antimemoirs* is strongly influenced by the autobiographical passages in *The Idiot*. Malraux escaped torture only because his dossier failed to arrive from Gestapo headquarters, and he was freed from prison when the Germans abandoned Toulouse in September.

Malraux commanded the Alsace-Lorraine Brigade under General Leclerc from September 1944 until February 1945, and took part in the capture of Dannemarie in November, the defence of Strasbourg against von Runstedt's offensive in December, the march on Colmar and Sainte-Odilie, and the triumphant entry into Strasbourg. Malraux received the Croix de la Libération and the Croix de Guerre with four citations for his distinguished service; but he had suffered great personal losses in the war. Both his half-brothers, Roland and Claude, had been killed; and Josette Clotis, who had borne him two sons, Gauthier and Vincent, was crushed and killed when she fell under a train in November 1944. It is hardly surprising therefore that just after the war C. L.

Sulzberger found Malraux "extremely nervous and rather dissipated looking: very thin, with dark shadows under his eyes and a long nose and face. He smokes American cigarettes constantly and refuses to sit down, walking about all the time. . . . He was constantly at an extreme point of tension."

VII

In 1945, Malraux, to the surprise and horror of his Left-wing admirers, accepted the Ministry of Information in De Gaulle's short-lived provisional government, and became the leading propagandist for De Gaulle's Right-wing party, the Rassemblement du Peuple Français. A number of scholars, notably Janine Mossuz, have attempted to reconcile Malraux's Gaullism with his prewar politics. But this task is impossible unless, like Mossuz, one defines the policies of Gaullism either as a tautology ("a faith in the future of another world which only Charles De Gaulle is able to construct") or as a synthesis of *Malraux's,* but not De Gaulle's, ideas. For Malraux, writes Mossuz, Gaullism "is not uniquely political but metaphysical, and is directed against an adversary, death, and against the train of certainties that accompany it: evil, oppression, servitude, chains of all sorts"—though one could argue that these "certainties" accompany life and are extinguished by death.

Denis Boak, who maintains a healthy scepticism about Malraux's career, is much closer to the truth when he places Malraux within the French literary-political tradition and states that it seems pointless to claim "his political attitude has never basically changed. . . . Communism and Gaullism have little in common except their authoritarian approach. . . . Certainly Malraux has moved sharply from Left to Right in politics; but this has been, especially in France, so common a development among writers as to be almost typical." Malraux himself has admitted in an illuminating remark in 1969, "There *is* a gap between my present views and the ideas of my youth. . . . I have replaced the proletariat by France." And he has rather subjectively defined Gaullism as "political passion in the service of France."

Malraux, like so many other disillusioned intellectuals on the Left, became hostile to "The God That Failed" after the Stalinist Purge Trials of the late 1930s, which eliminated virtually all the Russians who had served in Spain. Malraux equated Gaullism with anti-Communism and wrote that after the war "any movement born of the Resistance must be Gaullist if it did not want to be communist: because only the General was really prepared to set up an independent State and nation as an alternative to a communist State." Though Malraux denied with unusual modesty that De Gaulle said to him what Napoleon said when first introduced to Goethe ("Voilà, l'homme!"), the General lavished pompous praise on his Minister:

> On my right, then as always, was André Malraux. The presence at my side of this inspired friend, this devotee of lofty doctrines, gave me a sense of being insured against the commonplace. The conception which this incomparable witness to our age had formed of me did much to fortify me. I know that in debate, when the subject was grave, his flashing judgments would help to dispel the shadows.

In the *Antimemoirs* Malraux quotes his remark to De Gaulle that the Resistance led some "towards revolutionary romanticism, which consists in confusing political action with theatre." This extremely revealing remark is a perfect definition both of Malraux's direction of the Rassemblement's tasteless D'Annunzian-style rallies, which were held in the Paris Vélodrome (the six-day bicycle race stadium) during the late 1940s, and of his career as a Gaullist Minister when he disguised the authoritarian politics of the Fifth Republic with a stream of theatrical oratory. Jean Lacouture, who witnessed the political sound and light spectacles of the Rassemblement, writes that there were "projectors, platforms, waterworks, backdrops, music: for three years Charles De Gaulle was a giant Gallic druid ... with an invincible silhouette and a resounding voice—floodlit and recorded in stereophonic sound by the producer of *L'Espoir*." The later speeches in *Oraisons funèbres* "give the impression of an orator of the seventeenth century who had dreamed of Lautréamont and studied diction with Sarah Bernhardt," says Lacouture. But the orator of the postwar Rassemblement has

> nothing written. No plan. Some telling phrases—heroic slogans or fine words—serve as the *leitmotiv* of his discourse. Having this material in his head he begins to expound the parallels between Goya and the Grand Turk, between the Marquis de Sade and Maurice Thorez, between the cathedrals and the slaughterhouses of Chicago, or between De Gaulle and François I.

Though few people in the enormous crowd could follow the dazzling flow of words that had once awed André Gide, Flanner confirms that Malraux created a tremendous, if confusing, impression:

> He made what was undoubtedly the most exciting, excitable speech, feverishly kneading his hands, as is his platform habit, extinguishing his voice with passion and reviving it with gulps of water, and presenting an astonishing exposition of politico-aesthetics that seemed like fireworks shot from the head of a statue.

Though successful as theater, these rallies were useless as practical politics, and the Rassemblement collapsed of *hubris,* gigantism and inertia in 1952.

After the war Malraux resumed his passionate study not only of Eastern art but also of his favourite painters—Rembrandt, Vermeer, Goya and Braque—a study that reflected the serious discussions of aesthetic questions in both *The Royal Way* and *Man's Hope*. The results of his lifelong interest in art were published in the lavishly illustrated *Voices of Silence* (1951), *The Imaginary Museum* (1952–1954) and *The Metamorphosis of the Gods* (1957), immensely long and complex yet intuitive and personal books, which suggest a cultural synthesis and unity in all works of art. Though received rather coldly by academic art historians, Malraux's unique and original work reveals a characteristic breadth of scope and range of learning, and is highly suggestive and stimulating.

When De Gaulle returned to power in June 1958, Malraux became his Minister of Cultural Affairs, and attempted to implement a number of political and aesthetic programs. During the Algerian crisis in 1958 Malraux had the idea of sending the three French Nobel Prize-winners, Martin du Gard, Mauriac and Camus, to Algiers "as a kind of permanent ambassador of the French conscience in the name of De Gaulle." But this project was never realized, perhaps because Camus preferred to retain and represent his own conscience. Malraux believed "The only thing we can save [in the colonies] is a kind of cultural empire, a domain of [French] values"; and he helped to enforce the policy of decolonization, proclaimed the independence of four new African states, and was nearly murdered during the Algerian war of 1962 by Right-wing extremists who opposed the policy of De Gaulle.

As Minister of Cultural Affairs he continued to travel extensively and to represent France in countries throughout the world. He restored palaces, cleaned the façades of buildings and transformed the appearance of Paris. He directed art exhibitions and reorganized the National Theaters; and dismissed the popular Jean-Louis Barrault, the director of the Odéon Theater, for openly sympathizing with the students during the May Revolution of 1968. And in a program that recalled the Soviet projects of the 1930s, he created Houses of Culture in some provincial cities.

While he was a Minister, in 1961, Malraux's two sons, like their mother, were killed in a violent accident. In 1965 Malraux separated from his second wife, Madeleine, the widow of his half-brother Roland, whom he had married in 1948. And in the summer of that year, after a serious illness, he took a recuperative sea voyage to Egypt, India and China. In Peking the Right-wing Minister and connoisseur of Eastern art met and revered Mao Tse-tung, the revolutionary who had obliterated the ancient culture of China. Malraux used this round-the-world voyage to structure the narrative of the first volume of his enigmatic and strangely unrevealing *Antimemoirs* (1967).

When Malraux left the government with De Gaulle in 1969, after eleven years in office, he explained his decision by an imperfect analogy to Republican Spain: "Do you see me remaining with 'them' after the departure of the General? It is as if, at the end of the Spanish war that he had won, Negrin had asked to become a colonel in the Guardia Civil"—though the Gaullist Malraux was much closer to the Guardia Civil than the Socialist Negrin.

Though freed from ministerial responsibility, Malraux continued to be active in both politics and art. In *Fallen Oaks* (1971) he created an idealized representation of his last meeting with De Gaulle in 1969 that is embarrassing in its fulsomeness and often absurd in its apotheosis. In 1972 Malraux was the subject of a series of French television programs, "The Legend of the Century"; he tutored Nixon for his interview with Mao Tse-tung; and at the age of 71 he offered to found a school of guerrilla warfare in Bangladesh or to lead its army of independence against Pakistan—just as in 1919 Lawrence had offered to break Ibn Saud's Wahabi movement with ten tanks and Moslems from the Indian army. Malraux, who deserved the Nobel Prize more than any other writer, but did not receive it because of his political association with De Gaulle, published his earlier essays on Laclos, Goya and Saint-Just in *Le Triangle noir* (1970) and his ministerial speeches in *Oraisons funèbres* (1971), and was writing the second volume of *Antimemoirs* at the end of his life.

It is possible to interpret Malraux's life as a series of spectacular failures—in France, Indochina, Arabia and Spain—that paradoxically amount to a remarkable success. As he says of Mao's Long March, "it was a retreat, but its result was like a conquest." Malraux was not admitted to a *lycée;* his obscure early fantasies, lavishly printed in private editions, were almost completely unknown; he gambled away Clara's substantial inheritance; he was arrested for trying to remove Khmer sculpture from the Cambodian jungle and sentenced to prison; his journalistic and political career in support of the young Annam League was ephemeral and totally ineffective; he was never in charge of propaganda for the Kuomintang in Canton; he was unable to free Dimitrov from a Nazi jail; he did not discover the lost city of the Queen of Sheba; and though he created and organized the Escadre España out of nothing, it was eventually defeated by German and Italian planes. Malraux was twice captured and imprisoned in the Second World War; he was accused of betraying the Left by joining the reactionary government of De Gaulle; he never realized his ministerial dream of an extensive system of French provincial Houses of Culture; and both of his marriages failed.

What is so impressive about Malraux's life, however, is that his sensitive idealism was never diminished by his failures and for fifty years, from Saigon to Bangladesh, he fought for just causes. He achieved a heroic record in two wars and brought moral standards to political activity, but he was more committed to art than to action, more to legend than to truth. When the opportunities for adventure coincided with his inclinations, he was capable of heroism; when they did not, he escaped into mythomania. Though his political accomplishments were limited, Malraux created in *L'Espoir* what Koestler calls "one of the greatest films ever made"; he published a number of ambitious and exciting books that revealed a new way of seeing art, both individually and contextually; and he wrote three first-rate novels. *Man's Fate, Man's Hope* and *The Walnut Trees of Altenburg,* whose heroes represent an idealized image of himself, defined the political conscience of his age.

5

"To Die for Ireland": The Character and Career of Sir Roger Casement

For a brief moment during the Easter rebellion, the personal fate of Sir Roger Casement was linked with the destiny of a nation, and his complex character and career illuminate that particular phase of Irish history. His efforts on behalf of the rubber workers in the Congo and the Amazon brought him fame and a knighthood, but his attempt to aid Ireland led him to the gallows. His role in the independence movement was a paradigm of noble yet pathetic heroism, and his execution for high treason in August 1916 a moral and political tragedy. The pattern of his political life, a series of disasters that testify to his compulsive desire for death and martyrdom, suggests profound guilt about his homosexuality and a need for self-punishment. His private diaries were more fantastic than real, and he was hanged for his sexual as well as his political dreams.

Roger David Casement was born in Dublin on September 1, 1864. His father, a Protestant captain in the Antrim militia who had fought with Kossuth in the Hungarian revolution, died when he was six. His mother, a Catholic, died three years later, and the orphan boy was then brought up as a Protestant by an uncle in Northern Ireland, and educated at Ballymena Academy. He became a clerk in a Liverpool trading company when he was 18, and two years later, in 1884, he sailed for Africa where he served King Leopold's Congo Free State as an explorer, hunter, surveyor and administrator. He returned to England after five years of service, but was sent out again the following year to organize transport on the Lower Congo for the Belgian authorities. At this time Casement first met Joseph Conrad, who was running his "tin-pot steamboat" on the Congo River, and the novelist later described Casement with amazed respect as

> a Protestant Irishman, pious too. But so was Pizarro. For the rest I can assure you that he is a limpid personality. There is a touch of the conquistador in him too; for I've seen him start off into an unspeakable wilderness swinging a crookhandled stick for all weapons, with two bulldogs, Paddy (white) and Biddy (brindle), at his heels and a Loanda boy carrying a bundle for all company. A few months afterwards it so happened that I saw him come out again, a

little leaner, a little browner, with his stick, dogs, and Loanda boy, and quietly serene as though he had been for a stroll in the park.

Casement was a tall, extremely handsome man, of fine bearing, a muscle and bone thinness, wrinkled forehead, face deeply tanned from long tropical service, thick, curly black hair, full and long pointed beard, and brilliant blue eyes.

With his impressive and responsible experience in the Congo, the young Casement entered the service of the Nigerian Protectorate in 1892, and three years later he was appointed Her Majesty's Consul in the Portuguese colony of Mozambique. In Lourenço Marques, Casement first exhibited his eccentric patriotism and was officially reprimanded for using stationery marked "Consulate of Great Britain and Ireland." After service in Angola on the west coast, he was employed during the Boer War on special service in Cape Town, for which he received the Queen's South African medal. In 1900 he was appointed Consul at Boma in the Congo Free State, and in 1903 conducted the investigation of atrocities committed upon the rubber workers in the Upper Congo which brought him worldwide fame.

During this investigation Casement kept the first of his extant diaries, which were to play such a notorious and fatal part in the last year of his life. He was extremely responsive to the natural beauty of the country, and as he rode through the jungle on the flooded, swollen river he sighted splendid blue Emperor butterflies, colored macaws, tiny chattering green parrots, a black-and-white Egyptian ibis in full flight, and the lively monkeys screaming eternally in the trees. In the evening the children bathed in the river, and stars cooled the sky in the night. These physical surroundings provided a strong contrast to the terrible atrocities committed upon what Casement called "the poor, the naked, the fugitive, the hunted, the tortured, the dying men and women of the Congo."Africans, bound with thongs that contracted in the rain and cut to the bone, had their swollen hands beaten with rifle butts until they fell off. Chained slaves were forced to drink the white man's defecations, hands and feet were chopped off for their rings, men were lined up behind each other and shot with one cartridge, and wounded prisoners were eaten by maggots till they died and were thrown to starving dogs or devoured by cannibal tribes. One girl carried the bones of her parents clinking in a ragged canvas sack and testified that starving people ate peeling whitewash torn from old buildings and then vomited up a green bile filled with leeches. Another boy described to Casement how during a raid on his village he was wounded and "fell down, presumably insensible but came to his senses while his hand was being hacked off at the wrist. I asked him how it was he could possibly lie silent and give no sign. He answered that he felt the cutting, but was afraid to move, knowing that he would be killed, if he showed any sign of life."

Though he had official sanction from the King's Government in Brussels,

Casement suffered daily obstructions by the officials of the State whose very existence was threatened by his inquiries. He wrote to his friend Richard Morten that Africa "has been 'opened up' (as if it were an oyster) and the Civilizers are now busy developing it with blood and slaying each other, and burning with hatred against me because I think their work is organized murder, far worse than anything the savages did before them." His detailed record of the atrocities achieved great force through its moderate tone and objective style, which expressed Casement's passionate commitment to the oppressed. As he wrote to Edmund Morel, the founder of the Congo Reform Association: "If I get home again I should go to all lengths to let my countrymen know what a hell upon earth our own white race has made, and was daily making, of the homes of the black people it was our duty to protect."

After Casement had sacrificed his health to complete the report, he found further obstructions from his own Government. Some men in the Foreign Office, ignorant about the actual conditions in the Congo, felt that Casement had exaggerated his findings, and when the report was published, their "method of conducting the controversy with Leopold consisted largely in running away from their own charges and offering apologies for my report." Casement believed, with considerable justification, that he was becoming the pawn of political interests while the tyranny in the Congo continued unchecked. He was chosen to conduct the inquiry, and then "humiliated, insulted, deserted" after it was published. As an Irishman, he had felt a natural sympathy for the Boers in the South African War; and he became bitterly hostile to the British Government when it betrayed and abandoned him. But in 1908, after the creation of the Congo Reform Association, Casement triumphed; and world opinion, stirred by his discoveries, forced King Leopold to surrender his personal ownership of the Congo Free State, which became a colony of Belgium. Casement was rewarded by his Government and made Commander of St. Michael and St. George.

In 1906 his consular career shifted to South America when he was appointed Consul at Santos and at Para in Brazil, and then Consul-General in Rio de Janeiro; and in 1910 he was asked to conduct another investigation of atrocities committed upon rubber workers in the Putumayo region of the Peruvian Amazon. Casement's experiences in the Amazon were a nightmarish repetition of the Congo. Here, as in Africa, an immense river cutting through a remote jungle, far from Government control, was used to transport rubber collected by natives who were enslaved and brutalized by their white overseers. Casement reported that the Indian, with his gentle face, soft black eyes and far-off look of the Incas, was so terrified and "so humble that as soon as he sees the needle of the scale does not mark the [required] 10k., he himself stretches out his hands and throws himself on the ground to receive the punishment." The Indians were mercilessly flogged with strips of tapir hide sufficiently stout to cut them to pieces, and left to starve till they ate the maggots from their own wounds. They were suspended "with the feet scarcely touching the ground and the chain hauled taut, and left in this half-strangled position until life was almost extinct." Women held helpless in the stocks were publicly raped, men with smashed testicles were burned at the stake and children had their brains dashed out.

Casement was particularly horrified by the most sadistic torturer, a Peruvian overseer called Armando Normand, who symbolized the connection between colonial exploitation, physical brutality and sexual domination. Normand had cut off the arms and then the legs of a captured chief "who preferred to suffer such a death to betraying the refuge of those who had fled" from their persecutors into the jungle. He also "put two Indian boys on a kitchen fire and roasted them alive. The skin peeled off and they were baked—but still alive." Normand's tortures of the Indians represented a kind of supreme evil that became possible only when man's basest and cruellest instincts, suppressed in Europe, were released under conditions of absolute power in the wilderness. Conrad had described the same conditions in *Heart of Darkness* which, like Casement's reports, attacked the hypocritical justification of colonialism by revealing the inherent savagery of civilized man.

In his Putumayo report, Casement raised questions about the psychology and morality of atrocities similar to those asked about Nazi extermination camps during the Nuremberg trails. "It may be wondered," Casement writes of the victims' passivity, "how numerous assemblages of men, not individually cowards, could be so coerced and dealt with by a very small band of oppressors." And he explains that there is no cohesion among the various tribes who had always fought against each other; they had poor arms, or sometimes none at all; and their chiefs and elders were taken from them and killed. But the military factors were less important than the psychological reasons. Suddenly, and for the first time in their lives, the helpless Indians were confronted with an overwhelming evil. Powerful foreigners appeared in their villages, chained them together, and transported them to a strange and terrible place where they were tortured and forced to work as slaves under the most brutal conditions. If they resisted, entire villages were exterminated. It was the final solution to the problem of cheap labor.

Casement's second significant question concerned responsibility and guilt, for when confronted with their victims' accusations, the white men "only pleaded that these crimes had been committed under the direct orders of the superior agents of the Company, whom they were required to obey." An identical defense became familiar thirty-five years later at Nuremberg and when Eichmann stood in the glass booth in Jerusalem.

Casement had been in Africa for nearly twenty years when he began his investigations, and he was exhausted by long years of service in the tropics.

He was racked by lumbago and arthritis, and malaria and dysentery had ruined his constitution. He had contracted skin diseases, and in the Putumayo he could scarcely walk from the eczema on both feet. He developed eye infections, and the insects buzzed around his sores and covered his body with large bites. He knew from painful experience how the constitution and character of the white man inevitably undergoes a subtle process of deterioration when he is compelled to live for extended periods of time among primitive races and in savage conditions, and the precise minutiae of his diaries revealed his morbid fascination with the atrocities. Malraux has described "The endless succession of days under the dusty firmament of the heavy leaden sky of the Congo, the tracks of invisible animals converging on the water points, the exodus of starving dogs under the empty sky, the time of day when every thought becomes a blank, the giant trees gloomily soaring up in the pre-historic world." This deterioration, accentuated by physical isolation and mental depression, Casement combated with all the force in his power. For he had seen many men, the subjects of his investigation, revert to their ancestral nature and become thoroughly brutalized in mind, habit and temperament. His feelings in the Amazon were the terse but graphic: "Rain and packing up, very tired, very tired, very sick of everything." In 1911 Casement was knighted for his work and two years later he retired from the Consular Service, his health permanently ruined.

Casement's long experience with colonial exploitation in the tropics made him particularly sensitive to England's subjugation of Ireland, and as the agitation about Irish independence was reaching its climax, he joined the fight for the oppressed people of his own country. The Home Rule Bill had been passed by a majority in the British Parliament, but the Ulstermen in the North, led by Sir Edward Carson, still insisted that only total exclusion would satisfy them, that if Ireland were not divided into two nations there would be civil war, and their jingoistic slogan—"Ulster will fight and Ulster will be right"—reverberated from Belfast.

In April 1914, 40,000 German rifles for the Ulster Volunteers were illegally landed at Larne, and when orders were given by Asquith's Liberal Government to disarm this group, the British officers at Curragh, a military camp near Kildare, threatened to resign their commissions rather than fight the Orangemen. During this mutiny, for it was nothing less than that, the British Government, for the first time since the revolution of 1688, had lost the allegiance of the Army and was helpless to enforce either the law of the land or their own declared policy in Ireland.

Ulster was bursting with German Mausers after the landing at Larne, and none of these rifles was ever surrendered. The importation of arms continued and increased, for on August 16, after the outbreak of the War, the Arms Act was rescinded and the sole obstacle to the importation of weapons was eliminated. The vigilance of the police diminished and an uneasy truce settled over the land, but it was merely a postponement of the threat of bloodshed until the War was over.

While the Tory Party, in their endeavor to achieve power in England, supported the Ulstermen, the Liberal Party took no active steps to restrain their activities, which the Lord Chancellor called "grossly illegal and utterly unconstitutional." In July 1914 at Howth, in southern Ireland, the Nationalists landed 1,500 rifles to defend themselves against Ulster. And the British Army, which had refused to march against Larne, met the Nationalists at Bachelor's Walk in Dublin, fired into the unarmed crowd, killed three men and wounded thirty-two others.

Despite his Ulster and Protestant background, Casement had been an Irish Nationalist since boyhood. He had joined the Gaelic League in 1904, and, under a pseudonym, had written articles supporting Irish independence while still in the service of the British Government. But he revealed his astounding political naïveté in December 1913 when he addressed a Nationalist meeting in Cork and was foolish enough to call for three cheers for their political enemy, Sir Edward Carson. The angry crowd broke up the furniture and hurled it at him, and he barely escaped injury.

Casement called the "nauseous fraud of Home Rule ... a promissory note payable after death," and in July 1914 sailed to America to raise funds for the Nationalist cause. In late October, after the outbreak of the War which England had entered to protect Belgium, the oppressor of the Congo, Casement arrived in Norway with Adler Christensen, a gaudily dressed and flagrant homosexual, whom he had met in New York. Casement's adventures in Norway are the first of many bizarre events that marked the third and final phase of his extraordinary career.

When Casement left Christensen to conduct his business, the Norwegian sailor was suddenly accosted, taken to the British Legation, questioned by the British Minister, Findlay, given money, and told to return the following day. Christensen told Casement what had happened, and returned to see Findlay, who revealed that he knew Casement's identity. He then quite bluntly suggested that Christensen should "knock Casement on the head" or help get rid of him in any other manner. Christensen was also asked to lure Casement to a place on the North Sea where a British warship could pick him up, and to steal his letters, in exchange for the protection of the British Government and £5,000 in gold. Despite the sinister designs of Findlay, Christensen refused the substantial offer and remained loyal to Casement, who was outraged by the treacherous behavior of the English.

Casement safely reached Germany in November 1914, in order to enlist support for Irish independence, and remained there for a year and a half. He had some initial success when he arranged the German-Irish Treaty of December

1914 in which Germany recognized the State of Ireland and agreed to help her win independence. Casement later boasted: "I have committed Germany for all time to an Irish policy . . . that, in all the centuries before, no other Power ever gave forth to any Irishman." In order to create an Irish Army, all the Irish prisoners of war were collected in Limburg Lahn camp and addressed by Casement, who urged them to join the Irish Brigade to fight for Ireland. Despite the inducement of a distinctive green uniform, better rations and living conditions, and return to Ireland when circumstances allowed, only fifty out of 2,500 prisoners joined the Brigade. For the captured Irish soldiers had been part of the First Expeditionary Force, and were well-trained, disciplined and loyal troops. Casement's campaign met with derision, and he was frequently jeered, called a traitor and even physically assaulted. On one occasion he was forced to defend himself with his umbrella and was protected from injury only by the intervention of his German guards.

When he failed to persuade the Irish prisoners and when the Germans discovered that Casement had no great following in Ireland, they lost confidence in him. He in turn became offended because the Berlin Foreign Office did not trust him sufficiently. Soon afterwards, Casement began to deteriorate, both physically and mentally. The old infirmities of his tropical career surfaced once again, he suffered severely from attacks of malaria, and in the summer of 1915 he had to be placed in a sanatorium for two months. He experienced great anxiety even there, and was visited by an agent of the secret police who asked for a military pass he did not have. He gave the agent his police identification card but feared there might be a misunderstanding and that he would be taken to jail.

By 1916 he was in a desperate state, and at times seemed to act like a madman.

Just at this point his fortunes suddenly changed. In the early part of the war the Germans believed that a rising in Ireland might be successful, but as they grew weaker and could not give it their full support, this belief began to fade. By 1916 they wished only to create a military diversion. During his year and a half in Germany Casement had repeatedly asked that arms and men be sent to Ireland and the Germans had always refused. But when they learned of the Irish plans for a rebellion on Easter Monday, April 4, 1916, they suddenly summoned Casement and offered to land him on the Irish coast with two other Irish soldiers in Germany, Captain Robert Monteith of the Irish Republican Army and Private Daniel Bailey, who had been recruited at Limburg Lahn camp.

Accordingly, on April 11, the three Irishmen were driven to the War Office and given railway tickets for Wilhelmshaven. They were put on submarine U-20, which had sunk the *Lusitania,* and steamed into the North Sea on schedule, but were forced to return to Heligoland because of an accident. They then boarded submarine U-19, and came round Shetland, through the British naval patrols, to the southwest coast of Ireland.

At the same time that Casement was sailing toward Tralee, the Germans sent another ship to assist the rebels, loaded with 20,000 Russian rifles of the 1905 pattern (whose ammunition could never be replaced in Ireland), captured during the war on the eastern front. But the German messages had been intercepted and their code deciphered, and on April 17 the British Admiralty received warning of the arms shipment and imminent rising. Four days later, on Good Friday, the destroyer *Bluebell*, cruising off Tralee, sighted a suspicious ship flying the Norwegian ensign. When signaled for her destination, the ship replied she was the *Aud* of Bergen, bound for Genoa. She was then ordered to follow the *Bluebell* to harbor, and did so after a shot was fired across her bows. But the next morning, just outside of Queenstown, the *Aud* stopped her engines, and the crew blew up her hull and abandoned ship. The German crew of nineteen men and three officers lowered their boats, pulled toward the *Bluebell* and surrendered. Their ship sank almost immediately.

Like Casement's landing and the Easter rebellion itself, the *Aud's* attempt to deliver arms was a hopeless failure. First, the time fixed for the landing was changed by the rebel leaders *after* the *Aud* had left Germany. Second, the *Aud* had no wireless equipment and so was unable to make contact with the Irish after the rendezvous had failed. Third, the Irish pilot who was to bring in the *Aud* was so confident she would not arrive before Sunday that he took no notice of the strange steamer and its flashing lights. Fourth, no preparations were made in Tralee for the receipt of the arms. And finally, the two Sinn Feiners who were sent from Dublin to meet the *Aud* had a fatal accident while motoring down to the coast that Good Friday night. The driver took a wrong turning in the dark and ran his car into the river at Puck, a few miles from the rendezvous. He left the car and was captured, but his three passengers were drowned. The Irish leaders at first thought Casement, Monteith, and Bailey had been drowned; and Casement thought his two friends had perished with their driver while searching for him.

On the same day the *Aud* was captured, the U-19, after a rough nine-day voyage during which Casement was violently seasick and unable to sleep, approached as near as she could to the Irish coast, but the expected pilot ship again failed to appear. She therefore lowered the three men in a collapsible boat at about 1 a.m. The boat was swamped by the rough surf and overturned before it reached land, and the men had to wade ashore and then return several times for their equipment. The boat was too large to be destroyed or even hidden, and their small supply of arms, which was never used, was hastily and ineffectually buried in the sand. The men waited for daylight, and then Monteith and Bailey walked into Tralee to find help, leaving the exhausted Casement to rest.

On that Good Friday morning, an Irish farmer, John McCarthy, awoke in the dark at 2 a.m. and, for the first time in his life, walked along the shore to a holy well about a mile from his house in order to say his prayers. On the way back, as the tide was coming in at daybreak, he found the rowboat beached a few yards from the shore, a dagger in the boat, a large tin box with pistols and ammunition half-buried in the sand, and footprints all around. He went to summon a policeman and returned to find his small daughter playing with the pistols.

When Thomas Hearn of the Royal Irish Constabulary arrived, he searched the surrounding area and at 1:20 p.m. found Casement hiding on the beach in a place called McKenna's Fort. Hearn pointed his revolver at him and warned he would shoot if he moved. Casement said, "That's a nice way to treat an English traveller," and when asked what he was doing there replied, "By what authority do you ask this question? Am I bound to answer you?" When threatened with arrest under the Defence of the Realm Act, he said he was Richard Morten of Denham in Buckinghamshire and the author of *The Life of St. Brendon*. He claimed he had arrived in Dublin port at 8 o'clock that morning, but a first-class railway ticket from Berlin to Wilhelmshaven, dated April 12, 1916, was found in his coat pocket. Casement's bag contained a green Nationalist flag, a pair of field glasses, a flash signal lamp, 900 rounds of ammunition, a foreign map of Ireland, and some loose pages from a notebook which contained the notation: "11th of April, left Dublin for Wicklow. 12th of April, left Wicklow in Willie's yacht," the inveterate diarist's rather transparent way of describing his departure in the German submarine.

As Constable Hearn and Casement were leaving the Fort on their way to police headquarters, they passed a small boy in a pony and trap. The boy saw Casement tear up some papers and clumsily drop them behind his back, and after they had left, he went back, picked up the papers and brought them to the police. The torn papers were a typewritten German code with a five-digit signal number opposite the sentences: "Await further instructions. Send agent at once. Railway communications have been stopped. Will send plan for next landing. Further ammunition needed. Further rifles needed. Send another ship. Send cannons. Send explosives."

In Tralee, when Casement was medically examined, he tested the doctor's political sympathies, identified himself, and asked the doctor to tell Austin Stack, the local Nationalist commander, to rescue him. The doctor delivered the message, but Stack refused to help Casement for fear of starting the rebellion prematurely, though a rescue at that time would have been quite easy.

Casement was then taken to London through Dublin, and when the train stopped at Killarney station, the head constable said, "Did you hear what happened to the two lads at Puck? They ran into the tide and were drowned." As the train left the station Casement began to sob and continued for some time. He then said, "I am sorry for those two men; they were good Irishmen. It was on my account they came over here." In Dublin he asked if he would be given a bed when he arrived in London; he had been up for nine nights and was exhausted.

He was first jailed in the Tower of London, "prey to the most distracting thoughts a man ever endured and of sorrow for what I knew to be taking place in Ireland." After two weeks imprisonment, "his clothes were filthy ... his beard half-grown, his eyes red-rimmed and bloodshot, his arms, head and back swollen with insect bites from his verminous cell; he hesitated in speech and was unable to remember places and names.... His boots were hanging round his ankles, he was collarless and had to hold up his trousers. No natural light penetrated his cell." He thought he was going to be shot.

But he was transferred to Brixton Prison and then charged at Bow Street Police Station, where he was relieved to find that his confederates had not been drowned, for Daniel Bailey had been captured the day after Casement was arrested and appeared in court with him. After the charge was made, he pointed to Bailey and said: "That man is innocent. I think the indictment is wrongly drawn against him. If is it within my power to provide a defence for the man, I wish him to be in every way as well defended as myself."

After a thorough investigation by Admiral Reginald Hall of Naval Intelligence and Inspector Basil Thomson of Scotland Yard (neither of whom, oddly enough, testified against him), Casement was brought to trial in the High Court of Justice in London on June 26, 1916 and charged with high treason. He was accused of adhering to the King's enemies elsewhere than in the King's realm, that is, in Germany, contrary to the Treason Act of 1351, passed in the reign of Edward III.

The constitution of the court was extremely peculiar and singularly inappropriate for a state trial in time of war, the first such charge against a knight for several hundred years. The Lord Chief Justice, Lord Reading, while holding the office of Attorney-General, had been deeply implicated in the Marconi scandal of 1912 and had admitted, but only after the first investigation, that he had improperly speculated in the company's shares. But this did not prevent his elevation to the high bench.

In 1903 Colonel Arthur Lynch, who was charged with adhering to the King's enemies outside the realm, had been defended by Horace Avory, Lord Reading's associate justice, and prosecuted by Edward Carson. Colonel Lynch, an Irishman who had taken up arms against England in the South African War, joined the Boer forces, and fought in the field against the British Army, was the most recent precedent for Casement's trial. He was convicted of high treason and sentenced to death, but the sentence was subsequently commuted to life imprisonment, and he was pardoned after only a few months. He was elected to Parliament in 1907, and was serving in the House of Commons during

Casement's trial. The recent clemency and present prosperity of Colonel Lynch, MP, suggested that Casement should not be executed.

The Crown Counsel, Sir Frederick Smith, KC, Attorney-General, became notorious as "Galloper" Smith, Sir Edward Carson's second-in-command during the illegal gun-running at Larne, when Ulster threatened the tottering Liberal Government with civil war. He had, in fact, *before* the war, committed a similar crime—the illegal landing of German arms in Ireland to be used against a hostile British Government—for which Casement was now being tried *during* the war. This painful irony was obvious, but Smith, instead of remaining out of the case, deliberately led for the prosecution. Like Casement, he was tall, slender, muscular and attractive, but his icy character had none of Casement's gentleness and abstract idealism. He was a fierce political enemy of the prisoner, and brought considerable bias and personal animosity to the court. Smith's arrogance and intransigence, his cruel and devastating manner, was reflected in his penetrating cold gray eyes and in his brutal chin. He expressed his brilliant pomposity and intellectual superiority in a characteristic vein of subtle and restrained invective.

Casement's defense counsel, Arthur Sullivan, KC, was an Irishman with sharp, angular features, a furrowed forehead, and an immaculate mustache and goatee. Frail, and weary himself, he had a far weaker case than Smith, and was clearly no match for the overpowering rhetoric of the Attorney-General.

There were essentially two charges against Casement. First, that he endeavored to persuade British subjects, British soldiers, and prisoners of war in Limburg Lahn camp to forsake their duty and fight against Britain. And second, that he landed on the coast of Ireland with arms and ammunition for use against Britain. In a privately published pamphlet, *A Discarded Defence of Roger Casement* (1922), George Bernard Shaw suggested three possible lines of defense. Sullivan could contend, on the basis of Casement's diaries, that he was insane and unfit to stand trial; he could minimize the evidence, emphasize the positive aspects of Casement's conduct and plead for clemency because of his previous service and distinguished career; or, what Shaw considered most effective, he could argue that Casement be held as a prisoner of war and not tried as a traitor. But in the trial, Sullivan argued interminably on the grammatical as well as legal interpretation of the wording of the ancient Norman French Statute: that adhering to the King's enemies abroad did not constitute treason unless the offender was *in* the realm at the time of the offense. Casement did not testify on his own behalf, no witnesses were called for the defense, and Sullivan relied entirely on his own speech to the jury. The court ultimately decided that his interpretation was incorrect and that under the Statute a man could commit treason either inside the realm or, as in Casement's situation, outside the realm. Thus, the real political issue of the trial, whether the interests of Ireland were identical with England, and whether it was treason for an Irishman to support his *own* country, were buried by the legalistic quibbling about a technical point and never mentioned until Casement's speech *after* the verdict was delivered.

The jurors were a characteristic group of lower-middle-class Londoners, and the trial began with a humorous incident when some jurors with Irish names, who were challenged by the Crown, indignantly protested they were loyal Ulstermen and staunch supporters of Carson. Sir Frederick Smith opened for the prosecution with a characteristically dazzling speech. He explained the law of treason and the seriousness of the law; and recounted the notable consular career of the defendant with particular emphasis on the letter Casement wrote to the Foreign Secretary, Sir Edward Grey, when he received his knighthood:

> I find it very hard to choose the words in which to make acknowledgment of the honour done me by the King. . . . I would beg that my humble duty might be presented to His Majesty when you may do me the honour to convey to him my deep appreciation of the honour that he has been so graciously pleased to confer upon me.

Smith stressed Casement's "terms of gratitude, a little unusual perhaps, in their warmth, and in the language almost of a courtier," in order to show what he thought was Casement's sudden swing from loyalty to treason.

Smith described Casement's ardent but ineffectual activities in Germany, and his efforts that deliberately exposed the hungry, and sometimes wounded prisoners, "his inferiors in education, age and knowledge of the world, to the penalties of high treason." He narrated the capture of the *Aud* and the landing and arrest of Casement, and claimed that, "The prisoner, blinded by a hatred of this country, as malignant in quality as it was sudden in origin, has played a desperate hazard. He played it and he has lost it. Today the forfeit is claimed."

The prosecution then called six Irish prisoners of war who had been addressed by Casement in the Limburg Lahn camp and who, with an almost incredible irony, had been exchanged for German prisoners and were thus able to provide the evidence that proved Casement's treason.

The next day Smith called John McCarthy, the farmer who discovered the boat; Constable Hearn, who found and arrested Casement; Martin Collins, the boy who retrieved the torn papers; Constable Riley, who described the damaging code; Sergeant Butler, who took Casement from Tralee to Dublin by train; the Signalman of the *Bluebell,* who described the capture and scuttling of the *Aud;* a diver who recovered samples of the rifles, and a Russian colonel who identified them; and an English officer who identified the German maps of Ireland.

The defense counsel then presented his case—that the wording of this Statute of Treason did not apply to Casement—but his motion to quash the indictment was denied. Casement, not under oath and therefore not subject to cross-examination, was then allowed to correct several factual errors. He stated "the knighthood was not in my power to refuse," for a refusal would inevitably have meant the resignation of his diplomatic post and the end of his usefulness to the Indians of the Peruvian Amazon. He insisted that he had never asked or intended the Irish Brigade to fight for Germany, but only for Ireland; and he emphatically denied the insinuations that the prisoners' rations were reduced as punishment for not joining the Brigade and that he had accepted money from Germany. Finally, he objected to Smith's allusion to the Easter rebellion, which occurred after (and despite) his capture. Though Casement took no part in the rebellion, it was nevertheless an important factor in his conviction.

Sullivan began his closing speech for the defense with a rather awkward appeal to the jury's sense of fair play. He re-emphasized the point that Casement recruited the Irish Brigade to fight with the Nationalists against the Ulster army, when the war against Germany was over. He maintained the Crown had not proved that the *Aud* and Casement's landing were connected, so that their case rested solely on the first (yet sufficient) charge of suborning the prisoners of war. When Sullivan attempted to discuss the prewar gun-running in Ulster in order to explain and justify Casement's actions, he was interrupted by the Lord Chief Justice and told that no evidence of this had been given in court. Sullivan apologized abjectly ("I have been carried away too far, I am exceedingly sorry"), and rather incoherently attempted to continue his speech. He paused for a considerable time, and in one of the most dramatic moments of the trial, announced in surprisingly formal language, "I regret, my lord, to say that I have completely broken down."

The following day his junior counsel, Artemus Jones, concluded for the defense, but added little of substance to the case. He was dwarfed by the powerful closing speech of Frederick Smith, who summarized the argument of the defense and then tore it apart. He showed that the prisoner's intention was not, as had been stated, to land the Irish Brigade *after* the War, but rather to land them in Ireland *during* the War, "in order to evoke there once again, the hideous spectre of disunion, disloyalty and armed insurrection." He convincingly argued that Casement went to Germany to recruit an Irish Brigade; that if the Brigade had landed in Ireland it would certainly have aided Britain's enemies; and that he landed in concert with the *Aud*. Smith asserted that the Ulstermen "were never in his mind when he made these [recruiting] speeches, they never inspired the appeals he made . . . they are after-thoughts [invented] when it was necessary to exhume some defence." The most damaging piece of evidence was Casement's possession of the German code which, Smith emphasized, the prisoner intended to use "to assist the enemy in the war against our country." He forcefully concluded that "if these facts taken together: his journey to Germany, his speeches when in Germany, the inducements he held out to these soldiers, the freedom which he there enjoyed, the course which he pursued in Ireland, the messages which he contemplated as likely to take place between himself and the Germans, satisfy you of his guilt, you must give expression to that view in your verdict.... If you should come to the conclusion that the Crown has proved its case, however painful the duty, it is one from which you cannot, and you dare not, shrink. I have discharged my responsibility in this case; do you discharge yours."

The major point of dispute in the trial concerned Casement's intentions upon landing in Ireland. Though the prosecutor won his point, later commentators have insisted, incorrectly, that Casement landed in Ireland to stop the Easter rebellion. John Devoy, a contemporary Irish American leader, wrote in his *Recollections:* "Casement went to stop the insurrection if he could, believing that a fight at the time must end in disaster and that it ought to be postponed to await a better opportunity." Eva Gore-Booth, the sister of Countess Markiewicz, believed this; and three Irish writers, Leon O'Brien, Terence White and Roger McHugh, in *Leaders and Men,* have also maintained this view. But the Attorney-General won his case by denying this argument; Robert Monteith, a professional soldier and revolutionary who landed with Casement, escaped capture and was in the best position to judge Casement's intentions, denied that Casement landed to prevent the rising. And the most convincing evidence, which Casement himself wrote in the papers he attempted to send out of Pentonville Prison, is his rather romantic statement: "If I had been thirty-three instead of fifty-three, the arms would have been landed, the code would not have been found, and I should have freed Ireland, or died fighting at the head of my men."

The main purpose of Casement's activities during his years in Germany was to enlist German arms for Ireland, and his efforts were rewarded when Berlin decided to support the Easter rising. Casement was obviously disappointed that the Germans refused to send more substantial help—heavy arms, soldiers and especially officers—but was, nevertheless, eager to get a shipload of rifles and the assistance of a submarine. The *Aud* and the U-19 both worked to support the rebellion, and Casement rightly felt he would have a better chance of reaching Ireland by submarine. It was only *after* the *Aud* had sunk and he was captured that Casement realized the situation was hopeless (he had been in Germany and out of direct contact with Irish leaders), and tried to call off the rebellion. After his arrest, he asked to see the priest in Tralee and begged him, in order to avoid bloodshed, to get in touch with the Nationalist leader, John McNeill, and urge him to call off the rising. "Tell him I am a prisoner," Casement said, "and that the rebellion will be a dismal, hopeless failure, as the help they expect will not arrive." The final clause explains why, when in Ireland, not Germany, Casement thought the rebellion would fail.

O'Neill received the message, chose to ignore it, and went ahead with the rebellion in Dublin. But the leaders in southern and rural Ireland listened to Casement and canceled their military plans, and his countermanding order was an important reason for the failure of the Easter rising. Without national support, the fighting in Dublin lasted for a week, killed and wounded 3,000 men, wrecked the city, and incited English hatred of the Irish in general and Casement in particular. He was hanged, ironically, for the rebellion he tried—too late—to prevent.

After the conclusion of the Attorney-General's speech and the summing up of the Lord Chief Justice, the jury returned a verdict of guilty in fifty-five minutes. The convicted prisoner was allowed to address the court, and his speech, delivered with great passion and conviction, surpassed even the dazzling oratory of Frederick Smith. One juryman said afterwards that he would not have voted Casement guilty if he had heard his speech before the verdict was delivered.

Casement began by denying the jurisdiction of the English court and claimed his right to be tried in an Irish court by an Irish jury. He challenged the validity of the ancient statute, dug up "from the dungeons and torture chambers of the Dark Ages ... to take a man's life and limb for an exercise of conscience." And he condemned the formation of the Ulster Volunteer Movement in 1913 and justified the creation of the Nationalist Volunteers in opposition to them: when "the present Attorney-General asserted in a speech at Manchester [that] Nationalists would neither fight for Home Rule nor pay for it, it was our duty to show him that we knew how to do both. . . . I saw no reason why Ireland should shed her blood in any cause but her own, and if that be treason beyond the seas I am not ashamed to avow it, or to answer for it here with my life." He quoted the Ulster slogan, "Mausers and Kaisers and any King you like," and stated, with a direct reference to Smith, "the difference between us was that the Unionist champions chose a path they felt would lead to the woolsack [symbol of the Lord Chancellor]; while I went a road I knew must lead to the dock. And the event proves we were both right. The difference between us was that my 'treason' was based on a ruthless sincerity that forced me to attempt in time and season to carry out in action what I said in word—whereas their treason lay in verbal indictments that they knew need never be made good in their bodies. And so, I am prouder to stand here today in the traitor's dock to answer this impeachment than to fill the place of my right honourable accusers."

Like Casement himself, the speech was impressive but ineffectual; and the traditional black caps were placed on the heads of the justices as the sentence of execution by hanging was pronounced. Lord Reading's cap slipped to a grotesque angle and Justice Horridge, who suffered from a nervous twitch, seemed to be grimacing at the prisoner.

On July 17 and 18, the defense argued the appeal on the same legal grounds—the wording of the ancient Statute—as in the trial, and the argument was again dismissed. Casement could still appeal to the House of Lords, but another ironic twist to the judicial proceedings was revealed by the Criminal Appeal Act, which stated that no appeal to Lords could be lodged without the consent of the Attorney-General, in this case, the successful prosecutor. Smith later justified his refusal and said, "If I had given my fiat and the Lords had quashed the conviction on such a technicality, feeling against Casement was so strong that it might have brought the Government down."

Casement's last hope was a reprieve by the King on the recommendation of the Home Secretary, but this too was prevented by a startling discovery that added a strange and unexpected dimension to Casement's complex character. When he was brought to London after his arrest, the police found two trunks he had left in his old lodgings at 50 Ebury Street in Pimlico. When Inspector Thomson asked him to hand over the keys, Casement told him to break open the locks since there was nothing in them but some old clothes. In fact, the police found some personal black diaries for the years 1903, 1910 and 1911, the period of the Congo and the Amazon investigations, which recorded in frank, abundant and minute detail the homosexual activities of their political prisoner, and which radically changed the nature of the entire case.

Before the trial started, the prosecution suggested that the defense agree to produce the diaries in evidence, and that they cooperate in an attempt to obtain a verdict of guilty but insane. Sullivan, however, refused the offer: "I knew that it might save his life, but I finally decided that death was better than besmirching and dishonour." This decision was legally sound, for the diaries might have served as the basis of a separate action against Casement and would probably have destroyed his character without saving his life.

After Casement's conviction, extracts of the diaries were secretly circulated by Admiral Hall of Naval Intelligence, one of Casement's interrogators, among influential journalists, ambassadors, bishops and Members of Parliament, and were even shown to King George V. Before his appeal was decided, the newspapers publicized these private diaries, and one of them wrote: "It is common knowledge that Sir Roger Casement is a man with no sense of honour or decency. His written diaries are the monuments of a foul private life. He is a moral degenerate." The effect of this campaign was to extinguish the last remnants of public sympathy for Casement.

The passionate hatred of Casement was engendered even more by the "black" diaries than by the jingoistic patriotism and the hysteria of war. The sexual entries in the diaries occur nearly every day and are mixed in with descriptions of his daily work and social life, with observations about the weather and natural surroundings, and with his extremely detailed and exact financial accounts. For Casement, a compulsive and repressed personality, the spending of money was closely related to the spending of sperm, and the former often financed the latter in remote places where bed and boy were easily available. Casement's entries vary from vaguely homosexual longing, "A lovely pilot-boy on board—young (15) and face like girl—with long lashes and peach cheeks" to gross physical descriptions. Considering the enormous amount of work and travelling Casement did, the tropical climate, his physical and mental exhaustion, and normal (or even abnormal) limits of desire and satiation ("3 lovers had and two others wanted"), it is fairly obvious that most of the sexual entries were fantasies rather than actualities.

Casement constantly emphasizes the enormous and unreal size of the male genitals, passively observes other men's supposed erections and imputes sexual desire to all the boys he observes. He writes, for example, of a soldier "with erection under white knickers—it was half way to knee! *fully one foot long,*" and of a man who "had one below knees he could kiss." These entries suggest fears of his own inadequacy, for the sexual organs he describes are often twice as large as the usual size, always in a state of high excitement, and though erect, always *down* the leg toward the knee rather than characteristically upward.

Casement's passive observation is shown in entries like: "I hope almost at once to run across a good big one"; "Splendid testicles, no bush to speak of. Good wine needs no bush. Soft as silk and big and full"; and "one huge exposure, *red head and all,* and then Wicklow lad, knickers, 'His alright,' stiff." These are the admiring descriptions of a watcher, not an actor.

Finally, in an attempt to shed his guilt and to disguise the financial basis of his sexual encounters, Casement frequently projects his own desires on to those he observes: "Wanted it *awfully.* Literally begged for it" and "young dark boy, *huge,* wanted it awfully." Of course, there must have been numerous physical relations as well: "Breathed and quick, enormous push. Loved mightily, to hilt deep"; and "He stripped almost and went in *furiously.* Awfully hard thrusts and turns and kisses too, and biting on ears and neck. Never more force shown." But even here, the somewhat masochistic emphasis is on the epic of superhuman physical performance, which shows a desire to distinguish and therefore remember the specific sexual event amidst the blur of anonymous adventures and to experience in the retrospective recreation of the sexual encounter a sensation as great as the original excitement. It was emotion recollected in emotion.

The most convincing—and moving—entries are the shameful and confessional ones: "Getting loveless men up. ... Mine *huge* and he pulled it out. Others came so I fled. ... And so again I have sacrificed love to fear ... many stains on pants. I fear spoiled." When Colonel Sir Hector MacDonald was charged with homosexual practices in 1903 and shot himself in Paris on his way to face a court martial, Casement recorded: this is a most distressing case and "one that may awake the national mind to saner methods of curing a terrible disease than by criminal legislation."

Casement was a physically impressive and extremely virile-looking man, and until his diaries were seized no one had ever suspected he was a homosexual. His friends, and those who knew him best, never believed the accusations, and several books have been written to prove the diaries were forged by the English and that the homosexual entries were Casement's translation from the

Spanish diaries of Armando Normand, which Casement had made as part of the evidence against the sadistic torturer. The forgery theory has now been completely disproved.

Casement's diaries are the only evidence that he was a homosexual, and though the Belgians mounted an intensive campaign to discredit him after his Congo investigation, they never accused him of sexual inversion. If he had sodomized as many boys as he claimed in his 1903 diary, they surely would have found out about it and used it against him. He was under constant surveillance in Germany, but there was no evidence of homosexuality during that period of his life. The diaries, then, are more fantastic than real; the projections of a guilty and repressed homosexual that attempted to satisfy his unachieved desires.

When the British Cabinet (of which, of course, the Attorney-General was a member) debated the question of a royal reprieve after Casement's appeal was dismissed, several of the more astute ministers, who were concerned about pro-Irish opinion in America, at that time a necessary and neutral ally, thought it best to follow the advice of the British ambassador in Washington: "It is far better to make Casement ridiculous than a martyr" and a national hero, and to commute his sentence to life imprisonment. The Cabinet was evenly divided between clement and punitive factions (the latter strongly influenced by the diaries) when a decisive piece of evidence again appeared unexpectedly.

Casement had left a file of papers behind him in the courtroom, and these papers were returned to him—unread—in Pentonville Prison. Then Casement, with his customary yet incredible imprudence, sealed them up and asked the prison Governor to forward them to his solicitor. The Governor sent them instead to the Home Office for inspection, and the papers revealed that "the Irish Brigade might be employed in Egypt against British forces" if they could not be transported to Ireland. This was the decisive evidence that turned the Cabinet against Casement, despite political considerations.

After his appeal had been dismissed, Casement was officially deknighted and unofficially defamed—it only remained to hang him. On August 3, 1916, brave and dignified in the presence of death, he was taken from the condemned cell at Pentonville Prison in London and walked up the stairs to the gallows. The heavy rope was ritualistically placed around his neck, his head was hooded, and the trap sprung with a hideous crash. In accordance with prison regulations, he was left hanging on the scaffold for a superfluous hour. Among the last words he wrote were: "Do not let me lie here in this dreadful place," but his relatives, who had loyally assisted him to the very end, were denied his body. Instead his corpse was buried in a quicklime pit next to the gruesome murderer, Crippen. Some years later, in his epitaph of Casement, Yeats wrote, "The ghost of Roger Casement / Is beating on the door."

This ghost has never been laid to rest, and the violent controversy about his body, his diaries, his character and his reputation has continued until the present time. After prolonged and bitter negotiations, the Irish Government finally recovered his remains and he was honored with a state funeral in Dublin in 1965. Inspector Thomson had said the diaries "could not be printed in any age or in any language," but they were published in 1959 in English. They remained in the secret possession of the Home Office until the year of unauthorized publication, when they were first made available to qualified scholars who immediately verified their authenticity. Despite his homosexuality, Casement remains an honored Irish patriot.

There have been numerous books about Casement (T. E. Lawrence once wanted to write his biography), but his character and significance have never been satisfactorily explained. When asked about the German attitude toward him, Casement answered: "They could not understand me. They called me a dreamer." Casement was an emotional enthusiast who refused to see reality. He was idealistic and unselfish, and had considerable charm, but was high-strung and unstable, subject to periods of intense melancholy and self-pity, and to fits of hysterical weeping. His incredible lack of caution was more foolish than courageous, and he seemed doomed to leave a clear trail of incriminating evidence wherever he went.

Above all, Casement was an old-fashioned gentleman (he always commemorated Queen Victoria's birthday in his diary), intent on protecting and defending his honor even more than his life. During his interrogation he told Inspector Thomson: "I was not afraid to commit high treason . . . I face all the consequences. All I ask you to believe is that I have done nothing dishonourable." While drafting his final speech in the trial for his life, he made a sharp reference to the Attorney-General and then deleted it because "it might hurt his feelings." In his speech to the court he insisted that "a man, who in the newspapers is said to be just another Irish traitor, may be a gentleman." And after his conviction he affirmed: "I am already a dead man, but not yet a wholly dishonoured one."

In his last letter from the death cell to his closest friend, Richard Morten, Casement wrote:

> It is a strange, strange fate, and now as I stand face to face with death I feel just as if they were going to kill a boy. For I feel like a boy—and my hands are so free from blood and my heart always so compassionate and pitiful that I cannot comprehend how anyone wants to hang me.
>
> It is they—not I—who are the traitors filled with a lust of blood, of hatred of their fellows.

In the hour of his death, Casement reverted in his imagination to his pre-adolescent boyhood, a period of parental love and sexual innocence. His repressive Ulster-Protestant background would never allow him to reconcile his sexual instincts with the demands of society. Casement hated himself for his desires but succumbed to them, and he punished himself by a compulsive search for death and an elaborate preparation for the consecration of martyrdom that ended only on the gallows.

He left Germany unbalanced and exhausted, and called the Irish landing "a policy of despair." When asked by the German submarine captain if he needed more clothes, he replied, "Only my shroud." After his arrest, when informed he would be charged with treason, he laconically answered, "I hope so"; and then added, "I don't care what happens to me. I have long gone past that." And before his execution, he was more passionate and self-assured than ever: "They want my death, nothing else will do. And, after all, it's a glorious death, to die for Ireland. . . . I have felt this destiny on me since I was a little boy; it was inevitable; *everything in my life has led up to it."*

Casement's connection with Germany and the Irish independence movement led to a disastrous series of events that reveal his unconscious yet overpowering death wish: his liaison with the homosexual Christensen, Findlay's plot in Norway, the failure at Limburg Lahn camp, the collapse and hospitalization in Germany, the breakdown and return of the original submarine U-20, the rough and sleepless voyage, the deciphering of the German code, the capture of the *Aud,* the lack of a pilot boat in Tralee harbor, the swamped dinghy that could neither be hidden nor destroyed, the retention of the Wilhelmshaven railway ticket, the German code and his personal notebook, his immediate discovery by John McCarthy, the retrieval of the code by Martin Collins, the refusal of the local Nationalists to rescue him and his fatal order to call off the rebellion. This bizarre combination of events shows Casement as a hopeless idealist, magnificently unprepared for all military and political realities, and landing in a spirit of self-sacrifice that was virtually suicidal.

These ironies continued during his arrest and trial. As with the ticket and the code, he consistently refused to take the most obvious precautions, and left his incriminating diaries in London when he went to enemy territory for treasonable purposes in time of war. The composition of the court was strange: Avory (and Carson) involved in the Lynch trial, Reading smeared by the Marconi scandal, Smith deeply implicated in treasonable prewar gun-running, and Sullivan hopelessly ineffectual, arguing the weakest line of defense not only in the trial but also in the appeal. The release of the Irish prisoners by the Germans, the appeal to the House of Lords denied by the prosecuting attorney, the surreptitious circulation of the diaries, the campaign of defamation by the newspapers, the bloodthirsty hysteria of war, the capture of the incriminating prison papers—all this brought Casement to the scaffold where he knew he must end. Anything less would have disappointed him.

Ironically, he was executed because the public was made to believe that homosexuals should be hanged for treason. He died, like most patriotic martyrs, more for his dreams than for his actions. His hanging was a moral as well as political error, for if he had been, like Colonel Lynch, granted clemency and sentenced to life imprisonment, he surely would have been pardoned when political passions died down after the War or, at the very latest, when Ireland gained independence in 1922. Casement could have been an extremely valuable moderate leader in a country where many of the best men had been killed in rebellion or civil war, and he could have contributed to the settlement of the Irish problem, "the union of the shark with its prey," which remains bloody and insoluble even today.

Casement's two atrocity investigations helped to extinguish the cruel and exploitative colonialism in the Congo and the Amazon, and stand as one of the great humanitarian achievements of this century. Like his friend and contemporary, Joseph Conrad, Casement was one of the first men to question the idea of progress, a dominant idea in Europe from the Renaissance to the Great War, and to reveal in documentary reality the savage degradation of the white man in the heart of darkness.

Casement's achievement in Ireland, despite his succession of overwhelming failures, was serious and substantial, for his deliberate martyrdom helped the Irish to forge the uncreated conscience of their race. His landing was reported by an Irish farmer, an Irish boy picked up the pieces of the code, he was arrested by an Irish constable, Irish prisoners of war testified against him in court and he was betrayed by the Irishman who landed with him, for Bailey gave evidence in the pre-trial hearing and escaped prosecution himself. James Joyce was right when he said Ireland is a sow that devours her own farrow. Though the Irish helped convict Casement, the idea of a free Ireland was born during the Easter rising. When Casement realized his case was hopeless, he used his trial as a public forum to justify the rebellion and propagate the idea of Irish independence. He stands in the patriotic tradition of Wolfe Tone, who in 1796 attempted to overthrow British rule in Ireland with the help of the French Directory, and of Garibaldi, who in Casement's words, "went into the Navy of Piedmont to seduce the sailors from their allegiance, and was condemned to death as a traitor for that act."

Casement has found his justification in history, and in his final speech, which has a striking relevance today, he asserted:

> Ireland has seen her sons—aye, and her daughters too—suffer from generation to generation always for the same cause, meeting always the same fate, and always at the hands of the same power; and always a fresh generation has passed on to withstand the same oppression. . . . The cause that begets this indomitable persistency, the faculty of preserving through centuries of misery the remembrance of lost liberty, this surely is the noblest cause men ever strove for, ever lived for, ever died for. If this be the cause I stand here today indicted for, and convicted of sustaining, then I stand in a goodly company and a right noble succession. . . . An Empire

that can only be held together by one section of its governing population perpetually holding down and sowing dissension among a smaller but none the less governing section, must have some canker at its heart, some ruin at its root.

6

E. M. Forster and T. E. Lawrence: A Friendship

E. M. Forster and T. E. Lawrence first met in 1921 at the home of the Emir Feisal in Berkeley Square. Lawrence, whose successful campaigns against the Turks had made him world-famous, had recently been appointed by Winston Churchill to the Colonial Office as adviser on Arab affairs. He appeared, small and fairhaired, toward the end of lunch and was encouraging about prospects in the Middle East. Forster, whose smaller fame rested on his four novels, culminating with *Howards End* (1910), was pleased and impressed by the encounter with an intellectual man of action. He wrote this to Lawrence, received no reply, and soon afterwards left for a year in India as private secretary to the Maharajah of Dewas Senior. Three years later, Siegfried Sassoon asked Forster to read the as yet unpublished *Seven Pillars of Wisdom,* and the friendship began with Forster's long letter of brilliant criticism to Lawrence, who had by then enlisted in the Army Tank Corps under the name of "T. E. Shaw."

Though the difference in their lives—one on the plane of action, the other of thought—was often mentioned in their correspondence, they had some important things in common; and Forster, nine years older than Lawrence, was well qualified to judge the book. Forster had been at Cambridge, Lawrence at Oxford, and they had served in Egypt at the same time. While Lawrence was in Cairo, first as an intelligence officer at headquarters and then the Arab Bureau, where he helped to organize the Arab Revolt (1914–1916), Forster was a Red Cross volunteer in Alexandria (1915–1919). In 1921, two years after Lawrence participated in the Versailles Conference as counsel for the Arab cause, Forster was commissioned by the Labour Party Research Department to write on British colonial policy in Egypt. In his pamphlet *The Government of Egypt,* he described England's broken pledges and mistreatment of Egypt and recommended independence. The following year Forster published *Alexandria: A History and Guide,* as well as journalistic reports on Indian politics, and in 1923, *Pharos and Pharillon,* a series of sketches on ancient and modern Alexandria. Though

Forster had no experience of active life and no power of managing men, he had met English military and political leaders such as General Sir Archibald Murray and Sir Ronald Storrs and knew Orientals and Oriental life very well.

Forster recognized in *Seven Pillars* a masterpiece (though he wisely did not say so at once) and sent Lawrence an expert, incisive, sensitive stylistic analysis of particular sentences and paragraphs, which was the best criticism he ever wrote.[1] This was just the sort of frank and detailed advice that Lawrence desired and needed.

Forster divided literature into "fluid" and "granular" and placed Lawrence in the latter class. He observed that Lawrence presented an immobile and static series of pictures rather than a breathing, sliding reality and suggested that Lawrence should introduce more humor, more conversations to dramatize the characters, and more portrayal of his own character. Forster noticed that Lawrence very rightly had several styles—technical, narrative, reflective and emotive—and he showed by precise analysis that the slow-moving and mannered reflective mode was not sufficiently under control and tended to become strained and muddled. Forster copied out a passage of exquisite beauty in which the Arabs turn their backs on perfumes and luxuries to choose the eddyless wind of the desert (chap. iii, pars. 6–7). He praised Lawrence's etymological use of words, description of scenery and portrayal of pathos; he emphasized the unity of the book, and said no one would ever like the "great affair" more than he did. Later he wrote that

> round this tent-pole of a military chronicle T. E. has hung an unexampled fabric of portraits, descriptions, philosophies, emotions, adventures, dreams. He has brought to his task a fastidious scholarship, an impeccable memory, a style nicely woven out of Oxfordisms and Doughty, an eye unparalleled, a sexual frankness which would cause most authors to be run in by the police, a profound distrust of himself, a still profounder faith. (*Abinger*, p. 136)

Equally interesting is what the letter reveals about *A Passage to India,* with *its* several styles and dislike of "muddle." When Forster admired Lawrence's knowledge and use of geology, Lawrence praised the geological genesis of the caves, whose landscape was "despairingly well done." Reading *Seven Pillars* proved an inspiration to Forster, who was just completing his greatest novel, for Lawrence's work seemed to pull him together and help him finish his own book.

When Forster's letter arrived "a miracle happened." Though Lawrence had a bout of malaria, the fever suddenly left him and he sat up in bed to read the letter through. It was an extraordinary experience. He was intoxicated with pleasure and abnormally grateful about Forster's care and sensitivity, and asked for further comments when Forster had finished the entire book. He had been profoundly dejected by struggling through four versions in four years (the first "lost" in Reading station) and by squeezing actuality out of memory, and was stimulated and encouraged by Forster's praise. Later on, when Forster was depressed by being unable to write anything after *A Passage to India*, Lawrence's assurance that the novel could represent him for the moment, and that he would write just one good novel more, heartened Forster considerably. This was but one of many instances of mutual nourishment.

Lawrence followed Forster's advice about specific paragraphs, omitting two and rewriting a third in the final text. And he wrote to the novelist James Hanley:

> I found Forster a very subtle & helpful critic, over my *Seven Pillars*. Hardly anybody else (of the dozens of critics who dealt with that or *Revolt in the Desert*) said anything that wasn't useless pap. All Forster's notes on books or writing seem to me workmanlike. After all, he writes, & so knows what authors are up against. In himself he is a very witty, pointed, shy, emancipated person. I like him. (Lawrence, *Letters*, p. 738)

Their mutual interests were focused on their books, which they exchanged, read, criticized, praised, inscribed, dedicated and lent.

Much to Forster's discomfort, Lawrence insisted on keeping up the deferential guru-disciple side of their relationship in which Forster was the great artist and Lawrence the bungling amateur—"If the flea may assert a kindred feeling with the lion . . ."—and maintaining that he was better with a rifle and spade than with pen. Lawrence's inscription in Forster's copy of *Seven Pillars* was: "Not good enough, but as good, apparently, as I can do."

The two men were almost strangers at this first exchange of letters, and though Forster agreed that it was easier to write to strangers, it was inevitable that they should meet again. Forster went down to Dorsetshire, had a shy and rather awkward meeting with Lawrence, and was asked to Clouds Hill, the tiny four-roomed cottage that Lawrence and his fellow soldiers used as a retreat from military camp. Forster passed under the Greek inscription "I don't care" carved by Lawrence over the door, and returned often (once to meet Thomas Hardy) to enjoy the silence and happy casualness of the place.

Just after Forster's visit, during which he threw a stone at a noisy nightjar and smashed a tile on the cottage roof, Lawrence sent a fascinating letter on *A Passage to India*. He particularly praised the bitter scene at the Club following Adela's accusation, the roof-top conversation of Fielding and Aziz after the trial, and the orgiastic aspects of the Hindu festival. He called Forster one of the shining ones of the English language, admired the multiplicity of effects, the universal quality, and the superb rendition of setting: "One feels all the while the weight of the climate, the shape of the land, the immovable immensity of the crowd behind . . . all that is felt, with the ordinary fine human senses. A marvellous book" (*Letters*, p. 462).

Their response to each other's works was spontaneous and enthusiastic and enabled their personal affection to overcome natural reserve. They saw a great deal of each other and met at Clouds Hill, at King's College, and at Plymouth, walked around Mount Edgcumbe and went riding in Lawrence's speedboat. They met again in Lincoln, in London, and in Surrey, where Lawrence slyly exposed the identities of two important Secret Service men and suggested Forster ring them up to prove it. During this time Forster gave the popular and successful Clark Lectures at Cambridge, published them as *Aspects of the Novel* (1927), and brought out his stories, *The Eternal Moment,* in 1928. Lawrence meanwhile had re-transferred to the R.A.F. and served in India during 1926–1929, first in Karachi and then in Miranshah, ten miles from the Afghan border in Waziristan, where he began his translation of the *Odyssey.* In 1926 he privately issued *Seven Pillars* in a limited edition and published its redacted version, *Revolt in the Desert,* the following year.

Lawrence was so pleased with Forster's criticism of *Seven Pillars* that in the spring of 1928 he told Forster about his crude, unsparing, faithful notes on life in the ranks, very metallic and uncomfortable, which he hoped to make into a book by leaving them to sink down into his mind and then reviving his memory by their aid. Lawrence had given these notes, published as *The Mint* in 1955, to David Garnett and diffidently suggested to Forster that he might read these later and wiser writings.

The following summer, Forster sent Lawrence two long letters of incisive criticism on *The Mint.* He suggested that Lawrence begin the narrative much earlier, with his original dismissal from the R.A.F. (when his true identity was discovered), his time with the Army Tank Corps, and his re-admission. He liked the character of the drill sergeant Stiffy and the toughness, power and style of the first two parts, but was disappointed by the insipid conclusion and dissatisfied with Lawrence's desire to be fair to the Air Force. Forster thought, however, that the two most brilliant chapters were in Part III: the day of Queen Alexandra's funeral and a soldier's discovery of sexual experience in "Dance Night" (chaps. ix–x). When he suggested that Lawrence try to describe women, Lawrence evasively answered there were none to explore in Waziristan. (In his review of D. H. Lawrence's novels, T. E. Lawrence observed that both Lawrence and Forster gave their main parts to women whenever possible). Forster rightly judged *The Mint* unequal to *Seven Pillars,* discussed the problems of publication and, convinced of Lawrence's creative talent, encouraged him to write a third book.

Lawrence was once again delighted with Forster's analysis, but admitted that his friend's judgments were partial to his imperfections. He then told Forster about his method of composition. Each night in camp he would sit in bed with his knees drawn up and write down all that had happened during the day, hoping that memory and time would enable him to select the significant events. Five years later, while in Karachi, he completely rearranged the notes, using each one of them, and tied himself in knots trying to re-enact the imaginary scenes as he wrote them out.

The correspondence about *The Mint* elucidates the difficult question of Lawrence's motives for breaking off a brilliant career and plunging into the squalor of an Air Force depot. The East had been closed to him. Because of his torture and degradation at Deraa (*Seven Pillars,* chap. 80), he desperately wanted to escape respectability, to test his will, to hide and to suffer. The service was a great assoiler, a form of lay monasticism, a place for order and self-effacement. His own account is rather oversimplified. He wrote that his profound dejection about what he considered the failure of *Seven Pillars of Wisdom: A Triumph* broke his nerve and sent him into the service, where he found the sad substitute of a half-year's contentment. Another motive was his intense need for economic and personal security. A scruple prevented him from receiving any money for his work in the East and his writings about the Arab Revolt, and he felt disinclined to struggle for a living "on the outside." As early as 1928 he had safely mapped out his life and arranged for a job as night watchman in a London bank to begin in 1935, when he would be discharged.

Lawrence told Forster that he found his humble military life surprisingly satisfying. He liked the sun, the decent treatment and the private fireplace in the midst of Himalayan snows, and found there a measure of happiness. He found a bit of Arabia in India and commented: "Most of my time passes in reading and thinking, while I wander or sit upon the huge aerodrome, a flat clean stretch of sand, nearly a mile square. At night I lie down on my back in the middle of it, and speculate on the chances that some of you will perhaps see these same stars a few hours later over England. A gay life" (*Letters,* p. 531).

When in 1929 unfair newspaper publicity once again threatened his place in the Air Force, he was suddenly and secretly sent home from India, and had to go into hiding. "I am being hunted, and do not like it. When the cry dies down I'll come out of my hole and see people—unless of course the cry doesn't die down, and the catchers get my skin. I have a terrible fear of getting the sack from the R.A.F. and can't rest or sit still" (*Letters,* p. 641). But he saw he was too old to lead a boy's life much longer and of course realized the absurdity of his position: "It's like having a unicorn in a racing stable. Beast doesn't fit."

In his review of *The Mint* Forster explained, rather unconvincingly, why he thought Lawrence had exchanged comfort and distinction for fatigues and the square. "It was partly the desire to abase himself, to crash from the heights of commanding to the depths of obedience, it was partly the desire to hide, partly the itch for adventure. But believing him, as I do, to be true, I believe there was a deeper motive than these. He joined up because he wanted to get in touch with people, and felt he could only do this by doing the work they did, and by sharing their lives." His friendship with Forster was an exception to this rule.

Forster's explanation was put forth tentatively. He realized that Lawrence's character was very difficult to understand, that probably he did not understand himself, and that no one who knew him at all well would venture to sum him up. Although Lawrence was intensely reserved, had a crablike shell that often prevented him from revealing his thoughts and feelings, and liked to cover up mysteriously his own tracks, Forster eventually came to know him well. Because Lawrence had great breadth of interests and extraordinary flexibility of personality, he was particularly good at establishing successful relationships with a wide range of brilliant people. Though Forster fed buttered toast to his cat and lectured Cambridge "intelligenzanettes" while Lawrence, perspiring and greasy, clerked at aircraft engine shops in Waziristan, their minds were parallel. With Forster, Lawrence was sensitive and literary. They often discussed Beethoven and Tolstoy and wrote as one writer to another; indeed, Forster believed that Lawrence's deepest impulse was the desire to write. Because of Lawrence's sensitive adaptability, and perhaps to balance the view of him as a blood-thirsty egomaniac, Forster saw and emphasized the modest and humble, the selfless and tender side of Lawrence's personality. At Clouds Hill, Lawrence was always the kind and considerate host, providing hot-water bottles for his guests while he himself lived, as always, in ascetic simplicity. Lawrence had great powers of encouragement, and when they talked of the Arab Revolt he made Forster feel that he could almost have taken Damascus himself. Forster credited Lawrence with the three heroic virtues—courage, generosity and compassion—and suggested compassion as the lodestar to lead the reader through the psychology of *Seven Pillars*.

Though Lawrence was at times direct and open, he was more often, as he said of Forster himself, subtle, reserved and elusive. He threw up a great deal of verbal dust, loved bewilderment, leg-pulling, fantasy and teasing. (Forster could tease as well and once wrote, "Why June 26th? Ah. I can have my little secrets too, can I not?") Though it did not matter to Forster, Lawrence did not always tell the truth. Though Forster was frank with Lawrence, he was never equally frank in return; he could reveal only a little of himself and not arouse distrust. Yet in their letters, Lawrence is *more* frank than Forster. These are the qualities most prevalent in their obscured discussions of unpublished writings and homosexuality.

Forster has commented on Lawrence's sexual frankness. When he first read *Seven Pillars* he copied out three passages, one for its beauty and two others (chap. i, pars. 4–5, and chap. xcii, pars. 2–3) "for other reasons." The last two passages are very striking and direct descriptions of homosexual encounters: "friends quivering together in the yielding sand with intimate hot limbs in supreme embrace." When Forster cautiously asked Lawrence if he might keep these passages, Lawrence was not at all reticent and replied that he could do anything he pleased with the book. Lawrence later wrote that it seemed to him almost incredible that the learned *Royal Geographical Journal* and the *Journal of the Central Asian Society* both found *Revolt in the Desert* indecent. Yet when James Hanley's homosexual novel *Boy* was being prosecuted, Lawrence wrote the publisher that Forster was one of the few writers who might dare lead an attempt at help and said he did not understand why most of them were afraid of the word *sodomy*. Forster admired and would fight for men who published the kind of writing that he kept private.

A letter of Lawrence to Forster (September 8, 1927) reveals that in addition to the early unpublished story "The Rock," the lost play *The Heart of Bosnia* (1911), the unfinished novel *Arctic Summer* (1914) and the abandoned historical novel, Forster had written at least one long novel and one short story[2] he did not wish to publish in his lifetime because of personal reticence about their homosexual content.

Forster had sent Lawrence a copy of the very personal novel, Forster's "last keep," but he was afraid to read it for fear that his dislike of the book might carry over to Forster himself. "If you knew all about me," Lawrence wrote from India in 1927, "(perhaps you do: your subtlety is very great: shall I put it 'if I knew that you knew . . . '?) you'd think very little of me. And I wouldn't like to feel that I was on the way to being able to know about you" (*Letters,* p. 537). Both men hid behind their natural reserve and felt safer with each other that way. Lawrence's "if you knew *all* about me" probably refers to the less pleasant side of his character, perhaps the masochistic and cruel side that Forster had not really known. He had observed, however, that Lawrence did not like to be touched and "had some queer friends" whom Forster instinctively distrusted. At the age of fifty, Forster felt that love was overrated and the relation one would like between people is a mixture of "friendliness and lust."

"I'm sorry your short story isn't publishable," Lawrence wrote in 1927. "As you said, the other wouldn't do for general circulation. Not that there was a wrong thing in it: but the wrong people would run about enlarging their mouths over you. It is a pity such creatures must exist" (*Letters,* p. 537). He also looked forward to Forster's new collection of old stories and said, "If you dedicate anything to me I'll wear the first page of it as an identity disc."

Forster's next published letter, possibly in response to Lawrence's, is severely truncated, with the first and third of three paragraphs omitted. He wrote that he has decided to dedicate the volume of stories, *The Eternal Moment,*

> "To T. E., in the absence of anything else." The dedication can be given a wrong meaning, which you will enjoy doing, and I shall like to think of you doing it. The matter is decided therefore. One of the stories is a feeble timid premonition of the [unpublishable] one which is with you now and which is yours really, and that is what the dedication really means. If you ever inscribe anything to me, either good bad or indifferent, I shall be a lot annoyed. (This too can be given a wrong meaning. Care to have a try?) [*a paragraph omitted*]. . . . Yours, EMF. (*Letters to Lawrence,* p. 66)

This tantalizing letter raises two interesting questions, the meaning of the dedication and of the story written for Lawrence. The dedication suggests that the book is a compensation for the friendship, companionship, affection that Forster cannot give Lawrence while he is in India. It might also mean that the book is a substitute for a love that Forster is perhaps unwilling or unable to give Lawrence. As for the "wrong meaning," I leave that for the reader to devise for himself.

One is on equally tenuous ground when discussing the story that is a "feeble timid premonition" of the unpublished tale. Of the six stories in *The Eternal Moment,* it is most likely that the rather grim yet vague and elusive "The Point of It" (1911) is the premonition of the one about Lawrence. Forster wrote that his Bloomsbury friends did not like the story, and when they queried, What *is* the point? he did not know what to reply. This story portrays two modes of life, that of Harold (Lawrence?)—brief, violent and fulfilled—and the other that of Michael (Forster?)—respectable, though somewhat dull and empty.

Forster's story was strangely and unhappily prophetic. In Lawrence's very first letter to Forster, he said the only satisfaction he ever got was from the voluntary danger of high speed on a motorbike. In 1929 George Bernard Shaw anonymously gave Lawrence a large, powerful and apolaustic motorcycle which he described in "The Road" chapter of *The Mint:*

> A glance at the speedometer: seventy-eight. Boanerges is warming up. I pull the throttle right open, on the top of the slope, and we swoop flying across the dip, and up-down up-down the switchback beyond: the weighty machine launching itself like a projectile with a whirr of wheels into the air at the take-off of each rise, to land lurchingly with such a snatch of the driving chain as jerks my spine like a rictus.

It was on such a ride, on May 13, 1935, just after Lawrence had left the R.A.F., that swerving to avoid some cyclists he crashed and was killed.

Forster saw Lawrence for the last time at the National Gallery. They had fixed a date for Forster's visit to Clouds Hill that was confirmed by Lawrence's note of May 7, the next-to-last letter he ever wrote. Two years earlier, he had written to Robert Graves, "I think Frederic Manning, and an Armenian, called Altounyan, and E. M. Forster are the three I most care for."[3]

The correspondence of Forster and Lawrence provides a valuable contribution to the biography of Forster, of which we know very little, and to the cultural history of the modern era. Forster himself was the original editor of Lawrence's letters, and David Garnett took over the work only after Forster decided he could not go on with it. Though many of Forster's letters are not included (Lawrence refers to some of them) and nearly half of them have considerable omissions, made by Forster himself, they are the only Forster letters to be published and the most personal and revealing of his writings. In the letters Forster steps out of his fictional guise and stands in his own character—tougher, more practical, more intimate and introspective than he otherwise appears. They show a powerful and "workmanlike" critical faculty, inspired by a personal interest, that is more consistently perceptive than the rather precious essays and the sometimes mannered and casual *Aspects of the Novel*. They express valuable philosophical reflections on love, old age and the possibility of finding peace and happiness in a world of infinite suffering but of limited cruelty. They make us anticipate with keen eagerness the complete edition of Forster's letters and unpublished fiction that will undoubtedly clarify the homosexual intimations of "The Story of a Panic," *The Longest Journey* and *A Room with a View*. The most interesting of Lawrence's letters to Forster are those on his method of composition, his just and insightful criticism of Forster's books (compare this to Conrad's polite but extravagant praise of his friends' mediocre work) and revelations of his motivation and character.

Most important of all, the correspondence reveals the happy conjunction of two diverse and brilliant personalities from very different spheres of life (Lawrence had gone to places where Forster said he "should smash and scream in 30 seconds") and the development of their friendship and understanding. Their common ideals are expressed in Lawrence's original introduction to *Seven Pillars of Wisdom*, omitted from the final text:

> I have fitted those peoples in a degree for the new commonwealth in which the dominant races will forget their brute achievements, and white and red and yellow and brown and black will stand up together without side-glances in the service of the world.

7

D. H. Lawrence, Katherine Mansfield and *Women in Love*

"Every true artist is the salvation of every other."
D. H. Lawrence, *Women in Love*

D. H. Lawrence and Katherine Mansfield had a good deal in common. Both were outsiders in English society: Lawrence because of his working-class background, Katherine because of her colonial origins. Though they left their birthplace, they were strongly influenced by it and frequently recreated it in their work. They revolted against the conventional values of the time; and had considerable sexual experience in early life, though Lawrence had been strengthened and Katherine hurt by it. They spent many impoverished years on the Continent and maintained a European rather than an insular outlook. They had intuitive and volatile personalities, experienced life with a feverish intensity, were highly creative and passionately committed to their art, and achieved a posthumous fame far greater than their contemporary reputations. Most important of all, they were seriously ill for a great part of their adult lives, and made their pilgrimage from country to country in search of a warm climate and good health. They were subject to sudden fits of black rage, suffered the constant pain of disease and the fearful threat of death, and died of tuberculosis at an early age.

During their ten years of friendship, in which Lawrence and Katherine twice lived in neighboring houses—in the autumn of 1914 in Buckinghamshire and the spring of 1916 in Cornwall—they oscillated from profound attachment to extreme hostility and back again. When they did not see each other, they kept in touch through letters and news from their close common friends: S. S. Koteliansky, Mark Gertler, Dorothy Brett and Ottoline Morrell, and they read each other's books. Though Katherine was attracted to Lawrence's responsive vitality, she was also repulsed by his passionate enthusiasm and dogmatic obsessions, which intensified her natural inclination to retreat into her private world.

Because their temperaments were radically different in this respect, Katherine frequently appeared negative, cowardly, pallid and sickly to Lawrence, who blamed her for being ill; while to Katherine, Lawrence's extreme affirmations and condemnations seemed almost insane in their manic egoism. Their most serious estrangement occurred in February 1920 (some months before the publication of *Women in Love* in November), when Lawrence sent Katherine what Middleton Murry justly called a "monstrously" and "inhumanly cruel" letter. If we can understand why Lawrence sent this letter and how Katherine was able to forgive him after he had (as she said) "spat in my face and threw filth at me," we will be able to perceive the essence of their friendship.

The history of their relationship is a record of affection given and received, for both Lawrence and Frieda said the Murrys were their most intimate friends. But Lawrence had a tendency to quarrel with the people closest to him, and Katherine's response to his temperamental extremism inevitably caused a breach, with harsh letters and bitter recriminations. Though both Lawrence and Katherine recognized that he was the greater writer, she became more of a personal threat to him as her literary reputation increased.

Though Lawrence had great insight into the characters of his friends, he was intransigent about his prescriptions for their behavior. He could demonstrate, in long letters or personal harangues, his love for them and concern about what they should do with their lives. But if they chose to ignore his advice, Lawrence felt wounded and betrayed, and harshly rejected them. This conflict accentuated his sense of isolation and self-righteousness, and gave him license to abuse them viciously. In his essay on Lawrence, Bertrand Russell (who is satirized as the elderly sociologist, Sir Joshua Mattheson, in *Women in Love*) says that when he received one of Lawrence's violent letters in 1915 he actually felt like committing suicide for twenty-four hours—until common sense reasserted itself. If Lawrence could make Russell, one of the great minds and great egos of the century, feel suicidal, then the effect on Katherine must have been equally devastating. Katherine also appears in *Women in Love* as Gudrun; and Lawrence's transformation of an actual person into a fictional character provides some revealing insights about his creative imagination: the way in which he shapes his vision of the world and enforces his way of seeing on the reader.

In January 1913, when Lawrence (who was three years older than Katherine) had published *The White Peacock* (1911) and *The Trespasser* (1912), and Katherine *In a German Pension* (1911), she sent him a copy of *Rhythm,* the little magazine she was editing with Murry, and asked him for a contribution. Lawrence replied from Gargnano on January 29 offering several stories. When the Lawrences returned to England in June 1913, they looked up Katherine and Murry and liked them immediately. And when they discovered that neither couple was married and both women were waiting for a divorce (Katherine had married George Bowden on March 2, 1909, and left him the next day), it seemed they were made for each other. Frieda felt "theirs was the only spontaneous and jolly friendship that we had. . . . I fell for Katherine and Murry when I saw them quite unexpectedly on the top of a bus, making faces at each other and putting their tongues out." This was a charming but characteristically childish aspect of the Murrys' relationship. Frieda was then estranged from her young children; and Katherine, who had briefly adopted a child in Germany, was far more understanding than Lawrence about Frieda's maternal feelings. Katherine visited the children and took them letters, and Frieda "loved her like a younger sister." Later in the summer the two couples bathed on the deserted sands of Broadstairs, and Lawrence gave the Murrys a copy of *Sons and Lovers*.

The Lawrences returned to Italy in September, described their lonely life in Lerici as one long enchantment, and passionately urged the Murrys to join them. The great problem was lack of money, for Murry's small income depended on reviewing in London. If he had followed Lawrence's advice he would have had to live on Katherine's allowance of £100 a year, and that seemed "quite intolerable" to him.

Lawrence discussed and dismissed this financial problem in a long letter to Murry written in the autumn of 1913, which brilliantly analyzed the essential defect in Murry's marriage and, unlike his later letters, was both insightful and reasonable.

> When you say you won't take Katherine's money, it means you don't trust her love for you. When you say she needs little luxuries, and you couldn't bear to deprive her of them, it means you don't respect either yourself or her sufficiently to do it.
>
> It looks to me as if you two, far from growing nearer, are snapping the bonds that hold you together, one after another. I suppose you must both of you consult your own hearts, honestly. . . .
>
> You must rest, and you and Katherine must heal, and come together, before you do *any serious* work of any sort. It's the split in the love that drains you. . . .
>
> If you want things to come right—if you are ill and exhausted, then take her money to the last penny and let her do her own housework. Then she'll know you love her. You can't blame her if she's not satisfied with you. . . . But, you fool, you squander yourself, not for *her*, but to provide her with pretty luxuries she doesn't really want. You insult her. A woman unsatisfied must have luxuries. But a woman who loves a man would sleep on a board. . . .
>
> You've tried to satisfy Katherine with what you could earn for her, give her: and she will only be satisfied with what you *are*.

Lawrence saw that trust and love could overcome Murry's scruples about money, and that Katherine's "need" for luxuries was merely a false and insulting excuse. Lawrence, like Katherine, also understood that a true marriage would strengthen her art. "I believe in marriage," Katherine told her friend, Sylvia Lynd. "It seems to me the only possible relation that is really satisfying. And how else is one to have peace of mind to enjoy life and to do one's work?"

When Lawrence states that "a woman who loves a man would sleep on a board," he is alluding to Frieda, who abandoned her security, her comfort and even her children to run off with an impoverished writer. The weak and selfish Murry, who could never supply Katherine's material or emotional needs, knew that she was *not* satisfied with what he was. But Murry's own career was just as important to him as Katherine's; and he did not love her enough to make this sacrifice, or have sufficient faith in his own talents to believe that he could write while abroad or start afresh later on. Murry, who was extremely insecure, had a wife whom he had to support emotionally and also nourish as a writer (as Frieda nourished Lawrence). Since Murry was self-absorbed and had high, if unrealistic, literary ambitions, he was particularly unsuited to this sacrificial role.

Katherine agreed with Lawrence and later bitterly criticized Murry for his unwillingness to leave his literary career in London and live modestly with her in the Mediterranean until her health improved. As she wrote in her *Scrapbook* in December 1919: "We were not *pure*. If we had been, he would have faced coming away with me. And that he would not do. He would not have said he was too tired to earn enough to keep us here. He always refused to face what it meant—living alone for two years on not much money." When poor health forced Katherine to leave England every winter, she found it extremely difficult to bear the solitude during the separation from her husband, although she had temporarily replaced him with her lesbian companion, Ida Baker.

Murry must have resented the invidious comparison between Lawrence's marriage and his own (a comparison which Lawrence was very fond of making) as well as the attempt to direct his life, and he rejected Lawrence's argument as graciously as possible. Though Lawrence could rarely refrain from giving good, if tactless, advice, he understood Murry's feelings, was grateful for his forbearance, and wrote rather apologetically in April 1914: "I thought that you and Katherine held me an interfering Sunday-school superintendent sort of person who went too far in his superintending and became impossible: stepped just too far, which is the crime of crimes. And I felt guilty. And I suppose I am guilty. But thanks be to God, one is often guilty without being damned." Lawrence's "impossible" interference in their lives frequently went too far and was a major cause of their most bitter quarrels.

Katherine and Murry (who could not marry until 1918) were witnesses at the Lawrences' wedding in July 1914, when Frieda impulsively gave her friend her old wedding ring, which was buried with Katherine in 1923. In October 1914, when the couple lived an hour's walk from each other in Buckinghamshire, Lawrence introduced Katherine to the Russian law clerk and translator, Koteliansky (who became one of her closest friends) and began to expound his plans for the island community of Rananim, named after one of Kot's Hebrew psalms. Unlike the passive and dependent Murry, Katherine was too sceptical and individualistic to become a disciple of Lawrence, and she proceeded to deflate his idealistic dreams. Catherine Carswell reports that "when Katherine, not without realistic mischief, went and obtained a mass of detailed, difficult information about suitable islands, Lawrence fell sadly silent. . . . Hiding her fun behind a solemn face, [Katherine] proved by time-tables and guide-books that *Rananim* was impossible." Murry remarks that Katherine "had moreover, a lightly mocking but ruthless way of summing up various people over whom [Lawrence] was temporarily enthusiastic, which made him smile rather crookedly. At such a moment he was a little afraid of her."

Katherine's *Journal* entries for January 1915 suggest the difficulties of living in close proximity with the exciting yet exasperating Lawrences, and the extreme variations of her attitude toward them:

> In the evening Lawrence and Koteliansky. They talked plans; but I felt *very* antagonistic to the whole affair. (January 9)

> In the morning, Frieda suddenly. She had had a row with Lawrence. She tired me to death. . . . [At night:] L. was very nice, sitting with a piece of string in his hand, on true sex. (January 10)

> In the evening we went to the Lawrences'. Frieda was rather nice. (January 15)

> Walked to the Lawrences'! They were horrible and witless and dull. (January 16)

> Lawrence arrived cross, but gradually worked around to me. (January 19)

After a quarrel with Lawrence about her children, Frieda sent Katherine to tell her husband that she would not come back. "'Damn the woman,' shouted Lawrence in a fury, 'tell her I never want to see her again.'"

Katherine was also unhappy in love and having personal problems with Murry during that month. The handsome and dynamic painter, Mark Gertler, found Gilbert Cannan's party "most extraordinarily exciting," and told his sometime mistress, Dora Carrington, that "Katherine and myself—both very drunk—made passionate love to each other in front of everybody!" Lawrence's sense of propriety was outraged by Murry's shameless indifference to this performance, and he angrily asked his friend: "Are you blind! If not, how dare you expose yourself?"

In February 1915, Katherine left Murry for her lover Francis Carco, who resembled Lawrence in his ardent self-confidence and warm, high-spirited life, and was then in the French army near Besançon. The abandoned Murry came to see Lawrence, who had moved to Sussex, and during the long walk from the station his cold turned to influenza. Lawrence devoted himself to nursing Murry and enjoyed the opportunity to give strength and comfort to his ailing friend, for he and Katherine were tubercular, and this moment afforded Lawrence a gratifying reversal of his weaker and dependent role with Frieda. The episode inspired the passage in *Aaron's Rod* when Lilly nurses the sickly Aaron back to health. Lawrence's new bond of intimacy with Murry alienated him from Katherine, who spent most of that spring in France, disillusioned and bitterly hurt by the selfishness of Carco and the indifference of Murry. In May, Lawrence wrote to Kot: "Does Katherine depress you. Her letters are as jarring as the sound of a saw."

In September Lawrence and the Murrys started a new magazine, *Signature,* which published Lawrence's "The Crown" and Katherine's "The Wind Blows"; and by December he had revived his plans for Rananim and wrote about his hopes for a harmonious and purposeful life: "My dear Katherine, you know that in this we are sincere friends, and what we want is to create a new, good, common life, the germ of a new social life together." Katherine and Lawrence were drawn closer together that month during a tragic period of her life.

Her younger brother, Leslie, had come to England for training in 1915 en route from New Zealand to the battlefields of France, and they had spent some happy days together recollecting and idealizing their childhood. In October, a week after Leslie reached the front, he was blown up while giving a hand grenade demonstration. "Do not be sad," Lawrence wrote with an optimistic compassion that anticipates his poem, "The Ship of Death":

> It is one life which is passing away from us, one "I" is dying; but there is another coming into being, which is the happy, creative you. I knew you would have to die with your brother; you also, go down into death and be extinguished. But for us there is a rising from the grave, there is a resurrection, and a clean life to begin from the start, new and happy. Don't be afraid, don't doubt it, it is so. . . .
> Get better soon and come back, and let us all try to be happy *together,* in unanimity, not in hostility, creating, not destroying.

In an attempt to bring Katherine out of her misery, Lawrence offered his friendship and understanding, and the opportunity to join him in an idealistic and creative community. By contrast, Murry (to whom Katherine had returned after her brief affair with Carco) was reduced to insignificance by Katherine's morbid love for her dead brother and felt more cut off from her than ever.

In February 1916, Lawrence, who was then living in Cornwall, intensified the campaign, begun in Lerici, to get the Murrys to live with him; and he wrote to them in the guise of a courting lover: "I've waited for you for two years now, and am far more constant to you than ever you are to me—or ever will be." And in March he pleaded: "Really, you must have the other place. I keep looking at it. I call it already Katherine's house, Katherine's tower. There is something *very* attractive about it. It is very old, native to the earth." Though Katherine was strongly opposed to Cornwall and distrusted the very idea of a community, the Murrys allowed themselves to be persuaded by Lawrence's desperate pleas:

"No good trying to run away from the fact that we are fond of each other. We count on you two as our only two *tried* friends, real and permanent and truly blood kin."

The Murrys reluctantly left Bandol, where they had spent their happiest months together; and the Lawrences were overjoyed at their arrival in April. "I see Katherine Mansfield and Murry arriving sitting on a cart," Frieda later remembered, "high up on all the goods and chattels, coming down the lane to Tregerthen." And Lawrence, who loved to do manual work, wrote enthusiastically to Ottoline Morrell: "The Murrys have come and we are very busy getting their cottage ready: colouring the walls and painting and working furiously. I like it, and we all enjoy ourselves. The Murrys are happy with each other now. But they neither of them seem very well in health." Though the couples were irresistibly drawn to each other, they could not live together; and their second communal experience, like the first, ended in failure.

Lawrence was highly critical of the Murrys' relationship and prescribed a radically new foundation for their friendship. As Murry writes in his autobiography, *Between Two Worlds* (1935):

> Lawrence believed, or tried to believe, that the relation between Katherine and me was false and deadly; and that the relation between Frieda and himself was real and life-giving; but that his relation with Frieda needed to be completed by a new relation between himself and me, which I evaded.... By virtue of this "mystical" relation with Lawrence, I participate in this pre-mental reality, the "dark sources" of my being come alive. From this changed personality, I, in turn, enter a new relation with Katherine.

Their friendship inevitably degenerated as Katherine reacted against Lawrence's powerful influence on Murry. She quite naturally resented Lawrence's assaults on her liaison, and his attempt to revitalize it though a passionate attachment to Murry. If Murry turned toward Lawrence, Katherine's unhappy feeling of belonging to no one engulfed her completely. "I am very much alone here," she wrote Kot in May 1916, after a few gloomy weeks in Cornwall. "It is not a really nice place. It is so full of huge stones.... I don't belong to anybody here. In fact, I have no being, but I am making preparations for changing everything."

Lawrence's violent fights with Frieda and his humiliating dependence on her revolted the rather reserved Katherine far more than the bleak and rocky landscape, and soon drove her away. In a letter to Beatrice Campbell in May, Katherine gave a precise and vivid description of Lawrence's rages, which embroiled her emotions, exhausted her and made it impossible to concentrate and to work:

> Once you start talking, I cannot describe the frenzy that comes over him. He simply *raves*, roars, beats the table, abuses everybody. But that's not such great matter. What makes these attacks insupportable is the feeling one has at the back of one's mind that he is completely out

of control, swallowed up in an acute, *insane* irritation. After one of these attacks he's ill with fever, haggard and broken. It is impossible to be anything to him but a kind of playful acquaintance.

Katherine was frightened by the insane quality of Lawrence's outbursts, and felt that she had to humor him if she wanted to avoid the rages that had such a disastrous effect on his health. Though these eruptions were embarrassing and unpleasant, Katherine was most disturbed by the fact that they closely resembled the kind of behavior she hated and feared in *herself:*

> My fits of temper are really terrifying. I had one this . . . morning and tore up a page of the book I was reading—and absolutely lost my head. Very significant. When it was over J[ack] came in and stared. "What is the matter? What have you done?" "Why?" "You look *all dark.*" He drew back the curtains and called it an effect of light, but when I came into my studio to dress I saw it was not that. I was a deep earthy colour, *with pinched eyes.* I was *green.* Strangely enough these fits are Lawrence and Frieda all over again. I am more like L. than anybody. We are *unthinkably* alike, in fact.

After Lawrence's violent behavior with Frieda, attempt to possess Murry and mad ravings when he screamed at his friend: "I hate your love, *I hate it.* You're an obscene bug, sucking my life away," the break between the couples was inevitable. When the Murrys left, with suitable excuses, at the end of May, Lawrence wrote defensively to Ottoline Morrell and ironically suggested the proper setting for their unrealistic child-love: "Unfortunately the Murrys do not like the country—it is too rocky and bleak for them. They should have a soft valley, with leaves and the ring-dove cooing." And in July he sent Kot his usual depressing diagnosis: "I think—well, she and Jack are not very happy—they make some sort of contract whereby each of them is free. . . . Really, I think she and Jack have worn out anything that was between them. I like her better than him. He was rather horrid when he was here." In his autobiography, Murry responds to Lawrence's criticism and quite reasonably states that "he appeared to think that we, simply because we had nothing to correspond with his intense and agonizing sexual experiences, were flippant about sex. . . . It struck us as quite exorbitant that Katherine should be regarded as a butterfly and I as a child, merely because our sex-relation was exempt from agony."

Lawrence's friendship and affection for Katherine were justified by a famous incident that took place in the Café Royal in September 1916. Katherine was sitting with Kot and Gertler when she heard the novelist Michael Arlen and the Indian Suhrawardy, both of whom had been friendly with Lawrence, maliciously reading his new volume of poems, *Amores,* and publicly ridiculing them. Though Katherine was still feeling hostile toward Lawrence, she was nevertheless loyal to his work and outraged that it should be mocked by the *canaille.* So she snatched the volume from their hands, bore it triumphantly out of the café and symbolically rescued her friend from their scorn—exactly as Gudrun does in "Gudrun at the Pompadour," a chapter that was added to *Women in Love* just before Lawrence completed it in November 1916. Katherine also used this incident in her story "Marriage à la Mode." When William, the husband whose wife has abandoned him for a corrupt set of "bohemian" admirers, returns to the city, he sends his wife a love letter to set things right. But Isabel reads it aloud to her friends who mock the letter and become hysterical with laughter.

Katherine's gallant gesture did not prevent relations with Lawrence from deteriorating for the third time—perhaps because Lawrence had found out more about their reasons for leaving Cornwall—and in November he wrote angrily to Kot: "I have done with the Murrys, for ever—so help me God." In February 1917 Lawrence voiced his first direct, if ambiguous criticism of Katherine and told Kot, who was her staunchest friend and must have resented Lawrence's attack: "Only for poor Katherine and her lies I feel rather sorry. They are such self-responsible lies." And he repeated this charge, but much more violently, in a letter to Mary Cannan in February 1921: "The *Nation* said K's book [*Bliss*] was the best short story book that could be or had been written. Spit on her for me when you see her, she's a liar out and out. . . . Vermin, the pair of 'em. And beware." Katherine had published only six stories between 1916 and 1920; and *Bliss* was her first book in nine years and her first important collection. Lawrence's *Rainbow* had been suppressed in 1915 and *Women in Love* (though completed in 1916) was not published until 1920. He thought Katherine had only a minor talent, and must have been angry to see his own novels attacked and delayed while her stories received rave reviews in the leading weeklies.

Catherine Carswell's account of Lawrence's criticism of Katherine's work in 1918 gives some indication of what he meant by her lies: "It was his opinion that the author of *Prelude* would come in time to find a certain falseness so closely entwined with the charm in her literary fabric that she would herself condemn even the charm and write nothing further until she had disentangled herself from the falseness." In *Women in Love* Lawrence also condemns Gudrun's criticism of Birkin as a lie: "Gudrun would draw two lines under him and cross him out like an account that is settled. There he was, summed up, paid for, settled, done with. And it was such a lie. This finality of Gudrun's, this dispatching of people and things in a sentence, it was all such a lie." Lawrence seems to be suggesting that the "self-responsible" lies in Katherine's personal life—her "ruthless mockery," subtle malevolence, cynicism and negativism—were related to the falseness in her art, and that she would have to be more seriously self-critical of her character if she hoped to improve her work.

Katherine agreed with the truth of Lawrence's criticism, for (unbeknownst to him) she had recognized the element of falsity in her art and analyzed her faults in a surprisingly similar way. She was aware, for example, of her tendency toward detachment from life and escapism, and wanted to "learn to live . . . a far more truthful existence" and to establish a deeper contact with people. In December 1919 she compared her own lack of enthusiastic response to experience with Lawrence's vital engagement in life: "Lawrence wrote from Florence. He said Florence was lovely and full of 'extremely nice people.' He is able to bear people so easily. Often I long to be more *in life*—to know people—even now the desire comes. But immediately the opportunity comes I think of nothing but how to escape." Katherine also felt, at the end of her life, that she had to undergo a personal purification and "cure her soul" before she could clarify and perfect her artistic vision. Though she wrote "At the Bay," "The Voyage," "The Garden Party," and "The Doll's House" in a feverish burst of creativity between July and December 1921, a fundamental self-distrust made her lose faith in her work, abandon writing in July 1922 and turn toward the mysticism of Gurdjieff—her own version of Rananim.

Despite Lawrence's criticism in February 1917, he was certainly not done with Katherine "for ever," for he still believed in her fundamental integrity. Their friendship revived once again in August 1917, when Katherine told Murry: "I have read a long letter from Lawrence—He has begun to write to me again and in quite the old way. . . . I am so fond of him for many things. I cannot shut my heart against him and I never shall." In the autumn of 1918, when Lawrence came to London from the Midlands and saw Katherine for the last time, they forgot their quarrels and remembered their love for each other:

> For me, at least, the dove brooded over him, too. I loved him. He was just his old, merry, rich self, laughing, describing things, giving you pictures, full of enthusiasm and joy in a future where we become all "vagabonds"—we simply did not talk about people. We kept to things like nuts and cowslips and fires in woods and his black self *was* not. Oh, there is something so lovable about him and his eagerness, his passionate eagerness for life—that is what one loves so.

Katherine appropriately refers to Lawrence in spiritual terms, expresses her old admiration for him and praises his ardent response to life.

The following month, Lawrence sent Katherine a book by Jung and analyzed their marriages in terms of its mother-incest idea:

> At certain periods a man has a desire and tendency to return into the woman, make her his goal and end, find his justification in her. In this way he casts himself as it were into her womb, and she, the Magna Mater, receives him with gratification. This is a kind of incest. It seems to me it is what Jack does to you, and what repels and fascinates you. I have done it, and now struggle all my might to get out.

Lawrence recognized that Katherine was both repelled and fascinated by Murry's passive dependence and sentimental idealization of her because he himself had Murry's tendencies. But he could not resist the temptation to exalt his own marriage at Murry's expense.

A few months later, writing to Katherine from Derbyshire in March 1919, Lawrence returned to the marriage theme, realized that he had often offended her, reaffirmed his belief that some day they would all be harmoniously united, stated that the stormy months in Cornwall had brought him *closer* to her and illustrated this by means of a dream-parable:

> Frieda said you were cross with me, that I *repulsed* you. I'm sure I didn't. The complication of getting Jack and you and F. and me into a square seems great—especially Jack. But you I am sure of—I was ever since Cornwall, save for Jack—and if you must go his way, and if he will *never* really come our way—well! But things will resolve themselves.
>
> I dreamed such a vivid little dream of you last night. I dreamed you came to Cromford, and stayed there. You were not coming on here because you weren't well enough. You were quite clear from the consumption—quite, you told me. But there was still something that made you that you couldn't come up the hill here.

Katherine, who had her first hemorrhage in February 1918, was warned in October that she would die in a few years if she did not submit to the discipline of a sanatorium. In Lawrence's dream she is cured of consumption, but is not well enough to come up the hill to him. They do meet, however, go outside together to look at the brilliant sky, and are momentarily "pierced" and "possessed" by a "star that blazed for a second on one's soul." The blazing star unifies their souls in a moment of epiphany that transcends the common battle of their bodies against consumption. Two weeks before Lawrence told Katherine his encouraging dream he wrote sympathetically to Kot: "Poor Katherine—I'm afraid she is only just on the verge of existence."

In December 1919 Katherine's life was seriously undermined by the gravest crisis of her marriage. Katherine, who was ill and living unhappily with Ida Baker in Ospedaletti, sent Murry a desperate plea for security and love. When he responded with selfish indifference, she sent him her most moving poem, in which she portrays herself as a helpless child abandoned by her husband and "rescued" by death. When Lawrence sent his cruel letter to Katherine in February 1920 she was still separated from Murry, living in a clinic in Menton, in extremely bad health, and emotionally dependent on letters from her husband and friends. On February 4 she recorded in her *Journal:* "Horrible day. I lay all day and *half* slept in this new way—hearing voices"; and the following day she noted: "Couldn't work: slept again. Dreadful pain in joints. Fearfully *noisy* house!" In February 1920, Lawrence was living in Capri near Compton Mackenzie and Norman Douglas, embroiled in the unsavory affairs of Maurice Magnus and very much the "black self" that Katherine so dreaded. On February 5 Lawrence wrote to Catherine Carswell: "I am very sick of Capri: it is a stewpot of semi-literary cats. . . . I can't stand this island. I shall have to risk expense and everything and clear out: to Sicily, I think." In early February, then, Katherine was extremely vulnerable and Lawrence extremely angry.

On about February 7 Katherine, deeply wounded and embittered about the betrayal of their friendship, complained to Murry: "Lawrence sent me a letter today. He spat in my face and threw filth at me and said: 'I loathe you. You revolt me stewing in your consumption. . . . The Italians were quite right to have nothing to do with you' and a great deal more." According to Murry, Lawrence also said: "You are a loathesome reptile—I hope you will die." On February 10 Katherine told Murry: "I wrote to Lawrence: 'I detest you for having dragged this disgusting reptile across all that has been.' When I got his letter I *saw* a reptile, *felt* a reptile—and the desire to hit him was so dreadful that I knew if I ever met him I must go away *at once*. I could not be in the same room or house, he is somehow filthy. I never had such a feeling about a human being." Though Murry wrote to Lawrence that "he had committed the unforgivable crime," Katherine doubted Murry's adamancy and asked him at the end of March: "Will you one day forget and forgive Lawrence—smile—give him your hand?"

E. M. Forster, who speaks with the authority of a victim, asserts: "There is a vein of cruelty" in Lawrence. But F. R. Leavis, who is blind to Lawrence's faults (if to no one else's) attempts to justify and excuse Lawrence's violent letter to Katherine and states that it "was no more to be called 'cruel' than medicine would be. Lawrence's genius manifested itself in *sympathetic* insight and an accompanying diagnostic intelligence, and cruelty was not in him." But it is far more useful to explain than to excuse the motives behind Lawrence's terrible letter, which are intimately connected with the fact that he refused to recognize his own disease and saw Katherine, as his dream suggests, "clear from the consumption." Lawrence wrote to her in January 1916, for example: "I am always seedy nowadays—my old winter sickness and inflammation—very weary I get of it—sometimes contemplate my latter end."

Lawrence admitted that he was seedy, sick, inflamed; had colds, coughs and bronchials; and defensively joked about his death. But he would never admit that he had tuberculosis—even after his near fatal hemorrhage in Mexico in 1925—and would never allow himself to be treated for the disease until the very end of his life in Vence. Though he warned their mutual friend, Mark Gertler, of Ottoline's weekend parties: "I should beware of Garsington. I believe there is something exhaustive in the air there, not so very restful," he restlessly drove himself about the world. And though he wrote to Murry in 1925: "I hear poor Gertler is in a sanatorium," Lawrence—like Katherine—would never enter a soul-destroying clinic. In 1920 Lawrence was not, like Katherine, in the terminal phase of tuberculosis, and he never really believed in her illness any more than he did in his own. He preferred to ignore the disease and pretend it would go away, and his amazing vitality allowed him to do so for many years. But by 1920 Katherine had admitted her tuberculosis and feared she might die: "I cough and cough, and at each breath a dragging, boiling, bubbling sound is heard. . . . Life is—getting a new breath. Nothing else counts." Lawrence felt threatened by Katherine's admission and terrified that the same thing would happen to him (just as Katherine had been terrified by Lawrence's "black rages"), and he irrationally lashed out at what he considered to be Katherine's weakness.

In March 1921, a year after this letter, Lawrence again refused to face the reality of Katherine's disease, characterized her as a hypocritical Camille and told Kot: "I hear [Murry] is—or was—on the Riviera with K.—who is doing the last-gasp touch, in order to impose on people—on Mary Cannan, that is." And in November he wrote, "I see Murry and the long-dying blossom Katherine have put forth new literary buds. Let 'em." It is ironic that at the end of her life, after many unsuccessful medical treatments, Katherine (like Lawrence) turned away from the reality of her grave disease and assumed it was nonexistent. Neither Lawrence nor Katherine could give up freedom and endure (as she wrote) "being alone, cut off, ill with the other ill." This tragic refusal to submit to the regime of a sanatorium obviously hastened their deaths.

Though Katherine and Lawrence did not meet again after the autumn of 1918, his novels continued to evoke a powerful response in her. Katherine intended to review *The Lost Girl* for Murry's *Athenaeum* in December 1920, and when she became too ill to do so she sent Murry her notes on the novel:

> Lawrence denies his humanity. He denies the powers of the Imagination. He denies Life—I mean *human* life. His hero and heroine are non-human. They are animals on the prowl. . . . They submit to the physical response and for the rest go veiled—blind—*faceless—mindless*. This is the doctrine of mindlessness. . . .
>
> Take the rotten rubbishy scene of the woman in labour asking the Italian into her bedroom. All false. All a pack of lies! . . .
>
> Don't forget where Alvina feels *"a trill in her bowels"* and discovers herself with child. A TRILL—What does that mean? And why is it so peculiarly offensive from a man? Because it is *not on this plane* that the emotions of others are conveyed to our imagination. It's a kind of sinning against art.

Though Katherine had formerly praised Lawrence's vital response to life, she now felt he denied life and had descended into mindless animalism. Katherine, who had portrayed the gruesome details of childbirth in her *German Pension* stories, had been through a miscarriage and an abortion that prevented her from having the children she so desperately wanted. She therefore had little tolerance for Lawrence's male ignorance, and condemned as false the description of Mrs. Tuke in labor and of Alvina's discovery that she is pregnant.

Katherine also criticizes Lawrence's concept of love in a letter to Dorothy

Brett in August 1921: "What makes Lawrence a *real* writer is his passion. Without passion one writes in the air or on the sand of the seashore. But L. has got it all wrong, I believe.... It's my belief that nothing will save the world but love. But his tortured, satanic demon love I think is all wrong." Katherine praises Lawrence's vital passion through an allusion to Keats' ironic epigraph—"Here lies one whose name was writ in water"—for this quality makes him a genuine writer. But Katherine—who had not slept with Murry since her hemorrhage in February 1918—feels that Lawrence's demon love, with its extreme emphasis on the physical, is not the kind of love that will save the world. Her final judgment of Lawrence, however, is extremely positive. "He is the only living writer whom I really profoundly care for," she wrote to Kot in July 1922. "It seems to me whatever he writes, no matter how much one may 'disagree,' is important. And after all even what one objects to is a *sign of life* in him. He is a living man."

Two weeks later, after Katherine had read *Aaron's Rod* and found it vital and convincing, she emphasized their essential intuitive understanding, despite some differences in their ideas: "I do not go all the way with Lawrence. His ideas of sex mean nothing to me. But I feel nearer L. than anyone else. All these last months I have thought as he does about many things." The influence of his beliefs is apparent in Katherine's journal and letters of 1921–1922, where many of the entries sound more like Lawrence than Katherine; for Lawrence, with Murry, Orage and Gurdjieff, had the strongest contemporary influence on her ideas.

One passage from Katherine's journal of August 1921 reflects Lawrence's belief that the complementary union of masculine and feminine elements represents a return to an original wholeness that unifies man and woman in marriage: "We are neither male nor female. We are a compound of both. I choose the male who will develop and expand the male in me; he chooses me to expand the female in him. Being made 'whole.'" A second passage, from Katherine's letter to Murry in January 1922, quotes Lawrence's concept of friendship, which he felt was as solemn as marriage. Though Katherine found this idea fanatical when Lawrence expounded it, first in Cornwall and then in a letter of November 1918, she now recognized the importance of Lawrence's belief and found it much more convincing:

> I remember once talking it over with Lawrence and he said "We must swear a solemn pact of friendship. Friendship is as binding, as solemn as marriage. We take each other for life, through everything—for ever. But it's not enough to say we will do it. We must *swear*." At the time I was impatient with him. I thought it extravagant—fanatic. But when one considers what this world is like I understand perfectly why L. (especially being L.) made such claims.

And in a third passage in December 1922, written a month before her death in the Gurdjieff Institute at Fontainebleau, Katherine explains her mystical reaction against intellectual life in purely Laurentian terms: "I can see no hope of escape except by learning to live in our emotional and instinctual being as well, and to balance all there."

The final phase of Lawrence and Katherine's friendship took place in the spring and summer of 1922 when he travelled to Australia and New Zealand, and in May told Kot: "If you were here you would understand Katherine so much better. She is *very* Australian! or New Zealand. Wonder how she is." Katherine realized that Lawrence's rather frenetic travels were very like her own and closely related to his disease. As she told the stable Kot, who rarely left London, in August: "It is a pity that Lawrence is driven so far. I am sure that Western Australia will not help. The desire to travel is a great, real temptation. But does it do any good? It seems to me to correspond to the feelings of a sick man who thinks always 'if only I can get away from here I shall be better.'" That same month Katherine left Lawrence a book in her will, as a token of remembrance, forgiveness and love; and Lawrence, who had not communicated with her since the cruel letter of February 1920, pleased her very much by sending a postcard from her birthplace, Wellington, with just one word: "Ricordi." "Yes, I care for Lawrence," Katherine told Murry in October. "I have thought of writing to him and trying to arrange a meeting after I leave Paris—suggesting that I join them until the spring." And the following month, when the Lawrences had settled in New Mexico, she asked Murry: "Do you ever feel inclined to get in touch with Lawrence again, I wonder? I should very much like to know what he intends to do—how he intends to live now his *Wanderjahre* are over."

But Katherine's desperate wanderings ended seven years before Lawrence's. When in February 1923, he heard of her death, he wrote Murry one of his most moving letters, which recalls the letter to Katherine on the death of her brother, expresses his fear that her death foreshadows his own and confirms the profound importance of their friendship:

> Yes it is something gone out of our lives. We thought of her, I can tell you, at Wellington. Did Ottoline ever send on the card to Katherine posted from there for her? Yes, I always knew a bond in my heart. Feel a fear where the bond is broken now. Feel as if the old moorings were breaking all. . . . I asked Seltzer [his publisher] to send you *Fantasia of the Unconscious*. I wanted Katherine to read it. She'll know, though. The dead don't die. They look on and help.

In March 1929 chance brought the gravely ill Lawrence to the Hôtel Beau Rivage in Bandol, where Katherine had had her first hemorrhage in 1918. ("How I *loathe* hotels," she once wrote. "I know I shall die in one.") As usual, Lawrence kept up a brave front, tried to disguise the gravity of his illness and felt a certain morbid comfort from the association with Katherine. As he told Murry: "I'm pretty well, but a scratchy chest and cough as ever—sickening—but pretty well in spite of it all. I believe Katherine once stayed here, so perhaps you know the place." A year later, in March 1930, Lawrence finally succumbed to the same disease that had killed Katherine.

In *Between Two Worlds* Murry states that in 1921, when he read and reviewed *Women in Love* (which Lawrence was writing when he lived with the Murrys in Cornwall in 1916), he did not see any biographical similarities and "was really astonished when, one day, Frieda told me that I was Gerald Crich." And in his *Reminiscences of D. H. Lawrence* Murry writes that his friend had an imaginary rather than a realistic understanding of Katherine, which partially explains the difference between the fictional and actual character:

> I have been told, by one who should know [Frieda], that the character of Gudrun in *Women in Love* was intended for a portrait of Katherine. If this is true, it confirms me in my belief that Lawrence had curiously little understanding of her. She was to him—or so it always seemed to me—a bird of strange plumage, out of his ken. When he talked about her to me, as he sometimes did when she was away, he seemed to be talking about someone whom I had never known—an imaginary figure. Since he talked earnestly, even vehemently, about her, the figure was evidently very real to him; but it was utterly unlike Katherine Mansfield. And yet he was very fond of her, as she was of him. But she knew him far better than he knew her.

A number of other critics, including Richard Aldington, George Ford and Emile Delavenay, repeat Frieda's statement that Gerald and Gudrun are based on Murry and Katherine, but very few of them discuss this complex relationship.

Since Murry had a rather superficial and commonplace conception of character, his failure to recognize himself and Katherine is hardly surprising. For in the novel Gerald is a man of action: a soldier, explorer of the Amazon, engineer and Napoleon of industry who rules over the coal mines; while the weak-willed, abstract and sentimental Murry, who Katherine said "couldn't fry a sausage without thinking about God," was a pacifist and bookworm. Gerald is blond, aristocratic, aggressive, domineering, successful and wealthy; while Murry was dark, bourgeois, passive, timid, unsuccessful and poor. Gerald is not realistically based on the diametrically opposed character of Murry, but on Lawrence's highly subjective concept of his relationship with Murry. Like Murry, and despite his external triumphs, Gerald is an inherently weak character who "must go his way, and will *never* really come our way," refuses Birkin's offer of male friendship and chooses marriage with Gudrun, who is distinctly superior to him.

Katherine and Murry, like Gudrun and Gerald, "make some sort of contract whereby each of them is free." Katherine's flirtation with Gertler, which outraged Lawrence, and her brief and unhappy love affair with the egoistic artist

Carco, may have suggested Gudrun's attraction to Loerke and her rejection of Gerald. Gudrun and Gerald's intense struggle of wills reflects the extreme violence of Lawrence's own marriage, and represents his very subjective conception of Katherine's mistress-lover relationship with Murry: the violent, destructive and disintegrating "union of ecstasy and death" which provides a powerful contrast to the healthy and vital marriage of Ursula and Birkin.

Lawrence's rather dogmatic contrast of the two couples suggests a significant weakness in the novel. For the conflict between Lawrence's aesthetic desire to create a convincing character, and his personal urge to express his resentment about the failure of the friendship in Buckinghamshire and in Cornwall, results in a portrait of Gudrun that is too negative for his purely novelistic purpose. The contrast and imbalance between the fictional couples is too biased and extreme, for Lawrence allows no other mode of marriage than his own, and harshly condemns Gudrun and Gerald as he had Katherine and Murry. Lawrence used Katherine as an inspiration rather than as a precise model, and triumphs over the Murrys in *Women in Love* in a way that he never did in actual life.

Unlike Birkin, Ursula, Hermione Roddice and Sir Joshua Mattheson, who are clearly modelled on Lawrence, Frieda, Ottoline Morrell and Bertrand Russell, Gudrun is not clearly based on an identifiable person. Mary Thriplow in Huxley's *Those Barren Leaves* (1925) resembles Katherine in appearance, character and behavior, but Gudrun has almost no connection (apart from the Café Royal incident) with Katherine's life and looks. Gudrun really represents Lawrence's gross exaggeration of the negative aspects of Katherine's character: her self-destructive quest for experience and the bitterness of her *early* work, for she had published only the satiric *In a German Pension* before Lawrence completed his novel in 1916.

The earthy and passionate Frieda considered the more sensitive and ethereal Katherine as a younger sister; and Lawrence subtly differentiates the sisters in the novel by a gradual manifestation of Gudrun's destructive qualities as she becomes more deeply involved with Gerald. Though Katherine, like Gudrun, was an artist in miniature, was reserved, childlike, clinging, detached from life, restless, cynical and satiric; she was not, as Gudrun is in the novel, arrogant, insolent, outcast, sinister, corrosive, destructive and incapable of love.

Lawrence transformed Katherine into Gudrun in the same way that he changed Gertler into Loerke. Just as Loerke is not based on Gertler as he really was, but on Lawrence's theoretical conception of him as a Jewish artist, so his creation of Gudrun deliberately emphasized the negative aspects of Katherine's character. Gudrun bears a perverse relationship to her model, and Gudrun's deterioration reflects some of Lawrence's bitterness about his health, his poverty, his persecution by the military and legal authorities as well as his morbid despair about the war, the fate of Europe and the future of civilization. In *Women in Love* Lawrence transforms Katherine's delicate art into attenuated preciosity; her satire into corrosion; her reserve into negation; her detached and determined resistance to his demands into arrogance and insolence; her insecurity and loneliness into infantile dependence; her quest for love into destructive sterility; her restless search for health into a rootless outcast life; her illness into evil.

Lawrence was fascinated by Katherine, who was at once a contrast and mirror image of himself; and though he exaggerated her worst qualities in Gudrun, he made her evil attractive to Gerald. His portrait of Katherine is as extreme as his cruel letter, and he distorts her character not (as Murry claims) because he did not understand her, but because he deliberately portrayed her according to his imaginative conception. Lawrence was referring to his idiosyncratic way of creating character when he explained his fictional technique to Edward Garnett, in the famous letter of June 1914, and said, "You mustn't look in my novel for the old stable *ego* of the character."

> That which is psychic—non-human, in humanity, is more interesting to me than the old-fashioned human element—which causes one to conceive a character in a certain moral scheme and make him consistent. . . . I don't so much care about what a woman *feels*—in the ordinary usage of the word. That presumes an *ego* to feel with. I only care about what the woman *is*—what she IS . . . as a phenomenon (or as representing some greater, inhuman will), instead of what she feels according to the human conception.

In *Women in Love* Lawrence rejected as false and uninteresting the conventional and consistent conception of character (exemplified by Murry's statement that Gudrun "was utterly unlike Katherine"), and tried to discover and portray the more profound psychic essence, what he called the "single radically unchanged element." Though Frieda could truthfully say that Lawrence began with the reality of Murry and Katherine, his visionary interpretation of character transforms and transcends the actuality of the original models.

8

Murry's Cult of Mansfield

Middleton Murry's creation of the cult of Katherine Mansfield is unique in modern literature. In a repetitive torrent of forty books, articles, introductions, poems and letters to the press, published between 1923 and 1959, Murry expressed his anguished self-consciousness, deliberately constructed his myth of Katherine and established a posthumous reputation far greater than she had enjoyed in her lifetime. The motives for Murry's literary crusade were closely connected to his own character and his relationship to Katherine, and were determined more by emotional and financial needs than by intellectual convictions.[1]

I

Murry was excluded from Katherine's room during the fatal hemorrhage in January 1923, but took possession of her after death and transformed her into the docile woman he had always wanted. Her gravestone at Fontainebleau reads,

<blockquote align="center">
Katherine Mansfield
wife of
John Middleton Murry
</blockquote>

as if that were her great claim to fame. It also bears the singularly inappropriate epitaph from *I Henry IV* (II.iii), "But I tell you, my lord fool, out of this nettle, danger, we pluck this flower, safety," for Katherine's story, "This Flower" (1924), portrays a heroine who recognizes that she will never pass through the danger of disease to "safety" and hides this fact from her rather foolish husband.

In his own book on Keats, Murry writes with appalling egoism that: "Nothing more powerfully prepares a man's instinctive and unconscious nature for passionate love than prolonged contact with hopeless illness in a loved one."[2] A year after Katherine's death Murry married his second wife, Violet LeMaistre, who was born in 1901, looked astonishingly like Katherine, and self-consciously imitated her dress, hair style, handwriting and mannerisms in order to win Murry's love. Murry was still in love with the *idea* of Katherine, and since Violet wanted nothing more than to replace Katherine, they seemed well suited to each other. Murry, with his incredible obtuseness, took three years to discover that Violet was not Katherine, and admitted, "It never struck me for a moment that there was a great difference between Katherine when I first met her, and Violet now."[3]

Murry encouraged Violet's pathological attachment to his dead wife, and the spirit of Katherine hovered over their marriage. Murry, who was certainly not generous when Katherine was alive, gave Violet Katherine's engagement ring, bought their house with the thousand pounds in royalties from Katherine's books, lived on the five hundred pounds a year that Katherine's posthumously published works brought in, named their daughter Katherine, and published Violet's stories, as well as Katherine's, in his magazine, the *Adelphi*. When Violet contracted tuberculosis, she exclaimed, "O I'm so glad. I wanted this to happen.... I wanted you to love me as much as you loved Katherine—and how could you, without this?"[4] Just as Katherine had turned away from Murry to the Caucasian mystic, George Gurdjieff, at the end of her life, so Violet fell in love with his friend Max Plowman. After Violet died of tuberculosis in 1931, Murry pitifully asked, "Am I attracted only by two kinds of women—one that I kill, the other that kills me?"[5]

Murry's guilt about his selfish and irresponsible treatment of Katherine, which hastened her death, led directly to the egoistic enshrinement of his wife. As high priest of Katherine's cult, Murry wrote an *apologia pro sua vita;* glorified his own role, image and importance; exploited her tragic death at the age of thirty-four; created a sentimental and idealized portrait which obscured her literary qualities; and made a good deal of money by publishing her posthumous works. Only three of Katherine's books appeared during her lifetime; eleven others were edited by Murry after her death. When Constable sent Murry a royalty check for a thousand pounds for *The Dove's Nest* and *Poems* (both 1923), he recorded, "It was by far the biggest check I had ever received, and ten times as big as any Katherine had received for her own work."[6]

Though Murry's biographer F. A. Lea believes, "The greatest [of his virtues] and the least conventional, was his honesty,"[7] Katherine was far more perceptive when she wrote, "His very frankness is a falsity. In fact it seems falser than his insincerity,"[8] for she understood that his frankness was a *persona*, a pose from which to project a false image of himself. Aldous Huxley, who was Murry's editorial assistant on the *Athenaeum* in 1919, exaggerated this aspect of Murry, whom he characterized as Burlap in *Point Counter Point* (1928), but he is worth quoting for his wit as well as for the essence of truth in his satire:

> When Susan died Burlap exploited the grief he felt, or at any rate loudly said he felt, in a more than usually painful series of those always painfully personal articles which were the secret of his success as a journalist . . . pages of a rather hysterical lyricism about the dead child-woman. . . .
> At the end of some few days of incessant spiritual masturbation, he had been rewarded by a mystical realization of his own unique and incomparable piteousness. . . . Frail, squeamish, less than fully alive and therefore less than adult, permanently under-aged, [Susan] adored him as a superior and almost holy lover . . . [who would] roll at her feet in an ecstasy of incestuous adoration for the imaginary mother-baby of a wife with whom he had chosen to identify the corporeal Susan.[9]

Huxley quite accurately perceives not only the falseness of the cult and Murry's pitiful exploitation of his grief, but also the emotional immaturity and childish role-playing of both Katherine and Murry, and he describes the destructive aspect of Murry's mystical love in the metaphor of sexual perversion.

D. H. Lawrence's story, "Smile" (1926), is also based on Murry's response to Katherine's death, and portrays the selfish reaction of a man who sees his wife's body in a convent and feels an ambiguous mixture of guilt, self-pity, indifference and lust for a young nun: "He did not weep: he just gazed without meaning. Only, on his face deepened the look: I knew this martyrdom was in store for me! She was so pretty, so childlike, so clever, so obstinate, so worn—and so dead! He felt so blank about it all!"[10] Lawrence, who knew Murry well, emphasizes his passivity and confusion.

Murry's "In Memory of Katherine Mansfield," an atrociously sentimental poem in archaic diction and (like Shelley's "Adonais") in Spenserian stanza, published on the first anniversary of her death, is a fine example of the insincerity and idealization of Katherine portrayed by Huxley and Lawrence:

> For she was lonely; was she not a child
> By royalty and wisdom, captive made
> Among unlovely men, beating her wild
> Impetuous wings in anguish, and dismayed. . . .
> A child of other worlds, a perfect thing
> Vouchsafed to justify this world's imagining? . . .
> A princess manifest, a child withouten stain.[11]

Lea points out that these lines on Katherine's death "were eight-year-old verses, re-conditioned for the occasion."[12] The third and fourth lines idealize Katherine by alluding to Arnold's (inaccurate) description of Shelley as: "A beautiful and ineffectual angel, beating in the void his luminous wings in vain."[13] There are significant analogies between the legends of Shelley and Katherine, for as Richard Holmes writes, "where events reveal Shelley in an unpleasant light, the original texts and commentaries have attracted suppressions, distortions and questions of doubtful authenticity, originating from Victorian apologists."[14]

Though Murry knew about Katherine's bitter and destructive sexual experiences, her lesbianism, abortion and drug addiction—Virginia Woolf thought she "dressed like a tart and behaved like a bitch"[15]—he stressed her perfect purity and called her "a child withouten stain."

Murry had opposed Katherine's submission to the mystical rigors of Gurdjieff and insisted in 1951 that his "prejudice against occultism was great; and it is as deep-rooted now as it was then."[16] But he emphasized Katherine's "spiritual" qualities one month after her death when he described a mystical experience in that confessional mode which exasperated critics and embarrassed friends:

> Not many months ago I lost someone whom it was impossible for me to lose—the only person on this earth who understood me or whom I understood. . . . I became aware of myself as a little island against whose slender shores a cold, dark, boundless ocean lapped devouring. Somehow, in that moment, I knew I had reached a pinnacle of personal being. . . . The love I had lost was still mine, but now more durable, being knit into the very substance of the universe I had feared.[17]

This essay characteristically reveals far more about Murry than about his ostensible subject and provides a preview of the visitation which he later described in *God* (1929). Since Katherine had been dangerously ill ever since her first hemorrhage in February 1918, her death was probable rather than "impossible"; and in October 1922, three months before she died, Murry admitted his total ignorance of her thoughts and emotions: "I feel I don't *know* anything. You've passed clean out of my range and understanding: and so suddenly."[18] Murry's self-conscious response to this experience is aesthetic rather than personal, for he converts his experience into literary terms. His description of himself as a little island devoured by the ocean recalls Arnold's "To Marguerite," just as his feeling that Katherine is knit into the universe echoes Wordsworth's "A Slumber Did My Spirit Seal." But the typically egotistic point is that Katherine's death led *him* to a vague "pinnacle of personal being."

Only Murry could write a book called *God,* and only he could begin the book with a very long first chapter about himself. In this introductory chapter Murry, who claimed a deep-rooted prejudice against occultism, once again describes the "mystical" experience of February 1923:

> When I say that "the room was filled with a presence," the "presence" was definitely connected with the person of Katherine Mansfield. . . . The "presence" of Katherine Mansfield was of the same order as the "presence" which filled the room and me. In so far as the "presence" was connected with her it had a moral quality, or a moral effect: I was immediately and deeply convinced that "all was well with her."[19]

This awkward and meaningless passage merely proves that Murry could easily convince himself of anything he wanted to believe. But his conclusion that "All was well with her" echoes her *Journal* entry of October 10, 1922, which Murry used as the optimistic but misleading conclusion of that book: "With those words Katherine Mansfield's journal comes to a fitting close. Thenceforward the conviction that 'All was well' never left her."[20] Though Katherine's death only three months later suggests that all was *not* well, his "mystical" experience prompted him to reaffirm that statement against all contrary evidence.

Murry's final attempt to exorcise the guilt-ridden memory of Katherine occurred—rather oddly—in his Introduction to Ruth Mantz's bibliography of Katherine's works (1931), when he described his dream of her rising, like a Gothic heroine, from the flowers of her coffin: "As I watched, Katherine Mansfield raised herself wearily out of the shallow turfy grave. With her fingertips she took back the hair from her still-closed eyes. She opened them at last, and looked at the garden and the house, and smiled. Then, as though weary, she sank back to sleep again. It was peace; it was good; and what she had seen was also good."[21] Once again, after his *second* wife had died of tuberculosis, Murry has the dead Katherine absolve his guilt in the language of the God of Genesis, who divided the light from the darkness and "saw that it was good."

But Murry's virtuous and high-minded statements about Katherine were constantly undermined by his own selfish behavior and unscrupulous falsification of their relationship. In his book on Keats, which is also about Katherine, Murry praises Fanny Brawne, who "jealously cherishes, in a secrecy that is sacrilege to disturb, the memory of her love."[22] Yet when Murry lectured on Katherine at the University of Michigan in 1936, Professor Clarence Thorpe was amazed by his violation of their intimacy and wondered, "How could a literary man discuss his wife in such a way in a public lecture?"[23] Though Murry told Ottoline Morrell, "the only thing that matters to me is that [Katherine] should have her rightful place as the most wonderful writer and the most beautiful spirit of our time,"[24] he always confused the "writer" with the "spirit," emphasized her "purity" at the expense of her genuine qualities, bathed the reality of her life in pathos and pain, distorted her actual achievement and inflated her reputation.

All this quite naturally angered the friends who knew and admired the real Katherine Mansfield. S. S. Koteliansky, her closest male friend, maintained that when Murry published her letters and journals he "'left out all the jokes,' to make her an 'English Tchekov'";[25] and when Murry published the *Journal* in 1927, Kot wrote to Katherine's intimate friend, Ida Baker, to sympathize with her and to say that it marked the end of his relationship with Murry. In 1928 Lawrence wrote to Dorothy Brett, "I hear Katherine's letters sell largely, yet Murry whines about poverty and I hear he *inserts* the most poignant passages himself. Ottoline declares that in the letters to her, large pieces are inserted, most movingly."[26] Lawrence criticized Murry for assuming the role of acolyte chosen to bear the chalice of her fame, and warned that hyperbolic statements about Katherine would provoke a critical reaction against her: "You are wrong about Katherine. She was *not* a great genius. She had a charming gift, and a finely cultivated one. But *not more*. And to try, as you do, to make it more is to do her no true service."[27]

Murry, who was called "the best-hated man of letters in the country,"[28] misrepresented his relationship to Katherine. He claimed, "We fell in love and were married" in 1912, and Ruth Mantz repeated this statement in the biographical notes of her bibliography.[29] In fact, they lived together for six years and did not marry until 1918, when Katherine finally obtained a divorce from her first husband, George Bowden. But Murry, who felt that their liaison might sully the image of her "spiritual purity," obscured the truth to "protect" Katherine.

Murry also elevated the commonplace events of their life to the level of the mystical and the tragic. He writes of their unhappy stay in the cold, cramped and sordid Rose Tree cottage in Buckinghamshire in the fall of 1914, "[I] told her that I had a sense of an infinite beatitude descending upon me. So, she said, had she."[30] Their beatitude, however, was not quite infinite, for Katherine had an affair with Francis Carco in February 1915. And Murry writes of his departure from Katherine in Bandol in December 1915, "The anguish of separation had begun, the terrible feeling that our love was totally at the mercy of an alien world."[31] But Alpers says that in December Murry voluntarily "returned to London, jealous of [Katherine's] dead brother [who had been killed in the War] and consumed with shame for being so. Katherine wrote happy, vivid letters to him every day."[32]

Murry falsifies their attitude toward the War as well as the nature of his love for Katherine. In 1929 Murry emphasized their tragic involvement in the War and interpreted Katherine's disease in terms of his own feelings, "Katherine Mansfield's illness [was] as much a circumstance of the war as any death at the front; but it has become *for me* the personal symbol of that universal suffering";[33] but in 1951 he records their casual disregard of the slaughter, "It was not by any effort of the will that we ignored the war, which was then [April 1916] at one of its blackest periods—the carnage around Verdun. We did it spontaneously, and without a tremor of conscience."[34]

Murry exaggerated Katherine's attachment to him and categorically states, "The greatest obstacle she had to overcome in taking the plunge and making the final decision to enter the [Gurdjieff] Institute had been her fear of losing me.... By risking losing me, she had found her love for me: it was entire and perfect."[35] But on October 10, 1922, one week before she entered Gurdjieff's Institute for the Harmonious Development of Man, she analyzed their relationship and saw with a penetrating clarity the fundamental falsity of their marriage:

What have you of him now? What is your relationship? He talks to you—sometimes—and then goes off. He thinks of you tenderly. He dreams of a life with you *some day* when the miracle has happened. You are important to him as a dream. Not as a living reality. For you are not one. What do you share? Almost nothing. . . . Life together, with me ill, is simply torture with happy moments. But it's not life. [36]

Though Murry always glorified his "entire and perfect" love for Katherine, he asked Frieda Lawrence—with whom he had an affair after Katherine's death in 1923 and after Lawrence's in 1930—"Why, I ask myself, was it *you* who should have revealed to me the richness of physical love?";[37] and told Frieda, "I just didn't know what man-woman love could be until I met Mary," his fourth wife, in 1938.[38]

It is clear, then, that Murry used his very considerable authority as a critic as well as Katherine's husband, literary executor, editor, biographer and guardian of manuscripts to create a misleading picture of her character and their marriage. This, as we shall see, overshadowed and distorted her literary reputation and established the sentimental cult which still survives in France.[39] Murry is an indispensable but thoroughly unreliable guide to Katherine, for he could not disentangle himself from her legend, could not distinguish between the woman and the artist, and could never form an objective and consistent view of her work. The emotional confusion of his literary criticism also characterized his social, political and religious ideas, which he expounded at the same time.

Murry joined the Independent Labour Party in 1931 and resigned in 1934; wrote *The Necessity of Communism* in 1932 and advocated a defensive war against Russia after the war; joined the Peace Pledge Union in 1936, wrote *The Necessity of Pacifism* the following year and renounced pacifism in 1946; thought of taking Holy Orders in 1937 and abandoned the idea in 1938. He was always extraordinarily naive: in 1931 he expressed hope that Fenner Brockway, the Independent Labour Party leader, would become an "English Stalin," and in 1943, as George Orwell noted, he praised the Japanese invasion of China.[40] As he confessed to his son Colin, who quotes the remark in his autobiography, which condemns his father's weakness, selfishness and cowardice, "True, I have incessantly been mistaken."[41]

II

Murry's creation of the cult of Katherine can be traced through his evaluation of her work, posthumous publication of her stories, reprinting of *In a German Pension,* discussion of her relation to Chekhov, misrepresentation of her critical reception and literary career, and editing of her journals. Murry's seventeen-hundred-word essay on Katherine, published in the Literary Review of the *New York Evening Post* five weeks after her death, is a paradigm of all his repetitive criticism about her.[42] He laid the foundation of his thought in 1923 and rarely deviated from it during the next thirty-four years. Murry's essay, the first critical work on Katherine to appear in America, contains hyperbolic praise, unwarranted comparisons with far greater writers, factual errors and deliberate misinterpretations of her work; it exaggerates the fragile, exquisite, delicate, child-like, pure, and spiritual aspects of her life and art, and totally ignores the reckless and ruthless, the earthy and ribald, the witty and bitter side of her character. Lytton Strachey, who had known and liked Katherine at Garsington during the War, reacted violently to Murry's idealization and blamed Katherine for Murry's distortion of her character. When Murry published Katherine's *Journal* in 1927, Strachey exclaimed, "Why that foul-mouthed, virulent, brazen-faced broomstick of a creature should have got herself up as a pad of rose-scented cotton-wool is beyond me."[43]

Murry consistently uses emotionally-charged adjectives and speaks of Katherine's "sensitiveness and courage" and the "magical" quality of her "absolutely original" stories whose "brilliant clarity is almost intolerable" and "vivid beauty unique and incomparable." Though Katherine and Murry were contemporaries of Virginia Woolf, Joyce, Lawrence, Pound and Eliot, he calls her "the most perfect and accomplished literary artist of the generation to which I belong."[44] He asserts of the Hogarth Press edition of *Prelude,* "The day will come, I am persuaded, when it will be as precious as the blue-paper 'Adonais' of Pisa," and suggests that (like Keats in the *Quarterly Review* legend) she was wounded by the critics, kept silent for many years, and was a delicate flower too fragile to exist in the harsh world: "The killing of the fly [in the story of that name] was torture to her, unrelenting torture."

Murry stated that "the recognition of her literary power had been almost universal [and] penetrated quickly to Oxford" after the publication of her first book, *In a German Pension,* in 1911, and also the critics' unjust accusations of cruelty made her "shrink from open publication" for nine years until she was finally persuaded to publish *Bliss,* whose "recognition was immediate."[45] Finally, he claimed that "she had a truth in her keeping; she knew something about life which [her readers] did not know and desired to learn" and, at the same time, that Katherine felt "her truth was not wholly true and that her vision must be renewed."

Murry's posthumous publication of Katherine's minor stories in 1923 and 1924 was based on dubious principles and did not enhance her reputation, which rests on her mature stories, her journals and her letters. Though two-thirds of *The Dove's Nest,* which appeared only five months after her death, consisted of unfinished fragments, Murry made no distinction between these *Nachlassen* and the six stories published after *The Garden Party* in 1922 and 1923. "It seemed to me," he wrote in the Introduction to this collection, "that there is not a scrap of her writing—not even the tiniest fragment—during this final period which does not bear the visible impress of her exquisite individuality and her creative power."[46] Though Murry admitted, in his Introduction to *Something Childish* (1924), a mixed bag of stories which Katherine had deliberately excluded from her books during her lifetime (five of them were unpublished), "I have no doubt that Katherine Mansfield, were she still alive, would not have suffered some of these stories to appear,"[47] he also insisted, "there was no difference in kind between her casual and her deliberate utterances."[48] Like the Romantic poets, who left many fragmentary works, but unlike Katherine, Murry valued spontaneity of expression more than finished art. He spoke of Katherine's "pellucid unpremeditated phrases"[49] and paradoxically wrote (with Katherine in mind), "There is a terrible completeness about Keats. His frustrations are consummations. The imperfect is perfect."[50]

But Murry, in his self-absorbed adoration, did not realize that Katherine's unfinished works (with the exception of "A Married Man's Story") were trivial failures which did not advance her reputation, and that her very slight and previously uncollected stories (mainly published in *The New Age, Rhythm*[51] and the *Blue Review* between 1911 and 1917) did not satisfy her fastidious taste and were distinctly inferior to her best stories included in *Bliss* and *The Garden Party*.[52] By combining early, late, uncollected, unpublished and unfinished stories, Murry obliterated essential distinctions and perpetrated a critical confusion which still exists: the *Collected Stories,* first published in 1945 and still in print, presents the stories by collections rather than by chronology and inexplicably places her first book, *In a German Pension,* at the *end* of the volume. D. H. Lawrence, an intimate friend of both Katherine and Murry, was extremely perceptive not only about her stature as a writer but also about Murry's emotional failure and economic exploitation of her work: "Katherine Mansfield was worth a thousand Murrys! But he drove her sick, neglected her, wandered away from her till she died, and then he prowled back like a hyena to make a meal of her."[53]

Murry had to employ considerable critical ingenuity to justify his reissue in 1926 of *In a German Pension,* which had been out of print for fifteen years and which Katherine had "persistently refused to have republished."[54] In 1920, after the success of *Bliss* had aroused the publisher's interest in her work, she told Murry, with characteristically severe self-criticism and respect for her readers, "I cannot have *The German Pension* reprinted under any circumstances. . . . I can't go foisting that kind of stuff on the public. *It's not good enough.*"[55] Though some of the stories—notably "At Lehmann's" and "A Birthday"—were better than Katherine imagined, they were all associated with an intensely unhappy phase of her life. She had "ruthlessly destroyed" her "huge complaining diaries" from 1909 to 1914,[56] and did not wish to revive the painful memories of that period. She also felt, quite rightly, that "Prelude" and many of her later stories were distinctly superior to her *New Age* work, and that she wanted to abandon satire for more lyrical and evocative fiction.

Instead of explaining the biographical context and arguing the literary merit of the youthful book, Murry chose to exaggerate Katherine's precocity and her wounded anger at the critics who had wrongly accused her "of being hard and bitter and cruel."[57] Murry maintained, despite her savage satire—provoked by the miscarriage of her illegitimate child in Bavaria in 1909—that the Germans were "a people whom she loved,"[58] for it was acceptable to say this during the Weimar Republic. He claimed it was "a truly remarkable [book] to have written at nineteen,"[59] though Katherine was still in New Zealand at that age and actually wrote the stories when she was twenty-one.

In 1931 Murry recalled, "It amazed her that her stories should be called cruel, until she understood that the truth as felt by a sensitive heart is always cruelty to those incapable of tenderness."[60] In this casuistical passage Murry suggests that *Katherine* had the sensitive heart (an allusion to Francesca's *"cor gentil"* in *Inferno,* V. 100) and that the cruelty was manifest in those who perceived it in her and were themselves incapable of tenderness (*"Honi soit qui mal y pense"*). It was not until his posthumously published essay on Katherine that Murry fully acknowledged "the feeling of despair and hopelessness which had inspired her [early] writing . . . the savage and almost cynical realism of *In a German Pension."*[61] Until the very end of his life Murry refused to recognize the bitter and caustic element in Katherine's work, perhaps because he had frequently been the victim of her satire and cynicism (she said he "couldn't fry a sausage without thinking about God"[62]), and he encouraged Katherine to write and critics to praise her sentimental stories. As Leonard Woolf, who had published *Prelude* and knew Katherine and Murry well, shrewdly observed,

> Murry corrupted and perverted and destroyed Katherine both as a person and a writer. She was a very serious writer, but her gifts were those of an intense realist, with a superb sense of ironic humor and fundamental cynicism. She got enmeshed in the sticky sentimentality of Murry and wrote against the grain of her own nature. At the bottom of her mind she knew this, I think, and it enraged her.[63]

The reprinting of *In a German Pension* eventually led to a re-examination of Katherine's indebtedness to her acknowledged master, Anton Chekhov, who was much better known in England in 1926 than in 1911. A typical entry in Katherine's *Journal,* which is filled with quotations from her Russian idol, is, "Worked on Tchehov all day then at my story till 11 P.M."; and in December 1920 she recorded and then humbly retracted a doggerel couplet:

> Besides I am sure you will agree
> I am the English Anton T.
>
> God forgive me Tchehov for my impertinence.[64]

But Murry, as usual, wanted to have it both ways: to affirm Katherine's spiritual affinity and greatness by association with Chekhov and, at the same time, to deny any direct influence which might compromise her absolute originality. He wrote, somewhat mystically, in 1924, "Though Chekhov was dead, some essential communication seemed to pass between his spirit and hers. He was always living to her, always at her elbow to remind her of the necessity of that strange purity of soul which they shared."[65] But in 1927 he denied the obvious facts and declared: "In fact, Katherine Mansfield's technique is very different from Tchehov's. . . . Her method was wholly her own, and her development would have been precisely the same had Tchehov never existed."[66]

The important question of Chekhov's influence reappeared in the columns of *TLS* when E. M. Almedingen conclusively demonstrated that Katherine's "The Child Who Was Tired" was an unacknowledged plagiarism of Chekhov's "Sleepyhead." This story, published in 1903, when Katherine was at school in London, was included in R. E. C. Long's translation of *The Black Monk and Other Stories*. Murry's reply once again ignored the bothersome evidence and was disingenuous in the extreme:

> Katherine Mansfield read German easily; she was in Germany in 1909; and I believe *The Child Who Was Tired* was written there. . . . It may be that, as Miss Almedingen suggests, this was the real reason why Katherine Mansfield was so extremely reluctant to have *In a German Pension* republished. But, until it is proved that she could have had access to this story in either an English, French or German translation in 1909, judgment must be suspended.[67]

It was not, however, necessary to suspend judgment on a conclusive point; and scholars have subsequently revealed the full extent of Chekhov's influence on Katherine, which Murry so cavalierly denied.[68]

Murry attempted to increase Katherine's reputation not only by exaggerating her precocity and originality but also—though this contradicted his claim about the "universal recognition" of her "modern masterpiece," *In a German Pension*—by falsely portraying her as a frail genius struggling against the indifference and even hostility of family, critics and publishers (only Murry, it seems, really understood her). In a book published in 1959 Murry wrote, "Her family had, naturally, not the faintest belief in her capacity to succeed as a writer,"[69] despite the fact that his own biography of Katherine stated that her father had asked a New Zealand journalist to read three of her sketches, which were later published in the Australian *Native Companion* in the fall of 1907.

Her father had also written to the editor of that magazine assuring him that his eighteen-year-old daughter's work was precocious but entirely original: "Since she was eight years of age, she has been producing poetry and prose."[70] The successful literary career of Katherine's cousin, Elizabeth von Arnim, the author of the best-selling *Elizabeth and Her German Garden* (1898), and Katherine's publication in the *Native Companion,* significantly influenced her father's decision to allow her to return to London in August 1908 with an allowance of a hundred pounds a year.

In his first essay on Katherine, Murry insisted that the "frequent misconception of her motive and attitude had much to do with her silence during the years that followed the publication of *In a German Pension.* . . . When [*Rhythm*] came to an end [in the spring of 1913] she did not even try to get her work published." Not until *Signature* began in 1916 did the stricken deer "decide to come out into the open again."[71] And Murry declared that in 1912 "Katherine had broken with *The New Age;* she had been presented with a kind of ultimatum, calling upon her to choose between two journals, and she had chosen *Rhythm*.[72] . . . There followed a long period during which Katherine Mansfield wrote much and published nothing. Not until the publication of *Prelude* in 1917 [*sic:* 1918] was the silence broken."[73]

The actual facts, as revealed to some extent by Murry himself, are quite different from this highly-colored version. On the one hand, Katherine's failure to publish was entirely involuntary for, as Murry notes elsewhere; "The beautiful story, *Something Childish but Very Natural,* which she wrote in Paris in December 1913, was refused by every editor to whom she submitted it,"[74] and between 1911 and 1918 "it was only rarely and with the utmost difficulty that she could get anything published at all."[75] On the other hand, Katherine persisted despite rejections and actually published much more than Murry suggested. Though Murry emphasized his own role as her literary impresario and stated that in 1916, "*The Signature* died within two months, and again Katherine Mansfield had nowhere to write, until I became editor of *The Athenaeum* in 1919,"[76] he knew that Katherine had published four stories in his *Blue Review* in 1913, did *not* completely break with the *New Age* and published six stories in that magazine in 1917—between the folding of *Signature* and the publication of *Prelude*. (Three of the stories were collected in *Bliss* and three in *Something Childish.)* Murry also liked to claim, despite obvious contradictions, that Katherine was attacked by critics and rejected by publishers, and also that her brilliant masterpieces were recognized even unto Oxford: that during her lifetime her work was "for the most part damned by the reviewers"[77] (which was false) and also that "generous tributes to her genius [were] paid in public and private" (which was true).[78]

Murry created a holy trinity of Christ, Keats and Katherine (he wrote books on all of them), was fond of reflecting on the singular likeness of Keats and

Katherine, and frequently compared her to Romantic poets. As he wrote in 1933, "Katherine Mansfield did not achieve the conscious wisdom of Blake. But she was going the same path; as Keats, when he died, was going the same path."[79] And he also asked (and answered) with complete seriousness, "What has Jesus to do with Blake, with Keats, with Katherine Mansfield? He has everything to do with them."[80]

Although Katherine had a unique temperament and an original vision of the world, she clearly did not belong with the far greater genius of Blake and Keats; and it is a salutary experience to set Katherine's ruthless self-criticism against Murry's excessive adoration and to place her in a clearer perspective. Katherine felt "my talent as a writer isn't a great one—I'll have to be careful of it,"[81] and firmly rejected one untitled story by noting: "This story won't do. It is a silly story."[82] When *Bliss* appeared she honestly told Murry, "a great part of my Constable book is *trivial*. It's not good enough."[83] And Katherine, whose late works included "The Dove's Nest" and "The Canary," complained to her cousin Elizabeth, an inferior but far more popular writer, "I am tired of my little stories like birds bred in cages."[84] Katherine felt that even her best stories were not fully realized and considered "The Garden Party" "a moderately successful story, and that's all. It's somehow in the episode at the lane, scamped."[85] She constantly fought against her tendency toward superficiality and smartness, and admitted her faults in a well-known, insightful passage, "I look at the mountains, I try to pray and I think of something *clever*."[86] Murry's public dishonesty about the merit of her work was related to his well-intentioned but harmful habit of privately praising Katherine's stories in order to cheer her up and express his devotion to her art. But Katherine, who needed lucid criticism, was too shrewd to accept Murry's hypocritical encouragement, though she loyally praised his intolerably precious "poetic drama," *Cinnamon and Angelica* (1920).

We have seen how Murry's highly subjective criticism evolved from his personal weakness, his guilt and his greed; how he idealized Katherine's character, exploited her tragic illness, and inflated the value of her work, sometimes by inept comparisons with greater writers; failed to distinguish between her unfinished, unpublished and uncollected stories; exaggerated her precocity, minimized her caustic satire, and falsified the facts of her personal and literary life; denied the profound influence of Chekhov; frequently contradicted himself; and created the sentimental image of a pure and suffering soul which attracted a wide readership and led to the cult of Katherine. It also inspired ardent disciples like the English teacher, Miss Batterson, in Randall Jarrell's *Pictures from an Institution* (1954), who felt Katherine's "brilliant and universal" stories were "the precarious consummation of Fiction."[87] All these characteristics, as well as Murry's positive genius for editing and image-making, were synthesized in his controversial publication of her journals.

Murry's delicate and difficult role as executor was complicated by the apparent contradiction between Katherine's will and her final letter concerning the disposition of her papers. We have seen that Katherine destroyed her early "complaining diaries"; she declared herself "a secretive creature to my last bones";[88] and before leaving Switzerland for her final—hopeless—medical treatment in Paris, she recorded: "Torn up and ruthlessly destroyed much. This is always a great satisfaction. Whenever I prepare for a journey I prepare as though for death."[89] On the day of her first hemorrhage she found time to record: "How unbearable it would be to die—leave 'scraps,' 'bits' . . . nothing real finished";[90] and five months before her death she wrote to Ottoline Morrell about Chekhov's *Notebooks,* which had been published by Koteliansky and Leonard Woolf in 1921, "It's not fair to glean a man's buttons and pins to hawk them after his death."[91]

Katherine's will of August 14, 1922 (the same day she wrote to Ottoline about Chekhov), is entirely consistent with these statements, for she stated: "All manuscripts, notebooks, papers, letters I leave to John M. Murry. Likewise I should like him to publish as little as possible and to tear up and burn as much as possible. He will understand that I desire to leave as few traces of my camping ground as possible."[92] Murry seemed to agree with Katherine's beliefs and desires, and in his review of Chekhov's *Notebooks* rather pompously affirmed, "I am still old-fashioned enough to believe that it is almost a *crime* to make public fragments of an author's manuscripts which he obviously did not mean to show the world."[93]

Yet in a tender, unpublished letter to Murry, written one week before she made her will, Katherine seemed to encourage Murry's "criminal" tendencies. By leaving her manuscripts to Murry and urging him to destroy only what he did not use, she contradicted the emphasis of her will and left the way open for publication:

> All my manuscripts I leave entirely to you to do what you like with. Go through them, one day, dear love, and destroy all you do not use. Please destroy all letters you do not wish to keep and all papers. You do know my love of tidiness. Have a clean sweep, Bogey, and leave all fair—will you?
> Monies, of course, are all yours. In fact, my dearest dear, I leave everything to you.[94]

Acting, presumably, on this letter, Murry prefixed Katherine's photo to the first number of his magazine, the *Adelphi* (which sold over 15,000 copies) and published her stories, poems, journals and translations, as well as three of his essays about her, in virtually every issue from June 1923 to December 1924. The first edition of Katherine's *Journal* appeared in 1927 and the "Definitive" in 1954. Though the second edition contained new passages, the 1904–1911 diaries from Mantz's biography, the 1911 entries from William Orton's *The Last Romantic* (1937) and material from the *Scrapbook* (1939), it was still very far from complete. The "Definitive" edition was tastelessly dedicated "To Mary Arden," the pseudonym of Murry's second wife, Violet LeMaistre, who had lived with Murry on Katherine's royalties but had never met her idol.

In his Preface to his wife's *A Writer's Diary,* Leonard Woolf clearly warned the reader to "remember that what is printed in this volume is only a very small portion of the diaries and that the extracts were embedded in a mass of matter unconnected with Virginia's Woolf's writing. Unless this is constantly borne in mind, the book will give a very distorted view of her life and her character."[95] But Murry exposed himself to charges of falsification by his failure to inform the reader that he had skillfully compiled the *Journal* not, apparently, from a single volume, but from forty-four different notebooks and diaries. Murry had silently altered dates, changed the order of the entries, distorted the facts, and made considerable omissions in order to present his subjectively sentimental image of his wife and to create the Mansfield myth. This attracted more readers to the *Journal,* which was reprinted seven times between 1927 and 1930 and translated into several languages, than to her finest stories. As Ian Gordon writes:

> By selection and by manoeuvering the raw material, particularly by the juxtaposition of passages originally unconnected and by printing diary entries continuous with scraps of story drafting without indication of the change in his material, the editor has created something that was not in the manuscripts and notebooks, a *persona,* an idealised picture of his dead wife.... The Katherine Mansfield of the *Journal* is an intense and over-rarefied spirit, conjured up by piety and affection.[96]

And Waldron adds that: "The distortion of the text by Murry has in turn distorted the personality of the writer," for Murry omitted or toned down "material which would reflect Katherine Mansfield's tetchy, even bitchy personality or her less conventional sexual proclivities."[97]

Waldron, Gordon and Mantz are all highly critical of Murry's inaccuracy and deny the value of the published *Journal.* Gordon states that "any further critical or biographical work on Katherine Mansfield must be based on the original Notebooks and not on either of the present editions";[98] and Mantz, who has not seen the manuscripts since the early 1930s, claims the *Journal* has "artistic value, but as a source for biographical reference it might as well be classified as fiction."[99] Though Murry was undoubtedly inaccurate, he nevertheless did brilliant and vital work as the editor of her *Journal* (but not of her other works). He frankly published Katherine's condemnations of his own behavior, and did not attempt to defend himself against accusations which were sometimes inspired by her illness and depression. After examining the manuscripts myself, I found that he did not try to conceal intimate or unpleasant matters (the entries about Francis Carco are exactly the same as the published ones), and usually omitted what he could not decipher, what was trivial and what was libellous (in 1906 Katherine described her father, who had been keeping her in New Zealand against her will, as being "like a constantly offensive odour"). Almost all the ellipses are in the original manuscripts, which do not—unfortunately—clarify any of the crucial biographical issues. It is impossible to read the extremely difficult handwriting, to date the random entries or to explain the obscure allusions more accurately than Murry has done.

III

Murry's editing and criticism of Katherine's work was, as he had hoped and intended, the decisive influence in establishing her posthumous cult and reputation. Her stories, *Journal* and *Letters*—which were published in 1928 in an incomplete and heavily edited volume—have been translated into twenty-two languages; all her fiction is still in print; the Penguin paperback edition of *The Garden Party* continues to sell more than 12,000 copies a year; and to commemorate the fiftieth anniversary of her death, the BBC presented six programs, starring Vanessa Redgrave, which dramatized her life and work. As early as 1926 Gerald Bullett called her, "The one short story writer of indubitable genius who has appeared during the present century,"[100] and her technique and style have influenced (to various degrees) the feminine sensibilities of Elizabeth Bowen, Katherine Anne Porter, and Eudora Welty, all of whom have written about her. Carson McCullers' biographer reports that the librarian of Columbus, Georgia, "had to buy a new Mansfield book of short stories for the library because Carson had literally 'read the pages to pieces.'"[101]

Christopher Isherwood has written one of the best essays on Katherine's work and a novel—*The World in the Evening* (1954)—whose heroine, Elizabeth Rydal, is modeled on Katherine. Isherwood has recently said that he was attracted to her evocation of New Zealand and was moved by the poignant life of her *Journal:* by her wanderings and her disease. But he became disenchanted by her cuteness and smartness, and took her self-criticism, "I look at the mountains, I try to pray and I think of something *clever*," as a personal admonition. But Katherine's statement about her aesthetic point of view: "I've been a camera.... I've been a selective camera, and it has been my attitude that has determined the selection,"[102] probably influenced Isherwood's most famous sentence, which appears on the first page of *Goodbye to Berlin* (1939): "I am a camera with its shutter open, quite passive, recording, not thinking." The books about Germany by Mansfield and Isherwood are both satires that portray sexual corruption and take place at the edge of doom: before the Great War and before the Nazi regime.

In 1941 George Orwell harshly but honestly dissected her weaknesses while recognizing her influence and mentioned the decline of her reputation, which Lawrence had predicted, in the politically-conscious Thirties: "Nearly always the formula is the same: a pointless little sketch about fundamentally uninteresting people, written in short flat sentences and ending on a vague query.... The spirit of Katherine Mansfield seems to brood over most short stories of the past twenty years, though her own work is almost forgotten."[103] And Frank Swinnerton, who knew Katherine in the days of *Rhythm,* before the War, has perceptively commented on her reputation and originality:

> I think Murry had a genuine admiration for her, and that only on her death did he begin to cash in on her reputation. This reputation was increased by reports of her illness, and the belief that any writer who dies of consumption must be a genius. But the admission of her talent was by no means universal; and the wider knowledge of Tchehov's work which came when his tales were published in more than odd volumes led to diminution of her claim to originality.[104]

Murry's desire to protect Katherine's personal image rather than tell the truth about her provides a strong contrast to the current biographical method, which presents—and accepts—the irregular and even abnormal aspects of a writer's life. Although Murry established Katherine's reputation and created her cult by acting as her literary man-midwife, making a religion of her art and substituting the delicate and sensitive for the cynical and amoral side of her character, his hagiography offended her friends and admirers, and perverted critical values and judgment. By writing far more about Katherine than any other literary critic and maintaining exclusive control of her manuscripts until his death in 1957, he created a false legend which eased his guilt and filled his pockets. Since Murry's apparently authoritative account of Katherine is based on lies, distortions, evasions and contradictions, current biographers and critics must reject his conclusions and construct a new and accurate view of her personality and her art. When Murry's critical debris is cleared away, the Katherine that emerges from the ruins is a darker and more earthly, a crueler and more capable figure than in the legend.[105] A systematic examination of Murry's voluminous writings about Katherine, which are subjective "appreciations" rather than objective analyses and have very little value today, seriously undermines his stature as a literary critic, and it is both significant and appropriate that his reputation has declined at the same time that Katherine's has increased.

9

The Quest for Katherine Mansfield

A good biographical subject is difficult to find. The ideal criteria for selecting a modern author are the existence of significant and accessible unpublished material, the existence of family and friends who can be interviewed, and the absence of either a recent biography or a current biography in press. It is essential to choose a congenial and interesting subject who will sustain one's attention for several years. By explaining how I chose my subject, gathered information, tracked down obscure people, conducted interviews, solved the major mysteries of Katherine Mansfield's life and found a sympathetic publisher, I hope to provide a specific example of how to do research for a modern literary biography.

    I had to consider and reject several writers before deciding on Katherine Mansfield. My first choice was Wilfrid Scawen Blunt, about whom I had written a chapter in my book, *A Fever at the Core*. But Lady Longford was writing a life of Blunt, and though his will stipulated that his private papers in the Fitzwilliam Museum in Cambridge be opened to scholars fifty years after his death, in 1972, I was not allowed to see them. I then considered Norman Douglas, who interested me because of his homosexuality, his life in Italy and his friendship with D. H. Lawrence. Though several earlier biographers had given up on Douglas, I heard that Mark Holloway had completed an excellent book that was actually in press. I had done the Critical Heritage volume on Orwell for Routledge, who suggested Robert Louis Stevenson. His exotic life appealed to me, but as I began to investigate him James Pope-Hennessy published his life—and was then murdered. Routledge next suggested Tennyson, whose long dull life and poems did not attract me; and I was relieved to discover that Oxford had commissioned a biography and denied access to his papers until their book was published.

    I first learned about Katherine Mansfield through her association with D. H. Lawrence and soon found that she was the perfect subject, partly because she lived during the period I knew most about. She also came from an exotic background; was extremely attractive; had an adventurous bisexual life and a bizarre marriage to the critic and editor, Middleton Murry; was a close friend of Lawrence, Virginia Woolf and Ottoline Morrell; was a good writer of both short stories and autobiography (in her journal and letters); became attracted to mysticism at the end of her life; and fought bravely against tuberculosis, which killed her at the age of thirty-four.

There are always a number of other people "working" on a good subject. Though many have toiled for several years and claim to be "authorities," I found it better to evaluate my rivals rather than to be discouraged by them. There were two serious competitors. Claire Tomalin, then literary editor of the *New Statesman*, had published a successful life of Mary Wollstonecraft and had a contract with Oxford and Random House for a biography of Mansfield. And the New Zealander, Antony Alpers, who had published the first complete life of Mansfield in 1954, had been working on a revised version since then. Though I started later than both of them, I published my book before Alpers published his and Tomalin temporarily abandoned hers.

Once I decided to write about Mansfield, I drew up a three-page proposal about how I planned to do the book and gave it to my agent, Tessa Sayle, of Leresche and Sayle in London. She then submitted it to several publishers and got a contract from the Australian firm of Angus & Robertson, who had a special interest in antipodean authors. My advance was thirty times more than the one I had received for my first scholarly book, published in 1973, which reflects the current popularity of biographies.

When I began the biography I did not know much about Mansfield, apart from her friendship with Lawrence and Frieda, and Lawrence's unsatisfactory love-hate relationship with Murry. I first worked out my ideas about Mansfield and Murry in a long chapter about them in my book, *Married to Genius*. I then realized there were several mysteries in her life which had to be solved before I could write a full-scale biography: her relations with Garnet Trowell, which led to her first pregnancy; her six months in Wörishofen, Germany in 1909, where she had a miscarriage and another love affair with the Polish émigré, Floryan Sobienowski; her relationship with William Orton; her one-day marriage to George Bowden; the liaison which led to her second pregnancy and abortion; and Murry's affairs with Dorothy Brett and Elizabeth Bibesco. Most intimate information does not appear in printed sources, and must be discovered either in unpublished manuscripts or in personal interviews.

Before beginning my research I reread the best modern biographies—Painter's *Marcel Proust*, Deutscher's *Leon Trotsky*, Edel's *Henry James* and Ellmann's *James Joyce*—paid particular attention to their prefaces, acknowledgments and footnotes to discover their sources of information, and tried to learn about technique and theory from these superb models.

A biographer should combine the scholar's passion for learning about his subject and the period in which he lived with the detective's monomaniacal delight in facts for their own sake. He should be an exceptionally organized person who enjoys gossip and likes to ferret out secrets. When he has finished his research, contemplated his discoveries, and understood the intellectual and emotional life of his subject, he must be able to fit everything he has learned into a meaningful pattern and to satisfy his readers' natural curiosity about the life of an extraordinary person.

The first step in gathering evidence was to read everything Mansfield had written and everything that had been written about her. I found it worthwhile to consult several dissertations (available on microfilm) for their factual and biographical information. I also read a great many books about New Zealand, Chekhov (her most important literary influence), tuberculosis and Gurdjieff. I began to establish an exact chronology of dates, places and events, and typed each separate note on three-by-five slips, which could easily be arranged into subjects and chapters.

Since there was no bibliography of criticism, I compiled the first one, found 635 items in fourteen languages, and published it in the *Bulletin of Bibliography*. It would also have been possible to annotate this bibliography and publish it as a book with Garland Press, as I had previously done with T. E. Lawrence and George Orwell. Apart from providing new information, the bibliography revealed the leading scholars in the field, the journals interested in publishing articles about her and the development of her reputation. My own articles on Mansfield, some of which were later included in the biography, were published in several journals during the course of my research; and I also initiated and contributed an essay to the special *Modern Fiction Studies* issue on Mansfield.

After reading all the published material I wrote more than 100 letters in search of new information. I found the libraries that held the major collections of papers concerning Mansfield: the Alexander Turnbull Library in Wellington (for Mansfield's papers), the University of Windsor (for her letters to Garnet Trowell), the University of Texas (for letters to Ottoline Morrell), the Berg Collection in the New York Public Library (for letters to Virginia Woolf) and the British Museum (for letters to Koteliansky and the Schiffs). And I wrote to all these libraries asking them to describe their collection and requesting permission to read their papers.

Another way of discovering new material was to place "Information Please" queries in the *Times Literary Supplement, Notes & Queries, Book Collector, New York Times Book Review* and *New York Review of Books*. In this way I found out about an unpublished Mansfield letter at Cornell that describes her hitherto unknown meeting with James Joyce; and had offers from two young ladies in New York, who were devoted to Mansfield, to do research for me at the Public Library.

By writing to Constable and Knopf, her two publishers, I learned about the present location of her business correspondence with these firms and the sales figures of her books. I also received a personal reminiscence from Alfred Knopf, who met Mansfield in Dan Rider's London bookshop in 1912. A letter to the Public Record Office in London produced a copy of her certificate of marriage to George Bowden, which revealed his birth data and father's occupation as well as the fact that she had lied about her age (she was actually under twenty-one) in order to marry without parental consent.

When I found there was a Gurdjieff group in Boulder, I went to one of their meetings to discover more about their ideas and attitudes, and to look through their library for contemporary references to Mansfield. The visit to this odd group confirmed my belief that Gurdjieff was a fraud who deceived Mansfield, that his ideas were meaningless and that his disciples mistook his confusion for profundity.

I also wrote to Mansfield's family and friends (her sister, Murry's brother, her closest friend, Ida Baker), and to every person who had any connection with her, asking specific questions and requesting interviews. If I did not receive an answer to my first letter, I kept writing until I got a reply. I began with people with whom Mansfield had corresponded or who had appeared in earlier biographies, and tracked them down in *Who's Who,* through their publishers or by asking other people for their addresses. I also wrote to scholars in the field asking if they had or knew about any new material. I eventually received letters from many well-known writers: Gerald Brenan, David Garnett, Christopher Isherwood, Frank Swinnerton, Sylvia Townsend Warner and Rebecca West as well as from everyone alive who ever knew Mansfield.

I had particularly good response from the following sources, which helped me to solve the essential mysteries in Mansfield's life. The University of Windsor sent xerox copies of Mansfield's twenty unpublished letters to Garnet Trowell in 1908. They had just been made public, after the death of his widow, who had donated the letters. My German friend, Werner Alferink, contacted the town Archivist of Wörishofen in Bavaria and sent me new and very specific information about her stay in that town, which corrected a recent dissertation I had consulted. Herr Alferink also sent postcards and pamphlets about the town and its history as well as copies of all the precious correspondence between the Archivist and other Mansfield scholars. All this information helped me to reconstruct Mansfield's bitter mood, and the guilt, humiliation, mental agony and physical pain that she had suffered in Germany.

When I discovered that Floryan Sobienowski had translated Shaw's plays into Polish, I wrote to Professor Dan Laurence, the former literary executor of Shaw's estate, who sent me a great deal of new biographical material about Floryan. Professor Laurence's papers also revealed that Floryan had translated one of Mansfield's poems into Polish and published it in a Warsaw literary weekly in 1910. I wrote to the National Library in Warsaw about this, and they sent me a xerox copy of the poem and Floryan's critique—the first to be written on Mansfield. A friend translated the critique into English, and it became the basis of my essay "Katherine Mansfield's 'To Stanislaw Wyspianski.'"

Other inquiries produced useful if less spectacular results. Smith College, where William Orton had taught economics after leaving England in the early 1920s, sent an extensive biographical file and an unpublished photograph. King's College, Cambridge, where George Bowden had been a student with E. M. Forster at the end of the century, sent obituary notices, and I learned—just too late—that he had died in Majorca at the age of ninety-eight in 1975. Fordham University Medical School, where Victor Sorapure (Mansfield's favorite doctor) had taught, sent articles by and information about him; and I also tracked down his obituary in the *Lancet* and the *British Medical Journal*. A close friend of mine, Dr. Sheldon Cooperman of Boston, answered many medical questions with clear and specific explanations of the symptoms and treatment of Mansfield's tuberculosis.

I had learned that the man responsible for Mansfield's second pregnancy was related to the publisher William Heinemann. This was confirmed when a friend who wrote to Antony Alpers told me he said that he would refer to this recently deceased man only as "F. H." Though I wrote to Tara Heinemann, who advertised for information in *TLS,* I was unable to find out anything more about him and also referred to him in my book as "F. H."

A letter from John Manchester, Dorothy Brett's friend and biographer, confirmed Mansfield's suspicions—and my own—that Brett had an affair with Murry when Mansfield was living in Italy in the fall of 1919. And correspondence with Enid Bagnold, the author of *National Velvet,* who knew Elizabeth Bibesco well, again confirmed that Murry had a more serious affair with Elizabeth, which aroused Mansfield's fury and threatened their marriage early in 1920.

Most people gave me the generous assistance that made it possible to reconstruct a life and write a biography. The only ones who refused to help were the journalist, Patrick Campbell, the son of Mansfield's friends, Beatrice and Gordon Campbell, who never answered my letters; and the heirs of Walter De La Mare. Though the woman who was writing De La Mare's biography encouraged me to read Mansfield's letters to the poet, his family would not allow me to see them until her biography was published. Fortunately, these refusals did not concern vital information.

The next stage of research was the personal interviews, which provided an exceptional opportunity to meet many distinguished and unusual people who were invariably hospitable and kind. At the appropriate time I telephoned the people I had already written to, arranged a specific appointment and got directions to their homes. I had typed out a long list of questions, with space in between, took brief notes on the answers during the interview, and wrote out the complete answers from my notes soon after the meeting. I found it was better not to have a tape recorder, which seems awkward—especially to older people—is difficult to transcribe and collects a great deal of useless material.

I mostly interviewed people in their seventies and eighties, and found that they had good memories for the distant, significant past—though they often did not remember what happened yesterday. But they tended to repeat what they had written rather than what had originally happened, as if their memory had obliterated as well as recorded the primary experience. I usually brought photographs which helped to recall obscure incidents. Older people tend to become extremely tired after an hour's conversation, so rapport had to be established almost immediately. I had to convey the impression of being knowledgeable, serious and sympathetic, yet not appear to be prying into secrets they were reluctant to disclose. It was essential to stick strictly to the subject and prevent them from wandering from it, for time was precious. It was best to begin with rather general questions and then, once their confidence had been gained, to lead up to more personal ones. It was important to remember that people born in the nineteenth century have a very different idea of sexual morality than now exists, and can be easily shocked. At the end of the interview I always asked to see their books and letters by Mansfield; and if they had written a book I brought a copy (preferably a first edition) and asked them to inscribe it. Though many people claimed, in their letters or on the telephone, that they had nothing valuable to say and scarcely knew Mansfield, I never believed this and always insisted on the promised interview. Every conversation revealed something of value and allowed me to corroborate other written and spoken evidence. Personal interviews gave me the most vivid sense of what Mansfield was really like.

Dorothy Brett, a close friend of Mansfield and Lawrence, was ninety-three when I visited her rather squalid adobe house at the edge of the desert near Taos, New Mexico, in March 1976. She was extremely frank and friendly, said and meant "ask me anything" (though I did not have the nerve to say "Did you sleep with Murry fifty years ago?"), and enjoyed being interviewed and talking about her happiest days. Though she had been deaf all her life, she could now hear better than ever with her modern hearing aid. Brett was lively and sympathetic, adored Mansfield and Murry, and made me understand why so many brilliant people had sought her friendship.

Brett's friend Enid Hilton, who had been introduced to Mansfield by D. H. Lawrence in 1919, wrote the most vivid and perceptive letter I had received about Mansfield. After talking about her old friends, Mrs. Hilton showed me a large bag that Tony Luhan had made from the hide of Lawrence's horse Azul; and then took me to an Indian reservation, north of her home in Ukiah, California, where she had been a social worker for thirty years.

I had an interview in San Francisco with Ruth Mantz, who with Murry wrote a biography of Mansfield's early life in 1933. At first she was friendly and full of praise for my work (which I had sent her previously) and showed me her photograph albums about places associated with Mansfield. She refused to show me the manuscript of her unfinished biography, but later suggested that we collaborate. She misled me, perhaps deliberately, by stating that Floryan and not "F. H." had got Mansfield pregnant; and when I later wrote that the date of the pregnancy made Floryan's paternity impossible, she blandly said, "You are right." When I asked permission to read the papers she had sold to the University of Texas, this rather difficult woman refused her consent.

When I wrote to Christopher Isherwood, one of the writers most strongly affected by Mansfield, he suggested I telephone him in Santa Monica, generously answered a long list of questions and discussed her influence on his early work. I later discovered that Mansfield was the model for the heroine of his novel, *The World in the Evening,* and was the source of his famous phrase, "I am a camera."

Since most of Mansfield's papers were in Wellington, I applied for travel and research grants to the Guggenheim Foundation, the National Endowment for the Humanities, the American Council of Learned Societies and the Fulbright Commission as well as to my own University. I did, in fact, win two University of Colorado research grants for travel to New Zealand in the summer of 1976 and to England, for my final interviews, in December 1976. The University also paid for postage, xeroxing and typing the manuscript. On the way to New Zealand I visited Samoa, Tahiti and Tonga, and was disillusioned by the disparity between the exotic and romantic image—created by Gauguin, Melville, Stevenson and Michener—and the reality of sullen people in a steamy landscape.

It was important to acquire a good understanding of the New Zealand and Wellington background, and I followed Mansfield's footsteps through the still wild and Maori-speaking Urewera country, which had scarcely changed since her adventurous journey of 1907. I also saw her birthplace, her house in Karori (the setting of "Prelude") and her house in Day's Bay, but I was horrified to find that two of her grand nineteenth-century homes had been destroyed to make room for a modern motorway.

The most crucial person connected with my research was Margaret Scott, who was editing Mansfield's correspondence, for she had manuscript and typescript copies of letters from all over the world as well as Murry's unpublished letters to Mansfield. She very generously let me stay in her house and read all the letters while I was working in Wellington, which saved my travelling to libraries in Australia, England and America (as she had done) and reading the letters in Mansfield's difficult handwriting (which she had learned to decipher) instead of in clear type. She also showed me her copy of Mansfield's *Journal,* which indicated the unpublished entries, and her notes in Ida Baker's *Memories.*

But as the weeks passed and I worked furiously all day and late into the night—for it was winter in wet and windy Wellington, and I found it the most boring city on earth—Margaret Scott seemed to become jealous of my energetic achievement which contrasted so strongly with her own listlessness. She began to nag and pick quarrels with me, and we once had a tug-of-war with a pair of my trousers while debating whether or not she should iron them. Her overt hostility alternated with menacing sulks, but I was determined to put up with anything until I had finished reading the letters and cleared out just before the inevitable explosion.

I was, however, able to interview two of Mansfield's girlhood friends, who revealed a great deal about her years in Wellington and at Queen's College. The fragile Edie Bendall, who was ninety-seven and lived near the setting of "At the Bay," had had a brief but passionate love affair with Mansfield in 1907. During the interview she asked me to help her across the room to look at photographs of her daughter, but we had to turn back when she became exhausted. She inquired when my book would be published; I replied, "In a year or two," and she thought for a moment and then said, "Well, I don't know . . ." Ruth Herrick, who was a spry eighty-six and had commanded the New Zealand WRENS during World War Two, was more tough-minded and straightforward. She discussed Mansfield's attitude toward her father, sisters, the Trowells, Ida Baker and her teachers at Queen's College, and revealed that the aesthetic Mansfield had insisted on conversing in French with her although they knew only ten words between them. I also met Mansfield's second cousin, Henry Craddock Barclay, who told me some new things about her family and her father, and described how during her lifetime Wellington tended to dislike her works and preferred the more popular novels by her famous cousin, "Elizabeth."

The Alexander Turnbull Library (the National Library of New Zealand) has the largest collection of Mansfield books and manuscripts in the world, which they bought from Murry's fourth wife, Mary, after his death in 1957. While working there I made certain that my notes were legible and accurate, for it would be extremely difficult to check them once I had left. I had to get permission from the Mansfield estate (controlled by Mary Middleton Murry through the Society of Authors) to quote unpublished material; and was fortunately granted permission to use all but three of the quotes I requested, and these I paraphrased. My contract deliberately stipulated that the publisher, not the author, must pay for literary and photographic fees. During my stay in New Zealand I was photographed and interviewed by the Wellington *Evening Post*, which provided excellent publicity for my biography.

In December 1976 I went to England to complete the interviews, and was often surprised by the shabby circumstances of distinguished men like Murry's biographer, Frank Lea, and Murry's brother, Richard, who cooked a superb lunch and told me about his family background, his devotion to Mansfield, and her attitude toward her illness. Murry's fourth wife, Mary, and his son, Colin (who spoke to me for twelve hours and invited me to stay overnight) both defended Murry's behavior and helped me see things from his point of view.

Frank Lea, who was in great pain and clearly dying, showed me how much an intelligent man could admire Murry. After listening to him praise Murry for more than an hour (a useful corrective) I finally said, "Who but Murry could write a book called *God* and then spend the first thirty pages discussing himself, as if to put the Deity in proper perspective?" And Lea rather poignantly replied, "Let the Hampstead intellectuals sneer. I found it to be a moving and a profound book."

Julian Vinogradoff, the daughter of Ottoline Morrell, gave me her childhood impressions of Mansfield at Garsington and on the French Riviera. She also showed me the guest book of Ottoline's famous country home, replete with Bloomsbury signatures, and several impressive paintings by Mark Gertler and Augustus John. I managed to offend her Russian husband when I remarked that Sergei Aksakov was a minor writer.

Montague Weekley, the son of Frieda Lawrence, had met Mansfield when she acted as an emissary from his mother and brought him sweets and money as he emerged from St. Paul's School. Lady Juliette Huxley, who had been French tutor and companion to Julian Morrell, spoke of the atmosphere of Garsington, analyzed the character of Frieda and Koteliansky, and said the greatest crime in Bloomsbury was to be boring.

Frank Swinnerton, who was ninety-two but had a remarkable memory, and the publisher, A. S. Frere, both told me a great deal about Mansfield's cousin and rival, Elizabeth, Countess Russell. And both repeated, as an example of her caustic wit, the same anecdote. After the Great War, when Elizabeth was told of a man who had been wounded in seventeen places, she replied, "I didn't know a man *had* seventeen places."

When I first wrote to Mansfield's ninety-year-old friend, Ida Baker, a letter—signed, but clearly not written by her—answered my questions. It also said she did not want to discuss Mansfield and referred me to an obscure young man who managed her practical affairs. After an extremely unpleasant meeting with this officious guardian in the distant and dreary suburbs of London, he forbade me to interview Ida. But I felt I owed it to myself and to scholarship to try and see her, and decided to challenge his claim to speak for her—for she was the only person who could answer certain questions about Mansfield.

I decided to try my luck with Ida while staying with friends in Winchester, who lived near her home in the New Forest. I drove into the tiny village of Fordingbridge on a rainy winter afternoon and proceeded on foot down a narrow, muddy path to her thatched-roof cottage. There was a totally immobile cow outside her door and a stone-like dog lying before the gas fire. I peered through the window at the haggard profile of Ida, as she sat bent over in a deep chair, buried under a pile of old army blankets and surrounded by a ring of dirty tissues. My first thought, when she failed to answer the loud knocks, was that she was dead and that I was the first to find her. But when a weak voice bade me enter, I went in thinking of James' "The Aspern Papers." I introduced myself and handed Ida a bunch of limp sopping flowers, but she absolutely refused to say a word about Mansfield. When she insisted, "I'm tired. I want to rest," I had to restrain myself from saying "You'll soon have plenty of time to rest. This is the time to *talk*." I protested that I had come all the way from America to see her, and she coldly agreed, "Yes, you *have* come a long way." I found it extremely difficult to imagine the young and beautiful Mansfield in love with this musty and skeletal figure. The stone dog never moved, and I had to suppress a desire to pile a few more blankets on Ida and carefully go through her papers. But since she clearly would not speak to me, or even sign her book for me (she claimed blindness though there were books and spectacles on her table) I reluctantly took my leave. When my grandchildren ask if I ever saw Ida Baker, I will at least be able to answer that I did.

I had considerably more successful interviews with members of the Trowell family. Garnet's nephew, Oliver Trowell, a painter and art teacher, told me about his uncle, gave me an original photograph of his grandfather (who had been Mansfield's cello teacher in Wellington) and provided an introduction to his aunt. The most revealing talk of all was with Dorothy Richards, the younger sister of Garnet and Mansfield's beloved "Dolly." I had not known of her whereabouts until Oliver Trowell told me she was living in Cambridge. She was married to the brother of Vyvyan Richards, the friend of my hero T. E. Lawrence, and had an unpublished letter from Lawrence as well as a piece of metal from a Hejaz railway locomotive, which had been blown up by Lawrence and was now inscribed in Arabic and placed next to her front door. After discreet and careful questioning, she revealed that Garnet had not married Mansfield because she was thrown out of the Trowell house by Garnet's father, Thomas, when he discovered that Garnet had got her pregnant! Mrs. Richards thus provided the crucial link of evidence between Mansfield's life with the Trowells in St. John's Wood and her passionate love letters to Garnet, now in Windsor. She also helped confirm that Mansfield married George Bowden to provide a father for Garnet's child.

The next stage of research took me to the Humanities Research Center at the University of Texas in April 1977. There I read Mansfield's letters to Ottoline Morrell and others, and studied the collection of Lucy O'Brien, who had planned to write a life of Mansfield in the late 1940s but abandoned the project when she heard about Alpers' book and decided, instead, to have a baby. Apart from new bibliographical information, the O'Brien collection had several letters from George Bowden about his disastrous marriage to Mansfield, which corroborated the letters he wrote to Alpers (now in Wellington) on the same subject and clarified Mansfield's motives as well as his own. When I wrote to

Lucy O'Brien about her work, she kindly sent me several long letters, sale catalogs and photographs.

I completed the research in the summer of 1977 by visiting all the houses and places in which Mansfield had lived in London and on the Continent. I went to Wörishofen in Germany; Sierre-Randogne-Montana in Switzerland; Ospedaletti in Italy; Menton, Bandol and Fontainebleau in France; and took descriptive notes and photographs of all of them. Since photographs are extremely important for selling the book, I tried to find as many unknown ones as I could during the course of my studies. I was given original photographs by Oliver Trowell (of his grandfather), by Richard Murry (of Mansfield and Murry), by David Drey (of his mother, Anne Rice, a close friend of Mansfield), and by Stephanie Fierz (of Mansfield and her sisters at Queen's College); and I acquired unpublished photographs of William Orton and George Bowden from Smith College and the University of Texas.

I also arranged to give lectures on Mansfield at all the places I did my research: at the University of Auckland, the University of Wellington, the Alexander Turnbull Library, Queen's College, London, and the University of Texas. These lectures enabled me to earn modest fees to defray expenses, to test my ideas before a learned audience and to generate interest in my work.

I had originally signed a contract with Angus & Robertson, a Sydney and London publisher, though I was not happy about their reputation. But they promised that if I delivered the typescript by April 1, 1977, they would print it fast, publish it in September as their main autumn book and get copies to Australia and New Zealand by Christmas. When the editor came to New York to sell the American rights in January, I gave him the first 300 pages and he was delighted. But when I sent them the completed book of 420 pages on schedule in mid-March, I heard nothing for several weeks. He then telephoned from London and asked me to cut the book by twenty percent, though he did not specify where the deletions should be made or attempt to justify his request on literary grounds. I immediately realized that his figure came from a cost-accounting estimate of the optimum sale price, refused to reduce the book, took it away from Angus & Robertson and returned their advance. By doing this I lost a definite contract, and gave up the possibility of publication in the fall of 1977 and the certainty of appearing before Alpers, whose book was supposed to be published by John Murray in London early in 1978.

Meanwhile, an editor at Hamish Hamilton, who had read *A Fever at the Core,* asked me to do a biography of Wyndham Lewis and offered me a good contract for this book. When I decided to send the Mansfield biography to Hamish Hamilton, I risked the Wyndham Lewis contract, which they withheld until they had read and liked the Mansfield biography. In the end they agreed to publish both books, gave me excellent advice about revisions, twice as much money as Angus & Robertson had offered, and promised to publish it in May

1978. I then heard that Murray had rejected Alpers' manuscript, which meant that my book, now much improved, would still appear first and be published by an infinitely better firm who paid much more than Angus & Robertson.

Even if the publisher is reputable, I carefully oversee all the details of the publication of my book. I selected the photograph for the dust jacket, chose the binding, wrote the copy for the jacket and the publisher's catalog, asked for proof of the jacket, photographs and captions as well as of the text, and made up the list of complimentary and review copies. To do otherwise is to invite disaster.

All the material collected in the course of my research—especially letters from well-known people and original photographs—was valuable and could later be sold to private collectors or to one of the research libraries that has a substantial Mansfield collection. When I completed the book, I made a descriptive catalog of this material, offered it for sale and made xerox copies of everything I wanted to keep. Just before the book appeared I had the publisher send review copies to all the magazines to which I contribute or which have reviewed my previous books. I had then done all I possibly could do. It remained the publisher's responsibility to promote the book and sell the subsidiary rights, and the reviewers' duty to recognize its merits.

The Katherine Mansfield that emerged during my quest was very different from the sentimental and idealized portrait that had been created by Murry and reinforced by her previous biographers. Though illness gave her a frail and delicate appearance, her character was less exquisite than tough; and she was more rebellious and daring, more cruel and capable than the figure in the legend.

10

Memoirs of D. H. Lawrence: A Genre of the Thirties

I

When Lawrence died in March 1930 most obituaries described him as "morose, frustrated, tortured, even a sinister failure." *The Times,* which emphasized the "pornographic and scandalous" Lawrence of *Lady Chatterley's Lover* and the suppressed exhibition of paintings that seemed to illustrate the novel, expressed the prevailing view that the "bearded satyr" was obsessed with sex and had a diseased mind: "He confused decency with hypocrisy, and honesty with the free and public use of vulgar words. At once fascinated and horrified by physical passion, he paraded his disgust and fear in the trappings of a showy masculinity. And, not content with words, he turned to painting in order to exhibit more clearly still his contempt for all reticence."[1]

Lawrence's flotilla of Boswells, dissatisfied with this caricature and eager to present their own interpretation of his vehement and contradictory character, hastened into print with eleven memoirs (the first ten published between 1931 and 1935) that became a minor but significant genre in the Thirties. His sister, Ada Lawrence, and Jessie Chambers discussed his youth. Middleton Murry (in two books) and Catherine Carswell quarreled bitterly about his middle years, and Aldous Huxley supported Carswell. Mabel Luhan, Knud Merrild and Dorothy Brett described the New Mexico period. Earl and Achsah Brewster portrayed the last decade, and Frieda Lawrence, who was a major figure in nearly all the memoirs, presented a more complete picture of her life with Lorenzo from the prewar years to his death in 1930. A comparative study of these memoirs enables us to read them as they were written: not as isolated books, but in relation to each other.

Lawrence generated intense emotion wherever he went, and his pilgrimage was stormy as well as savage. He had the power to change people, to arouse intense love and hatred, to deepen his friends' awareness of themselves and the world. He challenged them to respond to him totally and to fulfill their own potential. His personality made a powerful impact on everyone, and his closest friends had to explain the greatest event of their lives by analyzing and recording their experience in print. All the memoirs have two things in common: the authors were close friends of Lawrence and wrote about him in the 1930s. Many of them imitated his impassioned style and quasi-mystical language. Most used the occasion to come to terms with Lawrence's influence and portray themselves in relation to him; they set out to write about Lawrence but were forced to include a self-portrait. The memoirs were often distorted by personal bias, had a strong element of self-interest, and revealed as much about the author as the subject. Lawrence was a kind of deity to his bizarre group of friends; after his death some continued to worship him while others tried to destroy the god that failed.

Lawrence's ambivalent relations with all his friends, which were often stranger than anything in his fiction, led to a bewildering proliferation of disparate images that appeared in the various memoirs like the dynamic succession of figures in Duchamps' *Nude Descending a Staircase*. Lawrence was bored by Ada but attached to her by bonds of blood and memory; unable to give himself to Jessie but strengthened by her love and her support; disgusted by Murry's spinelessness but drawn to his intelligence and charm; disappointed by Carswell's defeatism but grateful for her loyalty and friendship; scornful of Huxley's rationalism but stimulated by his mind; fearful of Mabel's will but attracted to her warm glow of life; aware of Merrild's limitations but fond of his undemanding companionship; irritated by Brett's adoration but pleased by her sacrificial helpfulness; critical of the Brewsters' Buddhism but respectful of their search for religious truth; frequently furious with Frieda but vitally dependent on her love and inspiration. The extraordinary insight of Lawrence's fictional portrayals of his friends is confirmed by their own self-portraits in the memoirs: for Miriam *is* like Jessie, Ursula like Frieda, Mrs. Witt like Mabel, Dollie Urquhart like Brett.

The personal relations of the authors, who were all intensely jealous of each other, had a Byzantine and sometimes comical complexity. Ada and Jessie were early rivals for Lawrence's affection. Ada fought a lawsuit with Frieda, who was portrayed in a novel by Huxley. Murry had brief affairs with Frieda and Brett, battled publicly with Carswell and was satirized by Huxley. Carswell retaliated against Huxley's editorial assistant, Enid Hilton. Frieda hated both Brett and Mabel, who warmly returned her hostility. Mabel despised Brett and Merrild; Merrild loathed Mabel. Frieda lost Lawrence's ashes after his cremation in Vence; Mabel tried to steal them in Taos. Frieda, Brett and Mabel all loved Lawrence and wrote their books while living near each other in Taos. As the hostile and sympathetic factions warred against each other and tore Lawrence apart, they exposed "what an Até of discord Lawrence was in his generation, and what an amount of bickering and bad ink he managed to breed."[2]

The value and quality of the memoirs vary enormously and depend on six factors: the time the authors knew Lawrence; at what stage of their lives or his (he was a very different man when Jessie met him as an adolescent and when Merrild encountered him in 1922); their intimacy and involvement with him (the intense memoirs of Jessie and Murry have a different kind of value than the less personal accounts of the Brewsters and Merrild); their honesty and insight about themselves and their relation to him (the memoirs of Murry and Mabel are much more biased and distorted than those of Carswell and Frieda); their ability to separate the man from the work, to distinguish the personal impression he made on them from their reading of his books and reflection about his ideas; the quality of their minds and of their style (there is a vast difference in this respect between Ada and Huxley, Brett and the Brewsters); their use of Lawrence's letters, essays and poems, and of original photographs that complement the verbal description of persons and places (the letters provide a valuable ballast of autobiography within the memoirs and reflect his own response to the authors).

Philip Larkin has written that Lawrence's "reputation has been made up of two great waves of admiration; the first for the man, that produced all the personal accounts of him after his death, the second for his works. . . . And each in its own way was genuine and justifiable: Lawrence was both a wonderful man and a wonderful writer, and he was recognized as such right from the start."[3] But this statement is both oversimplified and misleading. The memoirs by Murry, Mabel and Jessie (the first two manifestly unreliable) expressed hostility rather than admiration, and his "wonderful" qualities were not generally recognized until a quarter of a century after his death.

II

Ada, Lawrence's younger sister (who was portrayed as Annie in *Sons and Lovers*), was close to him in childhood. But she hardened into a respectable Nottingham matron and strongly disapproved when he ran off with Frieda in May 1912: "I think the thought of me is very bitter to her—and she won't speak of me to anybody." Though he spent Christmas 1915 with Ada's family in Ripley, he found it was a "real purgatory to be in her little house, with everybody and everything whirling around." He also felt he had become estranged from his family and alien to their existence: "It is very queer to be here—makes me sad. I am fond of my people, but they seem to belong to another life, not to my own life. . . . I am not really 'our Bert.' Come to that I never was. And the gulf between their outlook and mine is always yawning, horribly obvious to me."[4]

Ada was shocked by *Lady Chatterley's Lover*, and Lawrence advised her not to see the exhibition of his paintings at the Warren Gallery. Her visit to France in 1929 depressed Lawrence, who could "feel all those Midlands behind her, with their sort of despair."[5] Though Ada was not as bad as their sanctimonious sister Emily, whom Lawrence called "Pamela, or Virtue Rewarded," she was as jealous as her mother for his affection. She slights his youthful intimacy with Jessie Chambers, Louie Burrows and Helen Corke, ignores his friendships with Blanche Jennings, Willie Hopkin and A. W. McLeod, and describes herself as "the only constant friend Lawrence ever had until he met his wife." Ada continued to fight for Lawrence's love after his marriage. At her urging, he once locked Frieda out of his room, and Ada screamed at his wife: "I hate you from the bottom of my heart."[6]

Lawrence left no will, and in November 1932 Frieda successfully fought his brother and two sisters for the control of his estate in the Probate Court in London. The decisive evidence was provided by Murry, who testified that in 1914 Lawrence had in fact drawn up a will, which was lost in their travels, in Frieda's favor. Ada, already irritated by Frieda's "blackening" remarks about the Lawrence family, was furious and bitter when she lost the case.

Though rather crudely put together by Ada, with the help of a Nottingham journalist, Stuart Gelder, *Young Lorenzo: The Early Life of D. H. Lawrence* (January 1932) is a sympathetic and revealing effort. The title was probably invented by Pino Orioli, who published the first Florence edition, for Lawrence was not called Lorenzo when young. The memoir is complemented by many (inaccurately dated) letters from Lawrence, three poems, "Adolf"(a vivid sketch of a rabbit, which Murry had rejected for the *Athenaeum* in 1919), and two works of the Croydon period: "The Fly in the Ointment" and "Art and the Individual." The book, which identifies the originals of James and Alvina Houghton in *The Lost Girl*, concludes with a few pages on "Proper Names in Nottinghamshire Novels" that usefully relate the fictional settings to actual localities. There are sixteen photographs, most published for the first time, which have since become famous: Lawrence's family, his mother, the "young prig" on his 21st birthday, the moustached man of 27, Ada on the beach at Mablethorpe and many places used in the Midlands novels. The Orioli, but not the Secker edition, reproduces nine early paintings by Lawrence and includes his essay on Rachel Annand Taylor.

Despite the idealized portrait of Lawrence's childhood, described in sentimental schoolgirl prose, Ada presents intimate details of their family life and discloses the biographical basis of *Sons and Lovers*. She describes the crucial differences between Lawrence's parents, and their mother's response to the painful realities of marriage: "She did not recover from the first shock of realising that her life would be one of almost ceaseless monotony among endless ugliness and dirt. She escaped into herself, and when the children came, lived alone with them. He was a stranger in the house." The children idolized the mother and rejected the father, who cultivated crude habits to irritate his "superior" family and became a "brutal and coarse beast" when drunk. There was a terrible change in their mother after the death of her eldest son, Ernest.

Ada writes that Lawrence was a delicate, sensitive and even morbid child. She says he became attracted to the shy and serious Jessie Chambers because she eagerly listened to his ideas and accepted his beliefs, but ignores the fact that this was his first stimulating contact with a mind comparable to his own. His fondness for Jessie led to her rivalry with his mother, who feared the loss of her son and hated his girl. Ada also mentions Lawrence's love affairs with Louie Burrows and Helen Corke. Though she refers to Alice Dax, she incorrectly says that Clara and Baxter Dawes in *Sons and Lovers* are fictitious characters.

Ada discusses Lawrence's early paintings, his stunning achievement of first-place in all England and Wales in the teacher's examination, his classroom experience at Croydon, the impressive testimonial from his Headmaster and the story of the special copy of *The White Peacock* that Lawrence gave to his mother just before her death. Ada, who nursed him during his illness, connects his pneumonia of 1911 to his later consumption and quotes his pathetic sickbed statement: "Ada, I could die just this minute if I wished."

Ada begins defensively by admitting, "To some he was a writer of obscene books and a painter of obscene pictures," and points out that Lawrence (who hated Eastwood) was, like Byron, reviled by the people of Nottinghamshire. Ada's book is important for the information she provides about Lawrence rather than for her own views about him. By recounting Lawrence's youth and early influences, she corrects serious misconceptions about his character and motives, domesticates and humanizes the legendary monster of depravity and perversion.

Jessie Chambers, the model for Emily in *The White Peacock* and Miriam in *Sons and Lovers,* met the youthful Lawrence in 1896, was the first to recognize his genius and remained his closest friend until their traumatic break in 1910. Her book provides a vivid and detailed picture of Lawrence's adolescence and early manhood, which were rich in experience and achievement.

D. H. Lawrence: A Personal Record (May 1935), the most structured, coherent and moving of the memoirs, has a tragic theme: the destruction of an idyllic friendship and the eclipse of Jessie as Lawrence's star begins to rise. Jessie portrays Mrs. Lawrence as the villain, Lawrence as executioner and herself as victim; she reveals the blighting influence of the mother, the ruthlessness of the son and the disastrous effect of Lawrence's rejection. As Lawrence began to free himself from his mother's stranglehold after her death, by brief affairs, the composition of *Sons and Lovers* and his encounter with Frieda, Jessie, "the anvil on which I have hammered myself out," was inevitably sacrificed.

Jessie gives invaluable descriptions of Lawrence's family: the richness and warmth of the father, who is ostracized by the others; the vital, emphatic, self-righteous mother, who coldly disapproves of Jessie and clearly sees that she is separating the young artist from his home. Mrs. Lawrence did not want to see Bert "as a man of genius. It would remove him too far from her. What she saw was the loving and dutiful son she could claim and keep, and share the day to day joys and sorrows with. They were in close communion, swiftly responsive to one another." The overt hostility of the parents created a strong emotional tension that always made Jessie feel slightly sick when she visited their home.

Lawrence's eldest brother, the fairy prince of the family, was already a legendary figure; his early death seemed to seal the extraordinary intimacy of Lawrence and his mother. His sister Ada, who was Jessie's good friend at their teacher training college, assumed "conscious ownership" of her brother and, after their mother's death, was all too eager to take over her dominating role.

Like Huxley and Frieda, Jessie mentions Lawrence's unusual ability to transform ordinary tasks into vital experience and shows that the plan for an ideal community, the quest for Rananim, developed very early in his career. "I should like to have a big house," Lawrence said, "you know there are some lovely old houses in the Park with gardens and terraces. Wouldn't it be fine if we could all live in one of those houses, mother and all the people we like together?"

But the magical quality of their association, their bond of loyalty and love, were doomed by Lawrence's unnatural attachment to his mother. (Jessie was not at all keen to set up house with her.) Mrs. Lawrence forced her son to choose between them and to confess to Jessie: "I've looked into my heart and I cannot find that I love you as a husband should love his wife." Lawrence divided love into the spiritual and the physical, turned Jessie into a pure abstraction and insisted: "You have no sexual attraction at all, none whatever." Jessie believed that "the whole question of sex had for him the fascination of horror, and also that in his repudiation of any possibility of a sex relation between us he felt that he had paid me a deep and subtle compliment."

The effect of Lawrence's honest rejection was devastating. The humiliating denial of love destroyed their spontaneous feeling "like the slaughter of a foetus in the womb" and seemed to drain all meaning from Jessie's life. She tried to maintain a self-protective attitude ("We'll have nothing to do with one another") and, as self-righteous as Mrs. Lawrence, put the entire blame for the failure of their love on him.

Jessie, who had sent in the poems by Lawrence that Hueffer had accepted and published in the *English Review*, urged him to rewrite *Sons and Lovers* in order to free himself from the obsession with his mother. For their bond was even more powerful after her death, when any intimacy with Jessie seemed disloyal to her memory. When he showed her the completed manuscript, she made a futile effort to deny its artistic power: "It made me see him as a philistine of the philistines.... His significance withered and his dimensions shrank. He ceased to matter supremely." But this casual dismissal is contradicted by the revelation of her deepest feelings. "I was hurt beyond all expression," she exclaims, with considerable self-pity. "I felt that I had suffered a terrible inner injury. It required all my effort to avoid a collapse." Jessie confessed that when her intense connection with Lawrence was severed, "I saw also the extinction of my greater self."

Yet Jessie, who portrays herself as shy, reserved, clinging, possessive, prudish and prosaic, inadvertently justifies Lawrence's rejection of her love. Lawrence chastises her for omitting the phrase about a man who "keeps mistresses" when they are reading *Hedda Gabler,* and, when he gives her *Anna Karenina* (which foreshadows his life with Frieda) and says it is the greatest novel in the world, the country girl "felt most sympathy in those days with Levin and Kitty, and followed their experiments in farming with deep interest." She was certainly the proper girl for Lawrence at that stage of his life, but not the right wife for the man who insisted: "I must have opposition, something to fight."

Jessie was scarcely comforted by Lawrence's assurance that he discussed her endlessly with his wife, and it was highly ironic that Frieda and Freud helped Lawrence to see and to accept Jessie's point of view. Her insight about Lawrence's crippling relationship with his mother was confirmed by the novel that ruined her life. Though Jessie had no contact with Lawrence after 1913, her pain was still fresh in 1935, and her memoir conveys a deep sense of irreparable loss.

III

Middleton Murry was Lawrence's friend and his enemy.[7] He frequently disappointed and eventually betrayed Lawrence during his lifetime and tried to deny his achievement after his death. Though Murry had many faults, he was also an attractive, sensitive, intelligent, talented, ambitious and stimulating man. Lawrence, who was poor and struggling to establish his reputation when he first met Murry in 1913, was glad to have his encouragement. Murry assumed his characteristic role as editor and midwife to the works of Lawrence and of Murry's wife, Katherine Mansfield. They planned to share certain aspects of their lives and to found a magazine that would express their plans for the regeneration of society. But the *Signature* collapsed after only three issues in 1915, and Lawrence withdrew almost immediately from Murry's *Athenaeum* in 1919 and *Adelphi* in 1923.

Though Lawrence was a difficult ally, he achieved a moment of communion with Murry when he nursed him back to health in February 1915 and recorded this incident in the scene where Lilly rubs down Aaron in *Aaron's Rod*. But the attempts of the Lawrences and Murrys to live together—in the autumn of 1914 in Buckinghamshire and the spring of 1916 in Cornwall—both ended in bitter failure. For Lawrence's struggle to escape from his conflicts with Frieda and his belief that male love between himself and Murry could point the way to a more meaningful form of marriage between man and woman led to intolerable demands on Murry, threatened his relations with Katherine, frightened him and forced him to flee from Lawrence's domination. The inevitable break came when Lawrence, who felt Murry was sapping his emotional energy, burst out: "I hate your love, I *hate it*. You're an obscene bug, sucking my life away"[8]—an insult that combined his favorite image of corruption with the suggestion of perversion.

Murry was the most serious threat to Lawrence's marriage, both in 1916 when Lawrence was attracted to him and in 1923 when Frieda was. Though Murry rejected Lawrence, he gratified his morbid compulsion to sleep with Frieda after Katherine's death in 1923 and after Lawrence's in 1930. As the object of Lawrence's love and the lover of Frieda, Murry was in a privileged position to speak about the intimate details of Lawrence's sexual life and to hint that Lawrence's disease made him impotent during his final years. Though Murry felt no inhibitions about making severe judgments on Lawrence's incapacity, his biographer reports that Murry himself was extremely inept as a lover: "There were no caresses, no preliminaries; his love-making (such as it was) was a climax without a crescendo."[9]

Lawrence, who had a complex love-hate relationship with Murry and was fond of diagnosing his weaknesses, advised: "Spunk is what one wants, not introspective sentiment. The last is your vice. You rot your own manhood at the roots, with it."[10] After their final break in 1926, Lawrence condemned the cowardice and self-pity that had caused Katherine Mansfield so much anguish and warned Murry's sometime mistress, Dorothy Brett, about the "mud-worm": "Don't be Murryish, pitying yourself and caving in. It's despicable ... I do loathe cowardice and sloppy emotions. My God, did you learn *nothing* from Murry, of how NOT to behave?"[11] Murry was intensely jealous of Lawrence, who was everything Murry was not; manly, sensual, independent, confident, courageous, creative, indifferent to money and to fame.

Murry accurately characterized himself as "Part snob, part coward, part sentimentalist."[12] He was a kind of rancid Rousseau: his thought was equivocal and confused; he had an endless capacity for self-deception; he disguised his total egocentricity behind his mock-saintliness and was always eager to display his stigmata before the public. Murry was disingenuous enough to believe that he could dispose of his defects by acknowledging them. But Katherine, who saw through his pose, once wrote: "His very frankness is a falsity. In fact it seems falser than his insincerity."[13] Aldous Huxley, who was Murry's editorial assistant on the *Athenaeum* and satirized him as Burlap in *Point Counter Point* (1928), characterized his writings as "a more than usually painful series of those always painfully personal articles which were the secret of his success as a journalist."[14] Huxley captured the essence of Murry's sanctimonious praise and vicious condemnation of Lawrence when he called *Son of Woman* "a curious essay in destructive hagiography."[15]

Murry, eager to capitalize on disaster, was first off the mark with a memoir of Lawrence. *Son of Woman* (April 1931) attempts to reveal the faults of Lawrence's personality and of his art. Murry, who could not separate the artist from the work and was completely untrustworthy when personally involved with the subject, criticizes Lawrence on a personal level and tries to explain his psychology in order to assuage his own guilt about the failure of their friendship. Like Jessie, Murry was deeply hurt by Lawrence, but instead of honestly admitting his own pain and explaining their relationship, he attacks Lawrence for rejecting and wounding him.

The title of *Son of Woman* suggests that Lawrence's weakness came from his crippling relationship with his mother and that she turned him into a tortured and "sex-crucified" Son of Man. His book—a mixture of memoir, biography and literary criticism—is a labored and repetitive oedipal interpretation of Lawrence's life that treats all his novels as if they were factual autobiography. Murry's view is an extreme and rather tasteless version of what Lawrence had admitted to Jessie just after his mother's death.

> "You know—I've always loved mother," he said in a strangled voice.
> "I know your have," I replied.
> "I don't mean that," he returned quickly. "I've *loved* her, like a lover. That's why I could never love you."[16]

Murry does not believe that the death of Lawrence's mother and the meeting with Frieda freed him from emotional constraints and led him to sexual fulfillment: "His love had been taken by his mother and not even her death could restore it for him to give his wife." Lawrence, who had been damned during his lifetime as a prophet of sexual license, is now condemned by Murry as a sex-crucified homosexual. But Murry does not explain whether he believes Lawrence's marriage failed because of his latent homosexuality or whether he turned to homosexuality because his marriage failed. The most offensive aspect of Murry's book is not the falsity of his argument, but his own eagerness to reveal the intimate details of Lawrence's—and Frieda's—sexual life.

Murry is much more perceptive when he discusses sexuality in Lawrence's books than in his life. His most valuable point is that Lawrence's homosexual feelings are expressed in the escape from woman to man and in the quest for male love in novels like *The White Peacock, Women in Love, Aaron's Rod* and

The Plumed Serpent. He states that when Lilly is nursing Aaron and the women are far away, "the underlying tension of hostility which is always felt when Lawrence is describing a woman and a man together peacefully dissolves. . . . Lilly wants a homosexual relation with Aaron to complete his incomplete heterosexual relation with Tanny. This he calls 'extending' marriage. Other people might find another name for it." (The high-minded innuendo is typical of Murry's tone and method.)

Murry also emphasizes that most of Lawrence's characters—Morel, Birkin, Sisson, Somers and Mellors—are self-portraits and that Anna, Ursula, Tanny, Harriet, Kate and Connie are modeled on Frieda. He convincingly argues that Lawrence's novels present a struggle between power and love and attempt to reconcile the sexual and spiritual elements in man, that Connie's submission to Mellors is a fictional compensation for what Lawrence could never achieve in real life. But Murry's insights are weakened by a misguided evaluation of Lawrence's works. Murry, a model for Gerald Crich, condemns *Women in Love* as false and self-deceiving, *St. Mawr* as futile and incoherent; he finds *Aaron's Rod* Lawrence's greatest novel and *Fantasia of the Unconscious* his greatest book. Murry's admission that *Aaron's Rod* and *Fantasia* were the only works that he understood did not prevent him from writing two books about Lawrence.

In his Preface to *Son of Woman* Murry confesses that it is necessary to use "the language of judgment and condemnation" and admits that his judgment of Lawrence is also a judgment of himself. He combines a piteous *persona* and squeamish confessions of his own inadequacy ("my heart is wrung with anguish") with a meaningless pseudo-mystic style, and writes of the death of Lawrence's mother: "The bond which united him to the universe was suddenly snapped; he was cast out of life, derelict on the naked shore of the great sea wherein before he had moved and had his being."

Murry admits that his personal relations with Lawrence were "a miserable and tragic failure" because he lacked understanding of Lawrence's character and beliefs. He quotes Lawrence's prescient warning: "Do not betray me," which shows the depth of his commitment to Murry, and claims it never "ceased to echo in my soul." Yet these words made no impression on Murry when he condescendingly condemned Lawrence to the realm of psychopathology. According to Murry, Lawrence was a "greatly gifted, greatly tortured" man whose love inevitably turned into a "seething and bitter hatred of women." He was born to be a saint, had no business with sex at all and should have "become a eunuch for the sake of the Kingdom of Heaven."

Murry not only blames Lawrence, but also pities and reviles him. Sex was a torment for Lawrence, "a reminder of his own insufficiency and weakness and lack of courage." He suffered from persecution-mania, had less than normal sexual vitality, was incapable of loving a woman. He tried to escape into the realm of mindless sensuality yet could not reach the "goal of true sexual fulfilment." He was radically conscious of his failure as a male, for it was "not easy for a man incapable of begetting children to convince a woman of his perfect manhood." His real wish was to satisfy "his sense of doom and death and corruption." It is characteristic of Murry (who had four offspring with two wives) to ignore the likely possibility that Lawrence did not want children and to confuse sterility and impotence.

Murry's contemporary stature as critic, editor and intimate friend provided a spurious endorsement to his perverse interpretation. T. S. Eliot, who shared Murry's hostility to Lawrence (which he expressed three years later in *After Strange Gods*), gave his *imprimatur* to Murry's methods and conclusions in an influential review: "Mr. Murry has written a brilliant book. It seems to me the best piece of sustained writing that Mr. Murry has done. At any rate, I think I understand it better than most of his recent writings. It is a definitive work of critical biography or biographical criticism.... The victim and the sacrificial knife are perfectly adapted to each other.... [But] I cannot help wondering whether Mr. Murry was not compelled to write this book in order to expel the demon from himself."[17] Like all Eliot's criticism, this hesitant review is freighted with qualifications. His belief that it is Murry's best book and ("at any rate") less obscure than his recent work is faint praise indeed. And the uncertainty of Murry's approach and his malicious attitude toward the "victim" seem to undermine the book's authority. Eliot's recognition that *Son of Woman* was exorcism rather than criticism was best understood by Frieda, who burnt the memoir and sent the ashes to Murry. Though Murry frequently insists that he was Lawrence's friend, he stands condemned by his own book. He was motivated by jealousy of Lawrence's achievement, by guilt about his own betrayal, by a desire to revenge himself for Lawrence's scorn and rejection, and by a wish to profit by his death.

Catherine Carswell, born (like Mabel and Frieda) in 1879, reviewed *The White Peacock* in the *Glasgow Herald* in 1911 and met Lawrence three years later. Though she had "a special kind of love and admiration" for Lawrence, she did not make emotional demands on him or arouse Frieda's jealousy, as did Ada, Mabel and Brett. (She was, however, jealous of Enid Hilton, who helped Lawrence distribute *Lady Chatterley's Lover* and assisted Huxley in preparing the *Letters* for the press; and, when reading the proofs, she could not resist changing Enid's name from Hilton to Hamilton in the last paragraph of Huxley's Introduction—which had to be corrected in later editions.)[18] Carswell's favorable critique of *The Rainbow* led to the loss of her job when the novel was banned in 1915. She planned to collaborate on a novel with Lawrence, and always regretted that her marriage and child did not allow her to follow him to New Mexico. Just after Lawrence's death, on March 14, 1930, she defended him against hostile obituaries in a lively letter to *Time and Tide*:

> He did nothing that he did not really want to do, and all that he most wanted to do he did. He went all over the world, he owned a ranch, he lived in the most beautiful corners of Europe.... He painted and made things, and sang and rode. He wrote something like three dozen books, of which even the worst page dances with life that could be mistaken for no other man's, while the best are admitted, even by those who hate him, to be unsurpassed. [He was] without vices, with most human virtues, the husband of one wife, scrupulously honest.

The brilliant title of Carswell's *The Savage Pilgrimage* (published by Chatto in June 1932), came from a phrase in one of Lawrence's letters. The book draws upon the memoirs by Murry, Ada and Mabel as well as the "Reminiscences" by Murry that appeared in the *Adelphi* between June 1930 and March 1931 (and came out as a book in January 1933). Though the early chapters of her memoir were first published in the *Adelphi* between November 1931 and March 1932, her book became a devastatingly accurate attack on Murry's sincerity and veracity, his supposed friendship with Lawrence and his ability to judge his work.

Carswell exposes Murry's ill-concealed antagonism, his ruthless and tasteless attempt to annihilate Lawrence under the pretense of "intellectual sincerity," and his hypocritical assurance that "this hurts me more than it hurts you." The clear motive behind his venomous, treacherous book is to justify himself and discredit Lawrence. His style is vitiated by vague banalities, he muddles the chronology of *Women in Love* completed in 1916 but first published in England in 1921) and "announced—with what unmistakable relish!—the end of Lawrence, just as Lawrence was engaged upon the books which Murry was later to announce as his finest." Though Murry speaks at length of Lawrence's greatness (like most critics, he allowed Lawrence's genius but hated its manifestations), "he has neither permitted to his great man any of the qualities of greatness, nor has he himself been modified by contact" with Lawrence.

According to Carswell, Murry had an unusual capacity for arousing sympathetic feelings, and Lawrence at first felt closer to him than any other friend. But Murry betrayed their friendship, and Lawrence soon learned not to trust him. She gives a more positive view than Murry of Lawrence's belief in the need to renew "the sacredness between man and man" and rejects Murry's base suggestion that Lawrence was impotent. She hints that Lawrence was aware of Murry's affair with Frieda in 1923, and was probably aware of it herself, for she declares: "In Lawrence's marriage there was no place for any kind of lieutenancy." The chumminess of Murry and Frieda, when Lawrence first saw them together at the railroad station, "was enough to turn him greenish pale all over."

The dramatic peak of Carswell's book is a detailed account of the "Last Supper" in the Café Royal that year, when Murry bestowed the Judas kiss on Lawrence and admitted: "I *have* betrayed you, old chap, I confess it. In the past I *have* betrayed you. But never again. I call you to witness, never again"—and when Lawrence collapsed in a drunken stupor and had to be carried home. She is especially savage about Murry's premature offer to provide deathbed comfort in 1929. Murry objected to Carswell's strictures; after a thousand copies of her book were sold, his threatened lawsuit persuaded her publishers to withdraw the memoir. In December 1932 it was issued by Secker in a revised form.

Carswell's portrait of Lawrence is a powerful contrast and convincing rebuttal to Murry's. She admits that Lawrence and Frieda had many violent rows, but insists that he broke free from his mother's influence and led Frieda, even if he failed to dominate her. Carswell found Lawrence somewhat prudish (she gets a wigging for appearing in a buttoned-up bathrobe), but felt only such a man could have written *Lady Chatterley's Lover*. She warmly describes him as "a man who lived from a pure source and steadfastly refused to break faith with that source"; as a disciplined and impassioned artist, a wise and gentle man, who struggled bravely against poverty, neglect, obloquy and disease. Though Carswell spent a relatively short period of time with Lawrence and did not always write from first-hand experience, her distance from him provided a certain objectivity that was conspicuously absent from the memoirs of Jessie, Murry and Mabel. Carswell's memoir, which provides a poignant account of Lawrence's last illness, is the most balanced, sympathetic and intelligent book about him.

Aldous Huxley first met Lawrence in the Garsington circle in 1915. After a lapse of ten years. Lawrence wrote to praise his travel book, *Along the Road*, and they were often together during the last five years of Lawrence's life. Carswell writes that Lawrence was glad and grateful to find a highly intelligent fellow-writer "to whom he could talk and a heart on which he could rely. For the time that remained Huxley was simply and charmingly devoted to him, and proved dependable to the last." Huxley, who portrayed Lawrence as Rampion in *Point Counter Point* and Frieda as Katy in *The Genius and the Goddess*, quite simply said: "He is one of the few people I feel real respect and admiration for."

Huxley's Introduction to his extensive edition of Lawrence's *Letters* (September 1932), which present a sustained narrative of his life and are themselves a definitive refutation of Murry, is probably the best essay ever written on Lawrence. He firmly supports Carswell against Murry's denigrations and argues that *Son of Woman*, "for all its metaphysical subtleties and its Freudian ingenuities," is largely irrelevant because it ignores the fact that its "victim" is an artist and that his biography does not account for his achievement. He then attempts to answer two vital questions: what sort of gifts did Lawrence have and how did they affect his response to experience?

Lawrence's special gift, Huxley believes, "was an extraordinary sensitiveness to what Wordsworth called 'unknown modes of being.'" Lawrence, who had the ability to establish an intimate relationship with almost anyone he met, advocated spontaneous living rather than fixed principles. He was a clever man as well as a genius and was able to absorb himself completely in the experiences of ordinary life: "He could cook, he could sew, he could darn a stocking and milk a cow, he was an efficient wood-cutter and a good hand at embroidery, fires always burned when he had laid them and a floor, after Lawrence had scrubbed it, was thoroughly clean." (It is worth comparing the sharpness of Huxley's mind and prose, with Murry's flabby thought and style.)

Like Carswell, Huxley is also sensitive about the effect of Lawrence's illness on his life and work. The resurrection theme, which dominated the last phase of Lawrence's thought and art, was closely connected to his brave struggle against disease, for his life "was one continuous convalescence; it was as though he were newly re-born from a mortal illness every day of his life.... For the last two years he was like a flame burning on in miraculous disregard of the fact that there was no more fuel to justify its existence." In a personal letter of October 1932, Huxley describes Lawrence's physical dependence on his wife and her mysterious power to being him back to life: "I have seen him on two occasions rise from what I thought was his deathbed, when Frieda, who had been away, came back after a short absence."[19] Huxley's Introduction presents Lawrence as a sane rather than a tortured being, as an artist whose disease intensified rather than diminished his life.

Murry flung himself back into the controversy in January 1933 with his four-part *Reminiscences of D. H. Lawrence*. The book was hastily patched together and included a defensive preface on his relations with Lawrence, the "Reminiscences" reprinted from the *Adelphi* of 1930–1931, retaliatory notes on Carswell's condemnations and all the criticism he had published on Lawrence during his lifetime. Though Murry's intention was to enable readers to "form their own judgment of the truth, and of Mrs. Carswell's methods," his book actually substantiated her attack.

Murry's prefatory remarks were not likely to win sympathy, despite his characteristic strategy of cringing self-abasement. He confesses that he wronged Lawrence, he failed him, he did not understand him or his books; that their relation was, from the first, profoundly false; that he *was* "sucking the life out of him"—though the vindictiveness of Lawrence's words nearly made him physically sick. His self-declared mission was to be "the destroyer of Lawrence," but he dared not undertake this "act of self-liberation" until his friend was safely dead.

This confession continues in the "Reminiscences" where Murry admits that he promised Lawrence he would follow him to Lerici in 1913, to Taos in 1923 and to Spotorno in 1925—and that he never went to any of these places. He attacked *The Lost Girl* under the heading "The Decay of D. H. Lawrence" ("Lawrence would have us back to the slime from which we rose"). He attacked *Women in Love,* which elicited his "repulsion and weariness," yet denies (as Carswell rightly suggested) that he was motivated by malice and ignorance. He claims it was merely an "irony of fate" that his criticism appeared "precisely the year (1921) when he was writing what I regard as the two finest of his later books." It is scarcely surprising that their final break came, after many earlier quarrels, in 1926.

Murry fares no better in his direct disputation with Carswell. He attempts to demean her portrayal of the "kind, eloquent and wise" Lawrence as "a creation of feminine fantasy" and piety, and tries to replace Huxley's portrait of an artist "always intensely aware of the mystery of the world" with a "living dead man, leading a posthumous life." He maintains that Lawrence was possessive and dominating, yet insists (with childish pettiness) that "Lawrence meant much more to me than he ever did" to Carswell. He quotes Lawrence's letter from Mexico in 1923—"I wish you'd look after [Frieda] a bit: would it be a nuisance? She will be alone. I ought to come—but I can't"—as if to justify his version of his seven last words at the "Last Supper": "I won't promise not to betray you." It seems significant that Murry calls her Frieda at the beginning of the book and then shifts to the more formal Mrs. Lawrence after his betrayal. Lawrence's three satiric stories—"The Border Line," "Jimmy and the Desperate Woman" and "The Last Laugh"—concern his jealousy and posthumous revenge for Murry's affair with Frieda.

The reprinted reviews do nothing to support Murry's incredible claim: "I was the only English critic who took Lawrence with the impassioned seriousness that he deserved." For his criticism is overwhelmingly negative. *The Plumed Serpent* shows that Lawrence "has lost faith in his own imagination"; the *Poems* contain "a hard, bleak quality of dogmatic asseveration"; *Lady Chatterley's Lover* is "a deeply depressing book."

The crude disparity between Murry's protestations of friendship and the abundant evidence of his own persistent treachery reveals his profound confusion about Lawrence and his astonishing capacity for critical aberration. Yet the startling contrast between the affectionate anonymous obituary that Murry wrote for *TLS* on March 13, 1930, the guilt-ridden breast-beating of the *Reminiscences* which began to appear in June 1930 and the violent hostility of *Son of Woman* which came out in April 1931, is even stranger and more difficult to understand.

Though there is no firm evidence to explain the sudden changes in Murry's view of Lawrence, his attitude toward the *Adelphi* and toward Frieda are the key to his bizarre behavior. One of Carswell's main charges against Murry was that he did not, as he claimed, found the *Adelphi* in June 1923 as a platform for Lawrence's views and that he did not intend to hand over the magazine to him as soon as Lawrence agreed to become editor. In "Lawrence and Jesus" (August 1923), Murry boldly declared that Lawrence "is become, since Katherine Mansfield's death [in January 1923], incomparably the most important writer of his generation." But when Lawrence rejected the magazine that was, as its banner boasted, "run for and by a belief in Life," the *Adelphi* became devoted to establishing the posthumous reputation of Katherine. His apparently authoritative account of Katherine's career was based on lies, distortions, evasions and contradictions. He prefixed Katherine's photograph to the first number of the *Adelphi* (which sold 15,000 copies) and published works by and about her in virtually every issue from June 1923 to December 1924. As high priest of Katherine's cult, he glorified his own role, image and importance, exploited her tragic death and created a sentimental image of his wife that led to the Mansfield myth.[20] Murry, who was Katherine's heir, had received a £1000 check for her royalties and was living on the £500 a year that her books brought in, saw Lawrence and Katherine as literary rivals. When Lawrence died, Murry felt his first loyalty was to Katherine and probably calculated that it would be more profitable if he continued to use the *Adelphi* to enhance her reputation.[21]

F. A. Lea reports, without a trace of irony, that after Lawrence's death in March 1930 Murry sought out Frieda. He "sped to the South of France to pay his last respects to Lawrence. There, however, he met Frieda: and this time, there was no holding back. 'With her, and with her for the first time in my life, I knew what fulfilment in love really meant.'"[22] It seems clear that Murry was infatuated with Frieda when he proclaimed in the *TLS* obituary that appeared on March 13: "Lawrence was the most remarkable and most lovable man I have ever known. Contact with him was immediate, intimate, and rich. A radiance of warm life streamed from him. When he was gay, and he was often gay—my dominant memory of him is a blithe and joyful man—he seemed to spread a sensuous enchantment about him." There is absolutely no sign in this passage of the "living dead man" who appears earlier in Murry's book.

It also seems likely that the guilty "Reminiscences," which Murry began to write in the spring of 1930, express the remorse he inevitably experienced when he returned to his second wife, Violet LeMaistre, who was also dying of tuberculosis, after paying his "last respects" to Lawrence in Frieda's bed. Finally, it appears that the denigration in *Son of Woman* not only attempts to exorcise Lawrence and justify himself, but also reflects his extreme hostility to Frieda, who rejected Murry (as Lawrence had done) and chose to live with her former Italian landlord, Angelo Ravagli. Murry's volatile controversy with Carswell and Huxley reveals that his intensely personal attack on Lawrence's character and ideas in *Son of Woman* was prompted by his emotional involvement with Frieda as well as with Lawrence. The most influential memoir was also the least trustworthy, for Murry's contradictory writings were not based on critical principles but on emotion.

IV

Mabel Luhan, six years older than Lawrence, was the antithesis of the poor, provincial, puritanical Ada and Jessie. She was rich, sophisticated, hedonistic, sexually rapacious; she had four husbands, including Tony Luhan, the silent and rock-like cigar-store Indian. Two months after arriving in Taos, Lawrence described the contradictions in Mabel's character with deadly accuracy:

> She has lived much in Europe—Paris, Nice, Florence—is a little famous in New York and little loved, very intelligent as a woman, another "culture-carrier," likes to play the patroness, hates the white world and loves the Indian out of hate, is very "generous," wants to be "good" and is very wicked, has a terrible will-to-power, you know—she wants to be a witch and at the same time a Mary of Bethany at Jesus' feet—a big, white crow, a cooing raven of ill-omen.[23]

Throughout his life Lawrence was threatened by possessive women: his mother, Ada, Jessie, Alice Dax, Frieda, Ottoline Morrell and Dorothy Brett. From his experience with them he learned to see relations with women as an endless struggle of clashing wills in which man either maintains a precarious dominance or is overcome by humiliating defeat. Mabel was, therefore, precisely the sort of woman he disliked, satirized, wanted to avoid—and never could. By her own account, she was arrogant, vain, selfish, domineering, willful, manipulative, petty, parasitic, jealous and malicious. She was possessive about the Taos Indians; had an irritating mystical streak (a weakness for Gurdjieff and Jung); led a boring, empty, meaningless life; was often overcome by a dreadful sense of futility. The active and amusing Lawrence made life seem worthwhile, and she confesses: "I tried to seduce his spirit so that I could make it work for me instead of doing the work for myself." Mabel constantly provoked Lawrence and made him feel, as H. G. Wells felt about his mistress Elizabeth Russell: "when you've had her for a week you want to bash her head through the wall."[24]

Yet with all her faults, and there were many, Mabel did discover Taos, take a serious interest in the cultural life of the sun-worshipping Indians, recognize the importance of artists like Robinson Jeffers (to whom her book is addressed, as if she were explaining Lawrence to a sympathetic spirit), and Edward Weston (who provided brilliantly vivid photographs of Lawrence, Tony and Mabel for her book). Most important, after reading *Sea and Sardinia* and some poems later collected in *Birds, Beasts and Flowers*, she realized that Lawrence was "the only one who can really *see* this Taos country and the Indians, and who can describe it so that it is as much alive between the covers of a book as it is in reality." She wrote to Lawrence about the people, the town and the clear air of the Sangre de Cristo mountains, offered to lend him an adobe house, sent Frieda a necklace that "carried some Indian magic in it" and attracted them to Taos. She was primarily responsible for what Lawrence called "the greatest experience from the outside world that I have ever had"[25] and for all that ensued from Taos: "Mountain Lion," "Eagle in New Mexico," "The

Princess," "The Woman Who Rode Away," *Mornings in Mexico, The Plumed Serpent* and *St. Mawr* (in which Mabel is the model for Mrs. Witt).

In his first cautious response to her letter, Lawrence asked some practical questions and inquired if there was the same sort of "colony of rather dreadful sub-arty people" that had driven him from Capri. He said he wanted to connect himself with "the last dark strand from the previous, pre-white era" and liked the sound of Taos, which reminded him of Taormina. He also excited the interest of Mabel, who had been psychoanalyzed by Freud's pupil and American translator, A. A. Brill, by mentioning that he had just completed a book called *Fantasia of the Unconscious*. When she pursued the subject, Lawrence exclaimed: "You want to send Brill to hell and all the analytic therapeutic lot." Mabel's ultimate riposte to this outburst, based on her superior insight as an analysand, was the perverse judgment: "Lawrence died because he was what is called a neurotic and because he scorned to learn the mundane mastery that may insure a long, smooth life if the living impulse is emasculated and overcome."

Everyone, including Mabel, is portrayed negatively in her spiteful *Lorenzo in Taos* (February 1932). Lawrence criticizes her way of life, friends, egoism, idleness, dress—even her bread-making. ("'Better luck next time,' he said, kindly, and threw his piece into the fire.") He especially dislikes her "evil, destructive, dominating will." She claims that Lawrence quarrels with all his friends and is totally dependent on Frieda, the root of his existence: "he was keyed to her so that he felt things through her and was obliged to receive life through her, vicariously." He worries about Frieda's moods, jealousy, anger, and meekly submits to her commands; yet he also beats her and repudiates her as "the enemy of life—his life—the hateful, destroying female."

Frieda is caustically described as a "reposeful hurricane" with a mouth "like a gunman." She has a foolish grin and is painfully obtuse, yet exaggerates her influence on his art: "He has to get it all from me. Nobody knows that. Why, I have done pages of his books for him." She exercises complete control over Lawrence and *"never* lets him forget her."

Mabel also attacks her other great rival, Dorothy Brett, who came to New Mexico as a kind of buffer between Frieda and Lawrence. "She was an amusing and attractive grotesque, and her eyes were both hostile and questioning as she came slowly up to me, examining me, curious, arrogant, and English." She has a paranoic glare, "sat in the doorway of life with her mouth slightly open, like a paralyzed rabbit" and enviously spies on Lawrence. The deaf Brett offers to trim Mabel's hair, but slashes away and cuts off the end of her ear! The two Danish artists, Knud Merrild and Kai Gotzsche, are briefly dismissed as "simple unremarkable characters."

Surrounded by these harpies and dullards, Lawrence naturally turns to Mabel for comfort and understanding: "From the first, Lawrence and I knew each other through and through as though we were of one blood. In fact, he told me many times . . . that I seemed like a sister"—a dubious compliment. "We communicated silently," says Mabel. "He knew me through the pores of his skin." Despite this soul-merging and secret sympathy, there is something terribly wrong in their relations. On his visits to Taos from 1922 through 1925, Lawrence senses antagonism, menace and destruction in the air and becomes violently angry with Mabel. In less than two months he flees from "Mabeltown" to the ranches, seventeen miles above Taos, to find peace and get on with his work. After their first quarrel, Mabel assumes a chastened mien and becomes "like Mary before our Lord."[26] But her submission soon fades away, and she gets irritated when Lawrence pays more attention to Frieda and Brett than to herself. Mabel swears the quarrel is not her fault and blames Frieda for the rupture. In 1924 she generously gives Frieda the Kiowa ranch, because Lawrence would not accept it, and receives the manuscript of *Sons and Lovers* in return. Despite their conflict, Lawrence took Mabel seriously, admired her energy, tried to collaborate on a novel with her, remained a loyal friend—from a distance.

Mabel's memoir is extremely subjective and unreliable. But when she transcends her self-absorption, she has an undeniable liveliness that captures the essence of Lawrence's and Frieda's characters. Her description of their first hundred-mile car trip to Taos, when Lawrence and Tony Luhan are frustrated by the breakdown of the engine, and the sharp exchange between the Lawrences, are closely observed and convincing:

> "Take that dirty cigarette out of your mouth! And stop sticking out that fat belly of yours!"
> "You'd better stop that talk or I'll tell about *your* things"

—Frieda replied, threatening to expose some horrible intimacies that only a wife could reveal. The psychological interest of Mabel's book is generated by the tension between her condemnation of Lawrence and her pathetic desire to possess him, between her persistent claim to an intuitive "flow" and her admission that he twice fled from her revolting egoism.

Knud Merrild and Kai Gotzsche were adventurous Danish painters who drove across America in a rattletrap car, met Lawrence in Taos and spent the winter of 1922–23 as his guests on the Del Monte ranch. These modest and unpretentious men were honored by their friendship with Lawrence, respectful of Frieda and (after being snubbed by Mabel) delighted that Lawrence preferred their company to hers. They were a strong contrast to Witter Bynner and Willard Johnson, the arty homosexuals with whom Lawrence later travelled in Mexico and portrayed as Owen and Bud in the first chapter of *The Plumed Serpent*. Though Merrild was then 28 years old and Gotzsche 36 (only a year younger than Lawrence) they seemed very boyish and developed a filial relationship with the Lawrences. Frieda, who took motherly care of them and made sure they had enough to eat, inspired their profound affection. Lawrence, who also felt responsible for their welfare and commissioned them to do several dust jackets for his books, constantly played the benefactor and schoolmaster. He taught them riding, cooking and Spanish, commented on their music and art, judged their behavior and endlessly expounded his ideas. (Merrild supplements his account of Lawrence's conversations with many long quotes from his books, though he had not read any of them when he first met Lorenzo.)

In *A Poet and Two Painters* (June 1938), Merrild explains that when Lawrence became disgusted with the hateful Mabel—who bullied him into writing a book with her and surrounded herself with phony people and performing Indians—she lent him her Lobo ranch in the mountains. But after Lawrence asked the Danes to accompany him, she restricted him to only one cabin so there should not be room for all of them and forced him to rent two neighboring cabins from William Hawk on the Del Monte ranch.

Though Lawrence was clearly fond of the Danes, he also needed them to share the heavy work of the ranch and to act as a buffer between himself and Frieda during the long isolation of winter. The Danes made the strenuous horseback ride to Taos whenever necessary, brought back gossip from town, provided company and conversation, and owned a car that (weather permitting) would take Lawrence wherever he wished to go. (On one trip they were forced off the narrow road by a Mexican wagon and almost fell over a cliff.) As Merrild writes, with defensive modesty: "We did not possess the brilliance of his mind nor the abundance of his knowledge; we had only horse sense, and knew people and the world by experience. . . . We did not play up to him, and were not afraid of voicing our opinions, whether they were contrary to his or not. We did not hesitate to side with Frieda, either, when we thought him wrong." Their great virtue was loyalty to Lawrence and willingness to help when they were needed.

The Lawrence that emerges from Merrild's book is a dogmatic, critical, cantankerous, irascible yet admirable and impressive man. He forces the sick Merrild to drink horrible nettle tea. He tries to repaint the Danes' canvases, but they rebuff him. His puritan feelings are outraged when a woman innocently spends the night in the Danes' cabin. He becomes infuriated when they shoot a friendly rabbit in his garden, though he later shoots a porcupine. He angers the Danes by cruelly beating his dog, who had come into heat, followed her own dark gods and pursued an airedale lover. And he wants to murder Mabel: "I feel I could kill and that I should enjoy doing it. . . . I will kill Mabel first. . . . I will use a knife! . . . I will cut her throat!" Though Merrild sometimes resents his domination and recognizes his faults, he feels Lawrence "had a superiority that one could not deny and one had to admit that he had both strengthened and released something in one's life for which one could only have the deepest veneration." Despite Lawrence's difficult temperament, the Danes lived more closely with him than anyone else ever did and managed to establish "a unity of manly togetherness, understanding, fidelity."

After his great quarrel with Frieda in 1923, when she returned alone to England, Lawrence met the Danes in Los Angeles and travelled with Gotzsche to Mexico. But he longed for Frieda, feared she might leave him, and seemed to have lost his buoyancy and interest in life. Merrild, who refutes the Mabel-Brett portrait of the shrewish Frieda, believes she was an absolute necessity to him. Huxley's Preface to his book suggests Merrild's strengths and reveals the weaknesses of the more partisan feminine memoirs: "Most of the accounts of Lawrence hitherto published have been by women. In their own way some of these accounts have been quite excellent; but with the exception, remarkably enough, of Frieda Lawrence's, they have conspicuously failed to display this precious quality of disinterestedness. . . . They have tended to adopt a kind of proprietary attitude towards their subject. They write as though they had invented and patented Lawrence."

The proprietary Dorothy Brett, daughter of Viscount Esher and sister of the Ranee of Sarawak, had been deaf since childhood. She was a student at the Slade School of Art with Mark Gertler and Dora Carrington and first met Lawrence through Gertler in 1915. She was the only one of his friends to follow him on his second visit to New Mexico in 1924 and lived there until her death, at the age of 94, in 1977. Lawrence portrayed her in "The Princess" as Dollie Urquhart and in *The Boy in the Bush* as Hilda Blessington, "one of the odd borderline people who don't and *can't,* really belong."[27] Faith Mackenzie described Brett as "the least exacting of [Lawrence's] satellites, the best behaved, perhaps the most unselfishly devoted, and certainly the least critical."[28] When I visited Brett in her rather humble adobe house at the edge of the desert near Taos in 1976, she was lively and sympathetic, and spoke with adoration of Lawrence and Katherine.

In *Lawrence and Brett* (April 1933), she portrays herself as an extremely sensitive, timorous, and vulnerable figure, easily embarrassed by reference to sex, unconventional behavior and violent quarrels. Her deafness seems to intensify her concentration on Lawrence. She tries to attune herself to his moods, is fearful of annoying him and, desperate to gain his approval, always takes his side in the arguments with Frieda. She is also helpful and self-effacing, and does not even mind when Lawrence criticizes and changes her paintings. She writes her rather mawkish book as if she were speaking directly to Lawrence (just as Mabel addresses her book to Jeffers). She provides brief but vivid portraits of Katherine, Murry, Koteliansky, Gertler and Carrington, and more detail than Mabel about the actual events of their daily life in New Mexico: the cleaning, washing, and baking; the painting, writing, and singing; the bathing, fishing, and riding in the mountains.

To Brett, Lawrence is a gentle and sensitive, warm and affectionate man, whom "every woman and most men loved." She feels shy about the "responsibility" of having him all to herself when the others are away for the day, proud when she is able to establish a harmonious understanding with him. She describes Lawrence reminiscing about his days as a schoolteacher ("I never had much trouble. The boys, I think, liked me"), writing under a tree in the woods, exploring the Indian cave about which he wrote in "The Woman Who Rode Away" and putting on rouge in Mexico to disguise his deathly pallor.

The real villain in Brett's book, as in Mabel's, is Frieda. She is usually portrayed as slothfully lying in bed or jealously raging against the long-suffering Lawrence. Brett describes Frieda as changeable, nervy, shrill, unbalanced, cross, rude, truculent, furious and violent; she emphasizes that Frieda is clumsy on horseback, too fat for the seats in the train and sometimes mistaken for Lawrence's mother. Frieda returns Brett's hatred, calls her "an asparagus stick" and a beastly nuisance, objects to her "spinster and curate" connection with Lawrence, sends her away from Oaxaca, banishes her from the ranch (where she spies on the Lawrences with a telescope) and restricts her to three visits a week. Brett retaliates by renting a nearby cabin, ignoring the injunction and coming nearly every day.

Brett regrets that Lawrence's friends cannot protect him from Frieda's exhausting screams and fights, and she mentions that Lawrence finds it humiliating to have to beat his unruly wife. Though Brett does not, like Mabel, hope to replace Frieda in Lawrence's life (she is far too humble—and realistic—to entertain this aspiration), the implicit theme of her book is that the man the Indians call "Red Fox" would be far better off without his cumbersome wife, "Angry Winter."

V

Earl and Achsah Brewster, seven years older than Lawrence, were expatriate American painters with a private income, seriously interested in Buddhism and Pali scriptures. They met Lawrence in Capri in 1921 and invited him to Ceylon the following year. In 1927 Earl took a walking tour with Lawrence through the Etruscan towns and in a shop window in Grosseto saw a toy rooster leaving an egg that suggested the title for "The Escaped Cock." The Brewsters were philosophically inclined, gentle, formal and rather old-fashioned. They liked and admired Lawrence, travelled about with him at the end of his life, but were not emotionally involved with him. Their memoirs had no thesis to prove, argument to fight or vendetta to settle. Lawrence, on his part, was genuinely fond of the Brewsters, respected them (as he did Huxley), wished to live and work with them in harmony, frequently saw them during the last nine years of his life—and satirized their materialism in his fable "Things."

D. H. Lawrence: Reminiscences and Correspondence (February 1934) is divided in two equal parts. The first section contains 113 letters from Lawrence—mainly about Buddhism, painting, his frenetic plans for travel and search for a place to live—interspersed with amiable but not especially perceptive passages by Earl. The last twenty pages contain a complete and consecutive memoir by Achsah, generally more acute than her husband's comments and particularly good on their life in Kandy.

The Brewsters did not find Lawrence to be the agonized soul they expected to meet: "He was more delicate physically, and more compassionate, both gayer and sadder than his writings reveal." In many respects their portrait of Lawrence resembles Huxley's. He was "a puritan with profound religious conviction, a man with reverence for life . . . beyond our mere mental consciousness." He combined spiritual awareness with worldly wisdom, was practical about the details of ordinary existence, open-handed with gifts and money. They contradict the hostile descriptions of Lawrence's marriage by Murry, Mabel and Brett, and believe: "Only a woman as strong and generous as Mrs. Lawrence, with her love for vital experiences and indifference to small things, would have suited Lawrence. He was never happy to be long separated from her."

Lawrence liked to talk to the Brewsters about common friends, memories of the past, mysterious differences between men and women, lack of vitality in modern people. Lawrence said he had not done justice in *Sons and Lovers* to his father's "unquenchable fire and relish for living," and would like to rewrite the novel. He maintained that Jesus never expected to be crucified and "should not have allowed Judas to betray him: and that it was not enough to have said to Satan: 'Get thee behind me.'" He believed that psychic conditions caused physical illness and that the hatred aroused by his books actually struck him in the chest.

He felt he had fought too much and the passive Brewsters had not fought enough. Lawrence, who always wished the seated Buddha would *stand up*, thought the Brewsters saw oriental religion as "some sort of easy ether into which you could float away unrestricted and unresisting." He urged them to get off the high but baneful plane of "Buddha and deep breathing."

Though Lawrence was at first enchanted by the spectacular beauty of Kandy, he soon was horrified by the teeming life, hated the debilitating climate that made him feel his "heart's blood oozing away," became seriously ill and could scarcely drag himself about. He felt his impressions of Ceylon had been distorted by illness, and his six-week visit produced only the poem, "Elephant," about the religious procession in honor of the Prince of Wales. The Brewsters were tolerant of Lawrence's criticism of Buddhism and Ceylon, and their modesty and conspicuous lack of egoism made their account the most objective, though not the most incisive, memoir.

When Lawrence met Frieda in 1912 he felt that she was quite unaware of her husband, Ernest Weekley, and told her that she was "the most wonderful woman in all England." Six weeks later, she took the two girls and their devoted nurse Ida to Ernest's parents in Chiswick and ran off with Lawrence—who had only £11. She had often travelled to Germany to visit her family, and her children thought she had gone there alone. When they asked Ernest, after a few weeks, "where is mama?" he turned pale and left the room. The grandparents said: "Don't disturb your father now, he is worried." As in "The Virgin and the Gipsy," Frieda's name was never mentioned at home and she became a non-person.[29]

Frieda married Lawrence in 1914 and often quarreled bitterly with him. She had various affairs during their marriage, most notably in 1923 with Murry and in 1926 with Lt. Angelo Ravagli, whom she first saw in a smart uniform with gay plumes and blue sash. After Lawrence died she bought Angelo out of the Italian army and lived with him in Taos from 1933 until her death in 1956. Angelo then sold the ranch and Lawrence's paintings and manuscripts and returned to the patient wife he had left twenty-five years earlier.

The title of *Not I, But the Wind* comes from one of Lawrence's poems; the book (which had Frieda's family crest as the frontispiece) was privately printed in Santa Fe in July 1934 and appeared in London the following year. Frieda's version of *Look! We Have Come Through!* contains 90 letters from Lawrence to her mother, her sister and herself (the earliest ones, written to her in Germany, express his great depth of feeling when she was still uncertain about their future and flirting with German officers in Metz) as well as four poems and an essay on Keats' "Ode to a Nightingale." Though sketchy and disconnected, her memoir is both lyrical and commonsensical. It portrays the excitement and intensity of their marriage, avoids the more unpleasant aspects of their life, and it is more generous and warm-hearted than the bitter recollections of Jessie, Murry, Mabel and Brett.

Frieda's main theme is that "it was a long fight for Lawrence and me to get at some truth between us," to achieve the balanced human relationship that he prescribed in his novels; "it was a hard life with him, but a wonderful one," for he made her feel new and free. Lawrence, who believed he had to have a strong woman behind him, praised her genius for living and said: "You make me sure of myself, whole"—complete as a man and as an artist. Though Frieda fought for her personal freedom, she acknowledged Lawrence's creative genius and willingly took a subsidiary role to advance his artistic career. She thought "the greatest pleasure and satisfaction for a woman is to live with a creative man, when he goes ahead and fights." Lawrence's struggle for truth in his marriage was closely connected to his creative life.

She admits that they also fought each other openly and honestly, especially when she was torn by loyalty to her husband and to her abandoned children.

Lawrence was so jealous of her children, even when they were grown up, that he denied Frieda really loved them and once flung a glass of wine in her face to prove the point. (When Frieda's daughter asked Lawrence if he cared for her mother, he replied: "It's indecent to ask; haven't I just helped her with her rotten painting?") Despite these outbursts, Frieda maintains that Lawrence was essentially a tender and generous man. She rejects the claims of Murry that he was a brutal and ridiculous figure, and the contention of Brett and Mabel that he might have loved them and did not really care for her. "Try it then yourself," she challenged, "living with a genius, see what it is like and how easy it is, take him if you can." She detests Brett for her slavish adoration of Lawrence and good-humoredly offers to give Brett half a crown if she would contradict him (she never did). They had a ferocious quarrel in 1929 when Brett took it upon herself to sell the manuscripts that Lawrence had left at the ranch and Frieda exclaimed: "Do you not know how *dishonest* that was without telling Lawrence—criminal, you know, did nobody ever teach you honesty?"[30]

Frieda explains that Lawrence trusted his life completely to her and that she knew he would die before his time. In 1925, after his near-fatal hemorrhage in Mexico, when Lawrence was given only a year to live, she realized that all her strength and love would not be enough to make him well again—though she did help to keep him alive for another five years. Lawrence, who had always refused to face the gravity of his disease, understood how close he had been to death and told Frieda: "If I die, nothing has mattered but you, nothing at all."

When Frieda remembers how "nobody wanted Lawrence's amazing genius, how he was jeered at, suppressed, turned into nothing, patronized at best, the stupidity of our civilization comes home to me. How necessary he was! How badly needed!" The vital, responsive and independent Lawrence of her memoirs reappears in her Foreword to *The First Lady Chatterley* (1944): "He died unbroken; he never lost his own wonder of life. He never did a thing he did not want to do and nothing and nobody could make him. He never wrote a word he did not mean at the time he wrote it. He never compromised with the little powers that be; if ever there lived a free, proud man, Lawrence was that man."

Frieda's memoir triumphs over the destructive attacks on Lawrence and herself. It reveals that his art was stimulated by her love and that he was vitally dependent on her. Frieda believed in his genius, was intensely responsive to his work, helped him imagine fictional scenes, tested his ideas, was sympathetic yet critical about his books and inspired the heroines of almost all his novels from *The Rainbow* to *Lady Chatterley's Lover*. Frieda, most intimately involved with Lawrence, was also more honest and objective than most of his friends. She expresses no grief or regret at the end of her book and accepts his death as she had rejoiced in his life: "So proud, manly and splendid he looked, a new face there was. All suffering had been wiped from it, it was as if I had never seen him or known him in all the completeness of his being. . . . There had been the change, he belonged somewhere else now, to all the elements. . . . Lawrence, my Lorenzo who had loved me and I him. He was dead."

The eleven memoirs provided a kind of literary bazaar where contemporary readers could choose their own image of the ghoulish or gifted Lawrence. For the authors portrayed Lawrence in relation to themselves and could rarely see him objectively. This explains why a great flood of books was needed to capture his multifarious genius and why Edward Nehls' elaborate *Composite Biography* succeeds in presenting the living artist while the scholarly biographies do not. The memoirs had immense contemporary and historical significance. They replaced the writer with the man; revealed a more lively, human, compassionate and suffering character; laid the foundations of his biography; and set the combative tone of Lawrence criticism that has prevailed until today. But Murry's perverse books—which came out first, stirred the greatest controversy and were admired by the critics—reinforced the hostile obituaries, prevailed against the more sympathetic memoirs and eclipsed Lawrence's reputation until the phoenix rose from the flames in the mid-1950s.

11

Wyndham Lewis and T. S. Eliot: A Friendship

I

An impressive concentration of subtle minds took place when Wyndham Lewis first met T. S. Eliot, who became a lifelong friend, in Ezra Pound's little triangular sitting room at 6 Holland Park Chambers in Kensington, early in 1915. Eliot had made the acquaintance of Pound only a few days before, when Pound had proudly shown him Lewis' *Timon of Athens* drawings. The tall sibylline figure, "his features of clerical cut," greeted Lewis, the first artist he had ever encountered, with his characteristically prim manner and fastidious speech. The bombastic Pound, disappointed by the studied reserve of Eliot, who was less confident than his new friends, adopted his hillbilly dialect (perhaps to amuse Lewis and soften Eliot, for all three men had spent their childhood in America) and intimated to Lewis: "Yor ole uncle Ezz is wise to wot youse thinkin. Waaal Wynd damn I'se telling *yew*, he's a lot better'n he looks!"

Lewis, a vital and versatile painter, novelist, critic, poet, philosopher, traveller and editor of *Blast,* had founded the Vorticist movement and was completing his first novel, *Tarr*. Eliot soon discovered that Lewis was a brilliantly amusing talker with a powerful critical intelligence and an astonishing visual imagination. In his 1918 review of *Tarr* in the *Egoist,* he called Lewis, in a phrase that has become famous: "The most fascinating personality of our time.... In the work of Mr. Lewis we recognize the thought of the modern and the energy of the cave-man." In *One-Way Song* (1933) Lewis portrayed Eliot's stern features, pessimistic poetic voice and lugubrious religious inclinations with affectionate irony:

> I seem to note a Roman profile bland,
> I hear the drone from out of the cactus-land:
> That must be the poet of the Hollow Men:
> The lips seem bursting with a deep Amen.

"Appearing at one's front door, or arriving at a dinner rendezvous," Lewis recalled in his memoir of Eliot, "his face would be haggard, he would seem at his last gasp. (Did he know?) To ask *him* to lie down for a short while at once was what I always felt I ought to do. However, when he had taken his place at a table, given his face a dry wash with his hands, and having had a little refreshment, Mr. Eliot would rapidly shed all resemblance to the harassed and exhausted refugee, in flight from some Scourge of God."

Lewis published in the second (and final) *Blast* of July 1915 Eliot's "Preludes" and "Rhapsody on a Windy Night," which were his first poems to appear in England and contained the suggestive lines that Lewis especially admired:

>I am moved by fancies that are curled,
>Around these images, and cling:
>The notion of some infinitely gentle,
>Infinitely suffering thing.

But after the censorship of Pound's poem in *Blast 1,* Lewis refused Eliot's "Bullshit" and "The Ballad of Big Louise." He called them "excellent bits of scholarly ribaldry" but stuck to his "naif determination to have no 'words ending in -Uck, -Unt, and -Ugger.'"

After World War I, Lewis replaced the friendship of the exuberant Pound with that of the cautious and circumspect Eliot, with whom he had more intellectual and less temperamental affinities. Eliot, whom Ottoline Morrell called "The Undertaker," would say at tea: "I daren't take cake, and jam's too much trouble," and he showed a Puritan distaste for the sensual pleasures which Lewis so eagerly enjoyed. He resented being patronized by Lewis, who had greater vigor and vitality, and in a letter to John Quinn remarked on the temperamental difference between his friends, Pound and Lewis, and himself: "I consider that Pound and Lewis are the only writers in London whose work is worth publishing.... I know that Pound's lack of tact has done him great harm." Tactlessness was also one of Lewis' failings.

Just after he met Lewis, in June 1915, Eliot, in "the awful daring of a moment's surrender," began his disastrous marriage with Vivien Haigh-Wood, the daughter of a portrait painter who suffered from poor health and "nerves"—and eventually went mad. After two unhappy years as a schoolmaster, he became a bank clerk at Lloyd's in the City and remained there from 1917 until 1925, when he joined Faber & Gwyer and soon became a prosperous publisher. Eliot found the exuberant, if volatile, Lewis a welcome relief from his domestic and commercial enslavement. Lewis' wife, Froanna, who liked Eliot best of all their friends, said Lewis took Eliot to music halls and boxing matches.

Lewis frequently went to Paris to keep up with the latest developments in modern art and to see the work of Picasso, Braque and Matisse. In the summer of 1920 Lewis, who wanted to get away from his pregnant mistress, and Eliot, who wished to escape from his wife, went on holiday together to Paris (where they had an introduction from Pound to Joyce), to Saumur on the Loire, and then down the river through Angers and Nantes, and north to Quiberon and the Golfe de Vannes in Brittany, which Lewis had visited with his mother in 1908. Outside Saumur, Lewis, speeding along at a great pace, had a nasty bicycle accident: his handlebars snapped off, and he was thrown violently on the road and badly injured his knee. He returned to the town furious at the proprietor, who brazenly tried to recover money for damage to the defective machine. The travellers also visited a monastery in Saumur, which Eliot attempted to sketch under the critical eye of Lewis: "The porter told us the hours, and suggested that we fill in the time by visiting the church, a short way up the street. 'Ah you should see that!' he boomed. 'It is very fine.—It is *very old—c'est très ancien!*' Then detecting, as he thought, an expression of disappointment in our faces, he added hurriedly—*C'est très moderne!*" At the end of each day, when they drank their armagnac in the café, Eliot maintained the habits of a bank clerk and scrupulously entered the day's expenses in a small notebook.

Lewis and Eliot's first meeting with Joyce, which was engineered by Pound, was brilliantly described in Lewis' autobiography. Though Joyce's work had been praised by Pound, Lewis had read only a few pages of *A Portrait of the Artist* when it appeared in the *Egoist* and found that it was too mannered, too literary and too sentimental-Irish for his austere taste. But Joyce (also primed by Pound) was familiar with *Tarr* and Lewis' other works and gave a flattering start of recognition when Eliot introduced them. Both men seemed to be aware of the momentous occasion. Lewis found Joyce an oddity in patent-leather shoes and large powerful spectacles; and in his four drawings of Joyce he captured the extraordinary face, "hollowed out, with a jutting brow and jaw, like some of the Pacific masks." Joyce played the Irishman in an amusing fashion and Lewis "took a great fancy to him for his wit, for the agreeable humanity of which he possessed such stores, for his unaffected love of alcohol, and all good things to eat and drink." He later called Joyce "a pleasing, delightful fellow, with all his scholarly egotism and Irish nonsense."

The ostensible object of the visit was to deliver a large brown parcel which Pound had entrusted to Eliot. When Joyce received their message and came to their hotel room with his tall son Giorgio, "Eliot rose to his feet. He approached the table, and with one eyebrow drawn up, and a finger pointing, announced to James Joyce that *this* was that parcel to which he had referred in his wire, and which had been given into his care, and he formally delivered it thus acquitting himself of his commission.... James Joyce was by now attempting to untie the crafty housewifely knots of the cunning old Ezra.... At last the strings were cut. A little gingerly Joyce unrolled the slovenly swaddlings of damp British brown paper in which the good-hearted American had packed up what he had put inside. Thereupon, along with some nondescript garments for the trunk—there were no trousers I believe—a fairly presentable pair of *old brown shoes* stood revealed, in the centre of the bourgeois French table."

The shoes and jacket were undoubtedly Pound's response to Joyce's letter of June 5, 1920: "I wear my son's boots (which are two sizes too large) and his castoff suit which is too narrow in the shoulders." Pound meant well by sending the cumbersome gift; but because of the unexpected arrival of a check (which may have paid for his patent-leather shoes), Joyce's circumstances had significantly improved before the literary messengers arrived with the footgear. Pound's unintentional revelation of his penury before (two equally impoverished) *confrères* aroused Joyce's Irish pride. Though he accepted their invitation to dinner, he insisted on paying for several days of lavish drinks, meals, taxis and tips.

Eliot suffered a nervous breakdown at the end of 1921 and spent some time in a sanatorium in Lausanne. During the next three years (also an extremely difficult period for Lewis) he was sick, miserable and acutely depressed: fearful of poverty and overcome by self-pity. In a 1923 letter Eliot wrote Lewis: "I am ill, harassed, impoverished, and am going to have 5 teeth out. I have managed to avoid seeing anyone for a very long time. I have several enemies."

II

In 1922 Lewis was present at the first reading of *The Waste Land* in London, when a friend of Mrs. Eliot, with splotches on his face, proudly identified himself as the "young man carbuncular." Eliot published the poem in October 1922 in the first number of the *Criterion,* when he was editing that magazine and encouraging Lewis to contribute to every issue. Despite—or perhaps because of—Eliot's good will and practical assistance, Lewis quarreled with him in January 1925, when Eliot advertised but did not print a long part of the *The Dithyrambic Spectator.* The ever-suspicious Lewis had been publishing two Zagreus sections of *The Apes of God* in the *Criterion* (for which he received £43) and he warned Eliot, who was then friendly with Virginia Woolf and other members of the Bloomsbury set: "Should any of these fragments find their way into other hands than yours before they appear in book-form I shall regard it as treachery." Eliot explained that Lewis' 20,000 word essay was too long to print and that illness had prevented him from writing an explanation, and answered Lewis in a calm and disinterested manner: "Please do not think that I am pressing upon you . . . a reminder of supposed services. I consider that anything I do is equalised by any support you give to *The Criterion.* Furthermore I am not an individual but an instrument, and anything I do is in the interest of art and literature and civilisation, and it is not a matter for personal compensation. But in the circumstances I cannot help feeling that your letter expressed an unjustified suspiciousness." But when Lewis continued his attacks in March—"Since before Christmas you have been guilty where I am concerned of a series of actions each of which, had I done the same to you, would have made you very indignant"—Eliot showed some exasperation and appealed to Lewis' faith in his integrity and their friendship: "I cannot work with you so long as you consider me either the tool or the operator of machinations against you. . . . Until you are convinced by your own senses or by the testimony of others that I am neither conducting nor supporting (either deliberately or blindly) any intrigue against you, I do not see that we can get any further."

But Eliot, because of his sobriety and apparent equanimity, was a difficult man to quarrel with, and remained Lewis' loyal friend and staunch defender. He believed that Roger Fry and other critics had deliberately hurt Lewis' career, and placed him above Joyce as a prose stylist: "Lewis was independent, outspoken and difficult. Temperament and circumstances combined to make him a great satirist. . . . His work was persistently ignored or depreciated, throughout his life, by persons of influence in the world of art and letters who did not find him congenial. . . . [But he was] one of the few men of letters in my generation whom I should call, without qualification, men of genius. . . . Mr. Lewis is the greatest prose master of style of my generation—perhaps the only one to have invented a new style."

It was highly ironic that the eminently respectable Eliot became involved in a stormy public controversy when Lewis painted his portrait in 1938, for the poet had changed a great deal since the "Waste Land" days of 1920. Eliot's association with Faber, beginning in 1925, rescued him from economic hardship and led to prosperity; his reception into the Church of England and acquisition of British citizenship in 1927 provided new strength and security; and his separation from his wife in 1933 finally freed him from the tragic bondage of her mental illness. Eliot had firmly established his literary reputation; he was widely admired as the successor to Yeats and acclaimed as the leading poet of his generation.

Eliot's respectability, religion, success, wealth and fame impeded his friendship with Lewis—who had none of these acquisitions. Lewis emphasized the difference between Eliot and himself when he told Geoffrey Grigson that he once went to visit the poet and found Ottoline Morrell on her knees beseeching him: "Teach me how to pray!" Lewis may have felt residual resentment about his dispute with Eliot concerning the publication of his work in the *Criterion,* but both men remained fond of each other. Lewis spoke teasingly about Eliot, treated him with ironic affection and (mistakenly) thought he had a better understanding of the world. He believed he had a superior intellect and never quite understood why he could not make the same artistic impression that Eliot did.

Lewis, who strongly projected his character in his own works and damaged his reputation with his vehement political tracts, criticized his friend's theory of impersonality (which enhanced Eliot's magisterial image) in a chapter of *Men without Art*. He felt Eliot had made a virtue of becoming an "incarnate echo" and ought to express rather than repress his personality: "If there is to be an 'insincerity,' I prefer it should occur in the opposite sense—namely that 'the man, the personality,' should exaggerate, a little artificially perhaps, his beliefs—rather than leave a meaningless shell behind him, and go to hide in a volatilized hypostatization of his personal feelings." When Eliot first saw a review copy of Lewis' book he said: "Oh, I'm very interested in this," borrowed the volume, and seemed to accept the validity of Lewis' criticism. Eliot found Lewis rather difficult, for he disliked quarreling as much as Lewis enjoyed it. But he thought Lewis was the liveliest and most original of his contemporaries and always had the highest respect for his genius. Lewis was usually cautious and discreet about Eliot with mutual friends, quietly agreed when the poet was praised and tempered his criticism with admiration in writing about Eliot.

There was a great deal of conversation and laughter when Lewis was working on Eliot's portraits, for his remarks amused and entertained the poet. Lewis expressed his favorable first impression of the handsome Eliot both verbally and visually. He described Eliot as: "A sleek, tall, attractive transatlantic apparition—with a sort of Gioconda smile . . . a Prufrock to whom the mermaids would decidedly have sung, one would have said, at the tops of their voices. . . . For this was a very attractive young Prufrock indeed, with an alert and dancing eye— . . . bashfully ironic, blushfully *taquinerie*. . . . Though not feminine—besides being physically large his personality visibly moved within the male pale—there were dimples in the warm dark skin; undoubtedly he used his eyes a little like a Leonardo."

Lewis actually did two portraits of Eliot in 1938. The first (now in Eliot House, Harvard) is a study for the second and depicts the poet's head and torso against a blank background. The second and much greater painting portrays Eliot, in waistcoat and lounge suit, slouched in an armchair, with crossed hands. He stares slightly downwards and to the left with great intensity, and the planes of his face are more contrasted, his bold features more precisely delineated than in the study. A shadow from his head appears on the pale green panel behind the deeply etched parting of his sleek hair. The abstract designs on both sides of the panel suggest the power of his imagination, while his solemn composure and fixed concentration convincingly convey the strength of his intellect. Eliot greatly admired this portrait, which captured the essence of his mind and art, and told Lewis he was quite willing for posterity to know him by that image (a photograph of 1954, reproduced in Lewis' *Letters,* shows Eliot pointing to the portrait with smiling admiration).

Lewis submitted the portrait to the judges of the Royal Academy exhibition in the spring of 1938. But *Blast* never got inside Burlington House, and the painting was rejected on April 21. The refusal of the portrait caused a furor in the British press, enabled Lewis to strike back at the citadel of artistic orthodoxy, gain some useful publicity and—ironically—attract the attention of a wider public. The refusal of the Eliot portrait came at the end of a long series of rejections suffered by Lewis in the 1930s. But the controversy aroused interest in the painting (which was refused by the Trustees of the Tate) and in 1939 T. J. Honeyman of the Lefevre Gallery sold it for £250 to the Municipal Art Gallery in Durban, South Africa. This money enabled Lewis to escape from England and travel to North America.

III

During the late forties, the final phase of his artistic career, Lewis' painting seriously deteriorated because of his defective vision. The most important work of his late period was his second portrait of Eliot, who in 1948 had won the $40,000 Nobel Prize for Literature. Lewis dined frequently with Eliot, in Scott's on Mount Street or the Hyde Park Hotel Grill, where he ate oysters and dessert—and skipped the main course. Eliot used to send Lewis cases of champagne (he could drink nothing else at the end of his life), and Lewis meticulously noticed that it was not vintage. Still ignored and impoverished, he was inevitably jealous of Eliot's enormous success and resentful about the poet in his letters. He told Pound, who had been charged with treason, declared insane and confined to St. Elizabeth's Hospital in Washington: "You might almost have contrived this climax to your respective careers: yours so Villonesque and Eliot's super-Tennyson." And he wrote to his American friend, Felix Giovanelli: "Eliot is a solid mass of inherited slyness. . . . Eliot is no great favourite of mine in later years. Lesser poet than Pound, though not such an exasperating fool of a man. He *has* I agree kicked up a nasty stink around himself of *cult*."

When Lewis painted his second, much more bland and conventional portrait of Eliot (which lacks the sharp incisive planes of the earlier work) in March and April 1949, he was obliged to scrutinize him very closely. As he wrote in "The Sea-Mists of the Winter": "When I started my second portrait of T. S. Eliot, which now hangs in Magdalene College, Cambridge, in the early summer of 1949, I had to draw up very close to the sitter to see exactly how the hair sprouted out of the forehead, and how the curl of the nostril wound up into the dark interior of the nose. There was no question of my not succeeding, my sight was still adequate. But I had to move too close to the forms I was studying. Some months later, when I started a portrait of Stella Newton, I had to draw still closer and even then I could not quite see. This was the turning-point, the date, December 1949." Another minor problem, as Lewis told a St. Louis friend, was that Eliot (whom he had described as "wriggling his lean bottom" in *The Apes of God*) became drowsy and his bottom "went to sleep" when he was immobilized in one position.

The portrait was completed in time for Lewis' exhibition at the Redfern Gallery in May, when both artist and subject were interviewed by *Time* magazine. Lewis' description recalled his earliest impression of the poet, haggard and apparently at his last gasp: "You will see in his mask, drained of too hearty blood, a gazing strain, a patient contraction: the body is slightly tilted . . . in resigned anticipation of the worst." Eliot suggested that Lewis' intensity made him feel somewhat uneasy: "Wearing a look of slightly quizzical inscrutability behind which one suspects his mental muscles may be contracting for some unexpected pounce, he makes one feel that it would be undesirable, though not actually dangerous, to fall asleep in one's chair." When this portrait, like the earlier one of Eliot, was refused by the Tate, Lewis blamed the malign influence of Kenneth Clark. But it was eventually acquired by Magdalene College for £300, and hung on the narrow staircase of the dining hall, poorly lighted and difficult to see.

Lewis' last polemical book, *The Demon of Progress in the Arts* (1954), concluded his argument against abstract art and unleashed his final onslaught against Eliot's "melancholy ex-lieutenant," Herbert Read. If, for Lewis, Fry and Kenneth Clark were art dictators, Read was an ineffectual impresario and aesthetic buffoon, who led the dashing but dull rear guard of abstractionists, was besotted with theorizing, neglected the evidence of the eye and never really looked at a picture in his life. In *Wyndham Lewis the Artist* (1939), he charged Read with willingness to provide any art movement with instant respectability and exposed his weaknesses with deadly accuracy: "Mr. Herbert Read has an unenviable knack of providing, at a week's notice, almost any movement, or submovement, in the visual arts, with a neatly-cut party suit—with which it can appear, appropriately caparisoned, at the cocktail party thrown by the capitalist who has made its birth possible, in celebration of the happy event. No poet laureate, with his ode for every court occasion, could enjoy a more unfailing inspiration than Mr. Read; prefaces and inaugural addresses follow each other in bewildering succession, and with a robust disregard for the slight inconsistencies attendant upon such invariable readiness to oblige."

The intensely independent Lewis (who had an integrated vision in art and literature, and was consistent in his aesthetic theory and practice) stated the essential problem was that Read's rather tame and conventional literary work was exactly the opposite of what he daringly professed in the visual arts. Stephen Spender, who said that Read hated Lewis and thought he was evil, has explained that Read's conflicting duality was caused by the extinction of his imaginative powers: "The creative side of his talent has gradually been submerged, and the more this has happened the more depressed he feels about the arts in general. He has a line which is to support nearly everything that is experimental and he therefore gives his readers the impression of being in the vanguard, and someone in the vanguard is supposed of course to have burning faith and vitality: qualities which, in reality, H. R. lacks."

In *The Demon of Progress in the Arts,* which drew the reluctant Eliot into the controversy, Lewis repeated his accusations of 1939 and sardonically observed that Read's willingness to trim his sails to the prevailing aesthetic winds had finally earned him a knighthood in 1953: "In Sir Herbert Read we have a man who has been very recently knighted for being so 'contemporary'; for having been for years ready to plug to the hilt, to trumpet, to expound, any movement in painting or sculpture—sometimes of the most contradictory kind—which was obviously hurrying along a path as opposite as possible from what had appealed to civilized man through the ages."

Lewis' book finally stimulated Read's counterattack, which alluded to the title of Lewis' work and appeared in the *Sewanee Review* in 1955 as "The Lost Leader, or the Psychopathology of Reaction in the Arts." Read relegated Lewis to the ranks of the aesthetic rear guard and argued: "Reactionaryism is a negative doctrine. It vigorously denounces an existing trend—the historical present—and seeks to establish a contrary trend. It is revolution in reverse." And in a note on the first page of his essay, Read mentioned that Lewis had provoked his response and made the unconvincing assertion that his own essay was impersonal: "It may be no accident that these thoughts came to me after reading *The Demon of Progress in the Arts,* an attack on the contemporary movement in art by Wyndham Lewis. It should be obvious, however, for reasons given in the course of my essay, that my observations have no application to Mr. Lewis himself."

When Eliot saw this article, he defended Lewis and criticized Read's "psychological" mode of argument. Read, embarrassed at Eliot's censure, became apologetic, maintained that he had always admired Lewis and claimed that Lewis' treacherous attack came as a complete surprise—though Lewis had been condemning Read, with considerable consistency, for thirty years: "The footnote in the *Sewanee* was inserted at the request of the editor, who felt that his American readers would not otherwise see the relevance of my article. . . . I find it difficult to explain why a man for whom I have always had friendly and loyal feelings [*sic*] should turn on me with such bitterness and resentment. . . . Lewis attacked me in a direct and extremely vituperative manner. I was surprised, and I could not reply in kind because I did not feel that way about Lewis—I had hitherto regarded him as a friend. . . . I now regret that I added the footnote—I remember that I added it with reluctance. . . . The harm is that I have shocked you, and there is no one in the world for whose good opinion I have more respect."

Though Read was chagrined by Eliot's displeasure, he continued to attack

Lewis after his death in an abusive obituary, a negative review of the *Letters* which appeared under the appalling homiletic title: "A Good Artist But a Bad Friend" and in his 1966 memoir of Eliot. In the memoir Read asserted: "On one of the last occasions that I lunched with [Eliot] alone at the Garrick Club he confessed that in his life there had been few people whom he had found it impossible to like, but Lewis was one of them." It is significant that Read admitted there were no witnesses and did not publish his malicious story until after Eliot's death, for his account contradicted the entire tenor of the poet's forty-year relationship with Lewis. Lewis' April 1955 remark provided a convincing refutation of Read and a fitting conclusion to their longstanding controversy: "Not long ago Tom expressed to me his misgiving for having, in effect, given Herbert Read his start, encouraging him to contribute to *The Criterion* and publishing some of his books, saying that there was no one whose ideas he considered more pernicious, and I agree with Tom."

IV

Just as Pound had helped Lewis at the beginning of his career, so Eliot sustained him at the end. Though grateful for the assistance, Lewis maintained his ironic attitude as the ecclesiastical Eliot hardened into a national monument: "Tom's always been timid, and afraid of what 'people' will say, 'people' these days for him being 'bishops'. . . . Oh, never mind *him*. [Tom's] like that with everybody. But he doesn't come *in here* disguised as Westminster Abbey." Lewis also continued his rivalry with Eliot. P. H. Newby, who discussed with Lewis the fee for a proposed BBC broadcast, has recorded: "'I expect you give Tom Eliot much more than me,' Lewis said. 'No,' I replied. 'You would get the same. There are standard fees.' He was not disposed to believe that he would get the same fee as Eliot; I got the impression it was not the amount that mattered but the status it implied. . . . People were alarmed by him—but, in my experience, without justification."

Eliot lent Lewis £200 (which he repaid from his BBC commission) to go to Stockholm for x-ray diagnosis and therapy in June 1950. After Lewis became blind the following year, several friends (including Eliot and Naomi Mitchison) helped him get a Civil List Pension. Eliot encouraged Henry Regnery to publish American editions of Lewis' books in the early fifties and in 1964 offered to write a Preface to the paperback edition of *Self Condemned,* which he called "the best of Lewis' novels" and "a book of almost unbearable spiritual agony." Eliot read the typescript and proofs of *Monstre Gai* and *Malign Fiesta* (the last two parts of *The Human Age*), made suggestions about revising the novels, introduced the radio adaptations and published an essay on *Monstre Gai* in the 1955 issue of *Hudson Review,* which also contained a chapter of the novel. Eliot read the proofs of Lewis' last book, *The Red Priest,* and wrote a warm obituary in the *Sunday Times:* "The output was astounding. The views expressed were independent. . . . There is, in everything he wrote, *style*. I would even affirm that Wyndham Lewis was the only one among my contemporaries to create a new, an original, prose style. Most prose of my time, indeed, seems to me, when compared with that of Lewis, lifeless. A great intellect is gone, a great modern writer is dead."

The friendship of Lewis and Eliot was based on intellectual sympathy and mutual esteem. Lewis, who was six years older than Eliot and had a more forceful personality, tended to dominate. He used his failure and Eliot's success to his own moral advantage, for both men felt that Lewis had received much less recognition than he deserved. Eliot, somewhat embarrassed by his own fame, freely expressed his admiration for Lewis in a dozen books and essays published between 1918 and 1960. Once he was blind, Lewis became even more dependent on Eliot's friendship; and after his death in 1957, Eliot continued to praise his genius. Lewis sustained his long friendship with Eliot, as he did with Augustus John and Ezra Pound, because his respect for Eliot's artistic and intellectual powers restrained his caustic tongue and combative temperament. Lewis and Eliot, like Pound and Joyce, the other modernistic "Men of 1914" were all outsiders—three were American and one Irish—whose artistic ideals and imaginative innovations transformed, during the early decades of the century, the cultural life of England.

12

Wyndham Lewis: Portraits of an Artist

I

T. S. Eliot's statement that Wyndham Lewis was "the most fascinating personality of our time" is confirmed by his frequent appearance in the imaginative literature of the twentieth century. For authors who had encountered what Eliot called "the thought of the modern and the energy of the cave-man" could not resist portraying Lewis in their works. He was used by poets as a touchstone for their political and aesthetic ideas, and by writers to inject a certain vitality into their novels or to pay off old vendettas. Though Lewis is recognizable in all these works, his character reflects the personality and attitudes of the author as well as his own provocative figure.

Roy Campbell saw Lewis from the Right, Auden viewed him from the Left, Edgell Rickword satirized his violence and dogmatism, and Pound pieced him into a nostalgic mosaic of the prewar English *avant-garde*. Joyce represented him as a purely intellectual adversary, and Ford used Lewis' appearance and his art to camouflage and project an aspect of his own character. Huxley, in the most significant treatment, characterized the conflicts and ambiguities in Lewis' absurd but impressive personality; and Edith and Osbert Sitwell both anatomized his weaknesses in retaliation for *The Apes of God*. Most recently, Eliott Baker has paid homage to Lewis' intellect and his pride.

The poetic and fictional portraits of Lewis also reflect the extreme fluctuations of his personal and artistic reputation during his fifty-year career. From 1909 to 1920 he was known as the bohemian poet and abstract painter, the combative leader of the Vorticists, the iconoclastic editor of *Blast* and the author of the Dostoyevskian novel, *Tarr* (1918). In the early 1920s, when Ford and Huxley portrayed him, Lewis edited *The Tyro* (illustrated with grimacing caricatures) and then "went underground" to write the fiery and highly provocative works that established his literary reputation when they appeared in a massive array at the end of the decade.

In the 1930s Lewis' Fascist sympathies made him a notorious artist and a dangerous enemy, while his alienation intensified his pathological suspicion and fear of persecution. He permanently damaged his reputation by praising the future dictator of Germany in *Hitler* (1931); by his Right-wing political tracts, his contribution to Oswald Mosley's Fascist journal and his anti-Communist novel about Spain. His recantations in 1939, which still showed signs of his original beliefs, came too late and were thought to be unconvincing and even insincere. In *Men without Art* (1934) he continued his negative but effective literary onslaughts, directed at friends like Eliot, Bloomsbury "enemies" like Virginia Woolf, and Americans he considered overrated: Hemingway, "The Dumb Ox," and Faulkner, "The Moralist with a Corn Cob." His political intuition was always unreliable, and when he sailed for Canada in September 1939 he seemed to be abandoning his country when it was threatened by war and defeat.

Lewis spent the entire war in Canada and America, struggling to survive, painting for money, writing little and almost forgotten. He had become older and gentler when he returned to England in 1945, began to write generous art criticism for the *Listener* and had a successful art exhibition in 1949. He became blind in 1951, when he wrote his profoundly moving valediction to the visual world, "The Sea-Mists of the Winter."

In the 1950s—finally, but perhaps too late—Lewis began to receive the long overdue recognition that is expressed in Elliott Baker's story. He was awarded an honorary doctorate, a government pension and a commission from the BBC to complete the trilogy he had begun thirty years before with *The Childermass*. His thought seemed harder, his courage greater, as his strength grew less. While blind he attacked Malraux, Sartre and Orwell in *The Writer and the Absolute* (1952); wrote his finest novel, *Self Condemned* (1954), about his painful years in Toronto; and completed *The Human Age* with *Monstre Gai* and *Malign Fiesta* in 1955. He received retrospective honor with a controversial exhibition at the Tate in 1956, and died the following year.

II

The belligerent Roy Campbell, Lewis' best-known disciple, actively supported him in the controversy that followed *The Apes of God*. In the knock-out couplets and swaggering stanzas of his neo-Augustan satiric poem, *The Georgiad* (1931), Campbell decries Lewis' lack of recognition, praises him (in his favorite bullfight metaphor) for attacking D. H. Lawrence's primitivism in *Paleface* (1929), and refers to the suppression of his own review of *The Apes of God* by the craven editor of the *New Statesman*:

> For vainly may a Lewis sweat his brains,
> The masterpiece in darkness still remains,

> While any dolt whose industry's behind
> Can win the reputation for a mind. . . .
> Perhaps some Lewis, winged with laughter soars,
> And in his wake the laughing thunder roars
> To see the fear he scatters as he goes
> And hear the cackle of his dunghill foes.

Though Campbell (a Catholic convert) never actually fought in the Spanish Civil War, he narrowly escaped from his house in Toledo when the Revolution broke out and became an ardent apologist for the Nationalists. In *Flowering Rifle* (1939), his long poem about the war, he praises Lewis, with barbarous imagery and characteristic violence, for his independent opposition to literary fashions and lazy coteries. But his praise is debased by his doggerel verse and Fascist ideology:

> And few but Wyndham Lewis and myself
> Disdain salaaming for their praise and pelf,
> With cleansing bombs to air the stuffy dens
> Wherein they picked their noses with their pens.

W. H. Auden, who served briefly as an ambulance driver with the Republicans in Spain, expresses a grudging admiration for Lewis. In "A Happy New Year" (1933), he praises Lewis for his therapeutic provocations:

> But Wyndham Lewis disguised as the maid
> Was putting cascara in the still lemonade.

And four years later, in *Letters from Iceland,* Auden and MacNeice recognized the angry political isolation of Lewis, whose book in praise of Hitler had made him one of the loneliest intellectuals of the 1930s. They alluded to his Welsh ancestry, his notorious persecution complex, his aggressive blond-beast Nietzschean hero, Kerr-Orr of *The Wild Body* (1927), and his peculiar combination of intelligence and stupidity:

> There's Wyndham Lewis fuming out of sight,
> That lonely old volcano of the Right. . . .

> We leave the Martyr's Stake at Abergwilly
> To Wyndham Lewis with a box of soldiers (blonde)
> Regretting one so bright should be so silly.

Edgell Rickword, who is satirized as Hedgepinshot Pickwort in *The Apes of God,* wittily mocks Lewis' violent condemnation of homosexuals in *The Art of Being Ruled, Paleface* and other works by praising him in the *persona* of the homosexual aesthete Twittingpan in "The Encounter" (1931). Twittingpan, who had once championed Lewis' *bêtes noires,* Gertrude Stein and the Sitwells, now ironically links Lewis with the sentimental Middleton Murry as "the only moderns likely to endure" and masochistically claims that Lewis has altered his life. He rejects emotion, inversion ("now thrust in front all I had kept behind"), Bergsonian flux and Bloomsbury frivolity:

> Don't you think Wyndham Lewis too divine?
> The brute male strength he shows in every line!
> I swear if he'd flogged me in his last book but one,
> as some kind person informed me he has done,
> I'd have forgiven him for the love of art.

Ezra Pound, with characteristic generosity, did everything he could to help Lewis in the early stages of his career. He contributed to and collaborated on *Blast,* placed Lewis' works in Harriet Weaver's *Egoist* and Margaret Anderson's *Little Review* (which published *Tarr*), sold his paintings to the wealthy patron, John Quinn, acted as his agent when Lewis was fighting in France and wrote a great many laudatory essays about his work. Despite Lewis's attack on Pound as a "revolutionary simpleton" in *Time and Western Man,* they always remained friends, and Pound became the subject of one of Lewis' greatest portraits.

Lewis appears in seven of Pound's *Cantos* in an aesthetic rather than a political guise. In Canto 80 Pound fondly recalls that he was first introduced to Lewis in 1909 by the poet and Keeper of Oriental Paintings at the British Museum, Laurence Binyon. Lewis, who had lived in Spain in 1902 and affected Spanish dress and mannerisms, belonged to the young group of poets who admired Binyon and Sturge Moore and met at the Vienna Café, near the British Museum, on New Oxford Street. After the Austrian owner, Josef, was forced to close at the outbreak of the war, the Café was turned into a bank:

> There were mysterious figures
> that emerged from recondite recesses
> and ate at the WIENER CAFÉ
> which died into banking, Josef may have followed
> his emperor. . . .
> So it is to Mr. Binyon that I owe, initially,
> Mr. Lewis, Mr. P. Wyndham Lewis. His bull-dog, me,
> as it were against old Sturge M's bull-dog.

In the first version of Canto 1 *(Poetry,* June 1917), Pound praised Lewis as an innovator in the arts: "Barred lights, great flares, new form; Picasso or Lewis." In Canto 78 he spoke of Lewis as one of the three prophetic voices in modern art. Though Gaudier and Hulme were killed in the War, their art and aesthetic ideas (like Lewis') survived and became influential:

> Gaudier's word not blacked out
> nor old Hulme's, nor Wyndham's.

In Cantos 98 and 102 Pound associates Lewis with Yeats and Eliot, all of whom, Pound believed, "had no ground beneath 'em," as "Orage had," because they lacked the knowledge of economic history and theory that Orage and Pound had acquired from Major Douglas. In Canto 96 Pound states that Lewis recognized the aesthetic importance of the capital of the Eastern Empire, which plays such a significant role in Yeats' poetry:

> 'Constantinople' said Wyndham 'our star'
> Mr. Yeats called it Byzantium.

The final reference, in Canto 115, is the most moving. Pound refers to Lewis' refusal in 1950 to risk surgery that might impair his mental faculties and his stoical decision to accept blindness. Unlike the terrified European scientists and intellectuals:

> Wyndham Lewis chose blindness
> rather than have his mind stop.

III

When Lewis met Joyce in 1920 and brought him the famous pair of old shoes—a gift from Pound—they got on well together and often stayed out all night drinking. And in July 1930, a month after Lewis' second attack on Joyce, they dined together at Joyce's request and had a friendly discussion about the operatic career of John Sullivan. Lewis plays a significant role in Joyce's *Finnegans Wake* (1939), as the model for Professor Jones and the Ondt. But Joyce is mainly concerned with refuting Lewis' caricature of him as Jamesjulius Ratner in *The Apes of God* and his criticism of *Ulysses* in *Time and Western Man* as "a record diarrhoea." Frank Budgen writes that "Joyce's comment: 'If all that Lewis says is true, is it more than ten per cent of the truth?' seems to me to be a sufficient reply. In *Finnegans Wake* Joyce gives Lewis the Shaun treatment. He parodies, mimics, caricatures Lewis' stylistic mannerisms much as Lewis caricatures his victims in *The Apes of God.*" Joyce includes a great many ingenious puns on Lewis' works ("irony of the stars," "cattleman's spring meat," "art of being rude," *Spice and Westend Women*) and satirizes his preferences for "space" rather than "time" literature. In *Dublin's Joyce* (1956) Hugh

Kenner reveals how "innumerable details of the *Wake* have their key in Lewis"; and in *Wyndham Lewis* (1957) Geoffrey Wagner devotes a long chapter, "Master Joys and Windy Nous," to the personal, literary and philosophical relations of the two writers. Since Lewis's role in *Finnegans Wake* has been extensively and expertly discussed, I shall concentrate on the portrayal of Lewis in novels which have received much less attention.

Ford was the first editor to publish Lewis' works and three of his stories, later collected in *The Wild Body,* appeared in the *English Review* in 1909. Ford contributed the first chapter of *The Good Soldier* to *Blast;* commissioned in 1914 an abstract panel for the study of South Lodge, the house he shared with Violet Hunt; and helped introduce Lewis to literary London. Lewis, irritated by the delayed payment for his stories, told Sturge Moore in September 1909: "Hueffer is a shit of the most dreary and uninteresting type." And, with characteristic ingratitude, he angrily told Ford he was *passé:* "*Tu sais, tu es foûtu! Foûtu!* Finished! Exploded! Done for! Blasted in fact. Your generation is gone.... This is the day of Cubism, Futurism, Vorticism. What people want is me, not you." But Ford, like Pound, was intrigued by Lewis' megalomaniac personality and remained on good terms with him.

Lewis (who studied at the Heymann Academy of Art in Munich in 1906) appears as George Heimann in Ford's first postwar novel, *The Marsden Case* (1923), which deals with London bohemians and aristocrats just before and during the Great War. This minor novel begins in July 1914, the month *Blast* was first published, as Heimann, a handsome young man with a romantic appearance and violent temper, has a bitter dispute with the unscrupulous publisher, Mr. Podd, about payment for a German poem, *The Titanic: An Epic,* which he has translated. Podd's insinuations about Heimann's obscure origins (he is actually the secret son of an earl) reinforce Kenner's description of Lewis—when he first met Ford in 1909—as "This mystery man without a past." And Ford's description of Heimann reflects the Spanish *persona* (later perfected by Robert Graves) that Lewis adopted when he returned to London after seven years of bohemian life on the Continent:

> I gathered that the foreignness of his aspect, his high-crowned hat, his coat, black and buttoned-up round his neck, like a uniform—always a startling effect, his immense black Inverness cloak, his young beard and his long black hair drooping over his ears, all these things were the products of a sojourn in Bohemia, not of foreign birth.

The lecture that the narrator, Ernest Jessop, gives at the Ladies Club in chapter 5 recalls the ludicrous *dénouement* of the lecture Ford gave at Lewis' Rebel Art Centre in 1914. Lewis' patron and colleague, Kate Lechmere, described how "the event nearly ended in disaster, for this dignified literary figure had his efforts rewarded half-way through the talk by a sharp blow from one of

Lewis' largest paintings: it had been hanging on the wall behind Ford and suddenly pitched forward on top of him."

The Night Club in the novel is clearly based on Freda Strindberg's Cave of the Golden Calf, which Osbert Sitwell said was "hideously but relevantly frescoed" by Lewis in his prewar Vorticist style. "I just dimly had a vision of the lighted stage of the Night Club," Ford writes in the novel. "The walls were decorated with paintings of menlike objects that had the faces of enlarged ants and blue, reticulated limbs like rolled paper cylinders."

Though Heimann's appearance, milieu and paintings resemble Lewis', the complex but static plot has no real connection with Lewis' life. Heimann's character is actually an aspect of Ford's and the events of *The Marsden Case* are based on Ford's laceration by women, escape to German spas, military experience and shell-shock—which were rendered much more successfully in *Parade's End* (1924–1928).

Aldous Huxley's *Antic Hay* was written in 1923, the same year as Ford's novel. At that time Lewis had published only one book, *Tarr,* and had a reputation that was more scandalous than serious. The novel was directly inspired by the sexual rivalry of Lewis and Huxley, who were competing for the affection of the wild and beautiful Nancy Cunard, daughter of the wealthy shipping magnate. Huxley's biographer writes that he fell madly in love with Nancy—the model for Myra Viveash in *Antic Hay* and Lucy Tantamount in *Point Counter Point* (1928)—in the autumn of 1922 and that his feelings were unrequited: "What she wanted were men who were more than a match for her, strong men, brutes. Aldous was simply not her type. He was far too gentle, too unexcessive and, with her, too hang-dog, too love-sick." The stronger and "more magnificently brutal" Lewis—who had three successful art exhibitions, "Guns," "Group X" and "Tyros and Portraits" in 1919, 1920 and 1921—carried on a checkered affair with Nancy in the early twenties and spent October 1922 in Venice as her guest and lover. She was the model for the childish and rebellious Baby Bucktrout, the heroine of Lewis' novel *The Roaring Queen* (1936), who tries to seduce the gardener with a copy of *Lady Chatterley's Lover. Antic Hay,* Huxley's second novel, was written in two months in the late spring of 1923, just after his wife, Maria, forced him to leave England for Italy and to break off his anguished relationship with Nancy.

Casimir Lypiatt, the fullest fictional portrait of Wyndham Lewis, ranks with Huxley's satiric characterizations of Katherine Mansfield, Middleton Murry, D. H. Lawrence and Frieda Lawrence. Lewis once wrote to a publisher: "I have been painter, sculptor, novelist, poet, philosopher, editor (cf. *Blast, Tyro, Enemy*), soldier, war-artist, traveller, lecturer, journalist"; and when Lypiatt, who (like Lewis) writes the prefaces for his own exhibition catalogs, exclaims he is a painter, poet, philosopher and musician, the owner of his gallery warns: "There is a danger of—how shall I put it—dissipating one's energies." In 1923 Huxley told H. L. Mencken that Lewis was "a queer and very able fellow," and Gumbril expresses this condescending ambivalence when he thinks: "Dear old Lypiatt, even, in spite of his fantastic egoism. Such a bad painter, such a bombinating poet, such a loud emotional improviser on the piano! And going on like this, year after year, pegging away at the same old things—always badly! And always without a penny, always living in the most hideous squalor! Magnificent and pathetic old Lypiatt!" Though Lypiatt (like Lewis) is extremely ambitious and idealistic, wants to recapture the greatness of the old masters and believes that artists reveal the moral nature of the universe, he is (unlike Lewis) totally without talent and doomed to the disappointment of unsold pictures and bad reviews.

There are a number of references to Lewis' books and paintings in *Antic Hay*. The eclectic and rather precious critic, Mercaptan, alludes to Lewis' Dostoyevskian novel *Tarr* when he insists: "We needn't *all* be Russians, I hope. These revolting Dostoyevskys." But Lypiatt, who has a Russian first name, shouts back: "'What about Tolstoy?' ... letting out his impatience with a violent blast." The last word, of course, refers to Lewis' bombastic magazine of 1914, which contained his dramatic fantasy, *Enemy of the Stars,* and his manifesto of Vorticism. Lypiatt alludes to the former when he turns his eyes heavenwards and looks up at the Milky Way: "'What stars,' he said, 'and what prodigious gaps between the stars!'"; and he defines the latter when he speaks of his work as "enormous, vehement, a great swirling composition!" Another of Mercaptan's criticisms specifically condemns the extreme energy and excessive emotion that characterize both Lewis' personality and the deliberately provocative *Blast:* "'You protest *too* much. You defeat your own ends; you lose emphasis by trying to be over-emphatic. All this *folie de grandeur,* all this hankering after *terribilità!'*"

Lypiatt's abstract paintings resemble Lewis' violent vorticist drawings of Shakespeare's *Timon of Athens* (1913): "a procession of machinelike forms rushing up diagonally from right to left across the canvas, with as it were a spray of energy." His "violent grimace of mirth" reflects the savage *Tyro* portraits of 1921. And his picture of Myra Viveash is exactly like the famous portrait of Edith Sitwell (painted in 1923, now in the Tate): "He had distorted her in the portrait, had made her longer and thinner than she really was, had turned her arms into sleek tubes and put a bright, metallic polish on the curve of her cheek." Though Lewis, the first abstract painter in England, was artistically though not financially successful, Myra Viveash believes his paintings are bad because there was no life in them.

There are several biographical details in the novel that match Lypiatt with Lewis. Lypiatt, who is also forty years old, paints Myra Viveash in a dirty studio, down a cul-de-sac in a mews, which resembles the Lee Studio in Adam and Eve Mews, Kensington, that Lewis used between July 1921 and October

1923. Lypiatt's passionate rejection of "aesthetic emotions and purely formal values" refers to the frigid theories that Roger Fry applied to the art of Cézanne; and Lypiatt's angry response to his lack of critical recognition alludes to Lewis' damaging quarrel with Fry and his break with the Omega Workshops in October 1913. This dispute led to his lifelong fight with Bloomsbury and to his belief that he was being ignored and persecuted by Fry and Clive Bell: "It's not their malignity I mind; I can give them back as good as they give me. It's their power of silence and indifference, it's their capacity for making themselves deaf."

Lypiatt's aesthetic career is directly related to the extraordinary number of references to artists and paintings in *Antic Hay*. Huxley mentions more than thirty-five painters from Duccio and Giotto to Picasso and Matisse, as well as specific works by Piero della Francesca, Raphael, Michelangelo, Rubens and Ingres, and these masters form a standard of excellence which Lypiatt fails to achieve. The only picture that is discussed at length is *The Last Communion of St. Jerome* (1614) by Domenichino, who, like Lewis, was subject to contradictory judgments and a fluctuating reputation. The painting actually was, as Gumbril says, "Poussin's favourite picture"; and though the artist was praised by Goethe, Stendhal, Delacroix and Taine, his reputation suddenly declined when he was absolutely condemned by Ruskin in *Modern Painters* (1843). This "horribly obscure" painting, like those of Lypiatt, is ambivalently presented in a reverent and a blasphemous manner. Though the "robed and mitred priest held out, the dying saint yearningly received, the body of the Son of God," Gumbril had wondered (as a child), "why on earth that old bishop (for I did know it was a bishop) should be handing the naked old man a five-shilling piece." In a novel where there is no true understanding between characters, who remain isolated in their own petty worlds, Huxley uses the painting to contrast the theme of unfulfilled communion—both spiritual and secular.

Lypiatt is scorned by Gumbril, condemned by Mercaptan, rejected and insulted by Myra Viveash. He provides a powerful contrast to the traditional English virtues of modesty and reticence; and is a truculent, turbulent, titanic, exultant and extravagantly boastful man, who has no literary tact and recites his own verses at every possible opportunity (Lewis' first, unpublished works, were sonnets). But Lypiatt is also a serious and dedicated artist, while Gumbril abandons his teaching position and devotes himself to promoting his absurd pneumatic trousers. (When Boldero is sent by Gumbril to ask Lypiatt to draw an advertisement for these trousers, he is kicked down the stairs by the indignant artist.) Though Lypiatt lives in solitary squalor and contemplates suicide, he is much more alive and attractive than any other character in the novel. Huxley compensates for his emotional frustration with Nancy Cunard by linking Lypiatt's failure in art with his failure in love. Yet, despite the satiric portrait of the bruised heart beneath the veil of cynicism, the contrast in the temperament of Lypiatt and Gumbril suggests not only the enormous personal and stylistic difference between the emotional Lewis and the intellectual Huxley, but also Huxley's reluctant recognition of his rival's obvious merits.

Huxley shaped the satiric image of Lewis which was later adopted by Osbert and Edith Sitwell in their double-barrelled fictional attacks that appeared in 1937 and 1938, about fifteen years after *Antic Hay*. Sacheverell Sitwell has recently written that the Sitwells were Lewis' friends during the 1920s—until he suddenly and savagely attacked them:

> In the early 1920s I was a friend and great admirer of Wyndham Lewis. . . . [But in 1930] he launched, without warning, *The Apes of God*, a huge time-bomb meant to destroy my brother, my sister and myself. Since then, though still an admirer of this genius *manqué*, I want to hear no more about him. He was a malicious, thwarted and dangerous man. . . . There was no reason except envy and malice for Lewis suddenly writing that time-bomb against us. He was a dangerous, unpleasant man with a touch of genius. . . . We had the impression he was a friend until he tried to deliver this death blow.

The portraits of Lewis in Edith's *I Live under a Black Sun* and Osbert's *Those Were the Days* are based on their personal relations with him, but they are strongly influenced by Huxley's caricature and embittered by Lewis' public malevolence.

In his biography of the Sitwells, whom he adores, John Lehmann is forced to confess that Edith's "hypertrophied alertness to injury, real or imagined, never left her" and to admit "the violence of her instinct for revenge." Her only novel, *I Live under a Black Sun,* an inferior by-blow of her book on Pope, retells the story of Swift, Stella and Vanessa, places them in the twentieth century and concerns the theme of "hatred replaced with love." Yet Henry Debingham, the character based on Lewis, has no real function in the novel and is introduced only to give Edith the opportunity to attack her enemy. For as Edith writes, in a gratuitous comparison: "Swift was incapable of lying, and his hatred was the reverse side of love. Swift feared nothing and nobody. Lewis enjoyed lying, not only as a defence behind which he could hide, but as an idol.'

Debingham, like Lewis, works in a squalid studio, and wears his hat pulled down and his collar turned up as a refuge and protection against a hostile world. He is extremely fond of role-playing and disguise, and Edith echoes Huxley when she states that behind his aggressive *je-m'en-fichisme* "he was nothing but a great blundering, blubbering Big Boy, craving for Home and Mother":

> For this remarkable man, who was a sculptor in those moments he could spare from thinking about himself, and from making plans to confute his enemies, had a habit of appearing in various roles, partly as a disguise (for caution was part of his professional equipment), and partly in order to defy his own loneliness.

Though Edith recognizes that Debingham's desperate efforts to be impressive are inspired by his profound isolation and solitude, she—quite naturally—has no sympathy for him.

John Lehmann's assertion that "the essence of Osbert Sitwell's satire is his hatred of the insensitive and the philistine" does not apply to the treatment of Lewis, who appears halfway through Osbert's long and rather tedious novel and is the only interesting character in the book. Like Ford's George Heimann, there is an air of secrecy and mystery surrounding Stanley Esor, whose origins are obscure. Sitwell suggests that Esor is covertly Jewish in order to explain his anti-Semitism—an allusion to Lewis' attacks on Jews during the 1930s. But in all other respects, Esor represents the Lewis of the early 1920s, when most of the novel takes place. Like Heimann and Debingham, Esor wears a swashbuckling black cape and a sombrero, and is fond of Spanish oaths.

Like Huxley's Casimir Lypiatt, Esor attempts to be a poet, musician, painter, philosopher, sculptor and architect; but he lacks genuine talent and his paintings have "a singular quality of wooden stiffness." Esor is Nietzschean in his *"übermensch* pugnacity," his "granite" personality and his desire to shock. But he is also arrogant, bad-tempered and boorish. He sees life "as a perpetual sabre-toothed struggle of man against man, in which the most ferocious, objectionable and unscrupulous inevitably conquered"; and sees himself as "a strong man, self-willed, a solitary being of unique grandeur, defying the past and saluting the future."

Like Lewis—but in contrast to Lypiatt—Esor "irresistibly attracted" women. He has an affair with a married woman, Joanna Mompesson, who tactlessly brings him a present of new collars. She eventually leaves her husband, Jocelyn, and comes to live in Esor's disgusting Kensington studio. When Myra Viveash comes to Lypiatt's studio at the end of *Antic Hay,* he hears her knock but refuses to answer because he has been deeply wounded by her rejection and her insult about his art. In Sitwell's novel, Esor also hears Joanna's knock, but *he* controls the situation and does not let her in for fear of compromising his art and being burdened with a domesticated mistress. At the end of the novel Esor becomes friendly with Jocelyn and meets him for tea in A.B.C. shops—which Lewis frequently patronized and blessed in *Blast*.

Sitwell is more concerned with Lewis' life than with his art, and Esor reflects many aspects of Lewis' habits, career, friends and faults. Esor suppressed his Christian name (Lewis disliked "Percy" and claimed to have lost it in the war); he is tall and inclined to corpulence (Osbert later wrote that Lewis' "lean Spanish elegance" had been replaced by a "robust and rather jocose Dutch convexity") and he is the autocratic leader of several artistic movements, who "adopted the pose of a herdsman, a lonely figure far above the flock" (an allusion to Lewis' personal manifesto, "The Code of a Herdsman," 1917). Esor exalts Chaldean and Negro sculpture just as Lewis did when he was influenced by T. E. Hulme's theories; and he does not hesitate to secede and form a new rebel movement of his own, as Lewis did when he attacked the Futurists (his former allies) and formed the Rebel Art Centre in March 1914.

Despite this loyal "Praetorian Guard," Esor is subject to fits of helpless dejection when he is hypochondriac or ill, an allusion to Lewis' severe illnesses and operations during 1932–1937. And like Lewis, Esor is extremely suspicious and afraid of being observed, moves about frequently (in the 1930s Lewis received letters at the Pall Mall Safe Deposit in Carlton Street), and often withdraws from circulation and disappears for long periods to write his numerous books. These peculiar characteristics make Esor "that curious combination of fretting neurasthenic and genial cave-man"—a direct echo of Eliot's phrase about Lewis' modern thought and cave-man energy. Though Lewis was satirized in *Those Were the Days,* he remains—in Sitwell as in Huxley—the only vital and fascinating character in their novels.

Elliott Baker's story, "The Portrait of Diana Prochnik" (1974), is the only fictional work in which Lewis appears as himself and is portrayed positively. The story, which resembles Philip Roth's "Goodbye Columbus," creates a tragicomic contrast between vulgar Jewish-American materialism and dignified English culture, as embodied in the (anti-Semitic) Lewis. It takes place in Buffalo in the fall of 1939 when Lewis, short of funds and forced to live by his brush, was painting Chancellor Capen of the University of Buffalo.

Baker begins by refuting Hemingway's biased view (a direct response to "The Dumb Ox") that Lewis had the eyes of an unsuccessful rapist; and he portrays Lewis as formal, proud, composed, articulate and highly intelligent; as a dedicated man who "based his entire life on the accuracy and integrity of his vision." Lewis meets the beautiful Diana Prochnik when she is dancing with some other students at the Hotel Stuyvesant, where he is staying. He then brings some of his paintings to her home in order to convince her father, a wealthy junk dealer, to let him paint her portrait. When the gauche Mr. Prochnik says: "Let's see your samples," Lewis, "with a streak of masochism" but with impressive honesty, shows the ignoramus a work that closely resembles his great *Surrender of Barcelona* (1936) (which was influenced by Velázquez's *Surrender of Breda*) and gives a brief but impressive lecture on Vorticism.

Though Mr. Prochnik prefers the art of Norman Rockwell, he commissions the hundred-dollar portrait of his daughter with the proviso that "he was to be the sole judge of its satisfaction. If he didn't like it, Lewis would get nothing." When Lewis brings the completed portrait to Prochnik's house he is shown the trashy junkyard paintings of this petty ape of God, recklessly condemns them and passionately states his artistic credo: "You know nothing of colour, nothing of composition, nothing of form or texture. . . . You make a few vulgar scrawls that any child could make and want to be praised for it. Men devote their entire lives to art. And no-one has the right to cheapen and denigrate what others die for." Though Diana adores the painting, her outraged father vehemently rejects it: "Crap! I wouldn't give two cents for it! I wouldn't have it in my house if *he paid me!*"

The most effective aspect of the story is Baker's moving recognition and revelation of Lewis' humiliating and degrading quest for portrait commissions among the philistine rich. As Lewis wrote from New York, in an unpublished letter of December 15, 1939 that dramatized the role of the artist in modern society.

> I am here on a painting expedition—I am head-hunting. I desire to *portray*, in oils, chalks, irrespective of looks, age, colour. . . . It is not every day of the week that a painter with any pretensions to being an artist is moving round looking for subjects: for usually the "portrait-painter," whether here or in Europe, is little better than a colour-photographer. . . . If you know any *intelligent*, or *beautiful* people that indeed would be marvellous. But I want to paint pictures, and I will take on any mug that offers without insulting it. (No billiard-balls for eyes, *postiche* [false] noses or cauliflower ears! Such a job as Dürer or Bellini would have done, were they alive today.)

Baker's description provides an interesting contrast to the iconoclastic and hostile Lewis who inspired envy and hatred in England during the Twenties and Thirties. For the Lewis in America is now mellowed by age and opposed to a different kind of moneyed philistinism. Whereas the English literary portraits were all biased, the American one has no personal animus. It is sympathetic to Lewis and critical of his adversary, but still vividly conveys the aggressive and hypersensitive character who resembles the earlier fictional portraits.

The portrayals of Wyndham Lewis demonstrate the profound and persistent influence of his personality and art on a number of significant poets and novelists. They also reveal that he inspired considerable hostility in Huxley and the Sitwells; reluctant respect in Auden, Rickword, Joyce and Ford; and deep loyalty and admiration in Campbell, Pound and Elliott Baker. Lewis is intensely alive in both the hostile and the sympathetic portraits, for he has such a fascinating character and is concerned with so many significant aspects of modern life that he becomes a symbolic as well as a living artist.

13

The Quest for Wyndham Lewis

I

All my books seem cursed. Bound copies of my first work, *Fiction and the Colonial Experience,* had to be recalled from America and burned when I found that none of my proof corrections had been made by the printers, who transposed lines, omitted the notes for an entire chapter and left in hundreds of their own errors. The English editor of *The Wounded Spirit* failed to find an American publisher; and when McGill-Queen's wanted to bring out the book, he refused to agree to their terms. Additions to my perfect typescript of *T. E. Lawrence: A Bibliography* were made by the editor in his large sprawling handwriting and then printed by photo-offset. The "Reader's Guide" series was discontinued by Farrar, Straus just as my *Orwell* was published by their English counterpart, Thames & Hudson. The innovative editor of *Painting and the Novel* changed the titles of all books and paintings cited in the text to lower case letters and reduced the photos—which he published on matt instead of glossy paper—until the details were completely extinguished. Though I managed to correct the titles, I could do nothing about the photos; and one reviewer aptly commented that the reproduction of Holbein's elongated *Christ in the Tomb,* squashed under a page of print, resembled a ham sandwich. After the publisher's manifest incompetence, I broke my contract with Manchester and gave *Homosexuality and Literature* to Athlone. The American edition of *A Fever at the Core,* which was reviewed in the daily and Sunday newspapers in England, was published so secretly—by a subsidiary of the house that had originally refused the book—that no one every knew it had appeared. The publisher of *Married to Genius* ceased to function as soon as that book came out; despite prominent reviews, it was published and remaindered almost simultaneously. Though this book was also published in India, I received nothing from Rupa but an invitation to tea the next time I was in Calcutta.

My essay on writing *Katherine Mansfield,* published in *Biography* in the summer of 1978, ended on a prematurely triumphant note; for that book, which followed in the same lamentable tradition, was more difficult to publish than to write. After the text was printed in March 1978 a long series of *contretemps* led inexorably to the final disaster. My publisher Hamish Hamilton asked Mrs. George Bowden, the widow of Katherine's one-day husband, for permission to quote his unpublished letters; she objected to my statement that the fictional music teacher, Mr. Reginald Peacock, was based on her late mate. Without consulting me the editor changed my text to suit her wishes. After threats of a libel action, he submitted the bound proofs to a lawyer, who said I could not safely use the word "lesbian" to describe Katherine's 90-year old friend, Ida Baker. I agreed to the deletion of this work, the editor took this concession as a sign of weakness, and again changed many passages—deleting "intimacy," "friendship," "companion"—without my knowledge or consent. There was also a great row about a photograph which Katherine's brother-in-law had given me to keep and reproduce in my book. When the publisher requested formal permission (always a time of trials) to do this, it transpired that the photo was actually owned by a woman I had never heard of, who vehemently accused me of stealing her property! The photo was duly returned to her, with apologies; but when I called to explain the misunderstanding and request the same permission for the French edition, she slammed down the phone and refused to answer when I tried to call back.

I had requested proofs of the very thorough index, which had been made when I corrected the original page proofs and which included birth and death dates of the most important figures, but was told by my editor that there was no time to see them and that he had corrected them for me. I replied I must have them, despite the delay, and was surprised to find that the printed index, passed by the editor, contained thirty errors. When I also insisted on seeing the corrected proofs, I was horrified to discover another seventy errors. Many of my corrections had not been made, the transformation from American to English spelling was inconsistent, my punctuation had been changed and the editor, while altering the text about Bowden and Ida, had introduced a great many mistakes. Two of the photos were badly reproduced, one was omitted entirely and the captions did not always match the List of Illustrations. This was how Hamish Hamilton had dealt with my two years of painstaking research and careful writing.

Fighting off a nervous breakdown, I telephoned the managing director of the firm in London (at their expense) and made my position absolutely clear. The biography had to be published exactly as I had written it or returned to me for submission to another publisher. If they attempted to publish a corrupt text, I promised to sue them for damaging my reputation as an author. I complained that they had been extremely deferential to the wishes of Mrs. Bowden, to Ida Baker (who died in July, before the book appeared) and to the Estate of Middleton Murry (who had to approve the quotation of unpublished material by Katherine), but had consistently ignored my desire to have the book published as I wrote it. It was absurd as well as distressing to have to quarrel about having my work published correctly.

The managing director, who did not want me to withdraw the book and knew I would do so (I had already withdrawn it from Angus & Robertson), agreed to reprint the 5000 copies of the book (which cost them a fortune). Every day at 7:30 a.m., for an entire week, I had hour-long phone calls from London as we wrangled about the text and I fought bitterly but successfully to restore my original words.

While all this was going on, George Braziller, a small but high-toned publisher, offered me excellent terms for the American editions of both *Mansfield* and the projected *Lewis*. But the details of the written contracts were less favorable than what we had agreed on verbally; and when I called New York about this, I learned that Braziller had left for Europe—expecting me to sign without further discussion. Since I have an English but not an American agent, I rewrote the contracts and returned them to him. In London, meanwhile, he was warned by Hamilton that the book was potentially libellous, would have to be reprinted and would not be published until the fall. He then lost all confidence in and enthusiasm for the books, and cancelled the contracts. The lucrative but always unreal advances disappeared even before I had planned how to spend them. Braziller pitched up unannounced on my London doorstep in October and once again asked to publish my books. But when he refused to pay for the American permissions, as he had originally offered to do, I lost patience with him and refused to sign the contracts.

The publication of *Mansfield* was delayed from May to November 1978, and I had to have the proofs sent to me while travelling in Europe. When my plans suddenly changed after a four-car accident destroyed my new auto on the Nuremberg-Munich *Autobahn,* I had to queue for hours at a packed Provençal post office to call London, and make several other difficult and expensive calls from Spain when the proofs failed to arrive on time.

When *Mansfield* finally appeared in November I received thirty-five reviews in England and fifteen in New Zealand (where it was published by Hodder & Stoughton); I sold the French rights to Editions Stock and the American to New Directions. I was interviewed by newspapers and the BBC Overseas Radio, and would have been on the television program "Word for Word" if they had found someone to debate the book with me. But my troubles with Hamilton were not yet over. The managing director wrote that they would deduct £100 from my advance for my excessive corrections on the second set of proofs, though these were caused by their errors on the first set. But they eventually withheld £180 for legal expenses, though they had caused me great nervous strain, extra work, and money for calls and postage. When Hamilton refused to return the disputed £180 I tore up their contract for *Lewis* and immediately signed with Routledge, who had published my *Orwell* volume in the Critical Heritage series. (When I asked Routledge for a review of that book by C. P. Snow, which they had quoted in a *TLS* ad, they replied that Snow had never reviewed the book!) The final blow occurred when the first printing sold out in three months and Hamish Hamilton failed to reprint the book. For more than eight months, while the demand for *Mansfield* was at its height, my biography was out of stock. Despite the desperate rearguard action to defend the integrity of my work, I still managed to publish my biography before Antony Alpers published his (which was due out in January 1978). I hate to contemplate what must have happened to him.

II

Though the life and work of Mansfield and Lewis seem to be totally different, they were contemporaries and had some surprising similarities. Both were born in British colonies, came from wealthy families but were poor all their adult lives, lived a bohemian existence in France, had a cosmopolitan rather than an insular outlook, were strongly influenced by Russian writers and wrote their first, satiric books about Germans. Lewis decorated the Cave of the Golden Calf, where Mansfield performed as a *commère*. Both shared a hostile attitude toward Bloomsbury, and wrote for the *New Age*. Both were emotionally involved with Beatrice Hastings, were artistic allies of Gaudier, and friends of the Schiffs and the Dreys. Both were hostile to doctors and unwilling to face the reality of their diseases.

In September 1922, four months before her death, Mansfield and Lewis had a disastrous meeting at the Schiffs' London house. He was rude, perhaps brutally cruel to the dying woman during their heated discussions about the limitations of her stories and her fatal infatuation with Gurdjieff, whom Lewis accurately described as a "Levantine psychic shark."

My experience with Mansfield's biography was excellent preparation for writing the life of Lewis. She died at 34 and wrote relatively little; he died at 74, wrote 50 books and 360 essays, and was also the most important English painter of the twentieth century. Mansfield's character was consistent; her stories, journals and letters were homogeneous and easy to understand. Lewis passed through a number of distinct physical, temperamental and artistic stages in his life, and his capacity for change and development was one of the most fascinating aspects of his character. Books like *Tarr, The Art of Being Ruled, Time and Western Man, The Apes of God, Self Condemned* and *The Human Age* were massive, complex and extremely difficult. Mansfield's work was essentially autobiographical; her letters and journals were truthful and her dominant mode was self-revelation. Lewis was intensely secretive about his private life, covered his tracks and hid behind a series of masks and *personae*. The editor of his *Letters* has observed that: "The scholar concerned with the data of Lewis' life has found himself lost in a fog of rumour and half-proved fact, of conflicting statements and pure fantasy."

Mansfield has been dead for fifty years, Lewis for only twenty-three years. My life of Lewis was therefore more extensively based on personal letters and interviews. There are many more people now alive who knew him than knew her and his surviving friends, unlike hers, are distinguished by their impressive intellect and fierce loyalty to his memory. His scholarly disciples are a close-knit, rather than a diverse group; a few of them even imitate the style, mannerisms and politics of the Master. Almost all Lewis scholars are men; a significant number of Mansfield scholars are women. Some of the feminist reviewers, who resented my invasion of their territory and assumed a man could not really understand their Katherine, launched attacks on my book. One particularly nasty review was written by the friend of a rival biographer. Though I sympathized with Mansfield, I never felt I was like her in any way. But I found that Lewis and I had (at least) a similar physique, quarrelsome temperament, hatred of publishers, capacity for work and commitment to intellectual life. I had written a good deal about Mansfield's friends and milieu—Lawrence, Bloomsbury and Garsington—before I began her biography. But I had never done scholarly work on Lewis' closest friends—Pound and Eliot—and had to master the more experimental forms of modernism. Fortunately, with Mansfield and with Lewis, I became increasingly attracted to their characters and books as I discovered more about their life and work.

The reputations of Mansfield and Lewis provided another significant contrast. Mansfield's reputation, founded on the cult established by Murry immediately after her death, has steadily increased during the last fifty years. Though she is particularly admired in her native New Zealand and in France, scholars from all over the world have written about her work; her books are still in print and continue to prosper. Lewis, on the contrary, because of his unpopular satires and Right-wing political tracts of the 1930s, has attracted more hostility than appreciation. In North America, his advocates tend to be conservative Catholic scholars, like McLuhan, Kenner and Kirk, who publish with Henry Regnery and in the *National Review;* and he has been either ignored or attacked by the liberal New York literary establishment. Irving Howe, their representative spokesman, has exclaimed in the *Partisan Review:* "When a charlatan like Wyndham Lewis is revived and praised for his wisdom, it is done, predictably, by a Hugh Kenner in the *Hudson Review.*" Most of Lewis' books are out of print and difficult to find; and he has not enjoyed the academic prestige of his contemporaries—Pound, Eliot and Joyce—who freely acknowledged his genius. One of my ambitions was to attract new readers and restore Lewis' reputation.

The attractive biographical image of Katherine was established in 1931 by the Mantz-Murry biography of her early years and reinforced by Alpers' rather sentimental evocation of 1954. But there has been no biography of Lewis. Roy Campbell's book was printed and announced in 1932, but never published; biographies of Lewis were projected and abandoned by Walter Allen, Martin Seymour-Smith and Catherine Dupré; and Victor Cassidy, who began ten years ago, has not published a word. My biography, which brings the Enemy out of the shadows and shows him to be more sympathetic than menacing, was the first to appear.

III

Though I followed the same procedure for both biographies, Lewis' longevity, secrecy, complex books and varied careers as a vital and versatile painter, novelist, philosopher, poet, critic and editor made the research for his life much more difficult than for Mansfield's. While I slowly acquired Lewis' valuable books (and sometimes borrowed them from Hugh Porteus and Walter Allen), I compiled a 900-item bibliography of criticism about him and a detailed 14-page chronology of his life. I wrote and received several hundred letters about Lewis, including vivid accounts from Lord David Cecil, Lord Clark, Alistair Cooke, Admiral Sir Caspar John, Archibald MacLeish, Henry Miller, Sir Oswald Mosley, Anthony Powell, Laura Riding, Sir Sacheverell Sitwell, Allen Tate and Sir William Walton.

In May-June 1978 (during the Mansfield *débâcle*) I spent five weeks reading 8000 Lewis documents at Cornell University. Fortunately, the librarians allowed me complete access to their superb collection of Lewis letters and manuscripts and guided me through the complex task of studying them. Since only one other person had read everything at Cornell (and he moved to Ithaca and took a year and a half to do it), it seemed as if the long shelves of papers existed solely for my benefit. The considerable strain of reading manuscripts for eight hours a day and typing the notes all evening was alleviated by the exhilaration of continuous discoveries. I left Cornell with Lewis' stern warning echoing in my throbbing head: "When a person, who, like myself, has played a prominent part in the intellectual life of his country, in his time, comes to die, the circumstances of his life are liable, by way of biography, to be distorted and arranged according to the fancy of the biographer."

W. K. Rose, the superb editor of Lewis' *Letters,* who died of a brain tumor in 1968, left all his papers to Vassar College. Reading his correspondence with people who had died since his edition appeared in 1963 provided much new information; and his earlier letters to people I had written to allowed me to check the accuracy of their memories and confirm their stories. I also read Lewis' correspondence at Yale, the New York Public Library, the Morgan Library, the Museum of Modern Art, the British Library, London University Library, the

Tate Gallery and the Imperial War Museum. I gratefully received copies of letters from eight other libraries; and from his publishers—New Directions, Henry Regnery, Ryerson Press and Chatto & Windus—though his correspondence with most English publishers was destroyed, with their offices, in the Blitz. Dora Stone and Romilly John sent me *original* letters to copy; a number of other people allowed me to read Lewis letters in their possession; Sam Hynes provided a copy of a precious unpublished memoir by Kate Lechmere; and William Wees gave me a revealing tape-recorded interview with Helen Rowe, a model who had known Lewis before the Great War. I traced, with great difficulty and the help of a friend familiar with the Civil Service bureaucracy, Lewis' furious correspondence with the London County Council, which was trying to demolish his Notting Hill Gate flat at the end of his life, and was grieved to find that the file had been destroyed. When I first asked an Indian clerk if they kept correspondence from the 1950s, he said he could not tell me because he was not born then.

Though I succeeded in tracing hundreds of unpublished letters, I had severe problems with two libraries. Boston University, which owns important papers by the mother of two of Lewis' children, sent the least helpful letter I have ever received: "Our Iris Barry materials are restricted by the donor [Edmund Schiddel], and relative to his instructions we may not make this correspondence available for research, nor reply to queries concerning the contents of the materials." This seemed particularly absurd in view of the fact that the contents were described in the very useful National Union Catalogue of Manuscripts, the American equivalent of the National Register of Archives in London. Though the total and indefinite embargo of scholarly materials was (fortunately) unique in my experience, I did not—despite help from friends on the Boston University faculty—succeed in penetrating this sanctum.

With SUNY Buffalo, the second most important collection of Lewis papers and a lamentable contrast to Cornell, I had an infinitely more torturous experience. I first wrote to Buffalo asking to read their Lewis letters in September 1977, the month after my extremely pleasant and informative six-hour interview with the still-beautiful Mrs. Lewis. I took her out for lunch and a drive around Torquay, and she frankly answered all my questions, promised to send me her notes on Lewis' life and inscribed my copy of *Rotting Hill:* "To Jeffrey Meyers from G. A. Wyndham Lewis, Thanking you for a very enjoyable visit." (She had mellowed considerably since the early 1960s when she nearly drove W. K. Rose mad with her criticisms of his edition.) I looked forward, with craned eyebrows, to meeting her the following year.

Buffalo replied that written permission was needed to read the letters. I duly wrote for this to Mrs. Lewis and, after an alarming delay, was shocked to hear that she had suffered a disabling stroke in October. The Courts, acting on her behalf, would eventually take over the responsibility of the Lewis Estate;

until then, no one could supply the requisite permission. In May 1978 I stopped at Buffalo on the way to Cornell and found the Library was closed during the summer, precisely when scholars were able to visit. In July, when I went to London to write the book on a Guggenheim grant, the Library informed me that they would not supply copies of the letters—even if I got the necessary permission. (After Mrs. Lewis' stroke, in the fall of 1978, the last of Lewis' papers— his final keep—were sold to Cornell via Anthony Rota. Though Cornell and Rota were both willing to let me read these papers in London, before they were sent to America, I was prevented from doing so by a legal technicality.)

My hope for the Buffalo papers was briefly renewed in March 1979 when two of the three members of the committee advising the Society of Authors, which the Courts had appointed to administer the Lewis Estate, gave permission to get copies of the letters. In April the Director of the Library retired, they changed their policy and finally agreed to send the xeroxes. But Mrs. Lewis, who was 78 and had been in frail health for some time, died on April 12; and the committee's permission was suspended until the Estate was once again settled. I completed the biography on June 13, and in August finally received permission to get the letters from Mrs. Lewis' two heirs. Both of them have a serious interest in Lewis' work and had looked after her since his death.

In order to do justice to Lewis the artist I saw a great many of his paintings and drawings, which are scattered in museums throughout America, Canada, Britain, Australia and South Africa. I studied his work in Ithaca, Utica, New York City, Cambridge, Mass. and Windsor, Ontario; in seven London and eight provincial museums; in several art galleries (where I found biographical material in exhibition catalogs of Spencer Gore and Jessica Dismorr); and in the major private collections of Omar Pound, Wyndham Vint, Walter Michel, John Cullis, D. G. Bridson and David Drey. I wrote in advance to view paintings that were not on exhibition; and found it especially enjoyable to see the Tate's entire collection of Lewis spread out for my private view in their storage vaults. The British Institute of Recorded Sound and the BBC enabled me to hear readings by Lewis and broadcasts of *The Human Age;* and the Arts Council of Britain showed me a film on *Blast.*

IV

The most interesting aspect of the research was undoubtedly the seventy interviews I had with people who had known Lewis, though I had to be careful not to encourage informants to say what I wanted to hear. Those interviewed included three originals for *The Apes of God.* The blind poet, Edgell Rickword, who thought Lewis carried on a one-sided quarrel with him and got his own back in his ironic poem "The Encounter," was indifferent about his role in the

The Quest for Wyndham Lewis 209

satire. Stephen Spender, who wryly agreed that Dan Boleyn, a complete idiot, was based on himself, was amused by his fictional image. And Sacheverell Sitwell, who called Lewis a genius *manqué*, wanted to hear no more about the "malicious, thwarted and dangerous man" and—fifty years later—was still furious about his treachery.

In North America, Russell Kirk asked me to stay in his eclectic Michigan mansion and described his meeting with the blind old man; Father Stanley Murphy, who had invited Lewis to teach at Assumption College in the early 1940s, expressed great fondness for Lewis, told me about his effective teaching and identified the originals of *Self Condemned* as we looked across the Detroit River to the big American city. Marshall McLuhan, a loyal friend in the Forties and Lewis' leading disciple, described his publicity campaign for Lewis in Missouri, told how the enraged writer tore up a copy of his dangerous *Hitler* book—and how McLuhan got into Woody Allen's film, *Annie Hall*. I helped John Slocum, who lived in regal splendor in Newport, crack open his locked safe. There was no correspondence from Lewis, but we found dozens of forgotten letters from Pound. When my five-year-old daughter, accustomed to modest residences without long driveways and caged elevators, boldly inquired: "Hey Slocum, was this place once a palace?" he replied, in a deep and dignified voice: "My dear, it still is."

I smashed up my car on the way to dinner with Dora Stone and never reached Innsbruck; but I saw Roy Campbell's widow, Mary, in their crumbling villa above Sintra, and learned that Lewis' description of their wild wedding in *Blasting and Bombardiering* was strictly accurate and that Campbell considered their friendship one of the biggest events of his life. I also found Iris Barry's friend, Pierre Kerroux, in the Alpes Maritimes, heard about her final years and how her papers (including letters from Lewis and drawings by Picasso) had been stolen after her death.

In London, Rebecca West (the only person I met who knew Lewis before the Great War) gave me whiskey with dinner instead of wine, and talked about the days of Vorticism and *Blast* while sitting beneath her striking portrait that reveals a troubled intelligence in her strained expression and features. Paul Martin, the Canadian High Commissioner in London, made me aware of the damaging rumors that surrounded Lewis in wartime Canada: that he had been a conscientious objector in the Great War (instead of an officer at Passchendaele) and had been paid by Winston Churchill to leave England in 1939 (instead of going into voluntary exile). Martin's wife, Eleanor, explained—during a magnificent lunch—that the furious expression in her portrait was provoked by Lewis' cynical criticism of patriotism, the royal family, important politicians and military leaders while he was painting her. The Dowager Marchioness of Cholmondeley, a friend of Henry James, received me in her Kensington Palace

Gardens mansion, filled with portraits of herself by Lewis, Orpen and John. She had written love letters to Lewis in the early Thirties and described their secret meetings in his dingy Ossington Street flat.

Hugh Porteus, Lewis' longtime friend and disciple, was my liveliest and most indiscreet informant. In three long meetings (and a dozen letters) he told me of Lewis' keen interest in his own sexual affairs and how jealous he was of the closely-guarded Mrs. Lewis. Henry Moore, still handsome and energetic at eighty, dressed in a lilac shirt and affectionately stroking a piece of smooth-grained wood, expressed great admiration for Lewis as he showed me his studios and sculpture garden. As a young student, Moore was inspired by Lewis, whose books provided the stimulating gust of fresh air that liberated him from Bloomsbury's stranglehold on English art and confirmed his youthful hope that "everything was possible, that there were men in England full of vitality and life."

Moore's friend, Geoffrey Grigson, who impressively matches Lewis' fine presence and flashing intellect, also shares his reputation for stern standards and vitriolic severity. I approached Grigson with some trepidation and, as he assured me of Lewis' kindness, was surprised by the warmth, patience and generosity that belied his own fierce image. After a dinner cooked by his wife (a famous chef), we walked out under the stars of Wiltshire, his lamp guiding our way. As he wiped the mist from my windscreen, bade me safe journey and asked me back to see him in the spring, I could not forbear confessing that I found him exactly as he had found Lewis.

Though most people were astonishingly generous with their time and help—and I was surprised that so many eminent people agreed to see me—a few uncooperative ones did not answer my letters: Basil Bunting (a friend of Pound), Morley Callaghan (who knew Lewis in Paris and in Toronto), Malcolm Cowley (who met Lewis in New York), Henry Ford II (a patron in Detroit), Elsie Hirst (a friend of Mrs. Lewis, who had moved into a nursing home by the time I tracked down her address), Philip Johnson (a friend of Iris Barry), Alfred George Lewis (a New York relative), Rob Lyle (a friend of Roy Campbell), May Morris (an actress who lived next door in Notting Hill Gate), J. B. Priestley (who was drawn by Lewis), Lady Read (the widow of Herbert Read), William Roberts (a member of the Vorticist group and a total recluse), Martin Seymour-Smith, G. W. Stonier (a critic now living in South Africa), James Johnson Sweeney (who knew Lewis well in New York) and Pier van der Kruk (an elusive Dutch disciple). Perhaps some zealot can pin down and interview this remnant of witnesses.

The only people I was unable to find were Ida, the German model for Bertha in *Tarr*, who bore Lewis' first child and disappeared without a trace; and Alex and Ethel Lewis, Wyndham's half-brother and half-sister by his father's second marriage. Perhaps they will surface after the biography is published.

Besides Mrs. Lewis, Burgon Bickersteth, Edmond Kapp, I. A. Richards, Allen Tate, Ruthven Todd and Anton Zwemmer died while I was writing the book.

V

The research, correspondence and interviews enabled me to clarify, for the first time, the major mysteries of Lewis' life: his family background; his mistresses and children; his secret marriage; and the serious illnesses of 1914, the four operations of the mid-Thirties and the etiology of his final blindness.

The National Archives in Washington, D.C. supplied extensive documents about the military career of Wyndham's father, Charles Edward Lewis. The library of Nunda, New York, where Lewis' father grew up, sent information about his family and a copy of his article, "Escape from a Rebel Prison," published in the *Nunda News* of February 18, 1865. I eventually found his parents' marriage certificate in the Pennsylvania Department of Health, and his Will in the Philadelphia City Hall. Family letters in Cornell revealed that Lewis' parents separated when he was eleven years old because of his father's love affairs.

Lewis had five illegitimate children with three different women between 1909 and 1920, and abandoned all of them. Ida's child was born in December 1909. I knew, from Lewis' unpublished wartime letters to Pound, that two other children, a boy and a girl, were born between 1909 and 1915, but had never been able to trace them. After I had completed the biography and given it to Routledge, I went to Manchester to see a major collection of Lewis' drawings. The curator there, who was planning a major Lewis exhibition in October 1980, had through a mutual friend been put in touch with Lewis' daughter, who had told her about her mother, her childhood meetings with Lewis and his mother, and the later life of herself and her brother. Fortunately, I was able to meet Lewis' daughter and add this new discovery to the text before it was sent to the printer.

Iris Barry, an extraordinary woman, important film critic and founder of the Film Library of the Museum of Modern Art, was the mother of Lewis' last children, another boy and girl. Though Iris' close friends, Lord Bernstein and Ivor Montagu, were reluctant to discuss her, I found out about her life from material in the Museum of Modern Art and from interviews with other friends. Following up every vague lead, I telephoned a man whom I thought might be her son—a very delicate situation indeed—and he eventually agreed to meet me. He was a kind and cultured professional man, who had a difficult childhood and never knew Lewis. We became friends, I dined with him several times while I was writing the book, and he told me about his mother.

Lewis, who was a handsome man and had the gift of inspiring feminine devotion, possessed an impressive number of attractive and intelligent mistresses, most notably: Ida, the "Rose Fawcett" of *Tarr,* Kate Lechmere, Beatrice Hastings, the wealthy novelist Mary Borden, Augustus John's model Alick Schepeler, Sybil Hart-Davis, probably Helen Saunders and Jessica Dismorr, Iris Barry, Nancy Cunard and Agnes Bedford. From letters and interviews I was able to reconstruct their lives and relations with Lewis.

I found unpublished photos of Mary Borden and Iris Barry as well as of Lewis' father, his literary mentor Sturge Moore, his patron Sir Nicholas Waterhouse (whose unpublished memoirs I discovered), Marshall McLuhan and his friend Felix Giovanelli, and Father Murphy. I traced the photos of Lewis by John Vickers, which the subject described as unspeakable iconographic insults. In the files of the London *Times* I dug up two superb unpublished photos of Lewis: an early one of the young artist standing before his lost painting, *The Laughing Woman* (used on the dust jacket of my book), and a late one of the blind sage under his green eye shade. The Hulton Picture Library was also an excellent source of photos. In the *Times* and the Tate Archives I discovered six articles by Lewis that were not listed in the two recent bibliographies; a factual account of the Toronto fire described in *Self Condemned;* and two unrecorded interviews with the *Buffalo Courier* in 1939 and the *Daily Mail* in 1956.

The basic dates in Lewis' life, as listed in standard reference books like the *Dictionary of National Biography* and *Who's Who* (which erroneously states that Lewis was an advisor to the Library of Congress), are incorrect. He was born aboard his father's yacht in Halifax, Nova Scotia in 1882 (not in Maine in 1884 or 1886, as he liked to say, to compensate for the years he lost in the War); and the date of his marriage was 1930, not 1929. When Mrs. Lewis could not remember the date of their wedding, I recalled her fury when W. K. Rose asked if she had really married Lewis and thought she might be trying to hide something from me. Though Lewis met his wife in 1918 and began to live with her in 1921, most of his close friends, who often visited his flat, did not know she existed. I could not locate a marriage certificate for 1929, but found that a Percy Lewis had wed a Gladys Hoskyns in Bristol in September 1939; and thought they had married just before leaving for Canada—until I realized they had already sailed when the coincidental Bristol marriage took place. A second search produced another marriage certificate of October 9, 1930, in which Lewis, who always camouflaged his private life, deliberately falsified nearly all the details. He spelled his wife's name Hoskins and described himself as aged 44 (instead of 48), an architect living at 22 Tavistock Road, Paddington (instead of 53 Ossington Street, Bayswater), the son of an English Captain in the Warwickshire Regiment (instead of a long-retired brevet Captain in the Union Army). If I had not known that Mrs. Lewis' father was a deceased florist named Joseph, it would have been impossible to verify their marriage. It is worth noting that couples do not have to provide proof for the statements they make on their marriage certificates.

The most complex aspect of Lewis' biography was his medical history.

With the help of two close friends who are doctors and the Neuro-Pathology Department of Southampton University Medical School, to whom I lectured on Lewis' case history, I was able to determine that his disease of 1914–1915 was gonorrhea (not syphilis), to understand and explain the sequence and purpose of his four operations for cystitis and urethral abscess between 1932 and 1937, and to establish the connection between the early venereal disease, the bladder disease and the nephritis that caused his death. I found three doctors—Millin, McPherson and Meadows—who had treated Lewis and showed that the pituitary tumor which caused his blindness by crushing the optic nerve had no effect on his so-called "paranoid" behavior. Though hospital records and x-rays are systematically destroyed seven years after the patient's death (and must therefore be rescued by biographers before then), I found, held and examined Lewis' brain—the final remnant of a mighty intellectual life. In the Pathology Museum of Westminster Hospital, where Lewis died in 1957, Dr. Antony Branfoot explained the slow growth of his massive tumor (which did not, as Hugh Kenner put it, "invade vital areas of his brain") and his autopsy report. It is entirely characteristic that Lewis' death certificate incorrectly states that he was 72 (instead of 74) years old and that his tumor was a cranio-pharyngioma (instead of a chromophobe adenoma).

All this research was extremely expensive; during 1978–79 I spent more than $6000 for travel, postage and phone calls, xeroxes and photos, books and magazines, paper and typing. I will be fortunate to recover this money from the sale of the book; and will certainly receive nothing for the time (an average of twelve hours a day last year) spent on research, writing and typing the long first draft. The "merit increase" I received from the University of Colorado for writing *Mansfield* was negligible. Biography is a costly, laborious, exasperating and profitless work, and can only be sustained by demonic devotion to the subject.

At the fag-end of literary criticism, when all major authors have been exhaustively analyzed, four kinds of books are being written: rare original critiques, variations of existing ideas, thinly disguised repetitions of what has already been said, and sterile infatuations with structuralism and semiotics. In this decadent context a thoroughly researched biography, which is firmly based on extensive archival evidence and presents a massive quantity of new material as the basis for original interpretations, is perhaps the most valuable contribution to modern scholarship.

VI

The Guggenheim grant enabled me to spend 1978–1979 in London instead of in the intellectual isolation of Boulder. I took over a friend's old flat in Hampstead—village of writers and shrinks—and was intensely stimulated by the close proximity of Lewis' friends and my own. I soaked myself in Lewisian locales, from the Tour Eiffel restaurant (now the White Tower) of the Vorticist days to the Golders Green crematorium, where he made the final journey accompanied by a Hammond organ. I reviewed regularly for the *Financial Times* and *Spectator;* lectured at the University of Sussex and King's College, London. I built up an enormous momentum to finish the book, raced forward in joyous anticipation of Lewis' death—and my own release from the bondage of page and pen—and wrote the 500 pages in six months. My editor at Routledge, who swore he would not change a comma without my permission, rushed the book to press as their lead title for the spring of 1980 and planned to issue a paperback edition for Lewis' centenary.

While writing the biography I also arranged with Athlone and McGill-Queen's University Press to edit a collection of eighteen original essays on Lewis, which would stimulate critical appreciation of the depth and diversity of his fifty years of creative life and appear at the same time as my biography. I sent out the first invitations in December 1978 and had all the completed essays by July 1979. Though I got most of the contributors I wanted—including John Holloway, Marshall McLuhan and Hugh Kenner, old friends of Lewis, leading Lewis scholars and some younger enthusiasts—and they agreed to write on a well-balanced range of topics, this book involved much more work than I had anticipated. It was especially difficult to convince distinguished scholars, who had helped me in my research on Lewis, to make the revisions I suggested and raise all the essays to the highest standard. In the end, however, Athlone and I were well satisfied.

My previous work on modern literature from 1880 to 1950 was excellent preparation for the life of Lewis, whom Eliot called "the most fascinating personality of our time." I discussed the Great War in my books on T. E. Lawrence (a friend of Lewis); the politics and history of the Thirties and Forties in my books on Orwell (with whom Lewis quarrelled); the relation of art and literature in *Painting and the Novel;* and learned the methods of modern biography in *Katherine Mansfield*.

Like many geniuses—and Lewis deserves this title—he was a multifarious man who assumed many roles, and the disparate aspects of his character could not be focused in a single convincing image. But as the self-styled Enemy emerged from obscurity, he could be clearly seen as an independent, intelligent and courageous artist, and one of the most lively and stimulating forces in modern English literature. If he had not composed political tracts, had concentrated on perfecting his major works and had devoted more time to painting, his reputation would have been much greater. As his centenary approaches, it seems just and proper to include him in the literary mainstream with Joyce, Pound and Eliot—the "Men of 1914"—and as Auden said of Kipling in his elegy of Yeats, to pardon him for writing well.

14

Hemingway: Wanted by the FBI

We must have our man in Havana, you know. Submarines need fuel. Dictators drift together. Big ones draw in the little ones.
Graham Greene

The FBI file on Ernest Hemingway reveals that Hemingway organized a private spy network in Cuba during World War II; that the Bureau made unsuccessful attempts to control, mock and vilify him; that it feared his personal prestige and political power; and that, in a pathetic episode, it tracked him to the Mayo Clinic, just before he died. The file contains 124 pages—fifteen withheld "in the interest of the national defense," fourteen blacked out except for the salutation, a few almost illegible because of the faded original typescript. It runs from October 8, 1942 to January 25, 1974 (thirteen years after his death), and much of it has to do with the first year of Hemingway's wartime activities in Cuba. The file is extremely repetitive, and becomes unintentionally funny when the solemn bureaucrats report the bizarre behavior of the writer.

The characters in this tragicomedy include Hemingway's friends Spruille Braden (1894–1978), the American ambassador to Cuba; Robert Joyce, the second secretary, coordinator of intelligence activities and liaison with the FBI agents; and Gustavo Durán (1907–1969), who skillfully commanded Loyalist divisions in the battles of Boadilla, Brunete and Valencia during the Spanish Civil War. The villains are Raymond Leddy, the legal attaché (i.e., FBI agent) in Havana, who helped train men for the Cuban FBI; and General Manuel Benitez, chief of the Cuban police and extortionist on a grand scale, who had previously played Latin lovers in grade-B Hollywood films.

Braden was born in Elkhorn, Montana (Hemingway hunting country), graduated from Yale, married a Chilean, had a successful career as a mining engineer and entrepreneur in South America. He was ambassador to Colombia before assuming the post in Cuba in the spring of 1942. Though often pompous and self-righteous, he was an independent and effective diplomat; strongly anti-communist, he was praised by the historian Hugh Thomas as "an intelligent man, with considerable Latin American experience . . . a distinctly Radical diplomat, with strong views of social reform. He was regarded by many Cubans as the best ambassador the US ever sent to Havana."[1]

In his memoirs, *Diplomats and Demagogues,* Braden states that there were 300,000 Spaniards in wartime Cuba, of whom 15,000 to 30,000 were "violent Falangists." Braden claims that he asked Hemingway "to organize an intelligence service that will do a job for a few months until I can get the [additional] FBI men down. These Spaniards have got to be watched." Beginning in August 1942, Hemingway, according to Braden, "built up an excellent organization and did an A-One job."[2] His work ended with the arrival of the FBI operatives in April 1943.

Both Hemingway and the FBI state, more accurately, that Hemingway first approached Braden and volunteered to investigate the Spanish Falange with the aid of his Loyalist refugee friends. Supported by the ambassador, Hemingway discreetly established an amateur but extensive information service with his own confidential agents. He had twenty-six informants, six of them working full-time, and twenty of them undercover men. His expenses came to a thousand dollars a month and he had 122 gallons of scarce gasoline charged to him from the embassy's private allotment in April 1943.

Hemingway's greatest administrative coup was to recruit Durán to assist him in what he called his Crook Factory. He informed Braden that the highly cultivated Durán, the son of a Spanish engineer, came from a fine family, was an excellent musician and composer of ballet scores, and had been the music critic of important Paris newspapers. When the Loyalist cause collapsed in 1939, Durán escaped to Barcelona, was rescued by a British destroyer and taken to London. He married an American, moved to the United States in 1940 and worked for Nelson Rockefeller, who was coordinator of inter-American affairs for the State Department. According to Agent Leddy, in a letter written to J. Edgar Hoover on August 13, 1943, Hemingway described Durán to Braden "as the ideal man to conduct this work, 'an intelligence and military genius that comes along once in a hundred years.'" In *For Whom the Bell Tolls* (1940), Robert Jordan thinks of Durán to fortify himself before an attack: "Just remember Durán, who never had any military training and who was a composer and lad about town before the movement and is now a damned good general commanding a brigade. It was all as simple and easy to learn and understand to Durán as chess to a child chess prodigy."[3]

In October 1942 Durán was sent from Washington for the special purpose of assisting Hemingway. Two months later, according to D. M. Ladd, a senior FBI official, the general was getting out of hand and had already become a potential enemy of the FBI: "Durán's operations and attitude . . . assume proportions of domination and direction rather than assistance to the agencies properly engaged in investigating subversive activities." By August 1943 Leddy, unaware of the labyrinthine politics of the Spanish Left, was zealously conducting an investigation to determine whether Durán was an active member of the Communist Party and political infiltrator into the American embassy. (Durán, investigated and cleared by the State Department in 1946, had a distinguished career with the United Nations in Chile, the Congo and Greece between 1946 and 1969.)[4]

Braden, a fierce crusader against corruption in Cuba, also directed Hemingway to look into the involvement of Cuban officials in the pervasive local graft. Ladd, who called Braden "a very impulsive individual," warned Hoover on December 17, 1942, that this would be dangerous. If we get involved in investigating Cuban corruption, he said, "it is going to mean that all of us will be thrown out of Cuba 'bag and baggage'. . . . [Hemingway, like Durán,] is actually branching out into an investigative organization of his own which is not subject to any control whatsoever. . . . Hemingway's activities . . . are undoubtedly going to be very embarrassing unless something is done to put a stop to them." The FBI attempted to thwart Hemingway in two ways: by discrediting the information that was supplied to Braden and passed on to Leddy; and by claiming that Hemingway, like Durán, was a communist.

A week before the visit of President Batista to Washington in 1943, Hemingway warned that General Benitez was proposing to seize power when Batista was out of the country. Leddy looked into the matter and pointed out that no such preparations had been observed by FBI agents working "in daily contact" with those at police headquarters. But Braden reported in June 1944 that General Benitez, a habitual plotter, "was meeting in a house in the outskirts of Havana, making plans to throw out Batista."[5]

On December 9, 1942, Hemingway reported sighting a contact between a German submarine and a Spanish steamer, *Marqués de Comillas,* off the Cuban coast while he "was ostensibly fishing with [his millionaire friend] Winston Guest and four Spaniards as crew members, but actually was on a confidential mission for the Naval Attaché." The FBI duly investigated the incident and reported "negative results."

According to a Bureau memo from C. H. Carson to Ladd on June 13, 1943, Hemingway, after reading about a new type of oxygen-powered German submarine, investigated "the supply and distribution of oxygen and oxygen tanks in Cuba." Hemingway enthusiastically claimed (in the FBI's translation of his words): "At last with this development we have come to the point after months of work where we are about to crack the submarine refuelling problem." The FBI checked the supply and distribution of the island's oxygen and found everything properly accounted for. They gleefully announced, "Nothing further was heard from Hemingway about the subject," and noted the change in his attitude: "Hemingway's investigations began to show a marked hostility to the Cuban Police and in a lesser degree to the FBI."

Another ludicrous confrontation between the dogged Leddy and the exasperated Hemingway sounds like a scene out of Graham Greene:

> In January, 1943, Mr. Joyce of the Embassy asked the assistance of the Legal Attaché in ascertaining the contents of a tightly wrapped box left by a suspect at the Bar Basque under conditions suggesting that the box contained espionage information. The box had been recovered from the Bar Basque by an operative of Hemingway. The Legal Attaché made private arrangements for opening the box and returned the contents to Hemingway through Mr. Joyce. The box contained only a cheap edition of the "Life of St. Teresa." Hemingway was present and appeared irritated that nothing more was produced and later told an Assistant Legal Attaché that he was sure that we had withdrawn the vital material and had shown him something worthless. When this statement was challenged by the Assistant Legal Attaché, Hemingway jocularly said he was only joking but that he thought something was funny about the whole business of the box.

After this incident the Bureau was forced to conclude: "The 'intelligence coverage' of Hemingway consisted of vague and unfounded reports of a sensational character.... [His] data ... were almost without fail valueless." Though both Braden and the State Department praised the quality of Hemingway's reports, it seems clear that this information, however well intentioned, was (like that of Graham Greene's agent Wormold) based more on fantasy than on fact. The entire Crook Factory, which Hemingway's third wife, Martha Gellhorn, refused to take seriously, was most probably a charitable scheme to support a few dozen indigent Loyalists. Leddy noted, with considerable relief, that Hemingway's organization was disbanded as of April 1, 1943, because of a "general dissatisfaction over the reports submitted."

On October 8, 1942, Leddy had told Hoover that Braden "has acceded to HEMINGWAY's request for authorization to patrol certain areas where submarine activity has been reported . . . and an allotment of gasoline is now being obtained for his use." But Hemingway's sub-hunting expeditions, which replaced his spy network, were little more than an excuse for fishing and drinking with friends on his boat, the *Pilar*. Only the force of Hemingway's legend and overpowering personality could have convinced the ambassador, despite overwhelming evidence from the FBI, that his spy games had any value.

Leddy was both disdainful of Hemingway's activities and fearful of his power. Trained to see everything in black or white, without any subtle gradations of meaning, he was puzzled by the communist attacks on Hemingway, who had supported the Loyalists in the Spanish Civil War. The novelist clearly troubled the FBI just as the Bureau would later worry him; and Leddy wrote directly to Hoover about his difficulties with Hemingway. Like everyone else the FBI disliked, Hemingway was immediately suspected—and privately accused—of being a communist, though no evidence was—or ever could be—offered to prove this. The mood, tone, phrases and techniques of the FBI during the hot war in the early 1940s clearly foreshadow those employed by Senator McCarthy during the cold war in the early 1950s.

Leddy's first letter to Hoover, which opens the file on October 8, 1942, makes two charges against Hemingway. First, "when the Bureau was attacked early in 1940 as a result of the arrests in Detroit of certain individuals charged with Neutrality Act violations for fostering enlistments in the Spanish Republican forces, Mr. HEMINGWAY was among the signers of a declaration which severely criticized the Bureau."[6] (Ladd called this the "general smear campaign.") Second, "in attendance at a Jai Alai match with HEMINGWAY, the writer [Leddy] was introduced by him to a friend as a member of the Gestapo. On that occasion, I told HEMINGWAY that I did not appreciate the introduction."

Hoover dug into his files and answered in person on December 17 to enlighten and encourage his local agent: "Any information which you may have relating to the unreliability of Ernest Hemingway as an informant may be discreetly brought to the attention of Ambassador Braden. In this respect it will be recalled that recently Hemingway gave information concerning the refueling of submarines in Caribbean waters which has proved unreliable." Two days later Hoover added: "[Hemingway's] judgment is not of the best, and if his sobriety is the same as it was some years ago, that is certainly questionable."

On the same day that Hoover first wrote to Leddy, Ladd told Hoover that "Hemingway has been accused of being of Communist sympathy, although we are advised that he has denied and does vigorously deny any Communist affiliation." This was followed on April 27, 1943, by nine typed pages of Hemingway's "Activities on Behalf of Loyalist Spain," which made his humanitarian efforts to provide ambulances for the wounded, medical aid for the sick and asylum for the refugees seem like unconscionable acts. In the same report, under "Possible Connections with Communist Party," the Bureau, without any supporting evidence, accusingly states: "In the fall of 1940 Hemingway's name was included in a group of names of individuals who were said to be engaged in Communist activities."

Other FBI letters noted Hemingway's first and only political speech at the American Writers Congress at Carnegie Hall on June 4, 1937, attended by such suspicious characters as Archibald MacLeish, Senator Gerald Nye and Congressman John Barnard; Hemingway's threat to expose "fascist influences" in the State Department and the Vatican, which he claimed were responsible for the political "castration" of the 1943 film version of *For Whom the Bell Tolls;* and Hemingway's statement in *Look* magazine that there was "nothing wrong with Senator Joseph McCarthy (Republican) of Wisconsin which a .577 solid would not cure."[7]

This was the FBI's own internal "smear campaign"—but the Bureau did not dare to carry it out in public. The "communist" Hemingway, Leddy reported to Hoover, was himself attacked by communist newspapers in New York and Havana. In June 1943, *Hoy* (Today) quoted Hemingway as advocating "the sterilization of all Germans as a means of preserving peace" and claimed that *For Whom the Bell Tolls* was "directed against the Communist party and against the Spanish people."[8]

Moreover, as Carson explained to Ladd in an FBI memo of June 13, 1943, Hemingway's close friendship with Braden, his immense popularity in Cuba (where he was greeted like a popular monarch as he drove through the streets), his fame in America and his prestige abroad made it imperative to keep a safe distance from the rogue elephant. If molested, he was capable of inflicting serious wounds on the Bureau:

> Regarding Hemingway's position in Cuba, the Legal Attaché advises that his prestige and following are very great. He enjoys the complete personal confidence of the American Ambassador and the Legal Attaché has witnessed conferences where the Ambassador observed Hemingway's opinions as gospel and followed enthusiastically Hemingway's warning of the probable [i.e., unlikely] seizure of Cuba by a force of 30,000 Germans transported to the island in 1,000 submarines. A clique of celebrity-minded hero worshippers surround Hemingway wherever he goes, numbering such persons as Winston Guest, Lieutenant Tommy Shevlin (wealthy son of a famous Yale football player), Mrs. Kathleen Vanderbilt Arostegui and several Embassy officials. To them, Hemingway is a man of genius whose fame will be remembered with Tolstoy. . . .
> It is known that Hemingway and his assistant, Gustavo Durán, have a low esteem for the work of the FBI which they consider to be methodical, unimaginative and performed by persons of comparative youth without experience in foreign countries and knowledge of international intrigue and politics.[9] Both Hemingway and Durán, it is also known, have personal hostility to the FBI on an ideological basis, especially Hemingway, as he considers the FBI anti-Liberal, pro-Fascist and dangerous as developing into an American Gestapo.

On December 19, 1942, Hoover had already cautiously commented on the "impulsive" Braden: "The Ambassador is somewhat hot-headed and I haven't the slightest doubt that he would immediately tell Hemingway of the objections being raised by the FBI. Hemingway ["one of the real danger spots in Cuba"] has no particular love for the FBI and would no doubt embark upon a campaign of vilification."

Finally, the FBI realized that Hemingway, through his wife, Martha Gellhorn (a friend of Eleanor Roosevelt), had some influence with the president. Hemingway and Gellhorn had shown his pro-Loyalist film *The Spanish Earth* to the Roosevelts at the White House in July 1937. And on October 9, 1942, Leddy told Hoover with apparent awe: "During the week commencing October

12, 1942, Mrs. HEMINGWAY is to be the personal guest of MRS. ROOSEVELT during her stay in Washington." Braden took advantage of this visit to ask Martha to brief Roosevelt and Harry Hopkins about urgently needed funds to combat "the periodically reappearing enemy agents" in Cuba.[10] In view of all this, Carson concluded, it was best to prevent a direct confrontation with their formidable adversary: "The Legal Attaché at Havana expresses this belief that Hemingway is fundamentally hostile to the FBI and might readily endeavor at any time to cause trouble for us. . . . It is the recommendation of the Legal Attaché at Havana that great discretion be exercised in avoiding an incident with Ernest Hemingway"—one of the few people, it appears, who could successfully resist the hostility of the FBI.

Though Hemingway won the first round with the FBI and concentrated on submarine-hunting when the Crook Factory was dismantled after eight months, the FBI kept watch on him for the rest of his life. Reports continued to be placed in his file on his connections with General Benitez (1944) and Gustavo Durán (1947), his political activities and intelligence work (1949), his crack about Senator McCarthy in *Look* (1955) and even the quarrel of his fourth wife, Mary, with a Havana gossip columnist about whether or not lion steak was, as she claimed, a delectable dish (1954).

Matters became more serious at the end of Hemingway's life when his nostalgic support for the Spanish Left and distaste for the cruelty of Batista's regime (the police chief had still not overthrown the general) led to his naive and perhaps self-protective public support for the Castro government, which took power in January 1959 while Hemingway was away in Idaho and Spain. When he flew into Rancho Boyeros airport on November 3, 1959, as J. L. Topping of the embassy reported to the State Department, Hemingway told reporters:

> 1. He supported [the Castro government] and all its acts completely, and thought it was the best thing that had ever happened to Cuba.
> 2. He had not believed any of the information published abroad against Cuba. He sympathized with the Cuban Government, and all *our* difficulties.
> 3. Hemingway emphasized the *our,* and was asked about it. He said that he hoped Cubans would regard him not as a *Yanqui* (his word), but as another Cuban. With that, he kissed a Cuban flag.

These rash statements horrified his closest Cuban friends—Mayito Menocal, Thorwald Sánchez, and Elicín Arguelles—soon to be dispossessed and driven into exile by Castro, and forced them to break off all relations with Hemingway. (Shortly after his death in July 1961 his house, boat and other possessions were expropriated by Castro's government.)

The drama closes on a sad note. A letter from the special agent in Minneapolis to Hoover on January 13, 1961, reports that Hemingway had secretly entered the Mayo Clinic: "He is seriously ill, both physically and mentally, and at one time doctors were considering giving him electro-shock therapy treatments." (These treatments destroyed his memory and intensified his depression.) The psychiatrist treating him "stated that Mr. HEMINGWAY is now worried about his registering under an assumed name, and is concerned about an FBI investigation. [The doctor] stated that inasmuch as this worry was interfering with the treatments of Mr. HEMINGWAY, he desired authorization to tell HEMINGWAY that the FBI was not concerned with his registering under an assumed name. [The doctor] was advised that there was no objection."

Both A. E. Hotchner and Mary Hemingway have written that Hemingway, at the end of his life, imagined that he was being followed and spied on by FBI agents in Idaho and in the Mayo Clinic, and that no kind of argument or evidence could change his mind or alleviate his irrational—but quite terrifying—fears.[11] The doctor's ineffectual and absurd intervention could only have alarmed his patient. The FBI file proves that even paranoids have real enemies.

15

Memoirs of Hemingway: The Growth of a Legend

He looked at the one with the moustache again. "This guy is very tough," he told him. "He wants to shoot an Indian." "Listen, Hemingway, don't repeat everything I say. . . ." "I can't think of any reason why he should call me Hemingway," the big one said. "My name ain't Hemingway."[1]

Raymond Chandler, *Farewell, My Lovely*

I

Hemingway is the most famous example of the great writer and the commercial success. His public image, which he had helped create, sold his books, attracted the interest of Hollywood, and made his private life a subject for public consumption. But Dwight Macdonald, influenced by the publicity that surrounded Hemingway, was quite mistaken when he claimed that his "life, his writing, his public personality, and his private thoughts were all of a piece."[2] The public wants to believe in the existence of a phenomenal human being who fights, hunts, loves and *writes* so perfectly. This heroic image satisfies the needs of the public but is irrelevant to the real Hemingway; it tempted, corrupted and finally helped to destroy him.[3]

Hemingway not only helped to create myths about himself but also seemed to believe them. In the last decades of his life, the Papa legend undermined the literary reputation and exposed the underlying fissure between the two Hemingways: the private artist and the public spectacle. When his writing slacked off and he attempted to live up to and feed on the legend, his exploits seemed increasingly empty. His shotgun blast shattered the heroic myth—and led to a different *persona*. After his death, he became either the genius destroyed by accidents and doctors or a failed writer who had never achieved artistic greatness. To clear away these misconceptions and discover the truth about his life and art, we must first trace how these popular legends recur in the memoirs of Hemingway.

Hemingway always tended to exaggerate and embroider the events of his life. He wrote about his personal experience and could not invent without it. He believed he could write only about what he had actually seen and known, and his literary credo was to tell it as it was. But Hemingway combined a scrupulous honesty in his fiction with a tendency to distort and rewrite the story of his life. Given his predisposition to mythomania, his reluctance to disappoint either his own expectations or those of his audience, and the difficulty of refuting or verifying the facts of his life, he felt virtually forced to invent an exciting and imaginative alternative to commonplace reality.

Because of his tendency to obscure the distinction between fiction and his life, he was temperamentally primed for corruption by publicity and wealth. The boy who boasted in infancy that he was "'fraid a nothing," that he had once caught a runaway horse, began to establish his public *persona* while on the editorial board of his high school newspaper. He was not a great athlete or scholar but constantly reported his own minor exploits in the Oak Park *Trapeze*. He inflated his genuine heroism in war through newspaper interviews and public speeches while he was still in his teens. As a foreign correspondent, he learned how to create a romantic image and generate publicity. He had a literary reputation among expatriate writers before he had published a word of fiction. *The Sun Also Rises* (1926) created the most powerful literary image of Spain and of the Lost Generation and quickly influenced American youth. They "drank like his heroes and heroines, cultivated a hard-boiled melancholy and talked in page after page of Hemingway dialogue," Malcolm Cowley recalled.[4] By 1925 Ernest Walsh had celebrated Hemingway in verse as

> Papa soldier pugilist bullfighter
> Writer gourmet lionhead aesthete
> He's a big guy from near Chicago.[5]

A decade later in "The Snows of Kilimanjaro," Hemingway condemned Scott Fitzgerald for his infatuation with the rich in a story that reveals his own fears of corruption and predicts his spiritual death. He believed that he could (but feared that he could not) have money and remain private, enjoy luxury and write well.

Hemingway created his own personality by force of will. His war experience in Italy and expatriate life in Paris enabled him to diminish, if not sever, the powerful influence of Oak Park. He was, in his youth, confident about his physical strength and his creative powers. The need to recreate himself in his novels complemented the creation of his public *persona*. In *The Old Man and the Sea* he deceived himself about the profundity of his art in order to live up to his popular image. He diagnosed but could not avoid the danger even as he reaped the rewards. His insightful Nobel Prize speech, in which he confessed that a writer "grows in public stature as he sheds his loneliness and often his work deteriorates,"[6] is a sad acknowledgment of his personal tragedy.

Hemingway allowed himself to be photographed in his home for glossy magazines; endured foolish interviews when his books appeared; encouraged Walter Winchell, Earl Wilson and Leonard Lyons to gossip about him in their columns; let *Esquire* subsidize his sports and holidays in return for inferior articles; lived without expense in Sun Valley while lending glamor to the new resort; appeared at the Stork Club and in 21; became friendly with movie stars and helped choose the actors for his films; endorsed Parker pens and Ballantine beer; spent months fishing in Cuba and Peru to get proper pictures for the cinematic version of *The Old Man and the Sea*. In all these activities he was imitating a mythical image. Like a film star, he was handsome, glamorous, wealthy, well-travelled and much married. In later life he consented to be adored by young women, stayed in luxurious hotels, and made various attempts to return to earlier pastimes and settings he (and the public) associated with his dashing youth—poverty in Paris, bullfights in Spain, safaris in Africa. Ravaged by ailments, age and alcohol, he took a path to destruction that traced the pattern of a movie idol's career. But with Hemingway the debunking began almost as soon as the hero worship. For the exciting aura that surrounds the stars of public life also has its destructive side: the public discovers and learns to despise the weaknesses of eminent people. His pugnacious character helped to spread stories of a bullying, boastful loudmouth; unwashed, apparently uneducated and more at home with a gun than a pen.

Matthew Bruccoli notes "how difficult it is to establish the truth about virtually everything involving Hemingway," how "difficult to differentiate the public Papa from the private writer."[7] Though Carlos Baker's biography (1969) helped to distinguish the reality from the myth, the Hemingway legends remained in force: that he had Indian blood, was kept out of school for a year to play the cello, ran away from home, injured his eye while boxing, associated with gangsters, had affairs with the actress Mae Marsh and the spy Mata Hari, fought with the Italian *Arditi,* was fitted with an aluminum kneecap, kept a mistress in Sicily, reported the battles of the Greco-Turkish War in the wilds of Anatolia, killed Krauts in World War II, tried to land a plane on Mount Kilimanjaro. Virtually all the drinking, boxing, hunting, fishing and fornicating stories are exaggerations or fantasies.

In 1941 Edmund Wilson, who turned against Hemingway in *The Wound and the Bow,* wrote that he had already passed "into a phase where he was occupied with building up his public personality.... Hemingway has created a

Hemingway who is not only incredible but obnoxious. He is certainly his own worst-invented character."[8] Eighteen years later his long-suffering fourth wife, Mary, said he was then "on the skids from egotism and publicity seeking."[9] Unlike Orwell, whose *persona* strengthened and confirmed the image of an upright man, Hemingway's legend swamped and destroyed the real artist. Unlike Lowell, who could skillfully manipulate his public image, Hemingway could not attract publicity without damaging his integrity.

Hemingway's career inspired a series of seventeen personal memoirs (books written about him by people who knew him) that appeared between 1949 and 1980. Their viewpoints range from reverence and awe to condescension and hostility. They are distorted by personal bias, exude a strong element of self-interest and reveal more about the authors than the subject. They lack self-effacement, objectivity, perception; emphasize the legend at the expense of the artistic achievement. The authors of these memoirs were related by blood and friendship, connected by rivalry and hostility. A comparative study of these books enables us to read them as they were written: not as isolated works but in relation to each other.

These memoirs, which contained many photographs of Hemingway in bullring and battlefield, complemented the reviews and criticism of his work. They distorted the facts but laid the shaky foundations of his biography. As John McCaffery observed as early as 1950: "The personality of the subject has made a profound impact on the critic and has, in almost every case, affected the tone of the criticism."[10]

Yet the memoirs of Hemingway are valuable tools for biographical criticism; they describe important events in his life and reveal his character in relation to the authors. Even the works written by those who hardly knew Hemingway tell us something about the culture in which he lived. All the books reveal the idealized or debased personality. All have their eyes firmly fixed on the sales of their book and are far more concerned with themselves than with their ostensible subject.

The memoirs tend to fall into five general categories. The crassly commercial books by people who did not know him well—Kurt Singer, Milt Machlin, Jed Kiley, Jake Klimo, Peter Buckley—enhance the myth and debase the man. The books by hunting and fishing cronies—Lloyd Arnold and Kip Farrington—concentrate more on sport than on Hemingway. The family memoirs by Leicester Hemingway, Marcelline Sanford, Madelaine Miller and Mary Hemingway provide valuable information but show little understanding of the man. Gregory Hemingway's memoir, though more intelligent, participates in the debunking process by paying off old scores and trying to lay some troubling ghosts of his own. The professional journalists—Malcolm Cowley, Lillian Ross, José Luis Castillo-Puche—advance their careers with Hemingway's help or at his expense. Finally, A. E. Hotchner's book emphasizes Hemingway's tragic decline, while Adriana Ivancich basks in reflected glory and concentrates on herself.

II

Malcolm Cowley, who was a year older than Hemingway and had been a writer in Paris in the 1920s, won his respect with a number of favorable reviews and a perceptive introduction to the *Portable Hemingway* (1944). Cowley's "A Portrait of Mister Papa" was published in *Life* on January 10, 1949, and reprinted in McCaffery's critical anthology in 1950. It appeared at the end of Hemingway's fallow decade and prepared the basis of the legend. Cowley's epigraph resembles the transparent disclaimer that novelists customarily place in their books to avoid libel suits: "He asked me to state that he is not responsible for any inaccuracies or legendary accomplishments of any sort which may have been attributed to him."[11]

Cowley's postwar piece takes Hemingway's sub-hunting seriously and stresses his war service as roving correspondent and commando. But even Hemingway could not swallow Cowley's stories and asked his old comrade-in-arms, Buck Lanham: "Can you imagine anyone going around Hürtgen with a canteen of gin and one of vermouth? There wasn't any good vermouth in Paris even and who the hell would give vermouth canteen space in a war. That was just one of those old chestnuts from Malcolm's Life piece."[12]

Cowley also emphasizes Hemingway's physical prowess and patriarchal life in Cuba, the risks and scars of shooting and fishing on his boat, the *Pilar*, with a cadre of faithful followers. According to Cowley, Hemingway breaks his nose in a teenage boxing match with a professional but returns to fight again the next day. He no longer has fought with the *Arditi* (as Cowley had said in the *Portable Hemingway*), but still has an aluminum kneecap. Though *For Whom the Bell Tolls* was ideologically repugnant to the communists because it criticized Soviet tactics in Spain and was not translated into Russian until 1968 (and then with heavy cuts), Cowley dubiously claims it was used by Stalin's armies in World War II as a "textbook of guerrilla fighting." (This myth was probably based on the fact that T. E. Lawrence's *Seven Pillars of Wisdom* (1935) was used as a guerrilla textbook by Mao Tse-tung in the 1940s.) Though Cowley tried for accuracy and obtained information from Hemingway's friends as well as from his subject, his heroic view of Hemingway is very close to the way the writer chose to present himself to the public: he-man at the typewriter, experiencing and recording violent action.

Despite the tough image, Hemingway was a soft-hearted man. He corresponded with Philip Young and Charles Fenton and allowed them to quote from his work, though he violently opposed their critical studies which (he felt) were stimulated by Cowley's efforts to "embalm" him while he was still kicking. He was apparently persuaded to grant Cowley interviews in Cuba after the critic pleaded that his son's education was at stake and later reminded him that Cowley had written, when Hemingway was reluctant to let him do the *Life* article, that it would allow the boy to go to Exeter.[13] Hemingway regretfully told Dos Passos that he had a private life until Cowley intruded on it,[14] and halfheartedly tried to use Cowley as a stick to beat Young. As he told Young's editor at Rinehart: "There has been too damned much written about my personal life and I am sick of it. It was a very bad thing for me that Malcolm Cowley's article was published in LIFE."[15] Cowley's apotheosis of the Papa legend and McCaffery's book of essays aroused unrealistic expectations in critics who had waited a decade for Hemingway's latest novel and were savagely disappointed by *Across the River and into the Trees* (1950).

Lillian Ross met Hemingway in 1947 as she was working on her first *New Yorker* profile about his friend Sidney Franklin, the American bullfighter. Hemingway invited her to Idaho the day before Christmas and gave her generous help. In a letter of July 1948 he adopted the pidgin-English *persona* that disguised his respectable background: "I talk bad on account where and how brought up. Can talk properly. But I remember I asked you if you minded and you said no and so I talked naturally."[16] He was pleased to maintain a pugnacious stance and refused to speak and act like an intellectual—even if he thought and felt like one.

Ross spent November 16–18, 1949 with Hemingway—who had been threatened by a near-fatal illness in March of that year—and tried to set down exactly what she had seen and heard. In her profile, the celebrity flies into New York from Havana, sees Marlene Dietrich, drinks great quantities of champagne, buys a coat and slippers at Abercrombie's, goes to the Metropolitan Museum with his son Patrick and signs a contract with Charles Scribner. The title and leitmotif of the piece, which first appeared in *The New Yorker* on May 13, 1950, comes from Hemingway's frequent repetition of the meaningless phrase, "How do you like it now, gentlemen?" Hemingway put on a performance for Ross, expected her to see through his act and show the highbrow readers of her magazine the man behind the rather transparent mask. Instead, she accepted the façade, repaid his generosity with malice and established her reputation at his expense.

Though Hemingway treated the interview as a joke, assumed the role of dumb ox and constantly spoke with wisecracks and sporting metaphors, he was not quite as stupid and boorish as Ross' account suggests. She never recorded or revealed the serious and sensitive side of his character and chose instead to portray him as a boring braggart who keeps punching himself in the stomach. She did demonstrate, however, that he had followed a descending path—from the charming Paris flat above the sawmill in the early 1920s to the luxury and snobbery of the grand hotels of Venice in the late 1940s. And Mr. Papa's vainglorious boasts about his forthcoming novel invited disastrous retaliation:

> Book start slow, then increase in pace till becomes impossible to stand. . . . I started out very quiet and I beat Mr. Turgenev. Then I trained hard and I beat Mr. de Maupassant. I've fought two draws with Mr. Stendhal, and I think I had an edge in the last one. But nobody's going to get me in any ring with Mr. Tolstoy unless I'm crazy or I keep getting better.[17]

The defensive, disingenuous tone of Ross' Preface to her profile, which she hastily published as a book just after Hemingway's death in 1961, presented a notable contrast to the text. She claimed "it was a sympathetic piece" and affected surprise when some readers "thought that in describing that personality accurately I was ridiculing or attacking it." When Irving Howe condemned her book in the *New Republic,* she unconvincingly replied: "It was a loving portrait of a great and lovable man."[18] She had sent the Hemingways proof before publication and assumed, when they returned it with corrections, that they approved her work. In a taped interview with Patrick Hynan in 1970, A. E. Hotchner said that when Hemingway received Ross' proofs on the Monday of the week the essay appeared, it was too late to change anything.

Hemingway was apparently taken by, but not taken in by Lillian Ross. He chose—shrewdly if uncharacteristically—to ignore and forgive her attack. Privately, however, he was "shocked and felt awful." He told a publisher: "Lillian Ross wrote a profile of me which I read, in proof, with some horror. But since she was a friend of mine and I knew she was not writing in malice she had a right to make me seem that way if she wished."[19] In distant Paris, even the waspish Alice Toklas, who had always been jealous of Hemingway's friendship with Gertrude Stein, disliked Ross' "shooting an elephant" and expressed compassion for her old adversary: "It has strange revelations and exposures by himself and his wife—which were partially explained by Janet Flanner's telling me that he was mortally ill. . . . It is painful to know the present situation and the horror it must hold for him."[20]

Worse things than Ross awaited Hemingway, though he did not live to read them. Hemingway's life and novels aroused such intense interest that readers were not satisfied with the fiction itself. They took pleasure in knowing the intimate details of his life and speculating about how he transformed his experience into art. Hemingway's death allowed writers to exploit their connection with him and satisfy the American appetite for the legendary achievements of celebrities.

Kurt Singer—the author of 40 pulp books on spies, war and crime—actually felt guilty about rushing out his unspeakably vulgar *Hemingway: Life and Death of a Giant* by September 1961: "I felt like a prostitute, selling my inner feelings . . . a sort of ghoul feeding on the remains of a dead hero." Singer claims to have interviewed Hemingway at Sloppy Joe's bar in Havana (rather than in Key West), and his contradictory accounts make their meeting seem dubious. The first half of Singer's book covers Hemingway's "apprenticeship" and is taken (with many distortions) from Fenton's study of the 1916–1923 period. The second half, padded with quotations from Hemingway's works, is embellished by Singer's inane commentary and crude style: "Hemingway belched, wiped his nose with the back of his hand and farted."[21]

Singer, not satisfied to recount the sensational aspects of Hemingway's life, feels obliged to invent some spicy sexual anecdotes. He provides Hemingway, who "had his first woman when he was thirteen," with a series of fictional mistresses: a socialite in Oak Park, the drunken Maria in Chicago, the lusty sculptress Heloise in Paris, the starveling Rosita in Spain. Singer also describes an attempted homosexual seduction by his Cuban cabin boy. Singer confidently states that there are whorehouses in strait-laced Oak Park, that the Austrians held their fire when they saw *Captain* Hemingway's courage, that Hemingway's lawyer was Elmer Rice (adept with the adding machine), that Mary gave a Picasso to a grade school in Idaho.

Singer's literary taste is revealed in his dedication to "James Michener, the new champion who inherited the Hemingway crown." He stresses the "boats, booze, broads" at the expense of the books and gives a long paraphrase of *The Old Man and the Sea,* told to him in Spanish (though he says he does not understand that language) by an ancient Cuban fisherman. Singer's book is worth noting because it reveals the lower depths of publishing and the wildly distorted image of "Hemingway the Giant" that was offered to subliterate readers.[22]

In January 1961, Hemingway told a friend that Milt Machlin was a "complete jerk" and not worth writing about.[23] Machlin wrote negatively in "Hemingway Talking," which appeared in the September 1958 issue of *Argosy,* because he had tried to crash Hemingway's party and been thrown out. *The Private Hell of Hemingway* (1962) portrays "a way of living so colorful that it almost eclipsed the stories he wrote.... The brawling, boozing, battling years of America's greatest writer." The style is also crude: "He returned to a Paris that was wilder, more debauched and madder than the one he had left, if that was possible."[24]

Machlin's book, like Singer's, is made up of confused gobbets from other people's work. It treats Hemingway's legend and his fiction as if they were fact. Thus the Spartan Hemingway spars barefoot on rough cinders to toughen his feet while the hedonistic Hemingway spends $1400 a night at the Stork Club. The English nurse Agnes actually has a love affair with Hemingway, as in *A Farewell to Arms;* Martha Gellhorn is "The Blonde Peril"; and the title of Dos Passos' novel is reversed to become Kipling's *Soldiers Three.* Machlin's Cliff Notes biography, simple-minded and instantly produced, provides a "Private Hell" for the reader.

Leicester Hemingway, born in 1915, tried to imitate his older brother and traded on his name. "The Baron" was a failure in life, earned Hemingway's scorn and was estranged from him after World War II. Leicester has accurately defined their unequal relationship: "Ernest was never very content with life unless he had a spiritual kid brother nearby. He needed someone he could show off to as well to teach. He needed uncritical admiration. If the kid brother could show a little worshipful awe, that was a distinct aid." In 1953 Leicester published *The Sound of the Trumpet,* a mediocre war novel in which Hemingway appears as Rando Granham. He asked Ernest to approve his memoir in November 1959 and was refused permission to publish.

My Brother, Ernest Hemingway (1962), serialized in *Playboy* and translated into seven languages, reflects the good-natured hero worship of a brother who never knew Hemingway well and was absent from most of the events he describes. Leicester's claim that Hemingway abandoned Archibald MacLeish on a deserted island was categorically denied by the poet. Though his book is based on family correspondence, it offers vague statements instead of vivid details: "A great many bottles were uncorked that night. . . . Ernest roared with laughter and gave me a glancing punch on the shoulder."[25] The last sixteen years of Hemingway's life are covered in only fourteen pages, though there are some valuable facts about the disastrous shock treatments at the Mayo Clinic. In September 1982, Leicester shot himself, as his father and brother had done.

If Leicester, like Ernest, rebelled against the ecclesiastical propriety of Oak Park, his older sister Marcelline became an utterly conventional clubwoman. She was, like her parents, startled and disgusted by *Three Stories & Ten Poems.* When Dr. Hemingway read his son's first book, he wrote Ernest that "no gentleman spoke of venereal disease outside a doctor's office" and that he "would not tolerate such filth in his home."[26] (The six books he sent back to the publisher are now worth $11,000 each.)

Hemingway was dressed for several years as a girl to be the twin of Marcelline, who was held back for a year so she could go through school with him. She wisely leaves the rough stuff to Leicester (*her* book was serialized in the *Atlantic*) and emphasizes their happy childhood in *At the Hemingways* (1962). Hemingway is the cause but not the center of this old-fashioned, generally reliable domestic history, which describes the family, the schools and the good clean fun on Walloon Lake. Hemingway resented Marcelline's public lectures about him in Midwestern ladies' clubs (she also took notes at his funeral), had nothing to do with her in adult life and disappears from her book after his marriage to Hadley in 1921. Marcelline is honest about the suicide of her remarkable father in 1928, defends her mother (whom Hemingway called "the old bitch") and is more objective than Leicester and younger sister Madelaine.

Jed Kiley was a newspaper reporter on the Chicago *Examiner,* drove an ambulance during the Great War, ran a cabaret in Paris and was assistant editor of the *Boulevardier,* to which Hemingway contributed an essay, "The Real Spaniard," in October 1927. *Hemingway: An Old Friend Remembers* (1965) brings us back to the dream world of Singer and Machlin, for Kiley was not an old friend and did not remember. "A gag is a gag and a fantasy is a fantasy," Hemingway exclaimed in a letter to Kiley in December 1954, "but the *Ms.* you sent me . . . entitled Me and Ernest Hemingway is a long series of untruths, misstatements and falsehoods which I could not allow you to use even if it was labelled a fictional nightmare."[27] It was serialized in *Playboy* in 1956–1957 and published posthumously.

Kiley, like Leicester, portrays him as a swaggering drinker, gambler, adventurer and daredevil in Paris and Key West. He takes his chapter titles from Hemingway's fiction, uses a boxing metaphor throughout the book (the English edition is called *Hemingway: A Title Fight in Ten Rounds*) and lamely imitates the worst aspects of the tough guy style in *To Have and Have Not:* " 'The Snows of Kilimanjaro.' Get a load of that title. . . . Who the hell ever heard of snow in Africa?"[28]

A. E. Hotchner was born in St. Louis (home of three Hemingway wives) and trained as a lawyer. He met Hemingway in 1948 when Hotchner was sent to Cuba to convince him to write an absurd article for *Cosmopolitan.* Hemingway liked and trusted him. Hotchner was good fun, knowledgeable about New York literary and sporting gossip, and willing to assume Leicester's role of pupil, buffoon and factotum (more totem than fact). Hotchner accepted the nickname "freckles" and even joined Antonio Ordóñez's *cuadrilla* during a bullfight. He wrote successful television adaptations of several stories, a play and a novel by Hemingway—usually splitting the profits with the Master. They formed the Hemhotch betting syndicate, and he helped Hemingway cut "The Dangerous Summer" articles for *Life.* Castillo-Puche, who loathed and libelled Hotchner, records Hemingway's judgment: "He's a smart cookie. . . . He has lots of connections in television and the movies and knows his way around. . . . He's as faithful as a bird dog. . . . He's done a fine job of looking after my interests. . . . Hotchner's a good friend of mine, but he's a sharp customer."[29]

Mary Hemingway, who was then writing her own memoir, sued to prevent publication of Hotchner's book and lost her case in both the New York State Supreme Court and the Court of Appeals, in February and March 1966.[30] The court ruled that Hotchner was free to publish their conversations unless she could prove that Hemingway specifically told him not to do so.[31] Philip Young has summarized the decision:

> The judge's rejection of Mrs. Hemingway's case was based on three arguments. First, he ruled that conversations are not protected by common-law copyright. Second, he criticized her failure to realize that "random and disconnected oral conversations are given some semblance

of form only by virtue of their arrangement in the context of literary creation." Last, he objected to her legal silence during the three years that Hotchner was writing his book; when she did file suit it was so late that to stop the thing would have put a "disproportionate economic burden" on author and publisher.[32]

Since Mary did not have access to the Hemhotch correspondence, she did not know that Hotchner had used the letters to give the impression of tape-recorded dialogue. Hemingway's words were accurate, but most of them were not conveyed to Hotchner in conversation. The book is a compilation of "The Letters of Ernest Hemingway"—almost all Hem and no Hotch. When Hotchner diverges from Hemingway's correspondence, he tends to distort and invent.

Hotchner was genuinely interested in Hemingway as writer, friend and biographical subject. He was always ready to respond to his summons, listen to his exaggerated exploits (drunk or sober) and tolerate his abusive behavior. Hotchner never lost his reverential attitude, never ceased to marvel at Hemingway's superb skill and infinite patience. He provides a moving account of Hemingway's physical and mental deterioration during the last year of his life. But he makes no distinction between reality and fantasy and includes all the Hemingway legends. Despite or perhaps because of the unreliability of the book, *Papa Hemingway: A Personal Memoir* (1966) was serialized in the *Saturday Evening Post* in the spring of 1966, published by Random House in April, reached a sixth printing by November and was translated into twelve foreign languages.

In *Hemingway in Spain* (1974), the English translation of *Hemingway: Entre la Vida y la Muerte* (1968), the Spanish journalist-novelist José Luis Castillo-Puche tries to "go deeper and further than a coldly factual, scrupulously documented biography" by writing "a deeply felt, passionate, intuitive, personal book . . . a chaotic, hasty, Hemingwayesque confession" about "a pathologically devious man."[33] The memoir takes place during the nine days following his suicide as Castillo visits all the Hemingway locales in Madrid and offers his long-winded reflections on their meetings in Spain.

Castillo confesses that "sometimes it's more fun to invent a story than it is to live it in real life" and gives the impression that much of his book is fiction. Like Kiley and Klimo, Castillo exaggerates his friendship with Hemingway. His chronology is inaccurate and his text filled with errors. The real date of the funeral is pushed forward from July 5 to July 7 to coincide ironically with the opening of the San Fermín fiesta. Castillo unconvincingly calls Hemingway a pennypincher and speaks of his failure with women.

Castillo disapproves of the "Dangerous Summer" articles on bullfighting, which condemned Manolete's "cheap tricks" and aroused considerable hostility in Spain. He is critical and envious of Hemingway's friendship with Antonio Ordóñez, with Valerie Danby-Smith (the young Irish girl who assumed the role of Adriana Ivancich), with Bill Davis (the host at his celebrated sixtieth birthday party) and especially with Hotchner: "Two ridiculous figures hung around Ernesto every minute: Davis the jealous watchdog of his fame and fortune and Hotchner the exploiter of his reputation."[34] He irresponsibly calls Hotchner a hypocrite, a sickening toady, an obsequious bore, a clever exploiter. Though Castillo got away with this in the Spanish edition and Mary testified for Castillo's American publisher (in retaliation for her lost lawsuit), Hotchner won $125,000 in damages, but his libel award was subsequently thrown out by a federal appeals court.[35]

Lloyd Arnold, a photographer at Sun Valley, helped lure Hemingway—who provided excellent publicity—to Averill Harriman's new resort in 1939 and became his faithful hunting companion. Arnold's photographs, which include quantities of dead creatures, are excellent; and there are cameo appearances by Ingrid Bergman, Clark Gable and Gary Cooper. Arnold's homespun *High on the Wild with Hemingway* (1968) (severely cut in the paperback edition) portrays him in field and stream, bar and barbecue, but reveals almost nothing about him until the very end of the book: "He couldn't write any more, he was done with that; and though he didn't say so directly you got the message that they had tampered with his think machine back there, and loused it up, so it was no good, what he labored to put on paper."[36]

Kip Farrington's description of Hemingway's angling exploits in *Fishing with Hemingway and Glassell* (1971) complements the shooting achievements in Arnold's book and is the least revealing of all the memoirs. Only the first part of this book concerns Hemingway as fisherman. The second part describes the idle rich (whom Hemingway satirized in *To Have and Have Not*) fishing round the world to break previous records. The last part, on the depredations of Japanese commercial fishermen, has nothing to do with either Hemingway or Alfred Glassell—a Houston millionaire whose cameraman filmed him catching the world's biggest marlin. This sequence was used in the movie version of *The Old Man and the Sea*.

Farrington, who reprints Hemingway's introduction to his book *Atlantic Game Fishing*, met him in Bimini in 1935. Farrington attempts to defend his friend from "the best efforts of the literary sharks to tear him to shreds and drag him down" and presents a clean, well-mannered Hemingway who would have appealed to the stuffy Marcelline: "Ernest was cordial and gracious. . . . He was charmingly chivalrous . . . and wouldn't stand for bad language in front of ladies."[37]

Jake Klimo ran away from home in Iowa when he was eleven and spent his tender years as petty criminal and bum. He was a friend of Leicester and hung around the Hemingway circle in Key West and Cuba in the mid-1930s. Hemingway reassured his mother that Klimo "was a very good sort of bird" and got along well with Leicester.[38] The conjunctive title of the ghostwritten *Hemingway and Jake* (1972) suggests a relationship that never actually existed. But his connection with Hemingway, though tenuous, had a powerful impact on his character: "I had absorbed part of that personality; I found myself thinking in his patterns, talking in his way, parroting his words, even his style in violence."

Klimo—like Singer, Machlin, Leicester and Kiley—concentrates on the violent behavior of the fisherman, boxer, drinker and tourist attraction of Key West. Hemingway easily knocks a knife out of Klimo's hand during a mock attack; and Klimo—with an awe that matches that of Hotchner and Arnold— exclaims: "Man, he was powerful. He was a good fighter, too, a hell of a fighter. He laid me low, god damn."[39] Jake dislikes Pauline, who spoils their manly fun when she discovers Hemingway's affair with a woman in Havana and rushes over from Key West to protect her marriage. Klimo hints at something significant here but maintains an uncharacteristic discretion about Jane Mason that has continued through Baker's biography and up to the present time.

Madelaine, Hemingway's tomboy third sister, was born in 1904 and appeared as a character in "Soldier's Home." She named her son after him, became angry at anyone who exploited (Marcelline) or spoke ill of him (Gregory), and continued her childhood adoration throughout her life. *Ernie* (1975) consists of 42 short, subjective chapters ("Teen-age Fun—and Nicknames") and more than 130 family snapshots. She presents a reverential picture of her parents and emphasizes the idyllic life in Michigan rather than the stuffy existence in Oak Park. She is devoted to Hadley and bitter about Pauline, who not only broke up Hemingway's first marriage and brought disgrace upon the family, but also treated Madelaine as a servant when she came to Key West in 1928 to care for the newborn Patrick and type the manuscript of *A Farewell to Arms*.[40] Madelaine, who missed Hadley's wedding and her father's suicide, had a compensatory mystical experience at Hemingway's funeral: "On the carpet [of the church] was a perfect outline of Ernest's head, beard and all! It seemed as if his sad eyes were pleading."[41] Despite this vision, she was not invited to the reading of the will, which left everything—well over a million dollars—to Mary. Madelaine's amateurish effort is far less successful than the books by Leicester and Marcelline, whom she jockeys out of position as favorite sister. (The actual favorite was the silent Ursula.)

Gregory Hemingway—whose hostile memoir is diametrically opposed to Madelaine's—is Hemingway's youngest son by his second wife, Pauline. In 1951, when Gregory was a nineteen-year-old aircraft mechanic, he got into trouble for taking drugs. Pauline phoned Hemingway to tell him what happened, became involved in a violent quarrel and died the next day. Hemingway told Gregory that his trouble killed Pauline, and they never met again. When Gregory started medical school, he learned from her autopsy report that Pauline had died of a rare tumor of the adrenal gland and concluded: "It was not my minor troubles that had upset Mother but his brutal phone conversation with her eight hours before she died."[42]

Hemingway said many harsh things about Gregory, who was much more troubled than he suggests, in unpublished letters of the 1950s as well as in the posthumous *Islands in the Stream* (1970). In that novel Gregory appears as Andy:

"The meanest is Andy."
"He started out mean," Thomas Hudson said.
"And boy, did he continue". . . .
There was something about him you could not trust.[43]

Gregory, whose opinion of this book is not recorded, condemned *The Old Man and the Sea* as "sentimental slop." At Hemingway's funeral Gregory met Valerie Danby-Smith, with whom Hemingway had fallen in love in 1959 and had adopted as his "secretary." Castillo-Puche, who has a poor opinion of foreign women, criticizes Valerie's behavior: "She kept stroking herself, and constantly acted more or less like a little bitch in heat. She was a very pretty little creature, who was to lose a great many things at the fiesta."[44] Gregory, who had a crush on Mary Hemingway and once thought of "trying to posthumously cuckold papa" with Martha Gellhorn, eventually married the girl his father once loved. (In a similar compensatory fashion, Norman Mailer fastened on to the son after he had failed to meet the father, enjoyed bouts of ramlike head-butting with Gregory and wrote a short Preface to his book.)

The most agonizing, if not the most accurate, portrayal of Hemingway emerges from these tangled relationships. In *Papa* (1976), Gregory bitterly says he did not feel loved by his parents. They had wanted to have a girl and left Gregory with a horrible Germanic nursemaid when they travelled to Europe and Africa. As a child he wet his bed, found it difficult to read and write, became seasick aboard the *Pilar,* drank alcohol and was caught plagiarizing a story from Turgenev. As an adult he drank heavily, could not hold a job, failed to maintain a marriage, felt guilty about his mother's inheritance and spent it quickly on senseless slaughter (eighteen African elephants in one month).

Gregory's case history expresses a sense of tragic betrayal and makes a cruel judgment on the god that failed. He contrasts the heroic father of his childhood with the bully, sick bore and professional celebrity whose drunken revels with sycophants during the last decade of his life "merely anaesthetized the pain which had accompanied the loss of his talent." Since Hemingway's decline occurred after their quarrel in 1952, Gregory's jaundiced view corresponds with reality. But since he never saw his father after that year, his portrayal of the overbearing megalomaniac is not convincing: "It's fine to be under the influence of a dominating personality as long as he's healthy," though Gregory did not seem to like it even then, "but when he gets dry rot of the soul, how do you bring yourself to tell him he stinks?" (You wait until he is dead.) Gregory, like Leicester, desperately tried and failed to please Hemingway, and felt profound but guilty relief at his father's funeral: "I couldn't disappoint him, couldn't hurt him [or be hurt by him] anymore."[45]

Mary Welsh, a *Time-Life* journalist from Minnesota, met Hemingway in London in 1944, after his marriage to Martha Gellhorn had disintegrated, and married him in Havana in 1946. Though Mary told a friend, "she and Ernest promised each other she would not be a Boswell wife, so she never kept a record,"[46] Mary did keep a diary throughout their marriage. She poured all the intimate though trivial details into the leaden mold of *How It Was* (1976), whose title echoed *The Way It Was* (1959), Harold Loeb's memoir of expatriate days in Paris. Mary's book was originally submitted to Ernest's publishers, Scribner's; but when they offended her by recommending necessary cuts and revisions, she published it with the more tolerant Knopf.

Mary (Hemingway's literary executor) was the first to print in her book a substantial number of Hemingway's letters, written to her. They are sentimental, coy and curiously dull. Mary is honest about herself and the problems of her marriage. But she records few serious conversations, is incapable of psychological insight, conveys no sense of Hemingway as a complex human being and writes in the vulgar style of a ladies' magazine: "Lovely lunch, lovely people, and tonight, Venice, Venice, Venice—city of exquisite bridges, the moon just after full, coming up grandly over the Grand Canal. . . . That night my husband and I kept ourselves pleasurably occupied in bed."[47] The only torture worse than reading Hotchner on bulls is reading Mary on bulls.

Mary attempts to preserve her identity by telling the uninteresting story of her early life in the first part of the book. But she soon concedes: "I had been an entity; now I was an appendage." She had real doubts about marrying Hemingway and certainly knew what to expect after February 1945 when he placed a photograph of her Australian husband in the toilet bowl, blasted it with a pistol and flooded their room at the Ritz. But Mary finally accepts the man— and the legend. She gives up her professional career, adopts his sporting passions, entertains his coarse cronies, matches his numerous accidents with her own falls and fractures, tolerates his infatuation with two teenage girls: his "vestal virgin," Adriana Ivancich, and his *demi-vierge,* Valerie Danby-Smith.

Mary, a meek contrast to the willful and independent Martha Gellhorn, told Oriana Fallaci: "I didn't want to be Ernest's equal. I wanted him to be the master, to be stronger and cleverer than I, to remember constantly how big he was and how small I was."[48] This sacrificial self-effacement turned her into Hemingway's scapegoat and victim. Though Hemingway saves her life after a serious hemorrhage in August 1946 (he was at his best in emergencies), he also slaps her and throws wine in her face ("I guess my pride is expendable") when the disastrous reviews of *Across the River* coincided with the visit of the real-life heroine of the book in October 1950. But, like Robert Lowell's wife Elizabeth Hardwick, Mary has an infinite capacity for suffering. She tells him: "No matter what you say or do—short of killing me, which would be messy—I'm going to stay here . . . [until you] tell me truthfully and straight that you want me to leave." Mary tolerated his "neglect, rudeness, thoughtlessness, abusive language, unjust criticism, false accusations"[49] not only because she loved him and was loyal but also because she enjoyed playing the role of Sofia Tolstoy.[50] Mary was willing to endure almost anything to remain Mrs. Ernest Hemingway forever.

The photographer Peter Buckley, who shared a room with Hotchner during the crowded Zaragoza *feria* in 1956, "found so much wrong with that section of [Hotchner's] book that he has no faith in it as a whole."[51] Hotchner, on the other hand, recalled that Hemingway fiercely berated Buckley for intruding on Ordóñez' privacy while he was resting before a bullfight and that Buckley was never able to reestablish his sycophantic position.[52] In 1959 Hemingway called Buckley a jerk and told Lanham to pay no attention to him.[53]

Buckley's *Ernest* (1978) contains superb photographs (by himself and others) and is superior to the picture books by Leo Lania (1961), Lloyd Arnold (1968), Robert Gadjusek (1978) and Anthony Burgess (1978). But his derivative text, written in a simple-minded style, reveals an abysmal lack of perception:

> I wanted to pick him up, all six feet, 210 pounds of him, and put him here.
>
> Paris was very different from Oak Park.
>
> Make-believe is fun when everybody knows that's what it is.
>
> In 1956 Ernest sat and rested.

Buckley also offers the definitive word on Hemingway's style: "Ernest knew the short words and the long ones; he tried different sentences with different words, and he tried different paragraphs with different sentences."[54]

Adriana Ivancich was almost nineteen when she met Hemingway on a duck-shooting weekend in Italy. *La Torre Bianca* (1980) traces their relationship in Venice, Cortina, Paris and Havana from 1948 to 1954. Adriana's focus is herself: her friendship with Hemingway, her link to the character of Renata in *Across the River* and the scandal that followed its publication. Her self-regarding, impressionistic book is an expanded and much-padded version of her article, published in *Epoca* in July 1965, with the less ambiguous title: "La Renata di Hemingway sono io" (I am Hemingway's Renata). The tone of the book is bitterness mingled with pride: pride in her family background and her artistic achievements, in Hemingway's love and her inspiration of his art; bitterness about the effect of this friendship on her life.

Adriana's memoir is biographically important in several ways: for the self-portrait of the girl who was Hemingway's "true love"; for its new perspective on the events of his life; for its portrait of Hemingway. The editors of her *Epoca* article boast "at last we can give Renata a face." The book establishes her physical resemblance to Renata but denies any similarities in behavior. Adriana emphasizes that she was always chaperoned and protected. She clings to reflected glory yet needs to vindicate herself. The letters and conversations reported in the book suggest a friendship both paternal and flirtatious. But Hemingway maintains his role of passive suitor and their relationship does not develop.

When Hemingway flings the glass of wine in Mary's face, Adriana chastizes him, and he promises to behave. According to Adriana, the wine-throwing is provoked by Mary, who pesters him to dance "like a trained bear" and makes him lose his temper. Mary confides that she has been worried about Papa's infatuation but now feels that Adriana is a good influence. Adriana avoids the question of how her presence contributes to their domestic tension.

Yet there are many compensations for these *brutti momenti*. Hemingway goes out of his way to please Adriana: he gives elaborate parties and dinners, entertains celebrities and secures invitations to the Havana country club. She assumes this is her due. Throughout her book she describes herself at the center of his life: "What tenderness he had, my massive irascible friend!" The book never takes into account the feelings of other people, but treats every event from her narcissistic point of view.

Despite her assertions of affection, her portrait of Hemingway is negative. In Venice he is a tired, jaded, hard-drinking sentimentalist; in Havana, rude, dominating, obsessive; in their final meeting, shattered and tearful. Adriana's attitude to Hemingway remains ambivalent. She affirms her loyalty to him but describes herself as a victim of his love, burdened by the sheer number of his letters. She is tempted to burn them and be rid of "that Hemingway who had covered me with mud."[55] (Adriana, who sold the letters to a New York dealer for $17,000, hanged herself in March 1983.)

"What characterizes every book about Hemingway," Norman Mailer observes, "is the way his character remains out of focus."[56] None of these books has the intelligence and insight revealed in the memoirs of Ford on Conrad, Joe Ackerley on Forster, Stanislaus on James Joyce, Leonard on Virginia Woolf, or Jessie Chambers on Lawrence. Indeed, the radical defects, the standard of misconception, the Boswellian self-aggrandizement in these memoirs—*Ernie* and *Ernest, Papa* and *Papa Hemingway*—seem even stronger when they are read together and in retrospect. None of the authors distinguishes between the fictions and the facts of his life, and none of them has learned how to write from their long association with the Master. Instead of illuminating Hemingway's life, the memoirs present a composite autobiography of the people who knew him, were rivals for his favor, and enjoyed the vicarious residue of his fame and failure. The authors are divided by personal and commercial conflict, by a desire to write about themselves and by a need to focus on the subject who justifies the publication of their book.

The memoirs—by professional journalists, crass exploiters, hangers-on and emotionally involved family, lovers, friends—flow into two streams. They are symbolized by the gentle and tough images of the Hemingway hero, portrayed on the screen by Gary Cooper and by Humphrey Bogart. Malcolm Cowley, Marcelline Sanford, A. E. Hotchner, Lloyd Arnold, Kip Farrington, Madelaine Miller, Mary Hemingway and Adriana Ivancich attempt to give at least a glimpse of the inner man and present the more sympathetic Gary Cooper image. Lillian Ross, Kurt Singer, Milt Machlin, Jake Klimo, Gregory Hemingway and Peter Buckley rarely penetrate the façade and present the harsh Humphrey Bogart image—which is also reflected in Chandler's *Farewell, My Lovely*.

These memoirs allow us to trace the origin and evolution of the Hemingway legend, but are a minefield rather than a path through the tangled woods of Hemingway's life. The scholar concerned with the truth finds himself lost in rumor and half-proved fact, in conflicting statements and pure fantasy. His study of these exercises in egoism requires the utmost scepticism and vigilance. He turns, with considerable relief, to the rare seriousness of the *Paris Review* interview that portrays Hemingway's dedication to his art and reveals "a personality at odds with the rambunctious, carefree, world-wheeling Hemingway-at-play of popular conception."[57]

16

The Quest for Hemingway

The most complicated subject that I know, since I am a man, is a man's life.
                                    Hemingway, "The Christmas Gift"

I

My biography of Hemingway began as a life of Pound. Harvester Press offered me a contract to write a life of the "good Pound," up to 1920; and I had been trying to arouse enthusiasm for the project during long conversations with Allen Ginsberg, who had known and admired Pound at the end of his life. But the more reading and research I did the more I came to dislike his character and his work. I realized that I did not have sufficient sympathy with his poetry and politics to justify their peculiar logic. After visiting the Lilly Library at Indiana University, contemplating the 12,000 pages of letters and manuscripts written by Pound in his madcap backwoods dialect and realizing there were even more papers at Yale, I abandoned the project, with considerable relief, and spent the rest of the afternoon at the Kinsey sex museum. Soon afterward, I learned that Humphrey Carpenter (the biographer of Auden) was writing a life of Pound, and was glad that I did not have to compete with him and duplicate his effort.

When I visited the Hemingway Room of the John F. Kennedy presidential library in Boston, the capable curator, Jo Hills, told me that no one was presently engaged in writing a full-scale biography of Hemingway. The well-catalogued collection contains several thousand unpublished letters written by and to Hemingway, all his major literary manuscripts and thousands of documents, scrapbooks, clippings, reviews, tapes, photographs and memorabilia. The enormous amount of new archival material—donated by his fourth wife, Mary—as well as the timely publication of Hemingway's *Selected Letters,* Adriana Ivancich's autobiography *La Torre Bianca* and Bernice Kert's *The Hemingway*

Women, which printed but did not analyze or explain many important letters from his wives and mistresses, seemed to justify a fresh study of his life and art.

I had always been fascinated by Hemingway's life—which had inspired my travels and influenced my values—and had a longstanding interest in his art. I had taught Hemingway's works for twenty years, written articles and reviews about him and had chapters on him in my books, *Married to Genius* and *Disease and the Novel.* I had in addition published the 600-page *Hemingway: The Critical Heritage* and edited a book on *The Craft of Literary Biography.* I also had considerable experience in the Hemingway milieu. I lived for many years in the American West, crewed on a yacht in the Caribbean, spent two summers in East Africa, travelled extensively in France and Italy, and saw scores of bullfights while working as a professional writer in Spain.

Carlos Baker's *Ernest Hemingway: A Life Story,* the standard biography, appeared in 1969. Baker established the chronology and compiled a cautious and respectful encyclopedia of facts, with almost no analysis or interpretation of Hemingway's thought and character. He was constrained by writing an authorized biography, commissioned by Hemingway's wife and publisher, and by his inability to quote from Hemingway's letters. Baker was extremely reluctant to discuss sensitive matters—lesbianism, adultery, abortions, impotence, madness, family feuds—and cryptically confined the most interesting material to the footnotes. Having treated the fiction in an earlier book, he arbitrarily separated the two vital elements of a literary biography and did not show the relation of Hemingway's life and art. He failed to reveal a convincing and meaningful pattern in the life—an evaluation of relationships and comprehension of motives—or to illuminate the artist and inner man. Too close to and involved with his subject, Baker grew resentful, even hostile, and never resolved the conflict between his original hero-worship and the final emergence of the less attractive side of Hemingway's character. His book ends with the suicide shot; mine also considers the aftermath, the legend and the influence.

In order to secure a contract before I started the biography, I wrote a three-page proposal and sent it to six publishers. Norton, Viking, and Simon and Schuster were not interested. Robert Giroux kindly called to say he liked the idea but could not convince his colleagues to commission the book. Jason Epstein of Random House was keen but would not discuss details on the phone or suggest an approximate advance. Through his secretary, he ordered me to appear in New York, yet did not offer to pay my expenses. Several of my friends praised Ted Solotaroff, a writer as well as an editor at Harper & Row, and I accepted his contract for a critical biography of 160,000 words. When I sent in a typescript of 250,000 words, he accepted it without any requests for changes or cuts.

II

At first I was nearly paralyzed by the overwhelming amount of work I had to do, but I soon built up the obsessive momentum that enabled me to complete the research and writing in two years. Starting with the secondary works in Audre Hanneman's superb bibliography, I listed and read the enormous amount of biographical material on Hemingway. These works included a great many factual errors; some derived from Hemingway, others were invented by the authors. Dealing with the biographical evidence in Hemingway's fiction demanded careful critical judgment. He was an unreliable informant about his own life and invented many stories that had no factual basis, but he also wrote numerous works of fiction that were close to the truth and revealed a great deal about his personal life.

I had previously been offered a visiting professorship at the University of Massachusetts at Amherst, less than two hours from the Kennedy Library, which I frequently visited during the academic year. The spectacularly beautiful building, designed by I. M. Pei, is built on the windy shore of Columbia Point, in remote and dangerous Dorchester. The long, triangular, luxuriously appointed Hemingway Room has a fine view of Boston harbor and permits immediate access to the printed books and xerox copies of all the manuscript material. But work becomes difficult if anyone talks or types in the small room and nearly impossible when the curator is not on duty and the scholar is forced to move in with the researchers examining the Kennedy papers. The heating is uncomfortably irregular and the wide-open reading room is constantly bombarded by noise from the tourists in the museum below as well as from the slapdash staff, the talkative readers, the typewriters and the telephones. It was far easier to concentrate on the manuscripts in the rare book rooms at Princeton and Yale, which are sensibly sealed off from outside noise.

I studied additional Hemingway material at or from twenty libraries. The University of Maryland, Southern Illinois University and I Tatti kindly sent xerox copies of their letters, which could be read at home and at leisure. The rules about unpublished material are wildly inconsistent. The Kennedy Library did not permit copying, but the Library of Congress had a xerox machine available on the premises; and copies of some material restricted at the Kennedy were freely available at Princeton.

Beginning with the acknowledgments, notes and index in Baker's book, I gradually found out which of Hemingway's friends were still alive and where they lived, and wrote several hundred letters requesting information and interviews. The addresses of well-known people could be easily found in reference books, but the others had to be patiently stalked through a network of personal contacts. In contrast to the friends of Katherine Mansfield and Wyndham Lewis (the subjects of my previous biographies), who were responsive and eager to help, many of Hemingway's friends, frequently asked for their recollections, were unwilling to answer letters or talk about him. About forty acquaintances did not respond to my queries, and sixteen people (none of them crucial) did not agree to an interview. Some people enjoy being difficult and self-important; some are writing their own books and do not want to help rivals; some have genuine scruples about revealing personal matters. The biographer, like the journalist, is inevitably a suppliant—hanging on the end of a pay phone, subject to the whims and rudeness of his informants. He must tread the delicate line between pressing too hard for information and knowing when to withdraw.

I tried to contact Mary Hemingway through her lawyer Alfred Rice and her friends Connie Bessie, Tillie Arnold and George Plimpton, but all confirmed that she had completely lost her memory and would be a useless informant. Fortunately, Hemingway's sister Carol, his third wife, Martha Gellhorn, and Alfred Rice, who at first refused to see me, eventually agreed to be interviewed.

Letters are a distant form of interview and offer another chance to establish personal relationships. Correspondents are often surprisingly revealing, for letters give them the opportunity to relive the past and tell their own story. A few of my correspondents wrote brilliantly perceptive letters. Mario Menocal, Jr., the son of Hemingway's close friend, sent from Mexico City more than a hundred detailed pages about the Cuban period. Robert Joyce, who had been the intelligence officer at the American Embassy in Cuba during World War II, and now lived in Greece, illuminated Hemingway's private spy network and sub-hunting activities. Denis Zaphiro, a white hunter in Kenya, gave precise descriptions of the second African safari. Charles Collingwood of CBS recalled Hemingway's behavior as a war correspondent in France; and Lieutenant Leonard Krieger, who met Hemingway just before the liberation of Paris in August 1944, described how he recklessly drove into enemy territory ahead of the regular army. The Hemingway scholars, especially Michael Reynolds, were extremely helpful; and Norman Mailer wrote a valuable letter about Hemingway's son, Gregory.

Sometimes I did a great deal of work and got no results. When I learned that Caroline Moorehead, a columnist for the London *Times,* was the daughter of Hemingway's friend Alan Moorehead, I asked her if there were any Hemingway letters among her father's papers. She told me his papers were at Australian National University in Canberra; I wrote to them asking about the letters; and they said I needed permission from the estate before they could send copies. I duly secured permission, through Charles Scribner, Jr., from Alfred Rice, sent it to Australia, and asked them to search the files during the late 1940s. But they failed to find any letters from Hemingway.

I heard that a Robert Knutson had interviewed Hemingway while he was a patient at the Mayo Clinic and published an account of their talk in his high school newspaper. When I reached Rochester, Minnesota, I called five Robert

Knutsons until I got the wife of the right one. She told me he could not be contacted until he arrived home after work and he would be glad to help if I phoned at that time. I called every hour all evening, but the phone was off the hook. I even went to the house and found no one at home. When I finally reached his wife, after Knutson had left for work the next morning, she suggested I write to him and said she would urge him to reply. I duly wrote to the difficult and elusive man, who never answered my letter, and to his high school newspaper, which could not find his essay in its incomplete files.

III

Since the evocation of setting was vital in Hemingway's works, it was essential to see the places he had lived in and described. In Oak Park, a town (Hemingway said) of wide lawns and narrow minds, I saw his birthplace, the much grander house where he spent his boyhood, his high school and the public library, which contained significant biographical material. At Walloon Lake in northern Michigan, where the family had a summer cottage, I became totally immersed in my subject and swam a mile to see the house from the water. In nearby Petoskey (on Lake Michigan), the setting of *The Torrents of Spring,* I visited the rooming house where Hemingway lived in the fall of 1919, the public library where he lectured about the war and Braun's Restaurant, which was the model for Brown's Beanery in the novel.

In Paris I traced Hemingway's footsteps on the Left Bank and saw the Hôtel Jacob, 74 rue Cardinal Lemoine and 113 rue Notre Dame des Champs, where he lived with his first wife, Hadley; Gertrude Stein's flat at 27 rue de Fleurus; Sylvia Beach's bookshop, Shakespeare and Company, formerly on the rue de l'Odéon; Gerald Murphy's studio at 69 rue Froidevaux; and 6 rue Férou where Hemingway lived with his second wife, Pauline. Most of these places feature prominently in *A Moveable Feast.*

In Key West, a semitropical island that combines the characteristics of Nantucket and New Orleans, I toured Hemingway's luxurious house, studio, garden and swimming pool at 907 Whitehead Street, drank at Sloppy Joe's bar, and saw the books and photographs in the Martello Historical Museum and the Monroe County Public Library. I obtained special permission to visit Cuba from the U.S. Treasury Department, got a visa from the Cuban interests section of the Czech Embassy in Washington and found out about the expensive but unreliable charter flights from Miami. But when I learned that all of Hemingway's Cuban friends were now living in Florida, it did not seem worth the considerable trouble (I had been plagued by the communist bureaucracy in Prague and Budapest the previous summer) to see his home, the Finca Vigía, the Ambos Mundos Hotel, the Floridita Bar and the fishing village of Cojímar. I relied on my knowledge of the Virgin Islands, Puerto Rico and Mexico (as well as Hemingway's descriptions and several Cuban novels) to recreate the atmosphere of the country.

I visited the dreary town of Rochester, Minnesota, where few things begin and many things end, and inspected the Mayo Clinic and St. Mary's Hospital, where Hemingway was locked up in the psychiatric unit on the sixth floor. Finally, I went to Ketchum, Idaho (twelve miles from Hailey, where Pound was born), strolled around the bleak house at 400 Canyon Run Boulevard, where he shot himself, and paid homage at his grave, which is flattened by a tombstone so that tourists cannot steal the sacred dirt.

IV

I saw Hemingway's family and friends in New England, New York, Washington, Florida, Chicago, Minnesota, Montana, Idaho, Spain, France and England. The sixty-four interviews I conducted were the most interesting and revealing part of my research, and my book was nourished by the memories of many friends. Most of the people I met seemed to enjoy the interview and turned it into a social occasion that included a meal or an overnight stay. The famous were as likely to respond as the obscure; it all depended on the attitude of the individual.

In Deerfield Beach, Florida, I spoke to Hemingway's third sister, "Sunny," the model for Helen in "Soldier's Home." She looks like Hemingway, adores him and maintains a fiercely possessive attitude toward him. She complained about constantly being bothered by interviewers and urged me not to publish things that would hurt people. But she herself was extremely critical of others: her late sister Marcelline, a clubwoman who exploited the family name; Pauline, who treated Sunny like a servant; Gregory, who was hostile and irresponsible; Mary, who made her buy the Walloon Lake house after Hemingway had promised to give it to her; and Rice, who works hand in glove with Mary. Sunny had sold most of the family papers to Indiana University, but she still had Hemingway's high-school themes and some letters to her—which she refused to show me. I thought of tying her up and reading these papers, but decided that would be bad for her health and my reputation.

Hemingway's youngest sister Carol wrote a hostile reply and at first declined to see me, though she lived quite close to Amherst. But she relented after I had visited Sunny and invited me to lunch. Unlike Sunny, Carol (who had adored her brother as a girl and a young woman) was quite critical of Hemingway. She categorically denied his story that she had been raped as a child and explained his irrational hostility to her marriage. He threatened that he would never again see Carol if she married John Gardner and, despite many friendly overtures from Carol, callously kept his word.

Patricia Hemingway, the first wife of his brother Leicester, met me in

Washington and drove me to her house in Maryland. She had spent a decade mastering the history of the family and gave me her useful two-volume genealogy. She told me that she had been adopted by Uncle Tyler Hemingway (who got Ernest the job on the *Kansas City Star*), about the tribulations of her marriage to the feckless Leicester—who spent his life trying, and failing, to imitate Ernest—and about Leicester's second marriage and suicide.

Martha Gellhorn, still extremely hostile to Hemingway, had quarreled with a friend of mine whom I hoped would introduce me and was especially difficult to approach. I had missed her during a summer visit to England, when she was isolated in her Welsh cottage; and when I returned to London, she did not answer her phone. I went round to her flat in Cadogan Square, wrote a letter reminding her that we had corresponded about Wyndham Lewis' portrait of her mother and left it with the porter to slide under her door. Impressed by my dogged enterprise, Martha agreed to talk for an hour and a half. Tall and blond, with a good figure, soft skin and sharp tongue, she was still strikingly attractive at seventy-four. Her dislike of Bernice Kert's book made her suspicious of my work. Though she insisted that she would get stomach pains if she discussed Hemingway, she compulsively poured out her venom about his slovenly habits and abusive behavior.

I spent an entire week with Hemingway's three sons, who had followed their father's footsteps and lit out for the territories in the West. Though Patrick and Jack said they would see me, I had not heard from Gregory and his wife Valerie, who knew Hemingway well at the end of his life. When I got to the airport, Valerie was there to pick me up, Gregory was home for the weekend from his medical practice in the isolated town of Jordan and they invited me to stay at their house.

With them—and a few others—I established a curious and immediate intimacy that sometimes developed when I discussed intensely personal matters. I knew almost everything about Hemingway's life, and they apparently felt they could trust me. Within minutes we were talking about his sexual relations with Martha Gellhorn, and I soon learned the story of Gregory's bitter quarrel with his father. But the visit also had some awkward incidents. When Valerie and I were talking about Gregory in the cabin behind the main house where I slept, he quietly walked up to the door and overheard our conversation. Just as I remarked: "That must have been very difficult for you," a disembodied voice said: "Yes it was!" Like the biographer in "The Aspern Papers," I felt that I had been caught *in flagrante* and was reduced to strained silence.

Luck and timing were often crucial factors. After attending an opera with Valerie and a younger friend, we went out for drinks and he left to talk to some acquaintances at the bar. As Valerie was telling me the history of her friendship with Hemingway, the music was suddenly turned up very loud and I moved closer to hear what she was saying. Just as I was about to discover the precise nature of her relationship with Hemingway, the friend returned and interrupted our conversation. Later, as our conversation inched back to the subject, I was able to find out what I wanted to know.

Patrick, whose house is filled with sporting equipment and animal trophies, is a sympathetic, interesting and knowledgeable man with a manic laugh. In our twelve-hour talk he spoke of his serious illness in 1947, provided details of the second safari and emphasized that alcoholism was the key to his father's decline in the 1950s.

Since there was no direct flight from Bozeman to Ketchum, I took a spectacular 350-mile drive, through the western edge of Yellowstone. Jack, who looks like a blond version of his father, is vigorous and frank—though less intellectual than his younger brothers. We drove in his jeep down a dirt road and through the wilderness—no people, houses or cars—to a mountain stream, where he gathered shrimp for his trout pond from under the rocks: a trip that reminded me of the fishing expedition to Burguete in *The Sun Also Rises*. Jack's daughters—Margaux and Mariel (named for a French wine and a Cuban fishing port)—were not at home in Ketchum. But I played tennis with Jack on his own court and was struck by how the fifty-nine-year-old Jack was so vital and healthy while his father seemed so old when he died at the age of sixty-one. Talking to Hemingway's sons (disinherited by their father, who left everything to Mary) also revealed the family quarrels: Hemingway with his parents, his sisters Marcelline and Carol, his brother Leicester, and his son Gregory; his sons with Mary; Mary with A. E. Hotchner.

Hemingway's doctors were particularly difficult to see, and every one of them refused to answer questions about him. (I failed to convince his sons to obtain his medical records from the Mayo Clinic.) I was therefore surprised and delighted when Dr. Lynn Levy, a Hemingway enthusiast and friend of Jack's, invited me to a superb dinner of wild duck, and his partner Dr. George Saviers appeared as a fellow guest. Though the discussion of Hemingway was inevitably constrained, I did learn more about his injuries from the African plane crash of 1954, his admission to the Mayo Clinic and Mary's life after his death. The week out West, amidst perfect weather and magnificent scenery, was one of my best experiences, for I had fascinating conversations and learned a great deal.

V

It is common, when writing a biography, to become fascinated by certain figures in the subject's life who take on an independent existence and seem worthy of a full-length study. I became absorbed in the character and career of "Chink" Dorman-Smith, whom Hemingway met in Milan on Armistice Day, 1918, and who became one of his closest friends. While searching for information about

Chink in the histories of World War II, I came across an excellent chapter about him in Correlli Barnett's *The Desert Generals*. Barnett gave me the address of Chink's son Christopher, who kindly invited me to spend a long weekend at his home in Northumberland. He explained his father's unusual nickname and how Chink had won the Military Cross in the Great War; confirmed the influence of Kipling on Chink's character and values; showed me many unpublished letters from Hemingway and inscribed copies of his earliest books as well as Chink's annotations in the memoirs of World War II. I learned more about Chink from Field Marshal Lord Harding, Montgomery's biographer Nigel Hamilton, and the military historian M. R. D. Foot as well as from unpublished papers at King's College of London University, Manchester University Library, the Imperial War Museum and the Royal Military Academy Library at Sandhurst. From all these sources, I was able to show that Chink was a major influence on Hemingway, who refers to Chink in ten of his works, and that the destruction of Chink's career after he had drawn up the battle plans for the victory at the First Battle of Alamein was the direct inspiration and covert subject of *Across the River and into the Trees*.

Another brilliant military hero, also neglected in Baker's biography, was Gustavo Durán. A composer who became a Loyalist general in the Spanish Civil War, he was praised (as no other contemporary was ever praised by Hemingway) in chapter 30 of *For Whom the Bell Tolls*. Like Chink, Durán had a fascinating and little-known career after his life diverged from Hemingway's in 1944. I tried to trace Durán's family through the United Nations, where he had worked from 1946 until his death in 1969, but they were most unhelpful and did not even provide the address of his widow. In desperation, I wrote to the historian Hugh Thomas, who suggested I contact his friend Brian Urquhart, Deputy Secretary-General of the United Nations, about the scandalous obstructions I had encountered. Urquhart gave me the address of Durán's widow, Bonte, in Cambridge, England. She was eager to see me and to help; had many of Durán's papers, photographs and articles; gave me lunch and spoke to me for eight hours. She provided precise details of Durán's life, his role in Hemingway's Cuban spy network and his prolonged persecution by Senator Joe McCarthy. She had a painfully clear recollection of her encounters with Hemingway and Martha when their friendship with Durán had deteriorated and Bonte was their guest in Havana.

Brian Urquhart also put me in touch with Sven Welander at the United Nations archives in Geneva, who provided information about Durán's career in Chile, the Congo and Greece. *After Long Silence,* by Durán's brother-in-law Michael Straight, had some interesting if unreliable material about the strikingly handsome soldier, whose photograph I used in my book. All this information was supplemented by extensive interviews with Durán's sister-in-law, Dr. Belinda Straight, in Washington; his daughters, Lucy and Jane, in London; and his brother, Ernesto, in Madrid. Coincidentally, Chink's close friend Basil Liddell Hart introduced Gustavo to Bonte at Dartington Hall in 1939, just after Durán had escaped from Spain at the end of the Civil War.

I tracked down the documentary-film-maker Joris Ivens, who made *The Spanish Earth* with Hemingway in 1937, through the Dutch Consulate in New York. Though old and frail, suffering from asthma and from a recent hip operation, he was mentally vigorous and in his Paris flat spoke for several hours about the problems of filming during the Civil War, his quarrel with Orson Welles, his friendship with Martha Gellhorn, and described how Hemingway wrote and spoke the filmscript.

Another crucial and charismatic character, the wild and beautiful Jane Mason, who had been Hemingway's mistress in the 1930s, was also extremely difficult to trace. Jane's fourth husband, Arnold Gingrich, had been the editor of *Esquire,* and I tried to find her through the magazine. They could not help me, but one of the former staff members, Harold Hayes, thought Jane lived in Bergen County, New Jersey. After many phone calls and letters (for Mason is a common name), I finally found that Jane had died in 1981 and that her son Antony lived in Tuxedo Park, New York. During a weekend at Antony's house, I looked at Jane's photographs, scrapbooks and clippings, and saw home movies of Hemingway on his boat, the *Pilar*. I also read Jane's diary for the summer of 1934, which recorded her frequent engagements with Hemingway while her husband Grant was away on business.

I always felt it was worth meeting everyone who was willing to see me (I conducted only one telephone interview), for informants sometimes were quite different than I expected and often provided a single but crucial bit of information. While lecturing at the Library of Congress in the spring of 1984, I interviewed Evangeline Bruce, widow of the OSS colonel David Bruce. Though she had attended Hemingway's sixtieth birthday party in Málaga, she could not remember much about him. But she did give me the address in London of Henry Fonda's fourth wife Afdera, who was a lifelong friend of Hemingway's Italian love, Adriana Ivancich. Though Afdera forgot our appointment and was asleep when I arrived, she soon woke up, talked like rocket and confirmed (as I had suspected) that Adriana's suicide in 1983 was somehow connected to her involvement with Hemingway. Afdera explained that Adriana had had a nervous breakdown, drank heavily, quarreled with her second husband, was estranged from her sons and was deeply depressed by the failure of her book about Hemingway—a sad attempt to revive the past in order to compensate for the present.

The nature of Hemingway's relations with the bullfighters Antonio Ordóñez and Luis-Miguel Dominguín, whose personal and professional rivalry inspired "The Dangerous Summer" articles that appeared in *Life* in September 1960, had never been explained. I wanted to know what these two matadors thought of Hemingway, of his knowledge of Spain, of Spanish and of bullfighting. I found their contradictory answers to my questions revealed as much about Ordóñez and Dominguín as about Hemingway.

I had written twice to Ordóñez but received no reply. Still, when I phoned him from Marbella he was extremely friendly and responsive, and suggested we meet at the Hotel Inglaterra in the Plaza Nueva in Seville. He was charming and kind—the very qualities he praised in Hemingway. But he was unusually discreet and careful not to criticize his friend, and his brief answers tended to close off rather than develop the conversation.

The American novelist and screen writer Peter Viertel arranged my interview with Dominguín at his ranch near Andújar, three hours east of Seville. I drove several kilometers from the gate—past grazing bulls, a small bull ring, a few guest houses and an enormous dammed river—to a circular stone hunting lodge on top of a mountain. As with Ordóñez, I conducted the interview in Spanish. Dominguín had a world weary and dissipated look. He wore a knit shirt and shorts, and his legs were badly scarred with horn wounds. Cool and distant, much more critical of Hemingway than Ordóñez, he had not, like his brother-in-law and rival, been willing to play the son's role. He was still bitter about Hemingway's partiality to Ordóñez and about his criticism of Dominguín in "The Dangerous Summer" and said: "He never gave me any advice or encouragement about writing my memoirs. I threw away all his letters because I fear paper even more than I fear bulls."

Winston Guest, Archibald MacLeish and Leicester Hemingway had died in 1982, just before I began my research; and Adriana Ivancich, Toby Bruce, Robert Joyce, Joseph Losey, Joan Miró and Irwin Shaw passed away while I was writing the book. I was probably the last person to talk to most of them about Hemingway.

VI

I also had the good fortune to discover, partly as a result of the interviews, three important documents—psychological, political and historical—about Hemingway's life. In 1934, while Dr. Lawrence Kubie was treating Jane Mason after her suicide attempt, he was commissioned by the *Saturday Review* to write a psychoanalytic study of Hemingway. There was some acrimonious correspondence when Hemingway discovered this essay and managed to suppress it. After searching through Kubie's collected works, I contacted his colleague Dr. Eugene Brody, who put me in touch with Kubie's daughter, Anne Rabinowitz. She very kindly gave me copies of Kubie's essay and his correspondence with the editor of the *Saturday Review,* his lawyers, Charles Scribner and Hemingway, and she gave me permission to publish the essay, with my introduction, in the spring 1984 issue of *American Imago.*

I made the most interesting find by using the Freedom of Information Act to obtain a copy of the FBI file on Hemingway (as well as on Pound and Durán). These fascinating documents revealed that J. Edgar Hoover conducted a personal vendetta against Hemingway after the novelist had founded a rival spy network in Cuba during World War II, pursued him for the next eighteen years to the doors of the Mayo Clinic—Hemingway was quite sane when he said he was being followed by the FBI—and kept the file active until thirteen years after Hemingway's death. These revelations, which I published in the *New York Review of Books* on March 31, 1983, had wide repercussions. The article was translated into Italian and Portuguese, reprinted in Australia and parodied in the *Nation*. The *New York Times* story about my article was picked up by the wire services, was reprinted on the front page of the *San Francisco Chronicle,* and appeared in scores of newspapers in America, London, Hamburg, Milan and Sydney. I was interviewed a dozen times and gave a short summary of my findings to two million viewers on CBS-TV morning news. The discovery of the FBI file brought the publishers back to life. On the morning the *Times* story appeared, two firms offered me infinitely more money than I had accepted from Harper & Row. A week later, my brief moment of fame had passed.

An American Council of Learned Societies grant enabled me to complete the biography in the stimulating atmosphere of London. Though this seems an unusual place to write about an American novelist, I made many valuable discoveries while living there. From talking to Patrick Hemingway and writing to Mario Menocal, Jr. and Denis Zaphiro, I gathered several hints about a mysterious scandal, involving adultery and suicide, which took place in Kenya at the beginning of the century and which Hemingway heard about from his white hunter Philip Percival in 1934. By searching the London *Times* index, I came across a reference to the case in 1909 and followed it up in the Public Record Office at Kew. I discovered the full and hitherto suppressed story in the handwritten documents that had been sent that year from Kenya to the Colonial Office. In the *London Magazine* of November 1983, I explained what happened on that ill-fated safari and how Hemingway transformed the actual events into one of his greatest stories, "The Short Happy Life of Francis Macomber."

In London I was also able to interview the film directors Joseph Losey and Fred Zinnemann, the Labour M.P. Michael Foot and the authority on Spain Gerald Brenan. I learned other things from chance remarks at a dinner party. One evening, a friend of Martha's confided that she had some astonishing information about Martha's marriage to Hemingway but could not possibly disclose it. Of course I rang her up the next day and, after a long conversation, persuaded her to reveal her secret. While living in London, I lectured on Hemingway at the Royal Society of Literature, wrote about him in the *Literary Review* and *Critical Quarterly,* and aroused publishers' interest in securing the English rights to the book. At the Hemingway conference in Madrid in June

1984 I interviewed Ernesto Durán and Hemingway's Italian translator Fernanda Pivano, and saw many places—Bar Chicote on the Gran Vía and restaurant El Callejon on calle Ternera—that were associated with Hemingway.

VII

When I first began the biography, I hoped to write a livelier and more analytical book than Baker's. I thought Hemingway's life had been exhaustively examined in the seventeen memoirs published since his death and did not expect to make any startling discoveries. But my archival research, extensive correspondence and personal interviews produced a surprising amount of new material about Hemingway's wound in the Great War, the background of the Greco-Turkish War, his friendship with Chink Dorman-Smith, his periods of impotence, his quarrel with Carol Hemingway, his affair with Jane Mason (the model for Margot Macomber and Hélène Bradley in *To Have and Have Not*), his friendship with Gustavo Durán, the lesbianism of Jinny and Pauline Pfeiffer, his Cuban friends, his sexual problems with Martha Gellhorn, her supposed liaison with the jai-alai player Felix Areitio, his relations with Adriana Ivancich, his bitter fight with Gregory, his admiration for Slim Hayward and Jigee Viertel, his second African safari, his relations with Ordóñez and Dominguín, his affair with Valerie Danby-Smith, his medical problems and treatment at the Mayo Clinic, the reasons for his suicide and the aftermath of his death. I also explored the literary influence of writers outside the American tradition—Tolstoy, Kipling, Conrad, Joyce, D. H. Lawrence and T. E. Lawrence—and offered new interpretations of several major works: "The Short Happy Life of Francis Macomber," "The Snows of Kilimanjaro," *To Have and Have Not, Across the River and into the Trees* and *A Moveable Feast*.

I tried to portray the evolution of several different and distinct Hemingways, for he changed greatly from the confident genius of the twenties and the swaggering hero of the thirties to the drunken braggart of the forties and the sad wreck of the late fifties. But certain significant patterns, which recurred throughout his life, showed a consistency of character. He fell in love during wartime, became involved with his future wives while still married to his present ones, sought a scapegoat and reversed reality to fit his personal mythology, blamed others for his own faults, quarreled with those who helped him, had several military heroes—Dorman-Smith in the Great War, Durán in the Spanish War, Buck Lanham in World War II—and adopted a number of substitute sons: his younger brother Leicester, Gianfranco Ivancich, Antonio Ordóñez and A. E. Hotchner. At the end of his life he tried to repeat his earlier triumphs by returning to Africa, Paris and Spain and by falling in love with two nineteen-year-old girls.

The biographer is an investigative reporter of the spirit who enjoys the excitement of detection and discovery. By the time I completed the book—writing a hundred pages a month for seven months—I felt I knew not only Hemingway's tastes and habits but also how he would think and act in any situation. Hemingway was not always an attractive man, but his faults were an essential part of his character and he would be a far less interesting and exciting writer if he had been, for example, as perfectly polite as Archibald MacLeish. Though most books published after his death describe him as a boorish bully, I portray him as a surprisingly sensitive, pensive and intellectual artist.

17

Poets and Tennis

If racing is the sport of kings, tennis, in America anyway, is surely the sport of poets. Like poetry, tennis has strict rules and requires technical skill: it is individual yet social, aesthetically pleasing, intellectual, at times erotic. Even the feeble E. M. Forster, who fled from team games at school, boasted: "I play tennis with much energy."[1]

Tennis provided three generations of American poets with an outlet of aggression and a relief from the torments of artistic creation. The artists naturally carried their inflated egos from the study to the court and competed as ruthlessly in sporting as in literary life. Tennis appears in modern American poetry as a metaphor for social and sexual conflict, for individual ambition and narcissistic drive. Paradoxically, tennis also evokes a stable, harmonious and even courtly ritual in the work of European authors.

Robert Frost, who had a lifelong passion for the game, employed the tennis metaphor and embodied the competitive spirit. In his attack on Carl Sandburg's defense of modernistic poetry, Frost remarked that writing free verse was like playing tennis with the net down. He told an interviewer: "I've always thought of poetry as something to win or lose—a kind of prowess in the world of letters played with the most subtle and lethal of weapons."[2] At the Bread Loaf School in Vermont, young writers were expected to defer to the vanity of the aging bard and gracefully accept defeat on the court.

The most flamboyant and freakish player was Ezra Pound, who sported an enormous floppy beret—to distract his opponent as well as to shade his eyes. In *A Moveable Feast* Hemingway said: "Ezra, who was a very great poet, played a good game of tennis too."[3] And his tennis was as unorthodox as his poetry. Ford Madox Ford, a sometime opponent, famous for his tall stories, provided an endocrinological explanation of Pound's behavior:

> Mr Pound is an admirable, if eccentric, performer of the game of tennis. To play against him is like playing against an inebriated kangaroo that has been rendered unduly vigorous by injection of some gland or other. Once he won the tennis championship of the south of France, and the world was presented with the spectacle of Mr Pound in a one-horse cab beside the

Maire of Perpignan . . . followed by defeated tennis players, bull-fighters, banners and all the concomitants of triumph in the south.[4]

Ford's mistress Violet Hunt, who observed their game on the emerald turf court adjacent to their house in South Kensington, recalled Pound's chromatic costume and said his playing was "like a demon or a trick pony, sitting down composedly in his square and jumping up in time to receive his adversary's ball, which he competently returned, the flaps of his polychrome shirt flying out like the petals of some flower and his red head like a flaming pistil in the middle of it."[5] A Philadelphia friend compared Pound's energetic eruptions to those of "a galvanized agile gibbon."[6]

Since tennis can be played together by men and women, it has a sexual dimension lacking in most other sports. It offers a chance to flirt and enjoy physical proximity or an opportunity to struggle for sexual domination. Pound was especially agile and acrimonious when he played mixed doubles in London or Rapallo. Kitty Cannell, an early partner, noted: "Ezra ambled along in fawn pants and blue shirt. He motioned me back court and lay down near the net. From this position he would leap up and smash the ball over—marvellous when it came off. When it didn't, it was up to me. When I missed too, put off by blue streaks before my eyes, he would roar: 'Partner! Don't stand there gawping like one of those Rosetti females. Play!'"[7] Frederic Prokosch dramatized Pound's humiliating defeat at the hands of an Italian Amazon:

> The powerful Signorina smashed a lob of Ezra Pound's. "Shit!" said Pound. "I didn't hit the fucking ball high enough!" And then in an evil whisper, "She's a harpy, that woman!"
> He served a double-fault, then battled a ball into the net. *"Zero-quarante!"* cooed the Signorina, and Ezra Pound served an ace.
> "That will teach the scrawny bitch," he cackled triumphantly.
> The Signorina sent a powerful backhand drive straight at Ezra. He shrieked as he dipped his racquet in front of his abdomen.
> "Game and set!" cried the Signorina hurling her racquet in the air. Ezra glared. "She's trying to castrate me! She's a wolf in stork's clothing."[8]

Pound maintained his interest in tennis and played regularly with visitors and members of the staff while confined in Washington to St. Elizabeth's Hospital for the insane.

Hemingway was a keen tennis player in Paris, Key West and Cuba, and owned a court at the Finca Vigía. Though he had a bad eye from birth and a bad leg from a war wound, Hemingway (a kind of moveable beast) lurched around the court with more energy than form. In the early 1920s, he played Harold Loeb and William Carlos Williams on the red-clay grounds near the guillotine of the Santé prison on the Boulevard Arago. In his *Autobiography,* Williams recorded: "Played tennis with Hemingway and Harold Loeb, four sets. Hem and

I finally quit even, he unable to break my service and I, his: would have gone on till evening, perhaps. 'You've got nothing,' he told me. 'My knee gives out if I keep it up too long. Let's call it off.' "[9]

Hemingway responded to the aesthetic appeal of tennis, but deliberately transgressed the rules. He loved technical expertise and devised his own variation of traditional shots, using his bewildering "pig ball" service against Ezra's springbok tactics:

> I enjoyed the luxury of our tennis greatly and played with what was our conception of savage elegance. Ezra wore flannels. Ezra played better than I did, which is as it should be in tennis if you are to have pleasure. At that time, and up to a few years ago, I had a mysterious service called the pig ball. This landed flat and dead but with speed, and did not bounce at all. You can only serve a certain amount of pig balls since it is a slice which is stroked heavily on top with a very violent but caressing motion which is extremely destructive to the ligaments of the right shoulder.[10]

Hemingway was an aggressive player and a bad loser who always had to have his revenge. His first wife Hadley observed: "Ernest was as competitive in tennis as in everything else and whenever he missed a shot he would 'sizzle.' His racquet 'would slash to the ground and everyone would simply stand still and cower' . . . until he recovered himself with a laugh."[11]

Hemingway went in for blood sports in the 1930s, but returned to tennis when he acquired a young wife and good court in Cuba in the 1940s. He believed a few sets of fierce tennis with the Basque jai-alai players (who were political refugees after the Spanish Civil War) would boil the enormous amount of alcohol out of his system. A friend noted that his net game was as peculiar as Ezra's. Hemingway and Martha Gellhorn "played tennis a good deal, mostly doubles, and EH was an enthusiastic though unorthodox player. He took up his station at the middle of the net when his side was serving, and would insist on sterling net play, covering both sides of the court, ignoring his partner coming in after service."[12]

Tennis in Cuba often led to sexual strife. Hemingway criticized Martha's friends from *Time* magazine (she later married the editor) who came to the Finca "dressed in pressed flannels, to play impeccable, pitty-pat tennis." He also resented her flirtation with his handsome Basque rival Felix Areitio, who would carry Martha in his arms from the tennis court to the swimming pool. With the Basques, he introduced betting, devised imaginative variations of the traditional game and "played doubles against trios with the men at the net allowed to cross over and intercept the serve, and other special ground-rules."[13]

Though proud of Martha's style, he disapproved of her temperament. She could play well, but was bothered by the competitive atmosphere. As he wrote after their marriage had ended:

258   Poets and Tennis

> You had to let her *almost* win for her to be happy. If you *let* her win she became insufferable. You had to let her win sometimes insufferable or not. She played pretty good tennis, quite handsome to watch. But was lead-footed. She was not a competitor in sports, couldn't stand any kind of heat on, and being able to play quite well would play absolutely miserably, if there were social people around with expensive games. She used to play very well against me, alone with no one watching, and used to play really well sometimes with the Basques because she had a nice Bryn Mawr serve, and they, who served under hand when we first started playing all admired her serve and that built her up and made her shine.[14]

Hemingway's rather surprising interest in tennis as well as his early contests with Harold Loeb are reflected in *The Sun Also Rises* when Jake Barnes explains the destructive aspect of love and the high cost of Cohn's passion for Brett Ashley: "He loved to win at tennis. He probably loved to win as much as [Suzanne] Lenglen, for instance. On the other hand, he was not angry at being beaten. When he fell in love with Brett his tennis game went all to pieces. People beat him who had never had a chance with him."[15]

The poets of the next generation were both capable and competitive players. Theodore Roethke, who wrote delicate lyric poetry, was a huge, self-punishing, committed athlete. He coached the Lafayette College tennis team and played in serious tournaments. A boyhood friend in Saginaw maintained that he was not a natural athlete and lacked talent for the game, but overcame his limitations by fanatical practice and went into self-destructive rages:

> He was split high; his legs were thin; he moved in a series of lunges but he covered the court. Morley said, "He had this Prussian thoroughness. We had a practice board. If any of us did ten minutes on it, we had had enough, but I have seen Ted out there going bang! bang! bang! for three hours at a time. Pretty soon he was trying shots that only Tilden could have made." He played to win and, if he made a bad shot, would fly into a rage at himself and heave his racquet into the Tittabawassee River which was just over the fence. He even developed the skill—although this sounds implausible—of bursting the offending tennis ball by stamping on it.[16]

Stanley Kunitz, who frequently played against Roethke, described his awkward ferocity and sullen temper, and (like Frost) suggested convincing parallels between the poet and the player:

> We would fight it out on the courts for what we liked to boast, with a bow to Joyce, was the lawn tennyson championship of the poetic world. For all his six-foot-three, two-hundred-plus-pound bulk and his lumbering gait, he was amazingly nimble on his feet and ruthless at the kill, with a smashing service and a thunderous forehand drive. The daemon in him played the game just as it wrote the poems. Whatever he did was an aspect of the same insatiable will to conquer self and art and others. He could not bear to lose. If you managed to beat him by cunning and luck, you could not expect to be congratulated by him: he was more likely to smash his racquet across his knees.[17]

Since tennis pits individual against individual and exposes one's performance to public scrutiny, the game represents a challenge and an ideal, engages the mind as well as the body and forces the inner-directed player to dwell on limitations. For Delmore Schwartz, John Berryman and Randall Jarrell, the introspective sport encouraged self-analysis and self-laceration. Like Hemingway with Martha Gellhorn, Schwartz's conflicts with his wife Gertrude were accentuated by playing tennis together on the courts of Central Park. His notes for the unfinished "Story of the Tennis Ego" or "Tennis Christian" describe the progress of a quarrel in which the wife responds with resentment to her husband's critical remarks: "Secretly deriding her for being 'lazy, impatient, unskilled' and too easily discouraged, he would struggle to control his temper, and be so pleased with his 'new-found virtue' that he forgot his vigilance; 'the next second the suppressed anger gets out and is spoken.' This was the usual course of events, with Gertrude's sullen manner provoking Delmore's anger, always so near the surface."[18]

In one of his Dream Songs, John Berryman observed: "This world is a solemn place, with room for tennis."[19] But he talked about the game far better than he played it. As a fifteen-year-old Woody Allenish prep-school boy, he confessed not only to double but also to multiple faults: "I judge bounces very poorly, my foot work is terrible, I don't watch the ball closely enough, I am late getting in position, my strokes are incorrectly produced, my service is a series of double-faults, etc. In fact, I'm ashamed to appear on the court."[20] Not surprisingly, Schwartz beat Berryman (who should have played Gertrude). But he compensated for his defeats by engaging in verbal contests with Randall Jarrell. Berryman's first wife described "how they bragged! John, who ached to play well (but was temperamentally rather than physically unsuited to the game), bragged that he had once been ballboy for Helen Wills at Forest Hills. Randall could top that and did. They recalled games they'd seen, exchanged stories about memorable shots. Listening to them was like watching a match."[21]

Jarrell's lawyer and tennis partner wrote that "he loved music and sculpture, tennis and professional football.... He threw himself into each of his interests with all he had, as anyone who felt the impact of his fiercely competitive tennis appreciated."[22] The poet-translator Robert Fitzgerald, who often played evenly against Jarrell, also stressed Jarrell's aggressive play and the high seriousness with which he approached the game:

> Randall used to remind people that he had been trained as a psychologist ... and competitive tennis fascinated that side of him; then, too, he relished the craft and lore of the game, as of everything he took up. When he dropped the ball for his forehand shot in practice, you saw a small ritual performed with attention and gravity.
>
> I had the impression that for Randall this interest in tennis represented an attachment to common life.[23]

Fitzgerald later added that Jarrell was devoted to the sport but lacked stamina and power, and was not as good as he was cracked up to be. When Jarrell played in a tournament in Levanto, on the Italian Riviera, he was completely exhausted after two sets and totally dominated in the third. He had elegant form, good forehand and backhand strokes: a smart player but not tournament class.[24]

A poem and story by two contemporary American authors epitomize the attitudes of the previous generations. Robert Pinsky's "Tennis" (1975)—divided into The Service, Forehand, Backhand, Strategy, Winning—expresses, with a mystical tinge, the technical influence of professional coaching lore and how-to-do-it manuals. The poem has an ungentlemanly though typically American emphasis on victory and fear of failure:

> Walk, never run, between points: it will save
> Your breath, and hypnotize him, and he may think
> That you are tired, until your terrible
>
> Swift sword amazes. By understanding
> Your body, you will conquer fatigue.
> By understanding your desire to win
>
> And all your other desires, you will conquer
> Discouragement. And you will conquer distraction
> By understanding the world and all its parts.[25]

While Pinsky uses tennis as a metaphor for power and control, Paul Theroux's story "The Tennis Court" (1977), set in post-colonial Malaya where he had been a teacher, employs the competitive dynamics of the game to reveal prejudice and racial antagonism. The English players attempt to engineer a degrading tennis defeat in order to revenge themselves on Shimura, a despised Japanese "reciprocal guest" from a club in Singapore: "These Japs can't stand humiliation. If he was really beaten badly we'd be well rid of him." His character is expressed in his game and (like Hemingway and Roethke) he uses his racquet like a lethal weapon. He held it like a sword, chopped the air with it, "played a hard darting game . . . [and] barked loudly when he hit the ball."[26] The club members, resenting his style of play, hold him personally responsible for the torture, flogging, starvation and violence that took place during the Japanese occupation. But Shimura foils their plans by beating the well-trained but lower-class Malayan ball-boy. He sponsors the Malay in Singapore and, with oriental cunning, sends him back to the up-country club as *his* reciprocal guest.

The passion for tennis was not confined to American authors, but extended across the steppes and into Russia. Vladimir Nabokov's family had a court on their pre-revolutionary estate. In the nostalgic *Speak, Memory* he recalled his mother's charming manner, his father's well-intentioned advice and the exasperating regularity of his brother's game:

> Our current tutor or my father, when he stayed with us in the country, invariably had my brother for partner in our temperamental family doubles. "Play!" my mother would cry in the old manner as she put her little foot forward and bent her white-hatted head to ladle out an assiduous but feeble serve. After every exchange my father . . . pedantically inquires of my brother and me whether the "follow-through," that state of grace, has descended upon us. . . . The only game [my brother and I] both liked was tennis. We played a lot of it together, especially in England, on an erratic grass court in Kensington, on a good clay court in Cambridge. . . . Despite a weak service and an absence of any real backhand, he was not easy to beat, being the kind of player who never double-faults, and returns everything with the consistency of a banging wall.[27]

Even the austere post-revolutionary Alexander Solzhenitsyn—prevented from developing his game by internment in Gulag—realized a lifelong ambition and built his own tennis court when he retired into his barbed-wire compound in Cavendish, Vermont. As he told an interviewer: "When I was a boy in Ryazan I dreamed of playing tennis, but I never had enough money for a racquet. At the age of 57 [in 1975], I managed to allow myself my own court."[28] Solzhenitsyn preserved this ideal because tennis was not simply a game, but a formal ceremony that evoked the stability of the past.

Tennis as a metaphor for peace and order reappears in Donald Davie's "Shropshire" (1975), which nostalgically recalls the charming faults of his father as well as the threat of war in the fading light of peace:

> Our parents at their tennis-club. . . . A high
> Lob in the last light hangs like Nemesis
> On 1912! Deceived, my father's eye
> Forsees the easy smash that he will miss.[29]

In Thomas Mann's *The Magic Mountain* (1924), Hans Castorp and his tubercular cousin enviously observe the energetic and immaculately dressed youths playing tennis in Alpine Davos just before the Great War. The contrast between health and sickness is revealed in the symbolic phrase "coated with flour," which suggests both the menacing wintry snow that remains on the mountains in summer and the corpselike pallor of the moribund patients in the International Sanatorium Berghof: "Tennis was being played on several courts by long-legged, clean-shaven youths in accurately pressed flannels and rubber-soled shoes, their arms bare to the elbows, and sunburnt girls in white frocks, who ran and flung themselves high in the sunny air in their efforts to strike the white ball. The well-kept courts looked as though coated with flour." [30]

Katherine Mansfield, in long skirt and sun hat, played tennis in Regent's Park while a student at Queen's College, London, during 1903–1906. In her finest story "Prelude" (1918), the dreamy and disappointed Aunt Beryl is repelled by the coarse masculinity of the sweaty suitors provided by her brother-in-law: 'They are pulling up their trousers every minute—don't you know—and whacking at imaginary things with their racquets."[31]

John Betjeman's "A Subaltern's Love-song" (1945), an incantatory paean to the English summer, makes tennis both a social and sexual occasion. The predatory victory of an androgynous yet nubile opponent, playing in a garrison town, arouses the passion of a young subaltern who is excited by the sweaty body that repulsed Mansfield's Aunt Beryl. Though Americans, like Pound, feel defeat is a castrating experience, the Englishman finds it erotic to lose:

> Miss J. Hunter Dunn, Miss J. Hunter Dunn,
> Furnish'd and burnish'd by Aldershot sun,
> What strenuous singles we played after tea,
> We in the tournament—you against me!
>
> Love-thirty, love-forty, oh! weakness of joy,
> The speed of a swallow, the grace of a boy,
> With carefullest carelessness, gaily you won,
> I am weak from your loveliness, Joan Hunter Dunn.
>
> Miss Joan Hunter Dunn, Miss Joan Hunter Dunn,
> How mad I am, sad I am, glad that you won,
> The warm-handled racquet is back in its press,
> But my shock-headed victor, she loves me no less.[32]

Tennis expresses cultural as well as personal values. The life and work of modern poets reveal that Americans are competitive, egoistic, aggressive, even violent; eager for victory and angry in defeat. For European writers, however, tennis represents ritual and tradition. It is a social occasion for privileged people, an amateur pleasure, an aesthetic spectacle, a nostalgic recollection, a momentary state of grace, a memory of a lost world.

18

The Death of Randall Jarrell

What does being a poet mean? It means having one's own personal life, one's reality, in quite different categories from those of one's poetic work, it means being related to the ideal in imagination only, so that one's own personal life is more or less a satire on poetry and on oneself.[1]

Kierkegaard, Journals

I

The death of Randall Jarrell, who was struck by an automobile in 1965, has always been surrounded by mystery. The official verdict was "accident," but many familiar with the case concluded that it was suicide. A. Alvarez, Martin Seymour-Smith, Galway Kinnell and John Simon are perhaps the only writers to state Jarrell killed himself (though they offer no evidence for this assertion).[2] Recently discovered documents now make it possible to say exactly what happened to Jarrell and to suggest some reasons for his tragic end.

Jarrell belonged to a generation of poets, born between 1899 and 1917, who suffered from alcoholism and mental illness and died prematurely: Hart Crane, Theodore Roethke, Delmore Schwartz, Dylan Thomas, John Berryman and Robert Lowell. Roethke exalted insanity as part of the artist's fatal gift:

> What's madness but nobility of soul
> At odds with circumstance? The day's on fire!
> I know the purity of pure despair,
> My shadow pinned against the sweating wall.

But Berryman condemned the deity who devoured mad genius:

> I'm cross with God who has wrecked this generation.
> First he seized Ted, then Richard, Randall, and now Delmore.
> In between he gorged on Sylvia Plath.[3]

If, as Delmore Schwartz says (ironically paraphrasing Wordsworth): "We poets in our youth begin in sadness; / thereof in the end come despondency and madness,"[4] we must look to Jarrell's childhood for a partial explanation of his death. Frederick Hoffman could not be more mistaken when he maintains: "It is obvious that Jarrell had had a splendid childhood, though one wonders why it should flood his fancy in the last of his books [*The Lost World*], close to his death."[5] Though the facts about his childhood are often cloudy and contradictory, he clearly had good reason to be bitterly unhappy. He was born in Nashville on May 6, 1914, the second child (the first apparently died in infancy) of a nineteen-year-old mother and twenty-year-old father, who was then a bookkeeper.[6] Soon after Jarrell's birth, the family moved to Long Beach, California, where his father worked in a photographer's studio. His parents separated in September 1925, when his mother and younger brother Charles returned to Nashville, and Jarrell remained in Hollywood with his paternal grandparents and great-grandmother. Jarrell later recalled that when summoned to rejoin his mother "he hated to leave. 'How I cried!' he said. And he'd begged them so hard to keep him that when they wouldn't—or couldn't—he blamed them for being cruel and resolved never to think about them again."[7]

Jarrell's father soon remarried; his mother moved about frequently in Nashville, struggling to meet her financial obligations and to care for her two sons. Jarrell was forced to do what he considered "hellish" and humiliating jobs, like collecting money for newspapers and selling Christmas seals door-to-door: "*Imagine*, pestering people like that in their houses. Wasn't that a wicked thing to make a child do?"[8] In 1926 the lonely, handsome boy posed for the statue of Ganymede on the bogus Parthenon in Centennial Park. "His mother said the sculptors had asked to adopt him, but knowing how attached to them he was she hadn't dared tell him. 'She was right,' Randall said bitterly. 'I'd have gone with them like *that*.' "[9] During his childhood Jarrell lost his mother three times: when Charles was born and replaced him as her favorite, when he was suddenly severed from both parents and brother in 1925, and when his mother remarried in about 1930. After his mother's second husband was killed in a car crash in 1940, Jarrell (whose brother had moved permanently to Paris) had sole responsibility for her.

Blair Clark's insight about his friend Robert Lowell applies with equal force to Jarrell: "There were two dynamos within him, spinning in opposite directions and tearing him apart."[10] Though destined (like Hart Crane) for the candy business, Jarrell was sent by a wealthy uncle to Vanderbilt, where he became the favorite pupil of the most respected and influential poets of the

South: John Crowe Ransom, Allen Tate and Robert Penn Warren. These poets soon acknowledged his superior gifts, technical skill and formal mastery of verse. Tate remembered Warren "showing me some of the boy's poems. There was one beginning 'The cow wandering in the bare field' which struck me as prodigious; I still think it one of his best poems."[11] His precocious reputation as a "literary genius" led the youth to nourish great expectations.

Jarrell could be charming and gentle, but even friends like Elizabeth Bishop admitted that he "was difficult, touchy, and oversensitive to criticism." Berryman called him "a hard loser. He wasn't a man who liked to lose at all."[12] In an interview Tate angrily recalled: "Randall was the most difficult human being I ever knew. His vanity was absolutely astronomical. He insulted everybody. He would sneer at people."[13] Lowell (whose star eclipsed Jarrell's) tried to explain the acerbic character of the man who was admired by friends, worshipped in Greensboro, North Carolina (where he taught from 1947 to 1965) and accustomed to adulation: "In his own life, he had much public acclaim and more private. The public, at least, fell gravely short of what he deserved."[14]

Jarrell had published five volumes of poetry between 1940 and 1951, but there was a nine-year gap before *The Woman at the Washington Zoo,* one third translations from Rilke, appeared in 1960. In the 1960s, as his poetic inspiration diminished, he concentrated on translations, anthologies, criticism and children's books. In his essay on Wallace Stevens, written when he was thirty-seven, Jarrell observed that poets have no choice about waiting for the spark of heaven to fall: "A good poet is someone who manages, in a lifetime of standing out in thunderstorms, to be struck by lightning five or six times.... A man who is a good poet at forty *may* turn out to be a good poet at sixty; but he is more likely to have stopped writing poems."[15] And his second wife, Mary, wrote: "The half-alive poet/artist may reckon with arid and idea-less attacks, as Randall did, saying for a while, 'It's cyclical,' and writing 'Believe, my heart, Believe!' on scraps of paper around the house. Also, he can read—as Randall did—all that the Germans have to say about the crisis in the poet's ego that causes his creative paralysis."[16] But these attempts at resignation, incantation and reflection did very little good when inspiration failed. Jarrell suffered from that "morbidness which not infrequently casts a shadow on the mind of the ignored innovator."[17] In the mid-1960s he feared he might never recover his creative powers.

The loss of his mother and fear of sterility are poignant themes in the two beautiful children's books that he wrote during the final years of his life. As early as 1939, Jarrell had admiringly quoted from Collins' "Ode to Evening": "the weak-ey'd Bat, / With short shrill Shriek flits by on leathern Wing." In his *Bat-Poet,* the talented creature abandons his nocturnal habits and becomes isolated from the other mammals: "Toward the end of summer all the bats except the little brown one began sleeping in the barn.... So he had to sleep all alone.

He missed the others. They had always felt so warm and furry against him." As compensation he begins to write poetry; but when his work is criticized by the mockingbird and ignored by the other animals, he echoes Jarrell's earlier laments about the lack of an intelligent audience: "the trouble isn't making poems, the trouble's finding somebody that will listen to them." Though fluent at first, he becomes blocked when he tries to write about the color and song of the cardinal: "It was no use: no matter how much the bat watched, he never got an idea. . . . '[The cardinal would] make a beautiful poem; but I can't think of anything.'" When the unresponsive chipmunk remarks "how queer it must be to be a bat," the escapist, airborne poet replies: "No, it's not queer. It's wonderful to fly all night."[18]

Jarrell's brilliant illustrator, Maurice Sendak, said that his last children's book, *"Fly by Night,* is a strange story and a very personal one. . . . It is a painful dream about a little boy who misses his mother's presence, and I knew this was something that had always troubled Randall."[19] Jarrell writes: "At night David can fly. In the daytime he can't. In the daytime he doesn't even remember that he can. . . . 'If I remembered in the daytime I could fly in the daytime. All I have to do is remember.'" It seems clear that flying is a metaphor for the release of the imagination (as in dreams) and that his inability to remember represents the loss of poetic powers in the conscious world. The lonely David, in contrast to the bat, exchanges day for night. As he glides over his sleeping parents, his mother lies buried and obliterated under a mound of blankets and pillow. But he has the insight and power to see her dreams—and divine her true feelings about him. David's poetic flight, like the bat's, is exhilarating; but he must inevitably return to the sterile world of daylight. As the owl warns him: "You will fly / From your dark nest into the harsh unknown / World the sun lights." The outside world is "cold and hard and bare"; and at the end of the story, when he vainly tries to remember his furtive and suspect *vol de nuit,* he suddenly "opens his eyes and the sunlight blinds him."[20] Both children's stories are allegorical and convey an unusual sense of loss, isolation, sterility and frustration.

Jarrell's last and most autobiographical book of poetry, *The Lost World* (a world of lost parents, childhood and imaginative powers), was published in March 1965 and echoes the dominant theme of his earlier volumes: *The Rage for the Lost Penny* (1940) and *Losses* (1948). Ransom observed that Jarrell— who wrote of suicide in "Kirilov on a Skyscraper" and his note on Tuzenbach in *The Three Sisters*—"had a great flair for the poetry of desperation."[21] And Christina Stead (whose novel *The Man Who Loved Children* was enthusiastically praised by Jarrell) recently noted: "Some months ago in a bookshop in Canberra

I bought a volume of his poems and I was shocked to read in them a tendency to that act [suicide]."[22]

The Lost World (especially in retrospect) seems forlorn and foreboding. It is filled with images of illness:

> Forced out of life into
> Bed, for a moment I lie comfortless
> In the blank darkness;

of pain:

> His jerking body, bent into a bow,
> Falls out of the hands onto the table,
> Bends, bends further, till at last it breaks;

of mutilation:

> I lie here like a cut-off limb, the stump the limb has left;

of terror:

> there visited me one night at midnight
> A scream with breasts;

of derangement:

> But I identify myself, as always,
> With something that there's something wrong with;

of despair:

> The patients have in common hopes without hope;

and of death:

> I stand beside my grave
> Confused with my life, that is commonplace and solitary.[23]

Jarrell's morbid depression was all too apparent to close friends who met him in 1965. Hannah Arendt recalled: "When I last saw him not long before his death, the laughter was almost gone, and he was almost ready to admit defeat." And Stanley Kunitz notes: "He came north for a visit from Greensboro, with his beard deleted, and I saw at dinner for the first and last time the naked vulnerability of his countenance."[24] Although Jarrell had been severely depressed for several years (when his bearded mask was stripped away), Mary Jarrell was too close to her husband to foresee the disaster that occurred in February 1965 and confined Jarrell in a private hospital in Chapel Hill: "Randall's nervous breakdown was showing signs that all but we could see.... Before it was through with us, this ordeal called forth a desperate valor we'd never known we had.... When the doctors let him come home again, Randall was not as good as new, but he was recovering."[25]

The reviews of *The Lost World,* which appeared while Jarrell was in the psychiatric ward, must have intensified his depression. Friends like Philip Booth and William Meredith praised the book; and Jean Garrigue, Samuel Moon and W. J. Smith also wrote favorable notices. But the negative reviews, which repeated the old charges of sentimentality and self-pity, had a greater emotional impact on the hypersensitive invalid. Joseph Bennett wrote in the widely read *New York Times Book Review:* "His work is trashy and thoroughly dated; prodigiousness encouraged by an indulgent and sentimental Mamaism, its overriding feature is doddering infantilism." This savage judgment was reinforced by more persuasive and influential critics. Paul Fussell stated in the *Saturday Review:* "It is sad to have to report that Randall Jarrell's new book ... is disappointing. There is nothing in it to compare with the poems he was writing twenty years ago.... [His style] has hardened into a monotonous mannerism, attached now too often to the mere chic of sentimental nostalgia and suburban pathos." In the *Hudson Review* Roger Sale concluded: "If Lowell and Roethke are major poets, Jarrell is minor indeed." And Jarrell's younger rival James Dickey (who had come up to Vanderbilt when Jarrell was still the prototype of the brilliant promising poet) exposed in the *American Scholar* the crucial weaknesses of his poetry: "In Jarrell there is a pervasive and disquieting flatness.... He generally does not hold out long enough for the truly telling phrase, for the rhythm that matches exactly the subject, the image, the voice."[26]

II

Jarrell resumed teaching at Greensboro in the fall term but returned to Chapel Hill for further medical treatment on October 10. Four days later, while walking at night about a mile and a half south of town on the busy U.S. highway 15–501, which runs between Durham and Sanford and bypasses Chapel Hill, Jarrell was struck by a car. The composite newspaper reports are somewhat contradictory but give a full account of the incident. The front page of the *Chapel Hill*

Newspaper of October 15, 1965, which had a photograph of the damaged car, reported:

> Jarrell was walking south, facing oncoming traffic, when the accident happened at about 7:30 p.m. Graham Wallace Kimrey, 42, of Sanford, was identified as the driver of the car. Jarrell's head struck the right side of the windshield, breaking a large hole in the glass, and threads of his dark clothing were imbedded in the pane on the side of the car, the patrolman reported.
>
> Both Kimrey and his wife told the patrolman the victim seemed to whirl, "as I approached he appeared to lunge out into the path of the car." Most of the damage, estimated at $200, was at the windshield-door post on the right side of the car.
>
> Jarrell died instantly. Usually recognized as a bearded man, Jarrell was clean shaven when he died. Authorities said Jarrell was being treated at N.C. Memorial Hospital here for a skin graft by Dr. Earle Peacock, a Chapel Hill specialist. Jarrell had a two-day old pain killer prescription in his pocket when his body was found.
>
> Impact of the car spun Jarrell around and did not knock him more than three or four feet at most. The car was going at a speed below the 45-mile limit. No charges were expected to be lodged. . . .
>
> Dr. [Loren] MacKinney said he had inquired into Jarrell's background, pertaining to whether he had had periods of depression. However, Dr. MacKinney said his discussion on this line is considered medical, "privileged information."

This story provides some crucial facts and raises some unanswered questions. It is essential to note that Jarrell, most unusually, threw himself into the side of the car and went through the windshield, rather than under the wheels; that the evidence confirmed and the police accepted the Kimreys' statement that Jarrell lunged into their car; and that no charges were made against the driver. The pain-killer prescription suggested that Jarrell may have been drugged at the time, and the doctor's refusal to discuss his medical history implied that Jarrell had suffered periods of depression.

The *Winston-Salem Journal* of October 16 quoted author Peter Taylor in the misleading headline: "Friend of Jarrell Says Poet / Was Distraught About Bomb" and extracted more information from the State Trooper who investigated the incident:

> Gentry said the unlighted, wooded by-pass was a "weird place" for Jarrell to be walking. The spot was about a mile from where Jarrell was staying. "As the vehicle came abreast of the pedestrian," Gentry wrote in his report, "he lunged into the side of the vehicle, striking the left fender of the vehicle, his head striking the windshield, killing him instantly."
>
> After he had completed his investigation, Gentry said, he received later information that Jarrell was seen staggering on the edge of the highway about 10 minutes before his death. The couple who reported seeing him said it looked as if he were under the influence of a drug.

In this account, the policeman stated that the dark highway was a strange place to walk and provided additional evidence to suggest Jarrell may have been drugged.

The front page of the *Greensboro Daily News* had further information from the doctor:

> Dr. Loren MacKinney, deputy medical examiner, acting in the absence of Dr. Hubert Patterson, medical examiner, said last night that he had not completed his investigation of Jarrell's death. "Until I complete my investigation, I think it is better that I make no comment," Dr. MacKinney said. Hospital authorities said Jarrell had been undergoing skin treatment at Memorial Hospital.
> The body is at Hanes-Lineberry Funeral Home pending arrangements.

Finally, *The New York Times* of October 15—where most of the literary world read about Jarrell's death—emphasized the mysterious circumstances and was the first newspaper to state it was a suicide:

> [Jarrell] was struck by an automobile as he walked along the heavily travelled Chapel Hill bypass, U.S. 15–501. There was no immediate explanation for Mr. Jarrell's presence as a pedestrian on the highway.
> State Trooper Guy C. Gentry, Jr. said: "We are going on the assumption that it was suicide. He said witnesses reported that the victim had 'lunged into the side of the car that struck him.'"
> No charges were placed against the driver.
> The body was identified by friends of the poet on the campus at Chapel Hill.

The fact that the body was not identified by his wife suggests that she may have been away from Greensboro at the time. No further firsthand evidence is available, for the police reports at the Department of Motor Vehicles in Raleigh and the State Police Headquarters in Graham have been destroyed. And Guy Gentry, who left the State Police, worked for Martin-Marietta in Baltimore and moved to California five years ago, has disappeared.

The controversy about Jarrell began three weeks after his death when his grieving wife—who believed, "Readers are grateful for any knowledge you have, and they don't, about an artist they care for"[27]—responded to the brief obituaries in *Time* (October 22) and *Newsweek* (October 25). Both repeated the *New York Times* report that Jarrell "apparently 'lunged into the path' of a passing automobile" and was "an apparent suicide." She wrote to *Time* on November 5:

> The road he was walking beside is a narrow one-lane cutoff, not well lighted. My husband, who was dark-haired, wore dark clothes, including his gloves, and it was nighttime when the car brushed past him at about 45 m.p.h. bruising his shoulder and glancing the side of his head, causing instant death. The driver seems not to have been aware of my husband's presence at the roadside until he had hit him. His statement that my husband apparently "lunged into the path" of his car has a sinister ambiguity. . . . When no written evidence exists that a deceased person intended to take his life, it would seem more reliable and humane to assume death is accidental.

This account differs in several important respects from the newspaper reports, which were based on firsthand accounts by the driver, the policeman and the medical examiner. She describes the road as a "narrow one-lane cutoff" rather than a busy highway; says the car "brushed past him" rather than that he lunged into it; calls his injuries mere "bruising" and "glancing"; and, in contrast to the policemen's judgment, anticipates the line of legal reasoning that led to the official verdict of "accident."

Mary Jarrell added some new facts in her letter to *Newsweek* on November 22:

> My husband loved walks and naturally had taken several during his four-day stay at the Hand Rehabilitation Center in Chapel Hill, N.C. (He was receiving therapy for a nerve regeneration pain.) Except for the main street, Chapel Hill has virtually no sidewalks. . . . The medical examiner reported no broken bones, only surface contusions, and a skull fracture from an impact in the lower left back quadrant. The toxicologist's report revealed no evidence of sedation or tranquilizing medication.

Her statement that Jarrell loved walks does not explain why he chose the "weird place" on the dark highway instead of the pleasant campus of the University of North Carolina. The fact that he was "receiving physical therapy for a nerve regeneration pain" does not match Dr. Peacock's statement that Jarrell was having a "skin graft"—and neither one reveals the reason for this treatment. She maintains that Jarrell had no broken bones or lacerations; and repeats this in 1967 when describing the death of their cat who was also struck by a car: "Like Randall, the beautiful eyes and face, and the graceful body were not hurt in any way."[28] And she denies the rumors that Jarrell had been under the influence of drugs.

Though Jarrell's wife quite naturally wished to assuage the feelings of her family and friends after the incident by softening the grim facts of the case, there was far less reason to do so fifteen years later in a letter to the *New Leader*. On October 6, 1980 she contradicted John Simon's account of Jarrell's death in his review on September 8 of *Kipling, Auden & Co.*:

> In Simon's first paragraph he asserts that Jarrell "died of letting a truck run over him." The facts are:
> 1. It was not a truck, it was a passenger car.
> 2. Jarrell was not in the least "run over." He was sideswiped as he walked along the edge of the road, and flung upward across the hood.
>
> In his last paragraph Simon claims that Jarrell "was finally deflated into suicide," and that "Members of his family and friends who have tried to made his death appear an accident do him a disservice." Again, the facts are:
> 1. The doctors performing the autopsy found no other injury but a fracture at the base of the skull, which in their opinion killed Jarrell on impact.
> 2. The medical evidence, along with statements from persons in the car, formed the basis for

the coroner's report listing my husband's death as "Accidental" and making this a matter of public record on his death certificate.

This letter differs from her earlier accounts in which the passenger car bruised and glanced Jarrell's shoulder and head. It now places the blame entirely on the driver and claims Jarrell "was sideswiped . . . and flung upward across the hood." Jarrell's wife (who may not have read the complete autopsy report) repeats that the only injury was a fracture of the skull. Moreover, she states, for the first time, that the cause of death was officially recorded as "Accidental."

III

Three vital documents—Jarrell's Certificate of Death, Coroner's Report and Autopsy Report—finally enable us to cut through the multifarious contradictions in the newspaper and subsequent reports of Jarrell's death and to clarify the mysteries obscuring this incident. The Certificate of Death, signed by Dr. Loren MacKinney and dated Nov. 8, 1965, lists Jarrell's "Kind of Business or Industry" as "Poetry." It states the time of death: "7:30 P.M." (not 8 P.M.); the cause: "cerebral concussion"; the interval between onset and death: "less than five minutes" (not instantaneous); and the verdict: "accident."

The apparently contradictory Coroner's Report, filed in January 1966 by Allen H. Walker, Jr. (who, as was common at that time, was both a coroner and an undertaker) does not explain why the verdict was an "accident": "Kimrey's car was in the correct traffic lane, and when he came abreast of Jarrell, he suddenly lunged into the side of the car. Apparent evidence warrants calling his death accidental. No jury empanelled." But an interview with Walker in Hillsborough, North Carolina on June 10, 1981 reveals why he accepted Kimrey's statement that Jarrell lunged into the side of the car, yet called it an accident and felt there was no need for an inquest. Walker said a coroner's report was required on all automobile deaths and that the coroner was concerned only with the criminal aspects of the case. Following normal procedure, Walker did not examine Jarrell's body, did not talk to Kimrey and did not consult the medical examiner or the pathologist. He got all the facts from State Trooper Gentry. The decisive factors in his verdict were that Jarrell, in a rare kind of incident, hit the side rather than the front or front wheels of the car (though his lunge may have been mistimed); and that the legal verdict must be "accident" if there is no certain evidence—such as a written note—that suicide was intended. As *The New York Times* of November 9, 1965 reported: "Dr. Loren G. MacKinney, acting medical examiner, who signed the death certificate, said a three-week investigation of circumstances surrounding Mr. Jarrell's death had 'raised a reasonable doubt about its being a suicide.'"

The eighteen-page report of Jarrell's autopsy, authorized on October 15, contains startling revelations about his psychiatric history and the injuries sustained on the night of October 14. The pathologist, Dr. Fred Dalldorf, abstracts his findings in a clearly written two-page "Summary of Case":

> The patient had been seen at the North Carolina Memorial Hospital previously for psychiatric difficulties. He had been last hospitalized here [in May] approximately 5 months prior to his death with a manic depressive psychosis, and [in January] just prior to that hospitalization, he had attempted suicide by inflicting multiple cuts on his left arm. At the time of his death, he was receiving outpatient treatment here for these wounds.

Dr. Dalldorf gives the precise diagnosis of Jarrell's mental illness, reveals that he attempted suicide in January 1965 by slashing the bend and wrist of his left arm (the diagram on the first page of the autopsy report shows "two 4 cm scars left antecubital fossa" and "multiple 4 cm scars left wrist"), and explains that he was at the Chapel Hill Hand Rehabilitation Center in October to repair these severe wounds and restore the use of his left hand—which necessitated a skin graft and "physical therapy for a nerve regeneration pain."

The autopsy shows that "there was moderate atherosclerosis of both coronary arteries," which could have become a serious problem if Jarrell had lived; and "a minimal to moderate degree of fatty metamorphosis scattered throughout" the liver. More significantly, the autopsy reveals that the injuries to the left side of Jarrell's face, head and body—as one would expect when a man's head goes through the windshield of a car travelling at nearly 45 miles per hour—were much more extensive than previously reported. Bones were broken in his left foot and in his skull:

> Multiple ecchymoses [discoloration from bleeding into the skin] and abrasions were present over the face, the scalp, the left arm, the left side of the trunk, and the left lower extremity. The left foot was noted to be hypermobile on examination, and a portable x-ray of the left lower extremity revealed oblique fractures. . . . There was a 4 cm. laceration extending through the entire thickness of the scalp over the left parietal [side to back skull] bone. Multiple skull fractures were noted grossly and on x-ray examination involving both temporal bones, the left parietal bone, and multiple bones in the base of the skull on both sides. . . .
>
> At autopsy, severe and extensive injuries to the skull and the brain were found; and it is felt that his death may be attributed to these.

The multiple skull fractures caused hemorrhages, increased the cranial pressure, compressed the medulla and damaged the parts of the lower brain that control breathing and heart function.

The autopsy report also states: "There was no anatomical or toxicological evidence of any form of intoxication or of any other disease process which might have contributed to his demise," and proves that drugs were not a factor in

Jarrell's death. Finally, and contrary to all previous reports, Dr. Dalldorf concludes that "Death was not instantaneous; he remained alive for a short period of time after the accident though unconscious."

After Jarrell's death, a bizarre quarrel took place between the pathologists of Orange County (which includes Chapel Hill) and Guilford County (which includes Greensboro) about who should pay the $150 bill for his autopsy. Orange sent the bill to Guilford, quoting the North Carolina statute that the charge must be "paid by the county of legal residence of the deceased." Guilford ignored this point and wrongly claimed: "I fully appreciate that you cannot accept the financial burden of doing autopsies on every one who dies in Memorial Hospital and the referring counties should be asked to pay for them. But in this case, the decedent received his *initial* injury in your jurisdiction, and your police department conducted the investigation." Orange pointed out "that Mr. Jarrell did *not* die in this hospital, but at the scene of the accident," and correctly maintained: "As the law is stated, the place where an accident or death occurs and is investigated is not relevant." At this point, Guilford presumably conceded the issue and paid the bill.

Although Jarrell had been brought up as a Nashville Methodist, his funeral took place at the Holy Trinity Episcopal Church in Greensboro on October 17, when his body was cremated. His wife, two stepdaughters, uncle, aunt and mother (but not, apparently, his father or brother) attended the ceremony. The pallbearers included his oldest friends, Robert Lowell and Peter Taylor, his editor Michael DiCapua, his tennis partner Richardson Preyer, his colleague Robert Watson and other members of the College. His grave at New Garden Cemetery, near Guilford College, bears the inscription: "Randall Jarrell / Poet / Teacher / Beloved Husband / 1914–1965." He left an estate valued at $17,500 to his wife and also named her as literary executor. Adrienne Rich, whose early poems had been praised by Jarrell, spoke for all his friends when she called him "an irreplaceable piece of humanity."

The suicide of Jarrell—who died at 51, the same age as his gentle, vulnerable heroes, Proust and Rilke—had a powerful emotional impact on two poets, John Berryman and Robert Lowell, and may have loosened their tenuous hold on life. Berryman was stunned, confessed Jarrell's "death hit me very hard" and said he felt much worse later on when he read *The New York Times* report that called it a suicide. Nevertheless, Berryman thought Jarrell's iron self-confidence and childlike quality would have prevented him from killing himself.[29] In his elegy, written after further reflection, Berryman describes Jarrell's self-devouring torment, panic and frustrated ambition; and suggests he will soon give his friend a familiar greeting in the world of the dead:

> Let Randall rest, whom your self-torturing
> cannot restore one instant's good to, rest:

> he's left us now.
> The panic died and in the panic's dying
> so did my old friend. I am headed west
> also, also, somehow.
>
> In the chambers of the end we'll meet again
> I will say Randall, he'll say Pussycat
> and all will be as before
> whenas we sought, among the beloved faces,
> eminence and were dissatisfied with that
> and needed more.[30]

Lowell, who had often sent his poems to Jarrell in manuscript, recalled: "Randall had an uncanny clairvoyance for helping friends in subtle precarious moments—almost always as only he could help.... Twice or thrice, I think, he must have thrown me a lifeline." Unlike Berryman, Lowell had no doubts about Jarrell's suicide, and in "Ten Minutes" thinks he might end his loneliness in the same way as Jarrell did:

> I am companionless;
> occasionally, I see a late, suicidal headlight
> burn on the highway and vanish.[31]

In one elegy, Jarrell holds his slashed wrist as he had once held the black Persian cat that had also been struck by a car:

> They come this path, old friends, old buffs of death.
> Tonight it's Randall, the spark of fire though humbled,
> his gnawed wrist cradled like his *Kitten*.

In another elegy, Jarrell (whose nobility and innocence are suggested by "Child") walks in a trance on the highway, seeks death and "lunges on the windshield":

> lights, eyes, peering at you from the overpass;
> black-gloved, black-coated, you plod out stubbornly,
> as if asleep, Child Randall, as if in chainstep,
> meeting the cars, and approving; a harsh luminosity,
> as you clasp the blank coin at the foot of the tunnel.[32]

The facts about Jarrell's death are now known. But without an edition of his letters (promised since 1973), a biography (discouraged by his wife) and his psychiatric records (which cannot be released without family approval), we can only speculate on the causes of his death. Many factors contributed to his suicide: his unhappy childhood, the breakup of his marriage to Mackie Langham in 1951, worries about the health of his mother (who entered a nursing home in 1965), periods of sterility, fears that he would lose his poetic powers, hostile reviews of his last book of poems, division between his personal life and poetic ideal, realization that he had not fulfilled his brilliant promise and impossible hopes, severe nervous breakdown, manic-depressive psychosis and the earlier attempt to kill himself. Jarrell's uncharacteristic involvement of the driver and his wife, which risked their lives as he destroyed his own, was probably an attempt to make his suicide seem like an accident. Jarrell had always been an extremist: a man of passionate enthusiasm and extreme hostility. These traits were reflected in his all or nothing habits, friendship (with Tate and others), marriages, criticism—in his life and in his death. Jarrell was apparently not in full control of his mind and body when he lunged into the car on that dark night. But it was will, not fate, that determined his death.

Notes

2. Filial Memoirs of Tolstoy

References:

Ilya Tolstoy, *Tolstoy, My Father: Reminiscences,* trans. Ann Dunnigan (Chicago, 1971)
Leon Tolstoy, *The Truth about My Father,* [no. trans.] (London, 1924)
Aylmer Maude, ed. and trans., *Family Views of Tolstoy* (London, 1926)
Alexandra Tolstoy, *The Tragedy of Tolstoy,* trans. Elena Varneck (New Haven, 1933)
Sergei Tolstoy, *Tolstoy Remembered,* trans. Moura Budberg (New York, 1972)
Tatiana Sukhotin-Tolstoy, *The Tolstoy Home,* trans. Alec Brown (London, 1950)
Tatiana Sukhotina, *Tolstoy Remembered,* trans. Derek Cottman (London, 1977)

3. George Painter's *Marcel Proust*

1. *World Authors, 1950–1970* (New York, 1975), pp. 1107–1108.
2. Lewis Nichols, "Double Toil," *New York Times Book Review,* November 7, 1965, p. 8.
3. Phyllis Grosskurth, "An Interview with George Painter," *Salmagundi,* 6 (1983), 26.
4. Letter from George Painter to Jeffrey Meyers, January 13–28, 1986.
5. *World Authors,* p. 1108.
6. *Ibid.*
7. Letter from Painter to Meyers.
8. Simon Blow, "A Stake in the Past," *Guardian,* October 19, 1977, p. 10.

9. Grosskurth, *Salmagundi*, p. 36. For more information on Painter, see *Contemporary Authors*, volume 101 (Detroit, 1981), pp. 359–360, and *Who's Who* (London, 1985), p. 1466.

10. George Painter, *André Gide: A Critical and Biographical Study* (New York, 1951), p. 7.

11. Marcel Proust, *Remembrance of Things Past*, trans. C. K. Scott-Moncrieff (New York, 1934), 2: 130.

12. Letter from Painter to Meyers.

13. Grosskurth, *Salmagundi*, pp. 40–41.

14. *Ibid.*, p. 35.

15. Blow, *Guardian*, p. 10.

16. Grosskurth, *Salmagundi*, pp. 37–38. The first volume of *Chateaubriand* was dedicated, in part, to Marthe Bibesco.

17. *Ibid.*, pp. 39–40.

18. *Ibid.*, p. 28. It is worth noting that Painter's Foreword to *William Caxton: A Biography* (London, 1976), p. vii, remains unregenerate and asserts, like his Preface to *Marcel Proust*, that the sources for his life "have not as yet been adequately studied or interpreted"; that the biography is based on "an independent study of the primary sources"; that it is written "for the general reader, the student, and the specialist alike"; and that there are many new facts and new conclusions.

19. Letter from Painter to Meyers.

20. George Painter, *Marcel Proust: A Biography* (London, 1959), 1: xi-xii.

21. *World Authors*, p. 1108.

22. Grosskurth, *Salmagundi*, p. 37, relates that in *Other People's Letters*, Mina Curtiss "talks about the period when she went to Paris to collect Proust's letters and how she went to bed with the Prince Bibesco in order to obtain letters." Painter wrote a favorable review of Curtiss' edition in the *Listener*, 44 (December 21, 1950), 801. For Painter's reviews of books on Proust by Harold March and F. C. Green, see *Listener*, 41 (May 19, 1949), 861–862 and 42 (December 8, 1949), 1009, 1011.

23. Grosskurth, *Salmagundi*, p. 26.

24. See Marie Riefstahl-Nordlinger, "On Reading *Marcel Proust—A Biography*, Vol. 1, by George Painter," *X, A Quarterly Review*, 1 (July 1960),

203–209, and "A Reply to Mme. Riefstahl-Nordlinger from George Painter," *X, A Quarterly Review,* 1 (October 1960), 322–324.

25. George Painter, "Proust's Way," *Times Literary Supplement,* August 19, 1965, p. 715. See also Painter, "Proust's Way," *Times Literary Supplement,* September 9, 1965, p. 775.

26. Grosskurth, *Salmagundi,* p. 33.

27. This sentence and many others appear in "Proust's Way," Painter's Introduction to Proust's *Letters to His Mother* (London, 1956), pp. 32–48. In this essay, he presents a concise life of Proust and emphasizes the originals of his fictional characters.

6. E. M. Forster and T. E. Lawrence: A Friendship

1. The primary sources on the Forster-Lawrence friendship were the following: Lawrence's fourteen letters to Forster in *The Letters of T. E. Lawrence,* ed. David Garnett (London, 1938) and his references to Forster throughout the edition, some of them not in the index; Forster's twelve letters to Lawrence in *Letters to T. E. Lawrence,* ed. A. W. Lawrence (London, 1962), pp. 58–75; Lawrence's review, "Novels by D. H. Lawrence," *Spectator,* 139 (August 6, 1927), 223, in which he discusses Forster. Forster's four essays on Lawrence are: "T. E. Lawrence," a review of the trade edition of *Seven Pillars of Wisdom,* reprinted in *Abinger Harvest* (New York, 1936), pp. 134–140; a biographical memoir in *T. E. Lawrence by His Friends,* ed. A. W. Lawrence (New York, 1937), pp. 247–251; an elegiac description, "Clouds Hill," reprinted in *Two Cheers for Democracy* (New York, 1951), pp. 345–348; and a review, *"The Mint* by T. E. Lawrence," *Listener,* 53 (February 17, 1955), 279–280. Forster also discusses Lawrence in "English Prose Between 1918 and 1939" in *Two Cheers for Democracy,* pp. 274, 280.

2. Michael Holroyd, *Lytton Strachey* (London, 1971), p. 1010, quotes Strachey's letter of November 4, 1929, which mentions a second story: "Morgan was charming at the week-end—full of accounts of Africa from bottom to top. He read two stories to C. and me—improper—quite amusing."

3. Frederic Manning (1887–1935) was an Australian poet and novelist. Ernest Altounyan, a doctor, first met Lawrence in Aleppo in 1911. After Lawrence's death he wrote a book-length elegy, *Ornament of Honour.*

8. Murry's Cult of Mansfield

1. For a complete citation of Murry's writings about Katherine, see my article, "Katherine Mansfield: A Bibliography," *Bulletin of Bibliography,* 34 (July 1977), 53–67. For a discussion of the marriage of Katherine and Murry, see my book, *Katherine Mansfield: A Biography* (London, 1978).
2. J. M. Murry, *Keats,* 4th ed. (London, 1955), p. 28.
3. Quoted in F. A. Lea, *The Life of John Middleton Murry* (London, 1959), p. 140.
4. *Ibid.,* p. 144.
5. *Ibid.,* p. 187.
6. *Ibid.,* p. 124.
7. *Ibid.,* p. x.
8. Katherine Mansfield, *Journal,* ed. J. M. Murry (London, 1954), p. 296.
9. Aldous Huxley, *Point Counter Point* (London, 1965), pp. 170–172.
10. D. H. Lawrence, "Smile," *Complete Short Stories* (New York, 1964), 2: 584.
11. J. M. Murry, "In Memory of Katherine Mansfield," *Adelphi,* 1 (January 1924), 664–665.
12. Lea, *Murry,* p. 113.
13. Matthew Arnold, "Shelley," *Essays in Criticism: Second Series* (London, 1906), p. 252.
14. Richard Holmes, *Shelley: The Pursuit* (New York, 1975), p. 353 n.
15. Quoted in Quentin Bell, *Virginia Woolf* (New York, 1972), 2: 37.
16. Katherine Mansfield, *Letters to John Middleton Murry, 1913–1922,* ed. J. M. Murry (London, 1951), p. 642.
17. J. M. Murry, "A Month After," *Adelphi,* 1 (July 1923), 94–96.
18. Unpublished letter from J. M. Murry to Katherine Mansfield, October 1922, Alexander Turnbull Library, Wellington, New Zealand.
19. J. M. Murry, *God* (London, 1929), pp. 30–31.

20. Katherine Mansfield, *Journal,* ed. J. M. Murry (London, 1927), p. 255.
21. J. M. Murry, "Introductory Note" to Ruth Mantz's *A Critical Bibliography of Katherine Mansfield* (London, 1931), p. xv.
22. Murry, *Keats,* p. 76.
23. Quoted in Lea, *Murry,* p. 227.
24. Quoted in Sandra Darroch, *Ottoline: The Life of Lady Ottoline Morrell* (New York, 1975), p. 258.
25. Quoted in Beatrice Glenavy, *Today We Will Only Gossip* (London, 1964), p. 69.
26. D. H. Lawrence, *Collected Letters,* ed. Harry Moore (New York, 1962), p. 1105.
27. Quoted in Catherine Carswell, *The Savage Pilgrimage* (London, 1932), p. 198.
28. Quoted in Richard Rees, "John Middleton Murry," *Dictionary of National Biography, 1951–1960* (Oxford, 1971), p. 761. Gerald Brenan spoke for most of Bloomsbury when he wrote to me on October 3, 1975, "Everyone detested Middleton Murry."
29. J. M. Murry, "Katherine Mansfield," *New York Evening Post Literary Review,* February 17, 1923, p. 461 (hereafter cited as *Post*); and Mantz, *Bibliography,* p. 17.
30. J. M. Murry, *Between Two Worlds* (London, 1935), p. 311.
31. *Ibid.,* p. 375.
32. Antony Alpers, *Katherine Mansfield* (London, 1954), p. 210.
33. Murry, *God,* p. 14.
34. Mansfield, *Letters to Murry,* p. 85.
35. *Ibid.,* p. 699.
36. Mansfield, *Journal* (1954), pp. 332–333.
37. Quoted in Frieda Lawrence, *Memoirs and Correspondence,* ed. E. W. Tedlock (New York, 1964), p. 362.
38. *Ibid.,* p. 302.
39. Christiane Mortelier, "The Genesis and Development of the Katherine Mansfield Legend in France," *AUMLA,* 34 (1970), 252–263.

40. Lea, *Murry*, p. 198; and George Orwell, *Collected Essays, Journalism and Letters*, ed. Sonia Orwell and Ian Angus (New York, 1968), 2: 315.

41. Quoted in Colin Murry, *I at the Keyhole* (New York, 1975), p. 139. See also D. H. Lawrence, *Letters to Thomas and Adele Seltzer*, ed. Gerald Lacy (Santa Barbara, 1976), p. 52: "I know Murry too well to care what he says, one way or another."

42. The following quotations are from Murry, *Post*, pp. 461–462.

43. Quoted in Michael Holroyd, *Lytton Strachey* (London, 1971), p. 928.

44. In *Between Two Worlds*, pp. 317–318, Murry claims that Katherine "has written better stories than G[ilbert] C[annan] or D. H. L[awrence] have ever written in their lives, and better than they are ever likely to."

45. In 1921, Koteliansky and Leonard Woolf published their translation of Chekhov's *Notebooks*, but, as Kot explained to Ruth Mantz, "We did not use Katherine's name [she had helped Kot with an earlier version] because she was *not* then known as a writer." Quoted in *Katherine Mansfield: An Exhibition* (Austin, 1975), p. 44.

46. J. M. Murry, "Introductory Note" to *The Dove's Nest* (London, 1923), p. 10. See Lawrence, *Letters to Seltzer*, p. 111: "I think it's downright cheek to ask the public to buy that waste-paper basket."

47. J. M. Murry, "Introductory Note" to *Something Childish* (London, 1924), p. ix.

48. J. M. Murry, *Katherine Mansfield and Other Literary Studies* (London, 1959), p. 72.

49. J. M. Murry, "The Letters of Katherine Mansfield," *Listener*, 35 (April 4, 1946), 437.

50. Murry, *Keats*, p. 68.

51. In his "Introduction" to Katherine's *Journal* (1927), p. ix, Murry states that her first story in *Rhythm*, "The Woman at the Store," "caused a minor sensation." In fact, it was scarcely noticed.

52. I consider her best stories to be: "Prelude," *"Je ne parle pas français,"* "The Man Without a Temperament," "The Stranger," "The Daughters of the Late Colonel," "The Garden Party" and "The Fly."

53. Quoted in Witter Bynner, *Journey with Genius* (New York, 1951), p. 150. See also Edward Nehls, *D. H. Lawrence: A Composite Biography* (Madison, 1958), 2: 414.

54. Murry, *Post,* p. 461.
55. Quoted in J. M. Murry, "Introductory Note" to *In a German Pension* (New York, 1926), p. 8.
56. Mansfield, *Journal* (1927), p. 1.
57. Murry, *Post,* p. 461.
58. *Ibid.*
59. Murry, "Introduction" to *In a German Pension,* p. 8.
60. Murry, "Introduction" to Mantz's *Bibliography,* p. xvi.
61. Murry, *Katherine Mansfield and Other Literary Studies,* p. 75–76.
62. Quoted in Alpers, *Mansfield,* p. 194.
63. Leonard Woolf, *Beginning Again* (New York, 1964), p. 204.
64. Mansfield, *Journal* (1954), pp. 191, 226.
65. J. M. Murry, "The Weariness of Ivan Bunin," *Dial,* 76 (February 1924), 195. See also J. M. Murry, "Tchehov Revisited," *Adelphi,* 14 (1937), 19.
66. Murry, "Introduction" to *Journal* (1927), p. xiv.
67. J. M. Murry, "Chekhov and Katherine Mansfield," *TLS,* October 26, 1951, p. 677.
68. See Elisabeth Schneider, "Katherine Mansfield and Chekhov," *Modern Language Notes,* 50 (1935), 394–397; Eva Jacoubet, "Un curieux exemple d'identité littéraire: Katherine Mansfield et Tchekhov," *Études anglaises,* 3 (1939), 251–252; Sylvia Berkman, *Katherine Mansfield: A Critical Study* (New Haven, 1951), pp. 150–159; Ronald Sutherland, "Katherine Mansfield: Plagiarist, Disciple, or Ardent Admirer?," *Critique,* 5 (1962), 58–76; Don Kleine, "The Chekhovian Source of 'Marriage à la mode,'" *Philological Quarterly,* 42 (1963), 284–288; and Charanne Kurylo, "Chekhov and Katherine Mansfield: A Study of Literary Influence," dissertation, University of North Carolina, 1973.
69. Murry, *Katherine Mansfield and Other Literary Studies,* p. 74.
70. Quoted in Ruth Mantz and J. M. Murry, *The Life of Katherine Mansfield* (London, 1933), p. 275.
71. Murry, *Post,* p. 461.
72. Murry, *Between Two Worlds,* p. 204.

284   Notes to Pages 130–133

73. Murry, "Introduction" to *In a German Pension*, p. 8.
74. Murry, "Introduction" to *Journal* (1927), p. ix.
75. Murry, "Introduction" to Mantz's *Bibliography*, p. xiii.
76. Murry, "Introduction" to *Journal* (1927), p. ix.
77. J. M. Murry, *Katherine Mansfield and Other Literary Portraits* (London, 1949), p. 7.
78. Murry, *Post*, p. 462.
79. Mantz and Murry, *Life of Mansfield*, p. 7.
80. *Ibid.*, p. 11.
81. Mansfield, *Journal* (1954), p. 158.
82. Katherine Mansfield, Notebook, q MS/1903–1922 (36:5), Alexander Turnbull Library.
83. Mansfield, *Letters to Murry*, p. 544.
84. Katherine Mansfield, *Letters*, ed. J. M. Murry (London, 1928), 2: 268.
85. Mansfield, *Journal* (1954), p. 266.
86. *Ibid.*, p. 269.
87. Randall Jarrell, *Pictures from an Institution* (New York, 1960), p. 81.
88. Quoted in Lesley Moore (pseudonym of Ida Baker), *The Memories of LM* (London, 1971), p. 188.
89. Mansfield, *Journal* (1954), p. 292.
90. *Ibid.*, p. 129.
91. Unpublished letter from Katherine Mansfield to Ottoline Morrell, August 14, 1922, University of Texas.
92. Partially quoted in *Katherine Mansfield: An Exhibition*, p. 52, and in Lea, *Murry*, p. 113 n.
93. Quoted in Lea, *Murry*, p. 113.
94. Unpublished letter from Katherine Mansfield to J. M. Murry, August 7, 1922, Alexander Turnbull Library.
95. Leonard Woolf, "Preface" to *A Writer's Diary* (New York, 1954), p. ix.

96. Ian Gordon, *Katherine Mansfield,* rev. ed. (Lincoln, Nebraska, 1963), p. 119.

97. Philip Waldron, "Katherine Mansfield's *Journal,*" *Twentieth Century Literature,* 20 (1974), 12, 18.

98. Ian Gordon, "The Editing of Katherine Mansfield's *Journal* and *Scrapbook,*" *Landfall,* 13 (1959), 69.

99. Ruth Mantz, "K. M.—Fifty Years After," *Adam,* 370–375 (1972–1973), 127.

100. Gerald Bullett, *Modern English Fiction: A Personal View* (London, 1926), p. 114.

101. Virginia Carr, *The Lonely Hunter: A Biography of Carson McCullers* (Garden City, New York, 1975), pp. 51–52.

102. Conversation with Christopher Isherwood, July 31, 1976. The quotations are from *Journal* (1954), p. 269, and A. R. Orage, "Talks with Katherine Mansfield," *Century Magazine,* 87 (November 1924), 38.

103. George Orwell, "New Novels," *New Statesman,* 21 (January 25, 1941), 89–90. See also Orwell's more sympathetic review, "Sensitive Plant," *Observer,* January 13, 1946, p. 3.

104. Letter from Frank Swinnerton to Jeffrey Meyers, April 4, 1976.

105. The cult of Katherine still thrives in Helen McNeish's soppy edition, complete with soft-focus photographs, of the Mansfield-Murry correspondence, *Passionate Pilgrimage: A Love Affair in Letters* (London, 1976).

10. Memoirs of D. H. Lawrence: A Genre of the Thirties

1. Quoted in Ronald Draper, *D. H. Lawrence: The Critical Heritage* (London, 1970), pp. 23, 322.

2. Richard Aldington, *Pinorman* (London, 1954), p. 184.

3. Philip Larkin, "The Sanity of Lawrence," *TLS,* June 13, 1980, p. 671.

4. D. H. Lawrence, *Collected Letters,* ed. Harry Moore (New York, 1962), pp. 138, 547; D. H. Lawrence, *Letters,* ed. Aldous Huxley (London, 1932), p. 298; and quoted in Harry Moore, *The Priest of Love* (Carbondale, 1974), p. 453.

5. Quoted in Moore, *Priest of Love,* p. 465.

6. *Ibid.*, p. 416
7. For a thorough discussion of Lawrence's relations with Murry, see Jeffrey Meyers, *Married to Genius* (London, 1977), pp. 113–173; Jeffrey Meyers, "D. H. Lawrence," *Homosexuality and Literature, 1890–1930* (London, 1977), pp. 131–61; Jeffrey Meyers, "D. H. Lawrence, Katherine Mansfield and *Women in Love*," London Magazine, 18 (May 1978), 32–54; Jeffrey Meyers, *Katherine Mansfield: A Biography* (London, 1978), pp. 78–104.
8. Quoted in J. M. Murry, *Reminiscences of D. H. Lawrence* (London, 1933), p. 79.
9. F. A. Lea, *The Life of John Middleton Murry* (London, 1959), p. 31.
10. Lawrence, *Collected Letters,* p. 821.
11. *Ibid.*, p. 894.
12. J. M. Murry, *Between Two Worlds* (London, 1935), p. 80.
13. Katherine Mansfield, *Journal* (London, 1954), p. 296.
14. Aldous Huxley, *Point Counter Point* (London, 1965), p. 170.
15. Huxley, "Introduction" to *Letters,* p. x.
16. Quoted in Jessie Chambers, *D. H. Lawrence: A Personal Record* (London, 1935), p. 184.
17. T. S. Eliot, "Son of Woman," *Criterion,* 10 (July 1931), 768, 774.
18. Interview with Enid Hilton, Ukiah, California, June 25, 1976.
19. Aldous Huxley, *Letters,* ed. Grover Smith (New York, 1969), p. 364.
20. See Jeffrey Meyers, "Murry's Cult of Mansfield," *Journal of Modern Literature,* 7 (February 1979), 15–38.
21. In the eight years between the deaths of Mansfield and Lawrence, Murry published nine books by her: *The Dove's Nest* (1923), *Poems* (1923), *Something Childish* (1924), *The Journal of Katherine Mansfield* (1927), *The Letters of Katherine Mansfield* (1928), *Reminiscences of Leonid Andreyev* (1928; translated by Mansfield and Koteliansky), *The Aloe* (1930), *Novels and Novelists* (1930), and *Stories* (1930). Many of these books were first serialized in the *Adelphi*.
22. Lea, *Murry,* p. 165.
23. Lawrence, *Collected Letters,* p. 730.

24. Quoted in Meyers, *Katherine Mansfield*, p. 222.
25. D. H. Lawrence, "New Mexico," *Phoenix*, ed. Edward McDonald (London, 1936), p. 142.
26. See Helen Corke, *D. H. Lawrence's "Princess": A Memory of Jessie Chambers* (Thames Ditton, Surrey, 1951), p. 12: "Jessie was gentle—she treated him rather as Mary of Bethany might have treated Christ."
27. D. H. Lawrence and Mollie Skinner, *The Boy in the Bush* (London, 1963), p. 390.
28. Faith Mackenzie, *More Than I Should* (London, 1940), p. 33.
29. Interview with Barbara Weekley Barr, Chestfield, Kent, March 12, 1980.
30. Peter Irvine and Anne Kiley, ed., "D. H. Lawrence and Frieda Lawrence: Letters to Dorothy Brett," *D. H. Lawrence Review*, 9 (Spring 1976), 94.

14. Hemingway: Wanted by the FBI

1. Hugh Thomas, *Cuba, or the Pursuit of Freedom, 1762–1969* (New York, 1971), p. 730.
2. Spruille Braden, *Diplomats and Demagogues* (New Rochelle, New York, 1971), p. 283.
3. Ernest Hemingway, *For Whom the Bell Tolls* (New York, 1968), p. 335.
4. See "Gustavo Durán of the UN Dies; Was Associate of Hemingway," *New York Times*, March 27, 1969, p. 47.
5. Braden, *Diplomats*, p. 299.
6. See "Arrest of 12 Accused of War Recruiting: FBI Agents Seize Men and a Woman Indicted for Acting for Spanish Loyalists; Prosecutor Says Detroiters Lured Prospective Soldiers at Communist Meetings," *New York Times*, February 7, 1940, p. 8.
7. Ernest Hemingway, "The Christmas Gift," *Look*, 18 (May 4, 1954), reprinted in *By-Line: Ernest Hemingway*, ed. William White (New York, 1957), p. 450.
8. See Hemingway's ill-advised wartime assertion in his Introduction to *Men at War: The Best War Stories of All Time* (New York, 1942), p. xxiv: prevention of future wars with Germany "can probably only be done by sterilization."

9. See Ernest Hemingway, *Islands in the Stream* (New York, 1970), p. 215: there were "the inescapable FBI men, pleasant and all trying to look so average, clean-cut-young-American that they stood out as clearly as though they had worn a bureau shoulder patch on their white linen or seersucker suits."

10. Braden, *Diplomats,* p. 289.

11. A. E. Hotchner, *Papa Hemingway* (New York, 1966), pp. 273, 280; Mary Hemingway, *How It Was* (New York, 1977), p. 609.

15. Memoirs of Hemingway: The Growth of a Legend

1. Raymond Chandler, *Farewell, My Lovely* (1940) (New York, 1976), pp. 134–135.

2. Dwight Macdonald, "Ernest Hemingway," *In the American Grain* (New York, 1962), pp. 171–172.

3. For a history of Hemingway's literary reputation, see Jeffrey Meyers, *Hemingway: The Critical Heritage* (Boston, 1982); for an analogous discussion of D. H. Lawrence, see Jeffrey Meyers, "Memoirs of D. H. Lawrence: A Genre of the Thirties," *D. H. Lawrence Review,* 14 (Spring 1981), 1–32.

4. Malcolm Cowley, "A Portrait of Mister Papa," *Life,* 25 (January 10, 1949), reprinted in *Ernest Hemingway: The Man and His Work,* ed. John McCaffery (New York, 1950), p. 42.

5. Ernest Walsh, "Ernest Hemingway," *This Quarter,* 1 (1925–1926), 67.

6. Horst Frenz, ed., *Nobel Lectures: Literature, 1901–1967* (Amsterdam, 1969), p. 501.

7. Matthew Bruccoli, *Scott and Ernest* (New York, 1978), pp. 101, 155. Serious errors continue to appear in recent biographical books on Hemingway. Anthony Burgess, *Ernest Hemingway and His World* (London, 1978), mistakenly states that Hemingway's left leg was badly wounded at Fossalta, confuses Hemingway's friend Malcolm Lowrey with the English novelist, and says Valerie Danby-Smith was Scottish.

8. Edmund Wilson, "Ernest Hemingway: Gauge of Morale," *The Wound and the Bow* (New York, 1941), reprinted in Meyers, *Hemingway: The Critical Heritage,* pp. 304–305.

9. Quoted in Carlos Baker, *Ernest Hemingway: A Life Story* (New York, 1969), p. 550.

10. McCaffrey, Introduction to *Ernest Hemingway: The Man and His Work*, p. 8.
11. Cowley, "A Portrait of Mister Papa," p. 26.
12. Letter from Hemingway to Buck Lanham, December 27, 1954, Princeton University Library.
13. Letter from Hemingway to Malcolm Cowley, January 17, 1952, Kennedy Library. No such poignant pleas affected Faulkner. He refused to let Cowley, who was a good friend and had been instrumental in establishing Faulkner's reputation, follow the *Life* article on Hemingway with another on himself. See William Faulkner, *Selected Letters*, ed. Joseph Blotner (New York, 1977), p. 285.
14. Letter from Hemingway to John Dos Passos, October 30, 1951, Kennedy Library.
15. Ernest Hemingway, *Selected Letters*, ed. Carlos Baker (New York, 1981), p. 744.
16. *Ibid.*, p. 647.
17. Lillian Ross, *Portrait of Hemingway* (New York, 1961), pp. 25, 35.
18. Ross, *Portrait of Hemingway*, pp. 13–14; Lillian Ross, "The Hemingway Profile," *New Republic*, 145 (August 7, 1961), 30.
19. Quoted in Baker, p. 651; Hemingway, *Letters*, p. 744.
20. Edward Burns, ed., *Staying On Alone: Letters of Alice B. Toklas* (New York, 1973), p. 194.
21. Kurt Singer, *Hemingway: Life and Death of a Giant* (Los Angeles, 1961), pp. 10, 134.
22. In 1961 Singer also "edited" *The Secret Agent's Badge of Courage* by Ernest Hemingway, which was made up of five paragraphs from Clausewitz, published in Hemingway's *Men at War* (1942), and contained nothing at all by the putative author. See Audre Hanneman, *Ernest Hemingway: A Comprehensive Bibliography* (Princeton, 1967), p. 267.
23. Letter from Hemingway to Dave Lemke, January 18, 1961, Kennedy Library.
24. Milt Machlin, *The Private Hell of Hemingway* (New York, 1962), front cover, pp. 1, 61.

25. Leicester Hemingway, *My Brother, Ernest Hemingway* (New York, 1962), pp. 117, 213, 237. See also Donald St. John, "Leicester Hemingway: Chief of State," *Connecticut Review*, 3 (1970), 5–19.

26. Marcelline Sanford, *At the Hemingways: A Family Portrait* (London, 1963), p. 219.

27. Quoted in *The Fitzgerald-Hemingway Annual, 1972* (Washington, D.C., 1973), p. 354.

28. Jed Kiley, *Hemingway: An Old Friend Remembers* (New York, 1962), p. 107.

29. José Luis Castillo-Puche, *Hemingway in Spain*, trans. Helen Lane (New York, 1974), pp. 82, 182.

30. See "Mrs. Hemingway Loses Book Plea," *New York Times*, February 22, 1966, p. 7 and "Appeal on Hemingway Book," *New York Times*, March 18, 1966, p. 41.

31. Interview with Hemingway's lawyer, Alfred Rice, New York, December 21, 1982.

32. Philip Young, "I Disremember Papa" (1966), *Three Bags Full* (New York, 1972), pp. 64–65. Young, whose projected book aroused Hemingway's wrath in the early 1950s, was rehabilitated by Mrs. Hemingway in 1965 after he provided ammunition for her lawsuit against Hotchner. Young's devastating review of *Papa Hemingway* shows that Hotchner took passages from Robert Capa, Marlene Dietrich (though he may have originally ghostwritten her piece) and many others, and silently incorporated them into his own work.

33. Castillo-Puche, *Hemingway in Spain*, pp. xi, xiii, xiv.

34. *Ibid.*, pp. 351, 318.

35. See Arnold Lubash, "Hotchner's $125,000 Libel Award Upheld," *New York Times*, August 3, 1976, p. 20, and "Federal Appeals Court Throws Out $125,000 Libel Award," *New York Times*, March 24, 1977, p. 28.

36. Lloyd Arnold, *High on the Wild with Hemingway*, with a Foreword by John Hemingway (Caldwell, Idaho, 1968), p. 331.

37. S. Kip Farrington, Jr., *Fishing with Hemingway and Glassell* (New York, 1971), pp. viii, 68, 20.

38. Letter from Hemingway to Grace Hemingway, December 15, 1934, Indiana University Library.

Notes to Pages 235–239   291

39. Vernon (Jake) Klimo and Will Oursler, *Hemingway and Jake: An Extraordinary Friendship* (New York, 1972), pp. 141, 60.

40. Interview with Madelaine Hemingway Miller, Deerfield Beach, Florida, January 1, 1983.

41. Madelaine Hemingway Miller, *Ernie: His Sister 'Sunny' Remembers* (New York, 1975), p. 141. For more information on Madelaine, see Donald St. John, "Indian Indian Camp," *Carleton Miscellany*, 9 (1968), 95–109.

42. Gregory Hemingway, M.D., *Papa: A Personal Memoir*, with a Preface by Norman Mailer (Boston, 1976), p. 12.

43. Ernest Hemingway, *Islands in the Stream* (New York, 1972), pp. 10, 135.

44. Castillo-Puche, *Hemingway in Spain*, p. 184.

45. Gregory Hemingway, *Papa*, pp. 3, 100, 118. Gregory's book presents a strong contrast to the admiration expressed by his older sons. See Patrick Hemingway, "My Papa, Papa," *Playboy*, 15 (December 1968) and John Hemingway, "Memories of Papa," *The Student* (Winston-Salem, N.C.), (Winter, 1978), 29–34.

46. Fanny Butcher, *Many Lives—One Love* (New York, 1972), p. 430.

47. Mary Hemingway, *How It Was* (New York, 1977), pp. 282, 428.

48. Oriana Fallaci, "Mary Hemingway," *The Egotists: Sixteen Surprising Interviews* (Chicago, 1968), p. 153.

49. Mary Hemingway, *How It Was*, pp. 354, 604.

50. For a discussion of the marriages of Tolstoy and of Hemingway, see Jeffrey Meyers, *Married to Genius* (London, 1977), pp. 15–37.

51. Young, "I Disremember Papa," p. 66.

52. Patrick Hynan, *Hemingway* (Toronto: CBC, 1970), a two-record album, in the Kennedy Library.

53. Letter from Hemingway to Buck Lanham, September 16, 1959, Princeton University Library.

54. Peter Buckley, *Ernest* (New York, 1978), pp. 106, 120, 111, 156.

55. Adriana Ivancich, *La Torre Bianca* (Milano, 1980), pp. 170–171.

56. Norman Mailer, Preface to Gregory Hemingway, *Papa*, p. xi.

57. George Plimpton, Introduction to Ernest Hemingway, "The Art of Fiction," *Paris Review,* 18 (Spring 1958), 65.

17. Poets and Tennis

1. E. M. Forster, *Selected Letters,* ed. Mary Lago and P. N. Furbank (London, 1983), 1: 76.
2. Selden Rodman, "Robert Frost," *Tongues of Fallen Angels* (New York, 1974), p. 45.
3. Ernest Hemingway, *A Moveable Feast* (New York, 1964), p. 144.
4. Ford Madox Ford, *New York Essays* (New York, 1927), p. 45.
5. Violet Hunt, *I Have This to Say* (New York, 1926), p. 114.
6. Douglas McPherson, "Ezra Pound of Wyncote," *Arts in Philadelphia,* 2 (1940), 10–28.
7. Kathleen Cannell, "Two Essays on Ford Madox Ford," *Hemingway and 'The Sun' Set,* ed. Bertram Sarason (Washington, D.C., 1972), pp. 261–262.
8. Frederic Prokosch, "A Game of Tennis," *Visions: A Memoir* (London, 1983), pp. 99–100.
9. William Carlos Williams, *Autobiography* (New York, 1967), p. 218.
10. Ernest Hemingway, "African Journal," *Sports Illustrated,* 36 (10 January 1972), [p. 48].
11. Ruth Sokoloff, *Hadley* (New York, 1973), p. 61.
12. Notes on Carlos Baker's interview with Clara Spiegel, July 1964, Firestone Library, Princeton University.
13. A. E. Hotchner, *Papa Hemingway* (New York, 1970), p. 146.
14. Ernest Hemingway, *Selected Letters, 1917–1961,* ed. Carlos Baker (New York, 1981), pp. 642–643. A photo of Hemingway awkwardly hitting a backhand appears in Lloyd Arnold, *Hemingway: High on the Wild* (Caldwell, Idaho, 1968), p. 104.
15. Ernest Hemingway, *The Sun Also Rises* (New York, 1954), p. 45.
16. Allen Seager, *The Glass House: The Life of Theodore Roethke* (New York, 1968), p. 45.

17. Stanley Kunitz, "Remembering Roethke," *A Kind of Order, A Kind of Folly* (Boston, 1975), p. 79. Joyce's allusion to Alfred lawn tennyson is in *Ulysses* (New York, 1961), p. 50.

18. James Atlas, *Delmore Schwartz* (New York, 1978), p. 117.

19. John Berryman, *His Toy, His Dream, His Rest* (New York, 1968), no. 175.

20. John Haffenden, *The Life of John Berryman* (London, 1982), p. 44.

21. Eileen Simpson, *Poets in Their Youth* (New York, 1982), p. 112.

22. L. Richardson Preyer, "Tribute to a Gentle Flower," *Alumni News* (University of North Carolina at Greensboro), 54 (Spring 1966), 15. Preyer also reproduces a photo of Jarrell running for a backhand.

23. Robert Fitzgerald, "A Place of Refreshment," *Randall Jarrell, 1915–1965*, ed. Robert Lowell, Peter Taylor and Robert Penn Warren (New York, 1967), pp. 72–73.

24. Jeffrey Meyers, interview with Robert Fitzgerald, New Haven, Conn., December 16, 1982.

25. Robert Pinsky, "Tennis," *Sadness and Happiness* (Princeton, 1975), p. 16.

26. Paul Theroux, "The Tennis Court," *The Consul's File* (Boston, 1977), pp. 104, 102.

27. Vladimir Nabokov, *Speak, Memory* (New York, 1968), pp. 30, 190–191. Peter Quennell, ed., *Vladimir Nabokov: A Tribute* (London, 1979), p. 56 ff., provides a photo of the Russian tennis court with Nabokov's mother in the foreground.

28. "Homesick Writer Ends Silence," *Times* (London), December 12, 1983, p. 4.

29. Donald Davie, "Shropshire," *The Shires* (New York, 1975), no pp.

30. Thomas Mann, *The Magic Mountain*, trans. H. T. Lowe-Porter (London, 1957), p. 73.

31. Katherine Mansfield, "Prelude," *Stories* (New York, 1956), p. 95. Jeffrey Meyers, *Katherine Mansfield: A Biography* (London, 1978), p. 82 ff., reproduces a photo of Katherine in tennis garb.

32. John Betjeman, "The Subaltern's Love-song," *Collected Poems*, enlarged edition (London, 1972), p. 105.

18. The Death of Randall Jarrell

1. Søren Kierkegaard, *Journals,* trans. and ed. Alexander Dru (New York, 1959), p. 153.
2. A. Alvarez, *The Savage God* (New York, 1972), p. 238; Martin Seymour-Smith, *Who's Who in Twentieth Century Literature* (New York, 1976), p. 178; Galway Kinnell, *Walking Down the Stairs* (Ann Arbor, 1978), p. 103; and John Simon, "The Last of the Vine," *New Leader,* 63 (September 8, 1980), 20.
3. Theodore Roethke, "In a Dark Time," *Collected Poems* (New York, 1975), p. 231; John Berryman, *His Toy, His Dream, His Rest* (New York, 1968), p. 82.
4. Quoted in Robert Lowell, "To Delmore Schwartz," *Life Studies* (New York, 1964), p. 54.
5. Frederick Hoffman, *The Achievement of Randall Jarrell* (Glenview, Illinois, 1970), p. 17.
6. Information from a copy of Jarrell's birth certificate in the Berg Collection, New York Library.
7. Quoted in Mary Jarrell, "The Group of Two," *Randall Jarrell, 1914–1965,* ed. Robert Lowell, Peter Taylor and Robert Penn Warren (New York, 1967), p. 285 (hereafter cited as "Lowell").
8. *Ibid.*
9. *Ibid.*
10. Blair Clark, "On Robert Lowell," *Harvard Advocate,* 113 (November 1979), 11.
11. Allen Tate in "Lowell," p. 230.
12. Elizabeth Bishop and John Berryman in "Lowell," pp. 20, 17.
13. Irv Broughton, "An Interview with Allen Tate," *Western Humanities Review,* 32 (1978), 318.
14. Robert Lowell in "Lowell," p. 112.
15. Randall Jarrell, "Reflections on Wallace Stevens," *Poetry and the Age* (New York, 1953), p. 134.
16. Mary Jarrell, "Ideas and Poems," *Parnassus,* 5 (1976), 216.
17. Ford Madox Hueffer, *Ford Madox Brown* (London, 1896), p. 51.

18. Randall Jarrell, *The Bat-Poet* (New York, 1964), pp. 2, 15, 25, 41.
19. Quoted in Selma Lanes, *The Art of Maurice Sendak* (New York, 1980), p. 215.
20. Randall Jarrell, *Fly by Night* (New York, 1976), pp. 4–6, 21–22, 30.
21. John Crowe Ransom in "Lowell," p. 160.
22. Letter from Christina Stead to Jeffrey Meyers, June 3, 1981.
23. Randall Jarrell, *The Complete Poems* (New York, 1969), p. 290, 320, 323, 282, 317, 297, 280.
24. Hannah Arendt and Stanley Kunitz in "Lowell," pp. 8, 97.
25. Mary Jarrell in "Lowell," p. 297.
26. Joseph Bennett, *New York Times Book Review*, April 18, 1965, p. 24; Paul Fussell, *Saturday Review*, 48 (July 3, 1965), 31; Roger Sale, *Hudson Review*, 18 (Summer 1965), 306; James Dickey, *American Scholar*, 34 (Autumn 1965), 646, 648.
27. Mary Jarrell, "Reflections on 'Jerome,'" *Jerome: The Biography of a Poem* (New York, 1971), p. 9.
28. Mary Jarrell in "Lowell," p. 282.
29. John Berryman in "Lowell," p. 14; letter from John Berryman to Mary Jarrell, October 30, 1965, Berg Collection, New York Public Library.
30. Berryman, "Op. posth. no. 13," *His Toy, His Dream, His Rest*, p. 15.
31. Lowell in "Lowell," p. 112 and Robert Lowell, "Ten Minutes," *Day by Day* (New York, 1977), p. 108.
32. Robert Lowell, "Randall Jarrell" and "Randall Jarrell: 1914–1965," *Notebook*, 3rd, revised edition (New York, 1970), pp. 115–116, 50–51.

Bibliography

"Freud, Hitler and Vienna," *London Magazine*, 14 (August-September 1974), 67–79.

"Filial Memoirs of Tolstoy," *Biography*, 11 (Summer 1988), 236–252.

"George Painter's *Marcel Proust.*" *The Biographer's Art*. Ed. Jeffrey Meyers, London: Macmillan, 1989. pp. 128–148.

"André Malraux and the Art of Action," *London Magazine*, 14 (December 1974-January 1975), 5–34.

"'To Die for Ireland': The Character and Career of Sir Roger Casement," *London Magazine*, 13 (April-May 1973), 23–50.

"E. M. Forster and T. E. Lawrence: A Friendship," *South Atlantic Quarterly*, 69 (Spring 1970), 205–216.

"D. H. Lawrence, Katherine Mansfield and *Women in Love*," *London Magazine*, 18 (May 1978), 32–54.

"Murry's Cult of Mansfield," *Journal of Modern Literature*, 7 (February 1979), 15–38.

"The Quest for Katherine Mansfield," *Biography*, 1 (Summer 1978), 51–64.

"Memoirs of D. H. Lawrence: A Genre of the Thirties," *D. H. Lawrence Review*, 14 (Spring 1981), 1–32.

"Wyndham Lewis and T. S. Eliot: A Friendship," *Virginia Quarterly Review*, 56 (Summer 1980), 455–469.

"Wyndham Lewis: Portraits of an Artist," *London Magazine,* 20 (April-May 1980), 61–76.

"The Quest for Wyndham Lewis," *Biography,* 4 (Winter 1981), 66–81.

"Hemingway: Wanted by the FBI," *New York Review of Books,* 30 (March 31, 1983), 17–20.

"Memoirs of Hemingway: The Growth of a Legend," *Virginia Quarterly Review,* 60 (Autumn 1984), 587–612.

"The Quest for Hemingway," *Virginia Quarterly Review,* 61 (Autumn 1985), 584–602.

"Poets and Tennis," *London Magazine,* 25 (July 1985), 47–56.

"The Death of Randall Jarrell," *Virginia Quarterly Review,* 58 (Summer 1982), 450–462.

Index

Ackerley, J. R., *My Father and Myself,* 15
Adelphi, 120, 132, 155, 160, 163–164
Agee, James, 63
Almedingen, E. M., 129
Alpers, Antony, 124, 138, 141, 147
Apostolov, N., 21
Arendt, Hannah, 267
Arlen, Michael, 108
Arnaud, Joseph, 57–58, 59
Arnim, Elizabeth von, 145; *Elizabeth and Her German Garden,* 130
Arnold, Lloyd, 226, 240; *High on the Wild with Hemingway,* 234
Athenaeum, 113, 130, 156
Auden, W. H., 187, 199, 214; "A Happy New Year," 189, *Letters from Iceland,* 189
autobiography, 15, 17, 28, 150, 174; memoirs as autobiography, 239–240
Avory, Horace, 78, 88

Bailey, Daniel, 75, 76, 78, 89
Baker, Carlos, 225; *Ernest Hemingway,* 242
Baker, Elliott, 187; "The Portrait of Diana Prochnik," 198–199
Baker, Ida, 104, 123, 145–146, 202
Barclay, Henry Craddock, 144
Barker, Richard, 37, 39
Barrault, Jean-Louis, 67
Barry, Iris, 207, 209, 211
Barthoux, Jules, 56
Beauchamp, Leslie, 106
Bendall, Edith, 144
Benitez, Manuel, 215, 217, 221
Bennett, Joseph, 268
Berryman, John, 259, 263–264, 274
Betjeman, John, "A Subaltern's Love-Song," 262
Bibesco, Elizabeth, 141
Bishop, Elizabeth, 265
Blow, Simon, 31, 34

Blunt, Wilfrid Scawen, 137
Boak, Denis, 65
Bowden, George, 102, 124, 138, 140, 141, 146, 202
Braden, Spruille, 215–216, 217, 218, 220, 221
Brett, Dorothy, 101, 138, 141, 142, 149, 150, 151, 156, 166, 173; *Lawrence and Brett,* 169–170
Brewster, Achsah, 149, 150, 170; *D. H. Lawrence: Reminiscences and Correspondence,* 171
Brewster, Earl, 149, 150, 170
Brill, A. A., 166
Brooke, Rajah James, 49
Bruccoli, Matthew, 225
Bruce, Evangeline, 250
Buckley, Peter, 226, 240; *Ernest,* 238
Budgen, Frank, 191
Bullett, Gerald, 134
Bullock, Alan, 10
Burckhardt, Jakob, 2
Burgess, Anthony, 288 n7
Bynner, Witter, 167

Campbell, Roy, 187, 199, 206, 209; *Flowering Rifle,* 189; *The Georgiad,* 188–189
Camus, Albert, 67; *The Plague,* 54
Cannell, Kitty, 256
Carco, Francis, 105, 117, 124, 133
Carrington, Dora, 105
Carson, C. H., 217, 220, 221
Carson, Sir Edward, 73, 74, 78, 79, 88
Carswell, Catherine, 105, 109, 149, 150, 151, 159; *The Savage Pilgrimage,* 160–161, 162, 163
Casement, Sir Roger, 1; biography, 69–90, death, 86–87, 88, diaries, 70, 84–87, homosexuality, 84–89, in Africa, 69–71, in Brazil, 71–73, in Germany, 74–75, in Ireland, 73–78, 89–90, trial, 78–84, 88

Castillo-Puche, José Luis, 226, 232, 236; *Hemingway in Spain,* 233
Chamberlain, Houston Stewart, 5
Chambers, Jessie, 149, 150, 151, 152, 287; *D. H. Lawrence: A Personal Record,* 153–154
Chandler, Raymond, *Farewell, My Lovely,* 223, 240
Chekhov, Anton, 27, 125, 128–129, 134, 139, 283 n68; *Notebooks,* 131, 132
Chertkov, Vladimir, 16, 18, 19, 20, 22, 23, 24, 25
Chevasson, Louis, 51, 52
Cholmondeley, Sybil, 209–210
Christensen, Adler, 74
Clark, Blair, 264
Clark, Kenneth, 182, 206
Clifford, Sir Hugh, 50
Clotis, Josette, 61, 63, 64
Colleyre, Anne de, 38
Collingwood, Charles, 244
Conrad, Joseph, 69–70, 89; *Heart of Darkness,* 49, 54, 72; *Victory,* 54
Cookridge, E. H., 64
Corniglion-Molinier, Edouard, 55–56
Cowley, Malcolm, 224, 226, 240, 289 n13; Introduction to *Portable Hemingway,* 227, "A Portrait of Mister Papa," 227–228
Cunard, Nancy, 193
Curtiss, Mina, 37, 278 n22

Dalldorf, Dr. Fred, 272–273
Danby-Smith, Valerie, 233–234, 236, 237, 247–248
D'Annunzio, Gabriele, 47
Daudet, Léon, 41
Daudet, Lucien, 41
Davie, Donald, "Shropshire," 261
Davis, Bill, 234
Day, Douglas, *Malcolm Lowry,* 33
Debussy, Claude, 41
De Gaulle, Charles, 48, 65–66, 67, 68
Deutscher, Isaac, *Leon Trotsky,* 138
Devoy, John, *Recollections,* 82
Dickey, James, 268
Domenichino, *The Last Communion of St. Jerome,* 195
Dominguín, Luis-Miguel, 250–251
Dorman-Smith, Christopher, 249
Dorman-Smith, E. E. "Chink," 248–249
Dostoyevsky, Fyodor, 23; *The Idiot,* 64
Douglas, Norman, 137
Durán, Bonte, 249, 250
Durán, Gustavo, 215, 216–217, 220, 221, 249

Eastman, Max, 7
Edel, Leon, *Henry James,* 138
Ehrenburg, Ilya, 60–61
Eliot, T. S., 1, 187, 191; friendship with Wyndham Lewis, 175–185, obituary of Lewis, 185; *After Strange Gods,* 159, "The Ballad of Big Louise," 176, "Bullshit," 176, "Preludes," 176, "Rhapsody on a Windy Night," 176, *The Waste Land,* 178
Ellmann, Richard, *James Joyce,* 32, 33, 39, 138

Farrington, Kip, 226, 240; *Atlantic Game Fishing,* 234, *Fishing with Hemingway and Glassell,* 234
Faulkner, William, 289 n13
Fenton, Charles, 227, 230
Fitzgerald, F. Scott, 224
Fitzgerald, Robert, 259–260
Flanner, Janet, 56, 59, 66
Fonda, Afdera, 250
Ford, Ford Madox, 187, 199; *The Good Soldier,* 192, *The Marsden Case,* 192–193, *Parade's End,* 193
Forster, E. M., 1, 112, 255; friendship with T. E. Lawrence, 91–99, homosexuality, 96–99, 279 n2; *Arctic Summer,* 97, *Aspects of the Novel,* 94, 99, *The Eternal Moment,* 94, 97, 98, *The Heart of Bosnia,* 97, Letters, 98–99, *The Longest Journey,* 99, *A Passage to India,* 92, 93, "The Point of It," 98, "The Rock," 97, *A Room with a View,* 99, "The Story of a Panic," 99
Frere, A. S., 145
Freud, Sigmund, 1, 3, 6, 42; attitude to Vienna, 7–8, 12, Nazi attacks on, 11, 12, relation of thought to Vienna, 6, 13; *Civilization and Its Discontents,* 12, *History of the Psychoanalytical Movement,* 7, *Leonardo da Vinci,* 7, *Moses and Monotheism,* 5, 12, "The Psychology of Love," 7, *Totem and Taboo,* 7
Frohock, W. H., 37, 49
Frost, Robert, 255
Fry, Roger, 195
Fülöp-Miller, René, 20
Fussell, Paul, 268

Garnett, David, 98
Gelder, Stuart, 152
Gellhorn, Martha, 218, 220–221, 236, 237, 244, 247, 257–258
Gertler, Mark, 101, 105, 108, 112, 116, 117, 169
Gide, André, 44, 54, 60, 62, 67
Gilman, Richard, 37

Gordon, Ian, 133
Gosse, Edmund, *Father and Son*, 15
Götzsche, Kai, 166, 167, 169
Graf, Max, 4
Grigson, Geoffrey, 210
Gross, John, 38
Grosskurth, Phyllis, 31, 34, 37–38, 42
Guest, Winston, 217
Gurdjieff, George, 110, 114, 120, 122, 139, 140

Haas, Charles, 41
Hampshire, Stuart, 38
Hanisch, Reinhold, 9
Hanley, James, *Boy*, 97
Hartley, L. P., 36–37
Hemingway, Carol, 244, 246
Hemingway, Dr. Clarence, 231
Hemingway, Ernest, 1, 2, 61, 198; and the FBI, 215–222, 288 n9, as biographical subject, 241–254, as tennis player, 256–258, at Mayo Clinic, 215, 222, 231, Crook Factory, 216–218, legends, 224–225, 227–228, 230, 232–233, 235, 240, 254, life patterns, 253, memoirs of, 223–240, public image, 223–226, 240;
Across the River and into the Trees, 228, 238–239, 249, "The Christmas Gift," 241, "The Dangerous Summer," 232, 233, *For Whom the Bell Tolls*, 216, 219, 220, 227, 249, *Islands in the Stream*, 236, *A Moveable Feast*, 245, 255, *The Old Man and the Sea*, 225, 230, 234, 236, "The Real Spaniard," 232, *Selected Letters*, 241, "The Short Happy Life of Francis Macomber," 252, "The Snows of Kilimanjaro," 224, "Soldier's Home," 235, *The Spanish Earth*, 220–221, 250, *The Sun Also Rises*, 224, 258
Hemingway, Gregory, 226, 240, 246, 247; *Papa*, 236–237, 291 n45
Hemingway, Jack, 248, 291 n45
Hemingway, Leicester, 226, 246–247; *My Brother, Ernest Hemingway*, 231, *The Sound of the Trumpet*, 231
Hemingway, Mary, 221, 222, 226, 232–233, 234, 235, 236, 239, 240, 244, 246, 290 n32; *How It Was*, 237–238
Hemingway, Patricia, 246–247
Hemingway, Patrick, 248, 291 n45
Hemingway, Pauline, 235–236, 246
Herrick, Ruth, 144
Herzl, Theodor, 3, 6
Hilton, Enid, 142, 150, 159
Hindus, Milton, 38–39
Hitler, Adolf, 1, 3, 5; attitude to Jews, 9–10, 11, attitude to Vienna, 8–11, 13, political influences on, 5–6, 9; *Mein Kampf*, 8, 9

Hoffman, Frederick, 264
Hofmannsthal, Hugo von, 3
Holmes, Richard, 121
Hoover, J. Edgar, 219, 220, 252
Hotchner, A. E., 222, 226–227, 229, 232, 234, 240; *Papa Hemingway*, 233, 290 n32
Howe, Irving, 205, 229
Hunt, Violet, 256
Huxley, Aldous, 149, 199; relationship with Lawrence, 150, 151, 161; *Along the Road*, 161, *Antic Way*, 193–196, 197, *The Genius and the Goddess*, 161, Introduction to Lawrence's *Letters*, 161–162, *Point Counter Point*, 120–121, 157, 161, 193, Preface to Merrild, 169, *Those Barren Leaves*, 117
Huxley, Lady Juliette, 145

Ibsen, Henrik, *Enemy of the People*, 7–8
Isherwood, Christopher, *Goodbye to Berlin*, 134, *The World in the Evening*, 134, 143
Ivancich, Adriana, 227, 237, 240, 250; "La Renata di Hemingway sono io," 238, *La Torre Bianca*, 238–239, 241
Ivens, Joris, 250

James, Henry, 44
Janet, Pierre, 6
Jarrell, Mary, 265, 268, 270–272
Jarrell, Randall, 2, 259–260; character, 265, death, 263, 268–276, life, 264–265, suicidal, 266–268, 276; *The Bat-Poet*, 265–266, *Fly by Night*, 266, *The Lost World*, 264, 266–267, 268, *Pictures from an Institution*, 131, *The Rage for the Lost Penny*, 266, *The Woman at the Washington Zoo*, 265
Johnson, Pamela Hansford, 37
Johnson, Willard, 167
Johnston, William, *The Austrian Mind*, 4, 6
Jones, Artemus, 81
Jones, Ernest, 7, 12; *Freud*, 32
Joyce, James, 177–178, 185, 187, 199; *Finnegans Wake*, 191–192, *Ulysses*, 191
Joyce, Robert, 215, 218, 244

Keats, John, 130–131
Kenner, Hugh, 205, 213, 214; *Dublin's Joyce*, 191–192
Kert, Bernice, *The Hemingway Women*, 241–242
Kiley, Jed, 226, 231; *Hemingway: An Old Friend Remembers*, 232
Kirk, Russell, 205, 209
Klimo, Jake, 226, 234, 240; *Hemingway and Jake*, 235
Kokoschka, Oskar, 3, 4
Koteliansky, S. S., 101, 104, 105, 108, 109, 123, 282 n45

Kraus, Karl, 3, 4
Krieger, Leonard, 244
Kubie, Dr. Lawrence, 251
Kubizek, August, 8–9
Kunitz, Stanley, 258, 268

Lacouture, Jean, 66
Ladd, D. M., 216–217, 219
Langlois, Walter, 52, 57, 59
Larkin, Philip, 151
Laurence, Dan, 140
Lawrence, Ada, 149, 150, 151, 154; *Young Lorenzo,* 152–153
Lawrence, D. H., 1, 94, 188; attitude to friends, 102, 114–115, 150–151, 165, 168, characterization, 108–109, 116–118, fictional portraits of self and Frieda, 158–159, friendship with Douglas, 137, friendship with Mansfield, 101–118, memoirs of, 149–174, obituaries of, 149, 159, 163, 164, paintings, 152, personality, 149–150, portrays friends in fiction, 150, 166, 167, 169, 170, relationship with Frieda, 104, 107, 108, 110, 117, 162, 166, 167, 168, 169, 170, 171–173, relationship with Murry, 103–104, 105–108, 110–111, 112, 113, 138, 150, 155–156, 281 n41, tuberculosis, 101, 105, 112–113, 115–116, 117, 153, 162, will, 152;
Aaron's Rod, 106, 114, 156, 157–158; "Adolf," 152, *Amores,* 108, "Art and the Individual," 152, "The Border Line," 163, *The Boy in the Bush,* 169, "The Crown," 106, "Eagle in New Mexico," 165, "Elephant," 171, "The Escaped Cock," 170, *Fantasia of the Unconscious,* 158, 166, "The Fly in the Ointment," 152, "Jimmy and the Desperate Woman," 163, *Lady Chatterley's Lover,* 152, 161, 163, "The Last Laugh," 163, *Letters,* 159, 161, *The Lost Girl,* 113, 152, 162, *Mornings in Mexico,* 166, "Mountain Lion," 165, *The Plumed Serpent,* 158, 163, 166, 167, *Poems,* 163, "The Princess," 166, 169, *The Rainbow,* 109, 159, "The Ship of Death," 106, "Smile," 121, *Sons and Lovers,* 103, 151, 152, 153, 154–155, 167, 171, *St. Mawr,* 158, 166, "Things," 170, *The Trespasser,* 102, *The White Peacock,* 102, 153, 157, *Women in Love,* 101, 102, 109, 116–118, 157, 158, 160, 162, "The Woman Who Rode Away," 166, 170
Lawrence, Emily, 152
Lawrence, Frieda, 102, 103, 105, 106, 107, 111, 116, 117, 118, 125, 151, 152, 155, 159, 161, 163, 164; relationship with Lawrence, 104, 107, 108, 110, 117, 149, 150, 162, 166, 167, 168, 169, 170, 171–173; Foreword to *The First Lady Chatterley,* 173, *Not I, But the Wind,* 172–174
Lawrence, T. E., 1, 47–49, 55, 68, 87, 146; friendship with Forster, 91–99, homosexuality, 96–98; *Letters,* 98–99, *The Mint,* 94–95, *Revolt in the Desert,* 94, 97, *Seven Pillars of Wisdom,* 48, 57, 91, 92–93, 94, 95, 96, 99, 227
Lea, F. A., 120, 144, 145, 164
Leavis, F. R., 112
Lechmere, Kate, 192–193, 207
Leddy, Raymond, 215, 216, 218–219, 220–221
Lehmann, John, 40, 196, 197
LeMaistre, Violet, 119
Lewis, Charles Edward, 211
Lewis, Gladys Anne ("Froanna"), 176, 207, 208, 210
Lewis, Wyndham, 1, 2,; as biographical subject, 204–214, career, 187–188, children, 211, friendship with Eliot, 175–185, literary portraits of, 187–199, marriage, 212, medical history, 213, meeting with Mansfield, 204, mistresses, 210–211, portraits of Eliot, 180–182, portrait of Edith Sitwell, 194, posthumous reputation, 205, 214;
The Apes of God, 178, 188, 189, 191, *The Art of Being Ruled,* 188–189, *Blast,* 176, 187, 190, 192, 194, "The Code of a Herdsman," 197, *The Demon of Progress in the Arts,* 182, 183, *Enemy of the Stars,* 194, *Hitler,* 188, 189, 209, *Letters,* 184, 205, *Men without Art,* 180, 188, *One-Way Song,* 175, *Paleface,* 188, 190, *The Roaring Queen,* 193, "The Sea-Mists of the Winter," 188, *Self Condemned,* 184, 188, 212, *Tarr,* 175, 177, 187, 194, *Time and Western Man,* 190, 191, *Timon of Athens* (drawings), 194, *The Tyro,* 187, 194, *The Wild Body,* 189, *The Writer and the Absolute,* 188, *Wyndham Lewis the Artist,* 182
literary biography, 1–2, 30–40, 43, 44–45; choosing a subject, 137–139, 241–242, correspondence, 243–245, 249, 251–252, cost, 213, Freedom of Information Act, 252, interviews, 141–146, 207, 208–210, 243, 244, 246–253, publishing, 201–204, 214, 242, research methods, 139–141, 146–147, 206–208, 211, 212–213, travel, 143–144, 147, 208, 245–246, 252–253
Longford, Elizabeth, 137
Lowell, Robert, 1, 263, 264, 265, 274; "Ten Minutes," 274–275
Lowenthal, Marvin, 37
Lueger, Karl, 5–6

Luhan, Mabel, 149, 150, 151, 164–165, 168; *Lorenzo in Taos,* 166–167
Luhan, Tony, 165
Lynch, Arthur, 78–79

Macdonald, Dwight, 223
MacDonald, Sir Hector, 85
Machlin, Milt, 226, 240; "Hemingway Talking," 230, *The Private Hell of Hemingway,* 230
Mackenzie, Faith, 169
MacLeish, Archibald, 231
MacNeice, Louis, 189
Magnus, Maurice, 111
Mailer, Norman, 236, 239, 244
Malraux, André, 1, 47–68, 188; as government minister, 65–67, biography, 50–54, 55, 60, in Arabia, 55–60, 68, in Cambodia, 51–52, 54, 68, in the Resistance, 63–64, in Saigon, 52, 53, 68, in Spain, 60–63, 68, mythomania, 47–49, 53–60, wins Prix Goncourt, 54; *Antimemoirs,* 49, 56–60, 63, 64, 66, 67, *The Conquerors,* 54, *Days of Wrath,* 60, *L'Espoir* (film), 61, 62–63, 68, *Fallen Oaks,* 68, *The Imaginary Museum,* 67, "Lawrence and the Demon of the Absolute," 48, *Man's Fate,* 54–55, 60, 62, 68, *Man's Hope,* 61, 62, 66, 68, *The Metamorphosis of the Gods,* 67, *Oraisons funèbres,* 64, 66, 68, *The Royal Way,* 49, 54, 66, *Royaume farfelu,* 54, *The Temptation of the West,* 53, *Le Triangle noir,* 68, *Voices of Silence,* 67, *The Walnut Trees of Altenburg,* 47, 48, 63, 68
Malraux, Clara, 47, 51, 52, 54, 61, 68
Malraux, Claude, 50, 64
Malraux, Madeleine, 67
Malraux, Roland, 50, 64
Mann, Thomas, 12–13; *The Magic Mountain,* 261
Mansfield, Katherine, 1, 2, 261–262; as biographical subject, 137–148, 201–202, 204–206, as Gudrun in *Women in Love,* 102, 108–110, 116–118, death, 115, 119, 120, 121, 122–123, friendship with D. H. Lawrence, 101–118, influenced by Chekhov, 128–129, 283 n68, posthumous reputation, 119–120, 123, 125–130, 131, 133–134, 205, 206, relationship with Murry, 103, 104, 106, 107, 108, 110, 111, 114, 117, 124, tuberculosis, 101, 111–112;
Bliss, 109, 126, 127, 131, "The Canary," 131, "The Child Who Was Tired," 129, "The Doll's House," 110, *The Dove's Nest,* 120, 126, 131, "The Garden Party," 110, 131, *The Garden Party,* 127, 134, *In a German Pension,* 102, 113, 117, 125, 126, 127–128, 130, *Journal,* 105, 111, 123, 126, 128, 131, 132–134, 143, *Letters,* 134, 143–144, "Marriage à la Mode," 109, "A Married Man's Story," 127, *Poems,* 120, *Prelude,* 126, 128, 130, *Scrapbook,* 104, 132, *Something Childish,* 127, 130, "Something Childish but Very Natural," 130, "To Stanislaw Wyspianski," 141, "The Voyage," 110, "The Wind Blows," 106, "The Woman at the Store," 282 n51
Mantz, Ruth, 123, 124, 132, 133, 142–143
Mao Tse-tung, 67, 68
Marchand, Leslie, *Byron,* 32
Martin, Eleanor, 209
Martin, Paul, 209
Martin du Gard, Roger, 67
Mason, Jane, 235, 250, 251
Maude, Aylmer, *Family Views of Tolstoy,* 20–21, 23, 27
Maurois, André, 37
Mayrena, Marie-David de, 47, 49–50, 54
McCaffery, John, 226, 228
McCarthy, Joseph, 220
McCullers, Carson, 134
McLuhan, Marshall, 205, 209, 214
Menocal, Mario, Jr., 244
Merrild, Knud, 149, 150, 151, 166, 167; *A Poet and Two Painters,* 168–169
Miller, Madelaine Hemingway, 226, 240, 246; *Ernie,* 235
Monin, Paul, 52
Monteith, Robert, 75, 76, 82
Montesquiou, Robert de, 41, 42
Moore, Henry, 210
Moorehead, Alan, 244
Morrell, Ottoline, 101, 112, 117, 145, 179
Mossuz, Janine, 65
Murphy, Stanley, 209
Murry, Colin Middleton, 125, 144–145
Murry, John Middleton, 1, 102, 103–104, 105, 106, 110, 111, 112, 113, 118, 141, 152; as Burlap in *Point Counter Point,* 120–121, 155–156, as Crich in *Women in Love,* 116–117, cult of Mansfield, 119–135, 148, 163–164, on D. H. Lawrence, 149, 151, relationship with D. H. Lawrence, 103–104, 105–108, 110–111, 112, 113, 150, 155–156, 158, 162–163, relationship with Frieda, 156, 160, 163, 164, relationship with Mansfield, 103, 104, 106, 107, 108, 110, 111, 114, 117, 123–124, 127, 128, 138;
Between Two Worlds, 107–108, 116, 282 n44, *Cinnamon and Angelica,* 131, *God,* 122, "In Memory of Katherine Mansfield," 121, "Lawrence and Jesus," 163, *"Reminiscences,"* 160,

Index

162, 164, *Reminiscences of D. H. Lawrence,* 162–163, 174, *Son of Woman,* 157–161, 163, 164, 174
Murry, Mary Middleton, 144–145
Murry, Richard, 144
Musil, Robert, 3

Nabokov, Vladimir, 260; *Speak, Memory,* 260
Nagorny, Vera, 20–21
Nehls, Edward, *Composite Biography,* 174
New Age, 128, 130
Newby, P. H., 184
Nietzsche, Friedrich, *Thus Spake Zarathustra,* 55

O'Brien, Lucy, 146–147
O'Neill, John, 82
Orage, A. R., 114, 191
Ordóñez, Antonio, 232, 233, 250–251
Orioli, Pino, 152
Orton, William, 138, 141; *The Last Romantic,* 132
Orwell, George, 134, 188

Painter, George, 1; biography, 29–31, critical reception of *Proust,* 36–40; *André Gide,* 30, 31, *Chateaubriand,* 30, 31, Foreword to *Caxton,* 278 n18, *Marcel Proust,* 30–33, 40–45, 138, Preface to Volume I, 34–36, 38, "Proust's Way," 279 n27, *The Road to Sinodun,* 30
Petitjean, Armand, 61–62
Philby, St. John, 58–59
Pinsky, Robert, "Tennis," 260
Pliny, *Natural History,* 55, 58
Plowman, Max, 120
Porteus, Hugh Gordon, 210
Pound, Ezra, 175, 176, 177, 181, 185, 187, 199; as biographical subject, 241, as tennis player, 255–256, 257; *Cantos,* 190–191
Powell, Anthony, 37, 206
Prévost, Jean, 53
Prokosch, Frederic, 256
Proust, Marcel, 1, 30–33, 40–45; *Contre Sainte-Beuve,* 44, *Letters,* 37, 279 n27, *Remembrance of Things Past,* 29, 35, 40, 42, 44–45, *Swann's Way,* 29, 43, 44, *Within a Budding Grove,* 44

Quennell, Peter, 38

Ransom, John Crowe, 265
Ravagli, Angelo, 172
Read, Herbert, 182–184
Reading, Lord, 78, 81, 83, 88
Reynolds, Michael, 244

Rhythm, 102, 127, 130
Rice, Alfred, 244, 246
Rich, Adrienne, 274
Richards, Dorothy, 146
Rickword, Edgell, 187, 189, 199, 208–209; "The Encounter," 190
Riefstahl-Nordlinger, Marie, 39–40
Rimbaud, Arthur, 49, 55
Roethke, Theodore, 258, 263
Rose, W. K., 206, 207
Ross, Lillian, 226, 228–229, 240
Russell, Bertrand, 102, 117

Sachs, Maurice, 53, 54
Sale, Roger, 268
Sanford, Marcelline Hemingway, 226, 240; *At the Hemingways,* 231
Sartre, Jean-Paul, 63, 188
Sassoon, Siegfried, 91
Schönerer, Georg von, 5, 12
Schwartz, Delmore, 259, 263, 264
Scott, Margaret, 143–144
Sendak, Maurice, 266
Shattuck, Roger, 38
Shaw, Bernard, 98; *A Discarded Defence of Roger Casement,* 79
Signature, 106, 130, 155
Simon, John, 271
Singer, Kurt, 226, 240, 289 n22; *Hemingway,* 229–230
Sitwell, Edith, 187; *I Live under a Black Sun,* 196–197, 199
Sitwell, Osbert, 187, 193; *Those Were the Days,* 196, 197–198, 199
Sitwell, Sacheverell, 196, 209
Slocum, John, 209
Smith, Sir Frederick, 79, 80, 81–84, 88
Sobienowski, Floryan, 138, 140–141, 143
Solzhenitsyn, Alexander, 261
Sorapure, Victor, 141
Spender, Stephen, 60, 182, 109
Stack, Austin, 77
Stakhovich, Sofya, 21
Stead, Christina, 266
Steegmuller, Francis, *Flaubert and Madame Bovary,* 32
Stevenson, Robert Louis, 137
Strachey, Lytton, 126
Straight, Michael, *After Long Silence,* 249
Sullivan, Arthur, 79–80, 81, 84
Sulzburger, C. L., 64
Swinnerton, Frank, 135, 145

Taneyev, S. I., 22, 28
Tate, Allen, 265
Theroux, Paul, "The Tennis Court," 260

Thomas, Bertram, *Arabia Felix*, 56, 59
Thomas, Hugh, 216
Thorpe, Clarence, 123
Toklas, Alice B., 229
Tolstoy, Alexandra (daughter), 16, 17, 21, 28; *The Tragedy of Tolstoy*, 21–23
Tolstoy, Andrei (son), 22, 25
Tolstoy, Ilya (son), 17, 28; *Tolstoy, My Father*, 18–19
Tolstoy, Ivan (son), 22, 28
Tolstoy, Leo (novelist), 1; death, 21, 23, 24, 27–28, hypocrisy, 18–19, marriage, 15, 19, 21, 23–24, 27, relationship with children, 16–27, religious ideas, 15–16, 18, 20, 24–25, 27
Tolstoy, Leo (son), 17, 18, 22, 28; *Chopin's Prelude*, 20, *The Truth about My Father*, 19–20
Tolstoy, Marya (daughter), 18, 22, 26
Tolstoy, Sergei (brother of novelist), 20, 22
Tolstoy, Sergei (son), 16, 17, 21, 28; *Tolstoy Remembered*, 23–25
Tolstoy, Sofia (wife), 15, 16, 17, 25–26; attempted suicide, 18, 20, 24, diaries, 21–22, hysteria, 19, 21, 22–24, 27, 28
Tolstoy, Tatiana (daughter), 16, 17, 21, 22; *The Tolstoy Home*, 20, 25–26, *Tolstoy Remembered*, 27–28
Tomalin, Claire, 138
Trowell, Garnett, 138, 146
Trowell, Oliver, 146
Turgenev, Ivan, 18, 23

Urquhart, Brian, 249

Vergani, Ernst, 5
Vienna, 3–4; anti-Semitism in, 5–6, 7, 11–12, Jews of, 4–5, 7, 13, poverty in, 9, social conventions of, 6
Vinogradoff, Julian, 145

Wagner, Geoffrey, 192
Waldron, Philip, 133
Warren, Robert Penn, 265
Weekley, Ernest, 172
Weekley, Montague, 145
West, Rebecca, 209
White, Newman, *Shelley*, 32
Williams, William Carlos, *Autobiography*, 256–257
Wilson, Angus, 37
Wilson, Edmund, *The Wound and the Bow*, 225–226
Woolf, Leonard, 128, 133
Woolf, Virginia, 122, 178; *A Writer's Diary*, 133

Yeats, W. B., 191
Young, Philip, 227, 228, 232–233, 290 n32

Zaphiro, Denis, 244
Zweig, Stefan, 3; *The World of Yesterday*, 5–6